Inside the Local Campaign

COMMUNICATION
STRATEGY
AND POLITICS

COMMUNICATION, STRATEGY, AND POLITICS
THIERRY GIASSON AND ALEX MARLAND, SERIES EDITORS

Communication, Strategy, and Politics is a groundbreaking series from UBC Press that examines elite decision making and political communication in today's hyper-mediated and highly competitive environment. Publications in this series look at the intricate relations among marketing strategy, the media, and political actors and explain how they affect Canadian democracy. They also investigate interconnected themes such as strategic communication, mediatization, opinion research, electioneering, political management, public policy, and e-politics in a Canadian context and in comparison to other countries. Designed as a coherent and consolidated space for diffusion of research about Canadian political communication, the series promotes an interdisciplinary, multi-method, and theoretically pluralistic approach.

Other volumes in the series are

Political Marketing in Canada, edited by Alex Marland, Thierry Giasson, and Jennifer Lees-Marshment

Political Communication in Canada: Meet the Press and Tweet the Rest, edited by Alex Marland, Thierry Giasson, and Tamara A. Small

Framed: Media and the Coverage of Race in Canadian Politics, by Erin Tolley

Brand Command: Canadian Politics and Democracy in the Age of Message Control, by Alex Marland

Permanent Campaigning in Canada, edited by Alex Marland, Thierry Giasson, and Anna Lennox Esselment

Breaking News? Politics, Journalism, and Infotainment on Quebec Television, by Frédérick Bastien

Political Elites in Canada: Power and Influence in Instantaneous Times, edited by Alex Marland, Thierry Giasson, and Andrea Lawlor

Opening the Government of Canada: The Federal Bureaucracy in the Digital Age, by Amanda Clarke

The New NDP: Moderation, Modernization, and Political Marketing, by David McGrane

Gendered Mediation: Identity and Image Making in Canadian Politics, edited by Angela Wagner and Joanna Everitt

What's Trending in Canadian Politics? Understanding Transformations in Power, Media, and the Public Sphere, edited by Mireille Lalancette, Vincent Raynauld, and Erin Crandall

Inside the Campaign: Managing Elections in Canada, edited by Alex Marland and Thierry Giasson

Whipped: Party Discipline in Canada, by Alex Marland

See also:

Canadian Election Analysis 2015: Communication, Strategy, and Democracy, edited by Alex Marland and Thierry Giasson. Open access compilation available at http://www.ubcpress.ca/canadianelectionanalysis2015.

Inside the
Local Campaign

Constituency Elections in Canada

Edited by

ALEX MARLAND

and

THIERRY GIASSON

UBCPress · Vancouver · Toronto

31 30 29 28 27 26 25 24 23 22   5 4 3 2 1

Printed in Canada on FSC-certified ancient-forest-free paper
(100% post-consumer recycled) that is processed chlorine- and acid-free.

Library and Archives Canada Cataloguing in Publication

Title: Inside the local campaign : constituency elections in Canada / edited by
    Alex Marland and Thierry Giasson.
Names: Marland, Alex, editor. | Giasson, Thierry, editor.
Series: Communication, strategy, and politics.
Description: Series statement: Communication, strategy, and politics | Includes
    bibliographical references and index.
Identifiers: Canadiana (print) 2022022613X | Canadiana (ebook) 20220226490 |
    ISBN 9780774868198 (softcover) | ISBN 9780774868204 (PDF) |
    ISBN 9780774868211 (EPUB)
Subjects: LCSH: Canada. Parliament—Elections, 2021. | LCSH: Local elections
    —Canada. | LCSH: Political campaigns—Canada. | LCSH: Campaign
    management—Canada. | LCSH: Political candidates—Canada. | LCSH:
    Communication in politics—Canada.
Classification: LCC JL193 .I55 2022 | DDC 324.97107/4—dc23

Canadä

UBC Press gratefully acknowledges the financial support for our publishing
program of the Government of Canada (through the Canada Book Fund),
the Canada Council for the Arts, and the British Columbia Arts Council.

This book has been published with the help of a grant from the Canadian
Federation for the Humanities and Social Sciences, through the Awards to
Scholarly Publications Program, using funds provided by the Social Sciences
and Humanities Research Council of Canada.

UBC Press
The University of British Columbia
2029 West Mall
Vancouver, BC V6T 1Z2
www.ubcpress.ca

Contents

Acknowledgments

THIS BOOK IS THE third of consecutive volumes within the UBC Press Communication, Strategy, and Politics series that take an innovative look at a Canadian federal election through the lens of political communication. In 2015, we assembled sixty-six academics, students, and practitioners across Canada to write succinct, immediate reactions to that year's campaign, which resulted in the e-publication *Canadian Election Analysis: Communication, Strategy, and Democracy*. In 2019, fifteen academics paired with practitioner co-authors to reveal behind-the-scenes aspects of a federal election for *Inside the Campaign: Managing Elections in Canada*, which UBC Press published as open access. For this third volume, we built upon these experiences and suggestions from past contributors to produce a work anchored in the 2021 campaign that brings us closer to familiar methods of scholarly output while preserving our interest in timely documentation of the hidden sides of Canadian federal elections. *Inside the Local Campaign* is the first book to look at constituency-level elections in Canada within a digital communication environment. It is a more conventional academic book in that it draws on in-depth interviews with people directly involved with grassroots electioneering, but it features some twists, such as an academic co-authoring with a sitting MP, another with an unsuccessful nomination contestant, and a third with local journalists. Much like a campaign team, it represents a considerable group effort.

The editors would like to thank the contributors for following our firm editorial guidelines and for submitting their contributions within two weeks of the conclusion of the Canadian election in

2021. We appreciate the assistance of the professional and amateur photographers whose photos captured in the Appendix bring to life what an election campaign looks like on the ground across Canada. We are grateful for the timely, detailed, and thorough reviews of a draft manuscript supplied by three external referees; for the meticulous copyediting by Dallas Harrison; and for the striking cover designed by Kimberley Devlin. As with previous volumes, this book was only possible with the vision and goodwill of the fine personnel at UBC Press – including but not limited to Laraine Coates, Katrina Petrik, Melissa Pitts, Randy Schmidt, and Carmen Tiampo – who share our interest in prompt publication of assessments of Canadian elections. In addition to their commitments, publication of this book was possible with the help of a grant from the Canadian Federation of Humanities and Social Sciences, through the Awards to Scholarly Publications Program; a financial award from Memorial University of Newfoundland via its Publications Subvention Program, administered by the Office of Research Grant and Contract Services; and funding from the Groupe de recherche en communication politique, based at Université Laval. Thank you also to the Institute for Research on Public Policy (IRPP) for serializing drafts of select chapters that were published in *Policy Options*. Alex would like to thank Karly, and Thierry would like to thank Martin, Thomas, and Darren for making life that much more enjoyable.

Finally, thank you to readers of books in the Communication, Strategy, and Politics series.

Inside the Local Campaign

Introduction

Constituency Campaigning in Canada

Alex Marland

Abstract   In Canada, most voters prioritize national-level variables such as party leadership and party labels instead of local representation. As a result, local-level campaigning attracts relatively little scholarly attention. Nevertheless, there is growing interest in the work of candidates and their supporters because of competitive pressures and because political parties want them to collect and store information about constituents in a party-controlled database used for fundraising, volunteering, and voter mobilization. This introduction situates constituency campaigning in Canada, including observations about unique aspects of electioneering during a pandemic, and summarizes the ensuing chapters in the book.

Résumé   Au Canada, plutôt que d'accorder la priorité aux candidats locaux, la majorité des électeurs se concentrent sur des variables nationales telles que les chefs et les partis. Par conséquent, les campagnes menées localement attirent relativement peu l'attention de la communauté scientifique. Néanmoins, comme les partis politiques incitent les candidats et leurs partisans à recueillir des données sur les électeurs et à les conserver dans des bases de données qu'ils contrôlent, leur travail suscite de plus en plus d'intérêt. Ces informations sont ensuite utilisées dans le domaine du marketing de données, y compris pour la collecte de fonds, le bénévolat, et la mobilisation des électeurs. Cette introduction dresse un portrait des campagnes électorales menées dans les circonscriptions au Canada. Il présente notamment des observations sur les aspects uniques d'un processus électoral se déroulant pendant une pandémie et un résumé des chapitres qui constituent ce livre.

CANADIAN POLITICAL PARTIES are paying renewed attention to local-level electioneering, and so should the researchers who study national elections, political representation, and party politics. Since the age of television and the advent of public opinion polling, many have viewed canvassing for votes in electoral districts – defined geographical areas also known as ridings or constituencies – as a holdover from an era when Members of Parliament (MPs) were powerful public figures and electing a representative had significant local consequences. The diminishing political influence of MPs – coupled with the dominance of national media, party leaders, issues, and partisanship – reduced the perceived relevance of local campaigning. To cynics, electioneering by candidates and their supporters was ritualistic and irrational.

Technological changes paved the way for more centralized co-ordination by political parties that dispensed with direct, local contact with electors in favour of coordinated, national-level indirect communication, often via news management and advertising. Skepticism intensified in the late twentieth century with the proliferation of 24/7 television news, fax machines, email, and websites and the replacement of door-to-door voter enumeration with a permanent electronic list of electors.[1] Gradually, local candidates were subsumed within party brands dominated by the national leaders' personalities and media interest in their tours. Some of the most hardened doubters were political scientists who, since the 1940s, have used public opinion survey data to establish the prevalence of national-level variables.[2] Research studies suggesting that a candidate accounts for less than 10 percent of the vote[3] – with incumbents and rural candidates at the upper range – and the importance of partisanship, regionalism, and the electoral system have repeatedly affirmed the primacy of systemic factors that constrict the influence of local campaigns.[4] Withering party membership, waning civic responsibility, and declining volunteerism have contributed to less local engagement and lower voter turnout,[5] and the difficulty of examining district effects versus the comparative ease of focusing on candidate ratings has resulted in the marginalization of local electioneering in election studies and few academic publications on local political outreach, voter identification, or get-out-the-vote (GOTV) operations.[6] To many scholars, constituency campaigning is too difficult to study and less important than partisanship and party leaders, even though it is the local campaign that engages directly with Canadians, it is a local candidate whose name is on the election ballot, and it is Members of Parliament who represent citizens in the House of Commons.

In the twenty-first century, innovations in communication technologies have resurrected national-level interest in constituency campaigning. Suddenly, local campaigning is fashionable, even as candidates have morphed into party representatives who convey uniformity and follow directions from national war rooms. Between and during elections, political parties are harnessing web and mobile technology to assemble information about electors, which they are using to deploy cost-effective and targeted canvassing and messaging.[7] National parties now urge incumbents, candidates, local party workers, and volunteers to compile intelligence on constituents and upload it instantly into party databases and sometimes into an MP's private database. This coordinated management of "big data" has both centralized and energized local campaign operations.[8]

In today's hyper-competitive electoral marketplace, the surge of interest in the ground game has coincided with a drift away from national-level broadcast advertising and toward social media advertising and microtargeting of electors. The embrace of digital communications is one of the many reasons why quantitative researchers have recently investigated the election effects of constituency campaigning in Canada, with one study concluding that the happenings in local electoral districts "definitely matter for party support overall [and] should be integrated more fully into existing explanations of election outcomes in Canada."[9] Missing are descriptions of what actually occurs on the ground during a twenty-first-century campaign.

What localized work occurs in electoral districts during a Canadian federal election? *Inside the Local Campaign* sets out to answer this research question. The book's authors use the contest in 2021 as an anchor as they describe an assortment of local campaign activities in today's digital media ecosystem. Each chapter documents an aspect of constituency campaigning within a common organizational structure. Contributors concisely summarize the (often) limited Canadian scholarship on the profiled role or topic, then build upon theory by synthesizing applicable information from recent Canadian news stories to identify trends, and finally present fresh insights into what happens behind the scenes based upon new information compiled during the recent election. But first this introduction lays the groundwork by summarizing what is known about constituency campaigning in Canada.

The Resurgence of Local-Level Campaigning

In Canada's Westminster-style parliamentary system, electors vote for the representative of a political party in their electoral district. They rarely support independents. Executives in a party's local electoral district association (EDA), if one exists, are tasked with recruiting candidates and organizing a nomination contest so that local party members can select the person who will be the party's candidate on the ballot. The EDA, the candidate, and volunteers wage a local campaign to identify, mobilize, and persuade voters. The candidate who wins a plurality of votes in an electoral district during a federal election or by-election is elected to represent the area as an MP in the House of Commons, and the party that controls the most seats forms the government, with that party's leader becoming the prime minister and heading a cabinet. Each major party therefore attempts to run local candidates and mount competitive campaigns in as many districts as possible.

Campaigning is democracy's way of ensuring that aspiring office-holders and incumbents communicate their positions and initiatives with the electorate.[10] Outreach to electors raises their awareness of candidates, stimulates political interest among them, educates them politically, and informs them of policy positions. Information about campaigns is most evident on the national stage, where the media focus on party leaders, who tour the country making policy announcements and attending local rallies with the party faithful. Meanwhile, with comparatively little fanfare, local candidates and campaign workers try to secure votes from Canadians in

338 electoral districts. Under the shadow of a national campaign, they participate in local operations that put up signs, run an election headquarters, distribute brochures, knock on doors, place phone calls, and organize local rallies. Talking with electors on their doorsteps and by telephone to identify their vote intentions as "for," "unsure," or "against" is a pivotal aspect of GOTV mobilization used for identifying supporters who are urged to vote in advance polling and especially on election day. Provided that enough workers are available, the candidate's election team designates scrutineers to sit at polling stations to keep track of who has voted and to relay updates to the campaign headquarters so that workers can cajole identified supporters to vote before polls close. Well-resourced campaigns can offer transportation or child-minding services.

Political scientists who study political behaviour are prone to question the rationality of constituency-level campaigning, particularly in party strongholds. Their analyses of public opinion data, including use of the Canadian Election Study data set, demonstrate the primacy of partisanship, socialization, leaders, and other macro-level variables, reflecting the stark reality that, for most Canadians, there is little payoff in investing effort to assess individual candidates in a political system in which elected officials toe the party line. Consequently, constituency campaigning has often been treated as little more than a "ritual" with minimal effect on the election outcome.[11] Candidate factors are estimated to matter the most for partisans[12] and to make the difference between winning and losing in up to 14 percent of electoral districts.[13] Stories of candidates going to extreme lengths to solicit votes, such as flying by helicopter to remote areas or walking ankle deep in mud,[14] are treated as laudable efforts to inform electors with little bearing on the election result. Academics are also mindful that the national party provides local campaigns with graphic design specifications, increasing the message consistency and visibility of the party brand at the cost of marginalizing candidates' individualism.[15] Ultimately, there is scholarly consensus that constituency campaigning mostly matters in close races in which there is increased voter interest and turnout, decreased information search costs for voters, and greater party resources and tactical voting.[16]

A problem with this reductionist thinking is that scholars have struggled to measure adequately the effects of local electioneering on voting. Constituency campaigns encompass far more than candidate ratings. Academics who work with election survey data rarely consider whether local candidates influence leaders' ratings and rarely delve into electors' positions on local issues. We therefore know little about the true impact of constituency campaigning on voter behaviour. For example, on the surface, a candidate who visits a remote area to canvass for votes likely has limited direct effect on the vote outcome. However, we need to consider the communications value of the candidate being widely hailed as a deeply committed constituency representative, which can have a positive influence on how both the candidate and the party are viewed across the electoral district. Relatedly, candidates in neighbouring ridings might have vastly different approaches to adapting to national dynamics. As David Bell and Frederick Fletcher observed decades ago, understanding how effective campaign communication is requires recognition of "the extent to which local campaigns bring out the local significance of the major issues of the national campaign."[17] The focus on national variables in campaign studies results in knowledge gaps. Political scientists do not study, for example, how voters react when a local candidate departs strategically from the national campaign.

Treating constituency campaigning as foremost a vote-getting exercise ought to generate questions about and insights into the extent to which finite resources warrant redeployment from safe seats to marginal ridings. In some safe seats, a party's candidate reaches a margin of over 70 percent of the vote compared with the runner-up, whereas local campaigning and spending truly have an electoral impact in the small number of seats where the difference between winning and losing is a few hundred votes or less.[18] Moreover, prevailing in close races can make the difference between whether Canadians are governed by a majority or minority government, and in which party forms the government.[19] More broadly, candidates who secure a higher share of the vote, who build a local profile, and who make connections are seen as opinion leaders and augment their status within the party.

There has been some thawing in how academia considers local-level campaigning. In his presidential address to the Canadian Political Science Association in 2002, R.K. Carty advocated that we should look at Canadian parties as franchise organizations, whereby franchisors (the parties) enter licensing arrangements with local franchisees (the candidates) who leverage community networks and respond to the local marketplace.[20] The analogy is a good one given that it recognizes that political parties are professional operations that have invested in considerable brand architecture and that, as a result, their nominated candidates become brand ambassadors who behave as a sort of localized salesforce.[21] In a presidential address delivered in 2016, William Cross extolled the importance of local party activity in Canadian federal elections and advocated that researchers study localized aspects of party life. According to him, "we can only fully study many important aspects of Canadian politics by collecting riding level data to include in our analyses" that otherwise would be blurred by national-level impressions.[22] Practitioners are especially upbeat about local campaigns. They ascribe value to incumbency and voter outreach. They see competitive advantages in localized interpretations of national messaging, of the visibility of the candidate on doorsteps, and of GOTV field organization machinery. Between elections, the national parties encourage active EDAs and press their MPs to collect data on constituents, and in the lead-up to the campaign they organize candidate training. The perceived inability of political scientists to understand campaign dynamics is exemplified by one Canadian practitioner's claim that "an academic left alone to come up with the campaign plan ... [produces one] in a form that no one can comprehend."[23]

In any event, elections are about much more than getting candidates elected. Constituency campaigning is a fundamental democratic function that activates, engages, and includes electors and party workers in the process of selecting a representative, deliberating public policy, and indirectly selecting a prime minister and government. It causes politicians to interact directly with constituents, to listen to their concerns, and to integrate members of diverse communities who might ordinarily be left out of politics.

Indeed, many candidates have no chance of winning, meaning that their campaign workers are motivated by a sense of loyalty, promoting a political ideology, and the allure of social camaraderie that boosts supporter morale. Their engagement instills a sense of identity and belonging. When victors are declared, they are congratulated for running strong campaigns, whereas losers attribute their defeat to factors beyond their control. As one former MP puts it, "in the elections that I won, clearly people understood things properly. And then the elections that I lost, I guess I was a little underappreciated."[24]

One underappreciated reason that constituency campaigning is so vital to Canadian democracy is the challenge of connecting with the growing number of electors whose first language is neither English nor French. There are now more allophones than francophones in Canada, with more than 400,000 citizens in each linguistic group of Arabic, Cantonese, Mandarin, Punjabi, Spanish, and Tagalog, and many more collectively speak languages as diverse as Cree and Creole.[25] Reaching such a diverse population via mass media, social media, or so-called ethnic media is difficult, and community leaders often act as intermediaries.[26] But what has really fuelled interest in local campaigning has been political parties' drive to populate databases with identified supporters who might get involved, donate, canvass, and vote.

Awareness of the importance of blending traditional canvassing with digital campaigning was propelled by the machinery of Barack Obama's 2008 presidential election bid. The Obama team leveraged digital marketing, social media, and mobile marketing to empower grassroots supporters within a centrally coordinated national operation.[27] Enthusiasts were asked for their cellphone numbers so that the campaign could text them information, and they were constantly asked to supply additional details about themselves and their political interests in order to refine voter profiles. Using triangulation and global positioning system coordinates, the national campaign identified the locations of supporters who had installed an application on their smartphones and sent messages urging them to visit local campaign offices. Obama's supporters were encouraged to repurpose campaign content online, and volunteers were asked to phone their friends in battleground states and submit vote intentions to a national database. A community online portal was used to assemble information about local supporters, to host debate parties, to share personal stories, and to invite undecided voters. Volunteers could access a repository of names and phone numbers to knock on doors and call electors in their neighbourhoods. All of this bypassed the traditional role of the mainstream news media as an information filter and harnessed a digital army of volunteers across America.

Canadian political parties' interest in digital infrastructure was bolstered by trends in the United States. When Obama became president, the Conservative Party of Canada was being celebrated for its segmentation of citizens into like-minded cohorts, who could be reached through advertising on specialized media and by promoting boutique policies, and for its voter information database that archived donor status, lawn sign history, and political concerns that constituents identified on mail-back cards.[28] By the Canadian federal election of 2015, all major Canadian political parties were prioritizing database marketing, spurred in part by the Harper government's winding down of the per-vote election subsidy and drastically limiting the amount that estates can bequest to political parties.[29] The Conservatives and the Liberals rolled out smartphone and tablet apps so that canvassers could input information directly into the party's database while talking with constituents on doorsteps.[30] Global positioning system technology allowed the parties to monitor the areas of a riding being canvassed. Liberal digital architects harnessed information about elector preferences to refine messaging and disseminated information via email and social media to match the right messages with potential supporters.[31] The national parties – more so the Liberals than the Conservatives – have henceforth overseen local activities across the country and have harvested grassroots data for national purposes. More centripetal coordination and influence are being exerted over local operations, candidates, and incumbents than ever before.

It is now a norm that well-resourced campaigns mobilize a group of canvassers to knock on doors, to hurry the candidate over to greet a constituent, and to record information that is uploaded to the Cloud.[32] Talking to electors in person at their homes is perhaps the best way to identify potential supporters given that telephone canvassing is complicated by the abandonment of landlines and the fact that people screen their calls and because many Canadians do not engage with politics online. Canadian pollster David Coletto observes that

> going door to door is no longer just a tool to introduce a candidate to voters or to ask a household to put a lawn sign in front of their home. It has become an important, maybe the most important, source of market intelligence for Canadian political parties ... The rise of predictive analytics and digital advertising coincided with the decline of telephone-based direct voter contact. Somewhat ironically, "go knock on doors" in the age of digital first campaigning [has become] the "new" dimension in market intelligence for Canada's political parties.[33]

Today's constituency campaigners might not realize it, but the data that they are collecting is far more enduring and important to the party than focusing on a single election. Identifying the vote for GOTV operations, collecting email addresses, and encouraging supporters to take lawn signs have the post-election purpose of informing fundraising appeals and relationship building as part of the permanent campaign.[34] Increasingly, the canvassers who visit residences with a pencil and clipboard are the ones participating in a ritual of days gone by.

Trends in Local Campaigns

New profiles of local electioneering are needed to reflect these types of changing dynamics. Most of the descriptive research on constituency campaigning in Canada was conducted in a now-distant world before social media, smartphones, and wifi and before the social movements that sparked political reforms to address power imbalances that disadvantage women, Indigenous peoples, visible minorities, and LGBTQ2S+ citizens. Local news outlets have been closing, media conglomerates have been recycling stories, and urban-based national news organizations are paying scant attention to rural and remote communities. As well, election candidates are so entwined with their party's brand that it is difficult for them to express individualism and authenticity or to know when they can push back against the messaging that emanates from the national campaign.

In each election, a cadre of incumbents do not run again, creating openings for party candidates who are indoctrinated by the need to follow the leader and lack the institutional memory of how parliamentary politics works. The pressure for party unity raises a democratic predicament: If candidates do not think that they can speak up during an election campaign, then should we expect them to display independent voices when they are in Parliament? Wayne Easter was a long-time Liberal MP from Prince Edward Island who did not seek re-election in 2021. In the lead-up to that campaign, he bemoaned that the prime minister and to a lesser extent opposition leaders were surrounded by a growing sphere of political staffers armed with "a political science degree from somewhere" who complicate the role of MPs to represent constituents. Easter reflected that the House of Commons needs "a mix" of people and opinions so that "Parliament itself continues to reign supreme as a backstop to what government, or cabinet itself, may want to do."[35] Frustration with party shackles is a common refrain from parliamentary veterans in Canada, as the Samara Centre for Democracy and others have repeatedly found.[36] The turnover of so many seats in each Canadian federal election means that there is always a crop of new MPs struggling to learn how to navigate the parliamentary process and to find their voice.

As an election nears, each party's election machinery gears up, and key campaign positions are filled by trusted operatives. Although official titles vary, at the apex is the national campaign manager, typically followed by a chair or co-chairs who are prominent party trustees or elected officials and supported by regional campaign directors who might be political staffers on leaves of absence from their work on Parliament Hill and in ministerial offices.[37] On the ground, titleholders in EDAs are tasked with candidate recruitment and election readiness. The role of local party presidents in candidate recruitment can be significant, particularly with respect to encouraging women and racialized persons to run,[38] and they can become upset when national party operatives encroach on candidate selection. In 1972, party leaders were required to approve all party nominees standing for election, an authority that has been delegated since 2015 to representatives of the leaders. Disgruntled partisans invariably accuse a leader's circle of flouting party rules to anoint a preferred candidate or meddling in local affairs by dismissing an undesirable one. The tension over candidate selection has shifted from leaders interjecting to nominate women[39] to whether MPs have met party conditions for renomination. For example, the Bloc Québécois requires that its local associations in ridings held by the party raise $19,000, be debt free, and have a minimum of 350 party members, a requirement comparable to other parties' expectations of their incumbents.[40] Aspiring candidates, including incumbents, must pass a vetting process to be eligible to seek the nomination as the party's candidate. Those nominated in advance of the writ of election have the advantage of building name recognition and assembling a campaign team. In the case of a snap election, opposition parties and EDAs can be caught off guard and scramble to nominate a candidate, particularly in places where the party's support is weak. Internal scrutiny of the backgrounds and public remarks of potential candidates can be an irritant when it delays them from campaigning, and the time pressure to nominate a full slate increases the authority of the leader. The leader's agents can invoke urgency to change nomination rules and to appoint preferred candidates, which can anger local party members who perceive anti-democratic tactics,[41] and only those who pass central vetting are granted access to EDA membership lists and can begin fundraising.[42] In party strongholds, a nomination race for a popular party can be more intense than the election, whereas weaker parties can be so moribund that they parachute in a "paper" or "ghost" candidate who perhaps has never visited the riding and is unavailable to the media.[43]

Once nominated, a candidate assembles a campaign team, including appointing an official agent to ensure that the financial affairs stay within the rules. Well-resourced candidates might hire a seasoned campaigner to manage their runs for office, but many others are handled by a trusted colleague or family member. As the campaign gets under way, local media dutifully profile area candidates and report on all-candidates debates, and national media identify key seats to watch and comment on battleground areas that the national parties' seat triage has identified as priorities. Occasionally, a local contestant attracts attention for standing apart from the crowd, as with climate activist Avi Lewis in 2021. The grandson of a former New Democratic Party (NDP) leader, the son of a former leader of the Ontario NDP, and the husband of celebrated author Naomi Klein, Lewis was a vocal NDP candidate in Vancouver who attracted big crowds and endorsements from celebrities such as Jane Fonda and David Suzuki. His fame in a longshot riding with a party unlikely to form the government gave him added leeway to exert his independence. "I will never vote against my conscience ... I want to go to Ottawa to shake up the entire political establishment," Lewis said, as he proclaimed that he would champion a more aggressive green policy agenda than the one in his party's platform.[44] Although he made inroads by capitalizing on the Green Party's collapse, his third-place finish illustrates that constituency campaigning goes only so far, and the campaign experience of most aspiring legislators is a far cry from that of political stars. In Canada, even incumbents are involved with grunt work. "At 5:00am a week from the election I was out gathering a stack of about 10 defaced, sexualized, phallicized, large campaign signs alone with my dog – in the pouring rain no less," recalled Lenore Zann, a Liberal MP defeated in Nova Scotia.[45]

Party leaders are wary of local affairs drawing them into controversies that distract from national campaign management. In 2021, a campaign event held by NDP leader Jagmeet Singh alongside Manitoba candidates went awry when two First Nations leaders standing next to him endorsed a local Liberal. Elsewhere, some Green Party candidates shunned embattled leader Annamie Paul, whom they did not want visiting their ridings,[46] while in Quebec a Green candidate admonished her on Facebook.[47] Parties in contention to form the government are more likely to clamp down and control the message. Candidates who contradict the leader's position often issue public retractions or apologies and then abruptly disappear from public view in an attempt to deprive the media and critics of fodder to sustain the drama.[48] If a candidate is found to have exhibited egregious behaviour, such as a prejudiced social media post that opponents supply to the media, or even a complaint about an insincere apology, then the leader might be pressed to demand the candidate's resignation.[49] The party can try to lower the political temperature by encouraging its candidate to "pause" campaigning, whereas in other cases it will rush to recruit a replacement if time allows.[50] Likewise, the leader and/or candidates can publicly admonish campaign volunteers for unscrupulous acts.[51] However, coordination goes only so far: message discipline is difficult to enforce if multiple candidates break ranks, particularly if the voices of dissent come from incumbents in safe seats.[52]

The Pandemic Election of 2021

The Canadian federal election of 2021 will surely be known as the pandemic election. During the 43rd Parliament leading up to the election, MPs contended with a torrent of constituent inquiries and adapted to physical distancing health measures by hosting video meetings and digital town halls.[53] They held committee meetings via Zoom, and they voted on bills and motions via a hybrid set-up of some MPs voting in person in Ottawa and others voting electronically. For months, many worked from home without being able to meet colleagues or staff face to face, while those MPs who voted in person in Ottawa sometimes felt lonely, which complicated their ability to build relationships within the caucus, with members of other parties, and with senators. Parliament adapted to new technology by setting up Wickr Pro, an encrypted messaging app, for MPs to receive vote notifications, and caucuses created WhatsApp chats to enable MPs to connect. Staying in touch with constituents was difficult given that in-person canvassing of households and mingling in public forums were no longer viable. "Even just at events – at cultural events, at community events – when you just get to talk to people one-on-one and build those relationships in those ways, it's very different when you have to specifically book a Zoom meeting and you talk about a specific thing, right? You don't have a Zoom meeting to chit chat," lamented London NDP MP Lindsey Mathyssen just before the election was called.[54]

The need to avoid in-person interactions during a pandemic pushed many constituency campaign activities online, in some cases irrevocably. Candidates in large geographical areas experienced the convenience of video calls, and political organizers now know the benefits of hosting online debates, including keeping protesters at bay.[55] The trend toward digital options predated the pandemic, of course, but public health rules preventing normal in-person interactions sped up that trend. Some parties emailed supporters to urge them to consider running as candidates,[56] and social media advertising soared.[57] Many all-candidates debates were offered by Zoom or other video conferencing technology, resulting in greater accessibility to view more civil affairs now devoid of a crowd of partisan hecklers and candidates shouting over each other.[58] Conservative leader Erin O'Toole bucked participating in the leader's tour of electoral districts across the country by substituting two to three days of hosting virtual town halls from the controlled confines of a custom-built broadcast studio in an Ottawa hotel ballroom. The tactic enabled the party to reach voters directly in multiple regions and collect data on them, although a campaign post-mortem later criticized the leader for forgoing in-person engagement.[59] Reflecting on the Liberal Party's use of the Greenfly app, which helps social media influencers to share content online, a Liberal spokesperson quipped that "it's long been said that all politics is local, but the past year's unprecedented circumstances have also meant that 'all politics is digital' for the first time."[60] The pandemic election also saw a more intense effort to encourage supporters to vote in advance polls or to vote by mail.

A disconcerting trend that candidates must contend with is incivility. Some party candidates are given a hard time at public events, and all of them brace for being treated rudely on doorsteps. Almost every campaign expects its signs to be stolen or defaced, sometimes in an apparently coordinated manner soon after they are installed, and occasionally opponents are caught pinching election pamphlets out of mailboxes.[61] Seeking election requires a thick skin and the ability to endure harsh criticism, including being the target of toxic behaviour online that can spill over to in-person interactions. In the extreme, people hurl insults and vulgarities from their vehicles, and candidates in electoral districts where their party or leader is unpopular might fear canvassing alone.[62] In rare cases, they might be chased, receive death threats, or even be assaulted physically. According to MP Michelle Rempel Garner, the Conservative MP for Calgary Nose Hill, tactics of intimidation inhibited her ability to campaign in 2021. "This meant I can't advertise the location of my campaign office. I can't attend public events where my attendance has been advertised. I've had to enhance security measures. I'm on edge and feel fear when I'm getting in and out of my car, and out in public in general," she tweeted.[63] In Sudbury, a woman was charged with assault for allegedly pinning a male Liberal candidate against a wall and then kicking his car.[64] "Something has changed, and it has not changed for the good," Rempel Garner observed.[65]

Other pandemic activities were likely one-offs (see Appendix). Candidates who sought party nominations in the months before the election call tried drumming up support via telephone and social media, but signing up new members was complicated by not knowing how voting in a nomination contest would be held or how to mobilize those members to vote.[66] Fewer in-person public events were organized, with a preference for outdoor gatherings in line with public health guidelines. Politicians and campaign workers were scrutinized for wearing facemasks and whether they were vaccinated; some parties required that candidates and campaign workers be fully vaccinated or pass a daily rapid test.[67] When canvassers placed pamphlets in household mailboxes and rang doorbells, they stepped back to ensure physical distance and found that some housebound electors were excited about the opportunity for social interaction. In-person gatherings of volunteers talking politics over food and drink were scuttled in many campaign headquarters, which dampened worker morale, though it was mitigated somewhat by party operatives who posted upbeat messages to private

Facebook groups.[68] Door knockers arranged meeting points out-doors, their canvassing in apartment buildings was pared back, and telephone canvassers sat two metres apart or worked from home. In Winnipeg, a Liberal candidate did not publicly disclose the ad-dress of his headquarters in order to control unannounced visits,[69] while in Charlottetown a number of candidates speculated that the theft of lawn signs was linked to the inflated price of lumber.[70]

Local campaign teams were cautious about their GOTV oper-ations, such as considering whether drivers who offered constitu-ents transportation to the polls should be vaccinated and ensure that the vehicle's windows were open. Elections Canada experi-enced greater difficulty securing spaces for polling locations given that some locations, such as schools, were no longer available. The agency required that all in-person voters wear masks and allowed people to vote past the close of polls if they were in line. More time was required to count a higher number of special ballots, meaning that some races were not decided until after election day. Another aspect that might be temporal is the surprising popularity of the People's Party of Canada, which attracted support from nearly 5 percent of voters, many of whom were libertarians expressing dis-content with government COVID-19 policies.

To put the uniqueness of the pandemic election further in per-spective, we can consider some of the traditional constituency campaign activities that were normal a decade earlier.[71] In the lead-up to the federal election in 2011, MPs and nominated candi-dates had hosted roundtables and knocked on doors, and they had held grand openings for their campaign headquarters. Candidates canvassed in retirement homes, in shopping malls, and in restau-rants, and they attended all manner of local events, from library openings to garden shows, though there were also many instances of candidate no-shows at all-candidate debates. They flipped pan-cakes at community breakfasts, ate rubber chicken at luncheons, and delivered speeches at fundraising dinners. At the time, many candidates were beginning to experiment with social media and electronic town halls. The in-person engagements seem to have generated more controversial moments for critics to complain about and for media to report on.

Since then, candidates have continued to submit their public identities to their party and to the primacy of its leader, at centre stage in everything from the party's manifesto to advertising to the leaders' debates and the leader's tour. Local campaigns might be required to provide funds for party advertising and to relinquish as much as 100 percent of their post-campaign spending rebates to the national party,[72] and at their discrection centralized parties can deny candidates and MPs access to the local data that they collected on party members and supporters.[73] Even so, local flagbearers are championed when the leader is less popular, as occurred with Liberal Party advertising in 2021 that featured Quebec candidates talking about how "Team Trudeau is a tightly-knit team with a united vision."[74] A constant, regardless of the pandemic, is that the relationship between candidates and their parties is more complex and mutually beneficial than it might appear.

Goal and Structure of the Book

Inside the Local Campaign is an updated description of local-level campaign activities within a Canadian federal election. The earliest book-length academic treatment is likely Brian Land's *Eglinton: The Election Study of a Federal Constituency,* which meticulously details events in a prominent Toronto riding during the general election of 1962 and profiles an era when there was limited top-down party coordination.[75] Two notable volumes were commissioned as part of the Royal Commission on Electoral Reform and Party Financing in 1991. In *Reaching the Voter: Constituency Campaigning in Canada,* editors David Bell and Frederick Fletcher assembled a collection of regional case studies that drew attention to a crisis of declining political participation and found that local campaigns are often – but not always – microcosms of the national campaign.[76] In *Canadian Political Parties in the Constituencies,* R.K. Carty surveyed constituency-level party work and the role of EDAs and found variations across the country, with some district associations highly active and others dormant or non-existent.[77] Another influential book in this area was *Parties, Candidates, and Constituency Campaigns in Canadian Elections* by Anthony Sayers. His profiles of select BC ridings in the federal election of 1988 provided rich descriptions of local-level happenings and influenced our thinking of Canadian party candidates as fitting into one of four archetypes. According to Sayers, there are high-profile contestants who are political novices, local notables such as former municipal politicians who have a stable political base to draw on, party insiders who enjoy privileged status within the party, and stopgaps who have no prospects of winning and whose campaign teams might be family members sitting around their kitchen tables. A reread of these books shows that much campaigning remains unchanged from the late twentieth century to now.

Subsequently, R.K. Carty and Munroe Eagles published a quantitative analysis of constituency campaigning. In *Politics Is Local: National Politics at the Grassroots,* they find that many local party members derive satisfaction from participating in constituency elections and cast doubt on the normative view that the party centre exerts control over local affairs.[78] Another influential work is *Grassroots Liberals: Organizing for Local and National Politics,* in which Royce Koop looks at how the federal Liberal Party and its provincial cousins interact with EDAs and constituency-level campaigns. A spate of edited volume chapters and some journal articles enrich this small canon by looking at a variety of localized topics, ranging from LGBTQ2S+[79] and ethnoracial candidacy[80] to analysis of political behaviour indicating that local candidate factors make the difference in close races.[81]

New information is needed to understand how local campaigns operate in a faster-paced digital environment in which every mistake is magnified and party candidates amplify national-level messaging.[82] Nowadays there is more diversity among candidates. This results in different campaign experiences, such as new mothers who take breaks from canvassing to breastfeed in the back seat of a car[83] and visible minorities who are subject to media stereotypes that sometimes have a bearing on their electoral performance.[84] As well, the move to digital campaigning has had profound implications for local candidates who constantly communicate via social media, who put on virtual fundraising events, and who hold Facebook Live town halls.[85]

In this volume, we build upon *Inside the Campaign: Managing Elections in Canada* (UBC Press, 2020) by continuing to record what goes on behind the scenes in Canadian federal elections, this time in electoral districts. In the previous volume, academic authors collaborated with practitioners who had national-level experience. Although many practitioners shared inside information, the binds of partisanship and fears of career repercussions made it difficult for some to be objective about their campaign work or to disclose details, whereas academics often wanted to write more theory and integrate additional critical analysis. We decided for *Inside the Local Campaign* that the best way to generate inside information is to offer academics the choice of co-authoring with practitioners or compiling original data in some other manner. Another difference is our integration of some photographs to capture what local-level campaigning looks like across Canada (see the Appendix). Contributors were encouraged to prepare enduring content as opposed to documenting the pandemic election.

Holly Ann Garnett begins by building upon an insider's account of Elections Canada in the previous book[86] and her considerable research on election administration to understand how the directives issued by senior election administrators trickle down to the front lines. In Chapter 1, she looks at the essential role of Elections Canada workers, who have endeavoured to ensure that the election process is smooth, especially in the pandemic context of the election in 2021. Garnett observes that the integrated teamwork of national and local electoral managers delivers world-class election administration, notwithstanding occasional hiccups.

In Chapter 2, Angelia Wagner delves into the thorny topic of candidate ambition and the motivations of Canadians who consider standing for election. Past research has shown that people seek office because they are extroverts interested in a political career and want to influence public policy, or perhaps they are narcissists who pursue power.[87] Wagner's analysis of candidates in the federal election of 2021 finds that influencing public policy is the main reason that they run. There is also some variation in motivation depending on a candidate's gender or race.

In Chapter 3, Anna Lennox Esselment and Matthew Bondy investigate some of the ways that party operatives recruit aspiring candidates, drawing in part from Bondy's experience as a Conservative nomination contestant in Ontario. For some, a barrier to standing for election is the process within political parties to nominate candidates who want to run under the party banner, which according to the Samara Centre for Democracy many MPs think is a flaw in Canada's democratic infrastructure.[88] Incumbents have the inside track, but even so there is considerable jostling between national and local arms of the party over nomination contests and candidate selections. Electoral district associations compete with the agents of party leaders for influence, with one espousing the democratic role of grassroots members and the other concerned about protecting the party brand. Esselment and Bondy show that the lack of transparency in nomination contests is a cause for concern.

In Chapter 4, Cristine de Clercy veers from the Sayers archetype of Canadian election candidates by looking at the presence of star candidates.[89] She identifies dozens of local public figures who fit this categorization in the campaign in 2021, of whom about one in five was elected, and shows that commanding local attention is not necessarily a path to election victory. Her case study of a Liberal running in London enriches our understanding of high-profile contestants and fleshes out a category of the local candidate.

In Chapter 5, J.P. Lewis tackles the topic of ministerial incumbents, among the highest-profile type of incumbents. We know that incumbents enjoy an increased probability of victory of approximately 9–11 percent compared with non-incumbents, particularly those who enjoy positive reputations,[90] and that cabinet ministers have particular star power, nurtured by making a slew of spending announcements in the lead-up to an election that demonstrate political prowess to constituents. Drawing from half a dozen interviews with campaign managers and ministers, Lewis describes the special advantages enjoyed by ministers who seek re-election and dubs them "incumbents plus."

In Chapter 6, Mireille Lalancette, Vincent Raynauld, and Anthony Ozorai add an examination of the personalization of local candidates. In the last book, Lalancette delved into the role of a senior adviser to the leader on the leader's tour to illustrate the many calculations that go into image management, and Raynauld examined regional advertising.[91] This time they collaborate with a local practitioner to investigate how candidates establish public personas in their online communications. Looking at the hotly contested riding of Trois-Rivières, they discover that Prime Minister Justin Trudeau's social media use inspired the Liberal candidate's own use, but the medium was sufficiently flexible for the candidate to promote a personalized local image and work within national messaging.

Campaign messages stem from party platforms, and their construction was the subject of Jared Wesley's prior contribution.[92] Wesley co-authors Chapter 7 with Richard Maksymetz, a regional campaign chair with the Liberal Party. They direct attention to the role of a regional campaign chair, a position that reflects geographical variances and political cultures in a vast country where national-level issues can be less topical than local electors' concerns about provincial and local issues.[93] Their profile of the role of a regional campaign chair shows how the localized coordination function of party bosses has evolved over time.

Chapter 8 is by two scholars who have published much work on constituency campaigns in Canada. Royce Koop and Anthony Sayers draw on an array of interviews to describe the functions of local campaign managers, whose role focuses on optimizing voter identification and mobilizing supporters to vote at advance polls, by special ballot, or on election day. Among sundry duties is signing up volunteers; as one campaign manual puts it, this requires creating "anticipation about the excitement and possibilities of Election Day" to recruit workers to participate in GOTV operations.[94] Drawing from interviews with a handful of party campaign managers, the authors suggest that the work involves managing downward, upward, and outward.

In Chapter 9, Paul Wilson writes about the involvement of political staff in constituency campaigns. In the previous volume, he analyzed what ministerial political staff do during a campaign if they choose to remain in the minister's office for its duration.[95] Here

Wilson considers the work of political staff who take leaves of absence to participate in local campaigning. His interviews with party activists inform an updated look at the work on the ground carried out by individuals on local campaign teams. The profile is connected with Chapter 10, which illuminates what local canvassing entails. Jacob Robbins-Kanter interviewed eight local candidates and campaign managers to inform a description of how local volunteers are an important data-collecting resource for both local and national campaigns. He finds variations in approaches to canvassing and suggests that fundamental differences are forming between candidates who can afford new technologies to harvest local data and those who cannot.

Several contributors provide examples of how local candidates and their campaigns behave as franchisees by strategically distancing themselves from their party to generate ambiguity that benefits them and, ultimately, the party. In Chapter 11, Doug Munroe and Kaija Belfry Munroe leverage their past work on big data to profile how local campaigns from different political parties make use of their databases to inform their actions and decisions.[96] Contrary to past accounts of data marketing in Canadian federal parties, which tend to focus on large urban centres, their interviews with local candidates and campaign managers in Prince Edward Island reveal local resistance to using national databases. In Chapter 12, Erin Crandall extends her discussion on national-level party fundraising that appeared in the earlier book.[97] Joined by Liberal MP Kody Blois, Crandall reveals some of the inside practices of local fundraising by election candidates, using Blois's experience in Nova Scotia as a case study. In contrast to the database fundraising conducted by national parties, which use electronic appeals to collect small amounts from a large number of supporters, local fundraising is labour intensive and relies on a candidate's personal connections to solicit larger donations from a smaller pool of donors. In Chapter 13, Stéphanie Yates looks at the integration of national messaging into constituency campaigns, building on her work after the 2019 campaign.[98] She dissects efforts by the NDP and its candidates in Quebec to communicate a consistent message. Her conversations with NDP MP Alexandre Boulerice and his communications officer inform her view that candidates for a political party destined for the opposition benches can deviate from national messaging, though on delicate files this might result in their use of ambiguous language to avoid brand conflict. Readers of these three chapters will find variation from conventional views of candidates as party robots and evidence that incumbents are more likely than first-time candidates to challenge centripetal forces.

The two chapters that follow focus on media. In Chapter 14, Colette Brin extends her work from the previous book, which looked at how senior news editors make news judgments.[99] Joined this time by journalists François Cormier and Myriam Descarreaux, she looks at local media coverage during a federal election campaign, using the Quebec City region as a case study. The chapter shows how changes in news assemblage have consequences for information that voters receive about constituency campaigns. In Chapter 15, Brooks DeCillia writes about local all-candidates' debates, building upon his work on the national Leaders Debate Commission that appeared in *Inside the Campaign*.[100] He demonstrates that the absence of national standards and resources means that coordinating debates among local candidates makes for a hodgepodge of approaches and a cacophony of partisan voices hoping to embarrass opponents. His analysis of over 200 news stories and interviews with eleven local campaigners shows that the democratic idealism of debates creates the expectation that candidates participate even though many of them see more value in knocking on doors.

Participating in campaign sign wars is another ritual that constituency teams engage in and about which there is debate. In Chapter 16, Gillian Maurice and Tamara Small document the understudied and misunderstood practice of campaign signage in generating awareness of a candidate and, by extension, that an election is under way. Their profile of sign use by Greens in two Ontario ridings suggests that the long-standing activity performs an important symbolic function in local electioneering.

Finally, in Chapter 17, Thomas Collombat further fleshes out the challenge of local engagement. He discusses local advocacy and uses the Public Service Alliance of Canada (PSAC) as a case study, thereby contributing a localized extension of his *Inside the Campaign* study of national-level advocacy by PSAC.[101] Collombat discloses that even a well-resourced national advocacy group faces considerable complexities with local-level advocacy during a federal election.

The book wraps up with a conclusion by Thierry Giasson, in which he adds further context for the pandemic election of 2021 and reflects on the tensions of local campaigns. Themes underscoring contributions to this volume are the stresses of determining who should run for the party, the boundaries of message discipline emanating from the national campaign, and local resistance to data-driven campaigning. Giasson then synthesizes the lingering traditions of local campaigning before commenting on the editorial challenges of assembling *Inside the Local Campaign.*

Although contributors cover a lot of ground, inevitably there is a range of topics that could fill another volume. For example, we know little about how campaigning varies between party strongholds, where competition is weak or even non-existent, and competitive battlegrounds;[102] how candidates react to readjusted electoral boundaries;[103] or how political parties redeploy financial resources from their national offices to local constituency associations.[104] More research is needed on campaigning by the Bloc Québécois, on minor party and independent candidates, and on how canvassing works in sparsely populated areas of the country, including among concentrated populations of Indigenous peoples. As the following chapters show, there is still much to be learned about constituency campaigning in Canada.

Notes

1   See, for example, Wiseman, "Get Out the Vote – Not."
2   Black, "Revising the Effects of Canvassing."
3   Blais et al., "Does the Local Candidate Matter?"; Bodet et al., "How Much of Electoral Politics"; Clarke et al., *Political Choice in Canada,* 352–53; Krasinsky and Milne, "Some Evidence on the Effect of Incumbency"; Sevi, Aviña, and Blais, "Reassessing Local Candidate Effects"; Stevens et al., "Local Candidate Effects."

4 See, for example, Blake, "Constituency Contexts."

5 Nakhaie, "Electoral Participation."

6 See, for example, Bodet et al., "How Much of Electoral Politics."

7 Patten, "Databases, Microtargeting, and the Permanent Campaign."

8 Belfry Munroe and Munroe, "Constituency Campaigning in the Age of Data."

9 Bodet et al., "How Much of Electoral Politics."

10 This introduction integrates some information from Marland, "Constituency Campaigning: A Review."

11 See, for example, Mishler and Clarke, "Political Participation in Canada," 177.

12 Roy and Alcantara, "The Candidate Effect."

13 Stevens et al., "Local Candidate Effects."

14 Meisel, *The Canadian General Election of 1957,* 92.

15 See, for example, Flanagan, *Harper's Team;* Marland, *Brand Command.*

16 See, for example, Eagles, "Voting and Non-Voting," 13–14.

17 Bell and Fletcher, "Electoral Communications at the Constituency Level," 192.

18 Maloney, "'What Just Happened?'"; Westlake, "Ready or Not?"

19 For example, see Rana, "O'Toole Conservatives Missed Winning Government."

20 Carty, "The Politics of Tecumseh Corners."

21 Marland and Wagner, "Scripted Messengers."

22 Cross, "The Importance of Local Party Activity," 16.

23 Brook, *Getting Elected in Canada,* 164.

24 Chen, "'The Horizon, though Still Murky.'"

25 Statistics Canada, "Canada and Canada (Table)."

26 Flanagan, *Harper's Team,* 281.

27 MarketingProfs, "The Obama Playbook."

28 Turcotte, "Under New Management."

29 Bryden, "Political Parties in a Fundraising Frenzy."

30 Watters, "New Mobile Election Apps."

31 Delacourt, *Shopping for Votes.*

32 Koop, "Constituency Campaigning in the 2015 Federal Election."

33 Coletto, "Go Knock on Doors," 92, 104.

34 Marland and Mathews, "Friend, Can You Chip in $3?"

35 Mazereeuw, "'Far Too Much Control.'"

36 See, for example, Morden, *Real House Lives.*

37 Rana, "National Liberal Campaign Director."

38 Tolley, "Who You Know."

39 For example, Carbert, "The Hidden Rise of New Women Candidates."

40 Canadian Press, "As Bloc Prepares for Federal Election."

41 Moss, "Supporters Irked"; Walsh, "Liberal Party Triggers 'Electoral Urgency' Rule."

42 Rana, "Some Potential Liberal and Conservative Candidates."

43 For example, Zingel, "N.W.T.'s Conservative Candidate Has Never Visited."

44 Lalonde, "NDP's Avi Lewis Aims to 'Shake Up' Establishment."

45 Chen, "'The Horizon, though Still Murky.'"

46 Gilmore, "Annamie Paul Sticks to Toronto."

47 Raycraft, "Green Party Candidate in Quebec."

48 For example, Gilmore, "Tory Candidate Says She 'Misspoke.'"

49 For example, Canadian Press, "Imams Ask Conservative Candidate to Quit."

50 Kwong, Ballingall, and Hasham, "Liberals Ask Toronto Candidate to 'Pause' Campaign."

51 For example, see Tasker, "Conservative Candidate Banishes Campaign Volunteers."

52 For example, see Chen, "Conservative Election Ad Pulled."

53 Koop, Blidook, and Fuga, "Has the COVID-19 Pandemic Affected MPs' Representational Activities?"

54 Quotation and paragraph information from Ryckewaert, "Zoom Meet-Ups and Chat Groups."

55 Bachusky and Singleton, "Anti-Maskers Force Shutdown."

56 For example, see Boutilier, "Conservatives Email Supporters in Search of Candidates."

57 Bogart, "Spending on Facebook Ads Skyrockets."

58 Willing, "Ottawa Centre Debate."

59 Thibedeau, "Conservatives Say Their 'Virtual' Campaign Strategy Is Paying Off"; Thibedeau and Tasker, "Conservative Post-Election Report."

60 Levitz, "Liberals Pin Their Hopes."

61 McGarvey, "Voter, Opponent Shocked."

62 Patel, "'I've Never Seen So Much Division.'"

63 Canadian Press, "Aggression and Threats on Campaign Trail."

64 CBC News, "Marc Serré, Liberal Candidate."

65 Boisvert, "Canadian Politicians Warn of Political Violence."

66 Rana, "Aspiring Liberal Candidates for Don Valley East."

67 Bimman, "Conservative Candidates Warned."

68 Reynolds, "Grappling with How to Press the Virtual Flesh."

69 Some information in this paragraph was obtained from Robertson, "Six Feet of Separation."

70 Davis, "Signs, Signs, Nowhere a Sign."

71 Marland, "Constituency Campaigning in the 2011 Canadian Federal Election."

72 Stefanovich, Romualdo, and Thurton, "Some NDP Members."

73 Boutilier and Levitz, "Tories' Membership Database Locked."

74 NetNewsLedger, "New Liberal Ad."

75 Land, *Eglinton*. Land's research notes and ethnographic material are archived at the University of Toronto as part of the R. Brian Land fonds (UTA record 1462-B1997-0024-2).

76 Bell and Fletcher, *Reaching the Voter*.

77 Carty, *Canadian Political Parties in the Constituencies*.

78 Carty and Eagles, *Politics Is Local*.

79 Wagner, "LGBTQ Perspectives."

80 Black and Erickson, "Ethno-Racial Origins of Candidates."

81 Gidengil et al., "Does the Local Candidate Matter?"; Roy and Alcantara, "The Candidate Effect"; Stevens et al., "Local Candidate Effects."

82 Robbins-Kanter, "Undisciplined Constituency Campaign Behaviour."

83 Stoodley, "The Twists of Campaigning."

84 Tolley, *Framed*.

85 McGrane, "Campaigning in Canada during a Pandemic."

86 Lawlor and Mayrand, "Election Administrators."

87 Blais, Pruysers, and Chen, "Why Do They Run?"

88 Thomas and Morden, *Party Favours*.

89 In addition to Sayers, *Parties, Candidates, and Constituency Campaigns*, see Carty, Eagles, and Sayers, "Candidates and Local Campaigns."

90 Kendall and Rekkas, "Incumbency Advantages."

91 Lalancette, with Della Mattia, "Senior Adviser to the Leader"; Raynauld and Renauld, "Political Advertisers."

92 Wesley and Nauta, "Party Platform Builders."

93 For example, see Andrew-Gee, "Even in the Middle."

94 Liberal Party of Canada (Ontario), *Planning and Running a Successful Election Day*, 6.

95 Wilson, "Political Staff."

96 Belfry Munroe and Munroe, "Constituency Campaigning in the Age of Data."

97 Crandall and Roy, "Party Fundraisers."

98 Yates and Chenery, "National Campaign Director of Communications."

99 Brin and MacDonald, "News Editors."

100 DeCillia and Cormier, "Leaders' Debate Coordinators."
101 Collombat and Picard, "Third-Party Activism."
102 Bodet, "Strongholds and Battlegrounds."
103 See, for example, Pal and Choudhry, "Constituency Boundaries in Canada."
104 Currie-Wood, "The National Growth of a Regional Party"; Westlake, "Ready or Not?"

Bibliography

Andrew-Gee, Eric. "Even in the Middle of a Federal Election, in Quebec, All Politics Is Local." *Globe and Mail,* 16 September 2021. https://www.theglobeandmail.com/canada/article-even-in-the-middle-of-a-federal-election-in-quebec-all-politics-is/.

Bachusky, Johnnie, and Dan Singleton. "Anti-Maskers Force Shutdown of Innisfail Federal Election Forum." MountainView Today [Olds, AB], 8 September 2021. https://www.mountainviewtoday.ca/2021-federal-election-coverage/anti-maskers-force-shutdown-of-innisfail-federal-election-forum-4315942.

Belfry Munroe, Kaija, and H.D. Munroe. "Constituency Campaigning in the Age of Data." *Canadian Journal of Political Science* 51, 1 (2018): 135–54.

Bell, David V.J., and Frederick J. Fletcher. "Electoral Communication at the Constituency Level: Summary and Conclusion." In *Reaching the Voter: Constituency Campaigning in Canada,* edited by David V.J. Bell and Frederick J. Fletcher, 179–200. Royal Commission on Electoral Reform and Party Financing. Toronto: Dundurn Press, 1991.

–. eds. *Reaching the Voter: Constituency Campaigning in Canada.* Royal Commission on Electoral Reform and Party Financing. Toronto: Dundurn Press, 1991.

Bimman, Abigail. "Conservative Candidates Warned: Vaccinate or Test Daily, Party Email Shows." Global News, 18 August 2021. https://globalnews.ca/news/8121946/otoole-mandatory-covid-vaccines-tests-candidates/.

Black, Jerome H. "Revising the Effects of Canvassing on Voter Behaviour." *Canadian Journal of Political Science* 17, 2 (1984): 352–53.

Black, Jerome H., and Lynda Erickson. "Ethno-Racial Origins of Candidates and Electoral Performance: Evidence from Canada." *Party Politics* 12, 4 (2006): 541–61.

Blais, André, Elisabeth Gidengil, Agnieszka Dobrzynska, Neil Nevitte, and Richard Nadeau. "Does the Local Candidate Matter? Candidate Effects in the Canadian Election of 2000." *Canadian Journal of Political Science* 36, 3 (2003): 657–64.

Blais, Julie, Scott Pruysers, and Philip G. Chen. "Why Do They Run? The Psychological Underpinnings of Political Ambition." *Canadian Journal of Political Science* 52, 4 (2019): 761–79.

Blake, Donald E. "Constituency Contexts and Canadian Elections: An Exploratory Study." *Canadian Journal of Political Science* 11, 2 (1978): 279–305.

Bodet, Marc André. "Strongholds and Battlegrounds: Measuring Party Support Stability in Canada." *Canadian Journal of Political Science* 46, 3 (2013): 575–96.

Bodet, Marc André, Joanie Bouchard, Melanee Thomas, and Charles Tessier. "How Much of Electoral Politics Is in the District? Measuring District Effects on Party Support." *Canadian Journal of Political Science* 55, 1 (2022): 150–70.

Bogart, Nicole. "Spending on Facebook Ads Skyrockets amid Election, as Liberals Outspend All Other Parties Combined." CTV News, 3 September 2021. https://www.ctvnews.ca/politics/federal-election-2021/spending -on-facebook-ads-skyrockets-amid-election-as-liberals-outspend-all-other -parties-com%E2%80%A6.

Boisvert, Nick. "Canadian Politicians Warn of Political Violence after U.K. MP Is Stabbed to Death." CBC News, 16 October 2021. https://www. cbc.ca/news/politics/david-amess-canadian-reaction-1.6213606.

Boutilier, Alex. "Conservatives Email Supporters in Search of Candidates Ahead of Federal Election Call." *Toronto Star,* 14 August 2021. https:// www.thestar.com/politics/federal/2021/08/14/conservatives-email -supporters-in-search-of-candidates-ahead-of-federal-election-call.html.

Boutilier, Alex, and Stephanie Levitz. "Tories' Membership Database Locked." *Toronto Star,* 23 September 2021, A6.

Brin, Colette, and Ryan MacDonald. "News Editors." In *Inside the Campaign: Managing Elections in Canada,* edited by Alex Marland and Thierry Giasson, 85–97. Vancouver: UBC Press, 2020.

Brook, Tom. *Getting Elected in Canada.* Stratford, ON: Mercury Press, 1991.

Bryden, Joan. "Political Parties in a Fundraising Frenzy as Year Draws to a Close." CBC News, 30 December 2014. https://www.cbc.ca/news/ politics/political-parties-in-a-fundraising-frenzy-as-year-draws-to-a -close-1.2886299.

Canadian Press. "Aggression and Threats on Campaign Trail a Frequent Occurrence: Calgary MP." *CityNews,* 29 August 2021. https://edmonton. citynews.ca/2021/08/29/aggression-threats-campaign-trail/.

–. "As Bloc Prepares for Federal Election, Infighting Grows over Candidate Selection Process." CTV News, 8 August 2021. https://montreal.ctvnews.

ca/as-bloc-prepares-for-federal-election-infighting-grows-over
-candidate-selection-process-1.5539197.

–. "Imams Ask Conservative Candidate to Quit over Poor Follow-Up on Apology for Posts." Global News, 19 September 2021. https://globalnews. ca/news/8202753/imams-ask-steven-cotter-quit-islamophobic/.

Carbert, Louise. "The Hidden Rise of New Women Candidates Seeking Election to the House of Commons, 2000–2008." *Canadian Political Science Review* 6, 2–3 (2012): 143–57.

Carty, R.K. *Canadian Political Parties in the Constituencies*. Royal Commission on Electoral Reform and Party Financing. Toronto: Dundurn Press, 1991.

–. "The Politics of Tecumseh Corners: Canadian Political Parties as Franchise Organizations." *Canadian Journal of Political Science* 35, 4 (2002): 723–45.

Carty, R.K., and Munroe Eagles. *Politics Is Local: National Politics at the Grassroots*. Oxford: Oxford University Press, 2005.

Carty, R. Kenneth, D. Munroe Eagles, and Anthony Sayers. "Candidates and Local Campaigns: Are There Just Four Canadian Types?" *Party Politics* 9, 5 (2003): 619–36.

CBC News. "Marc Serré, Liberal Candidate for Nickel Belt in Northern Ontario, Assaulted in Campaign Office." 14 September 2021. https:// www.cbc.ca/news/canada/sudbury/serre-assaulted-campaign-office-1. 6175489.

Chen, Alice. "Conservative Election Ad Pulled, but Not before Being Panned by Party Members and Public Alike." *Hill Times,* 18 August 2021, 2.

–. "'The Horizon, though Still Murky, Was Beginning to Brighten': Defeated MPs Reflect on Losing Their Seats." *Hill Times,* 6 October 2021, 1.

Clarke, Harold D., Lawrence LeDuc, Jane Jenson, and Jon Pammett. *Political Choice in Canada*. Toronto: McGraw-Hill, 1979.

Coletto, David. "Go Knock on Doors: 'New' Dimensions in Market Intelligence." In *Political Marketing in the 2019 Canadian Federal Election,* edited by Jamie Gilles, Vincent Raynauld, and André Turcotte, 91–105. Cham, Switzerland: Palgrave Macmillan, 2020.

Collombat, Thomas, and Magali Picard. "Third-Party Activism." In *Inside the Campaign: Managing Elections in Canada,* edited by Alex Marland and Thierry Giasson, 185–95. Vancouver: UBC Press, 2020.

Crandall, Erin, and Michael Roy. "Party Fundraisers." In *Inside the Campaign: Managing Elections in Canada,* edited by Alex Marland and Thierry Giasson, 111–22. Vancouver: UBC Press, 2020.

Cross, William. "The Importance of Local Party Activity in Understanding Canadian Politics: Winning from the Ground Up in the 2015 Federal Election: Presidential Address to the Canadian Political Science Association Calgary, 31 May 2016." *Canadian Journal of Political Science* 49, 4 (2016): 601–20.

Currie-Wood, Rob. "The National Growth of a Regional Party: Evidence of Linkages between Constituency Associations in the Conservative Party of Canada." *Canadian Journal of Political Science* 53, 3 (2020): 618–37.

Davis, Tony. "Signs, Signs, Nowhere a Sign: Federal Election Signs Stolen from P.E.I. Riding." CBC News, 27 September 2021. https://www.cbc.ca/news/canada/prince-edward-island/pei-signs-stolen-election-sept-2021-1.6188989.

DeCillia, Brooks, and Michel Cormier. "Leaders' Debate Coordinators." In *Inside the Campaign: Managing Elections in Canada,* edited by Alex Marland and Thierry Giasson, 71–84. Vancouver: UBC Press, 2020.

Delacourt, Susan. *Shopping for Votes: How Politicians Choose Us and We Choose Them.* Toronto: Douglas and McIntyre, 2016.

Eagles, Munroe D. "Voting and Non-Voting in Canadian Federal Elections: An Ecological Analysis." In *Voter Turnout in Canada,* edited by Herman Bakvis, 3–32. Royal Commission on Electoral Reform and Party Financing, vol. 15. Toronto: Dundurn Press, 1991.

Flanagan, Tom. *Harper's Team: Behind the Scenes in the Conservative Rise to Power.* Montreal and Kingston: McGill-Queen's University Press, 2009.

Gidengil, Elisabeth, Agnieszka Dobrzynska, Neil Nevitte, and Richard Nadeau. "Does the Local Candidate Matter? Candidate Effects in the Canadian Election of 2000." *Canadian Journal of Political Science* 36, 3 (2003): 657–64.

Gilmore, Rachel. "Annamie Paul Sticks to Toronto as Some Green Candidates Reject Riding Visits." Global News, 10 September 2021. https://globalnews.ca/news/8181087/canada-election-annamie-paul-green-party-campaign/.

–. "Tory Candidate Says She 'Misspoke' in Opposing Vaccine Passports – Twice." Global News, 15 September 2021. https://globalnews.ca/news/8193354/canada-election-covid-vaccine-passports-conservative/.

Kendall, Chad, and Marie Rekkas. "Incumbency Advantages in the Canadian Parliament." *Canadian Journal of Economics* 45, 4 (2012): 1560–85.

Koop, Royce. "Constituency Campaigning in the 2015 Federal Election." In *Canadian Election Analysis: Communication, Strategy, and Democracy,* edited by Alex Marland and Thierry Giasson, 42–43. Vancouver: UBC Press, 2015. https://www.ubcpress.ca/canadianelectionanalysis2015.

Koop, Royce, Kelly Blidook, and Lesley Anne Fuga. "Has the COVID-19 Pandemic Affected MPs' Representational Activities?" *Canadian Journal of Political Science* 53, 2 (2020): 287–91.

Krasinsky, Michael, and William Milne. "Some Evidence on the Effect of Incumbency in Canadian Elections." *Canadian Journal of Political Science* 16, 3 (1983): 489–500.

Kwong, Evelyn, Alex Ballingall, and Alyshah Hasham. "Liberals Ask Toronto Candidate to 'Pause' Campaign after Dropped Sexual Assault Charge Was Revealed." *Toronto Star,* 16 September 2021. https://www. thestar.com/politics/federal-election/2021/09/16/liberals-ask-toronto -candidate-charged-with-sexual-assault-in-2019-to-pause-campaign. html.

Lalancette, Mireille, with Marie Della Mattia. "Senior Adviser to the Leader on Tour." In *Inside the Campaign: Managing Elections in Canada,* edited by Alex Marland and Thierry Giasson, 159–71. Vancouver: UBC Press, 2020.

Lalonde, Megan. "NDP's Avi Lewis Aims to 'Shake Up' Establishment." *Pique Newsmagazine,* 3 September 2021. https://www.piquenews magazine.com/local-news/ndps-avi-lewis-aims-to-shake-up-establishment -4273347.

Land, Brian. *Eglinton: The Election Study of a Federal Constituency.* Toronto: Peter Martin Associates, 1965.

Lawlor, Andrea, and Marc Mayrand. "Election Administrators." In *Inside the Campaign: Managing Elections in Canada,* edited by Alex Marland and Thierry Giasson, 31–43. Vancouver: UBC Press, 2020.

Levitz, Stephanie. "Liberals Pin Their Hopes on Social Media Influencers to Help Sway Voters." *Toronto Star,* 4 June 2021. https://www.thestar.com/ politics/federal/2021/06/04/liberals-pin-their-hopes-on-social-media -influencers-to-help-sway-voters.html.

Liberal Party of Canada (Ontario). *Planning and Running a Successful Election Day: A Manual for Campaign Managers and Election Day Chairs.* Internal party document, 2011.

Maloney, Ryan. "'What Just Happened?' Former Bloc Candidate Explains How It Feels to Lose by 12 Votes." CBC News, 16 October 2021. https:// www.cbc.ca/news/politics/bloc-patrick-ohara-brenda-shanahan-1. 6212127.

MarketingProfs. "The Obama Playbook: How Digital Marketing and Social Media Won the Election." MarketingProfs.com, 2008. https://www. marketingprofs.com/newprem/library/item.asp?id=2674.

Marland, Alex. *Brand Command: Canadian Politics and Democracy in the Age of Message Control.* Vancouver: UBC Press, 2016.

–. "Constituency Campaigning: A Review of the Literature and a Case Study of Ottawa Centre, 1997." Master's thesis, Memorial University of Newfoundland, 1998.

–. "Constituency Campaigning in the 2011 Canadian Federal Election." In *The Canadian Federal Election of 2011,* edited by J.H. Pammett and C. Dornan, 167–94. Toronto: Dundurn Press, 2011.

Marland, Alex, and Maria Mathews. "Friend, Can You Chip in $3? Canadian Political Parties, Perpetual Fundraising, and Relationship Marketing." In *Permanent Campaigning in Canada,* edited by Alex Marland, Thierry Giasson, and Anna Lennox Esselment, 87–107. Vancouver: UBC Press, 2017.

Marland, Alex, and Angelia Wagner. "Scripted Messengers: How Party Discipline and Branding Turn Election Candidates and Legislators into Brand Ambassadors." *Journal of Political Marketing* 19, 1–2 (2020): 54–73.

Mazereeuw, Peter. "'Far Too Much Control': Liberal MP Easter Pleas for Less PMO Control, More Ministerial Responsibility." *Hill Times,* 26 July 2021, 1.

McGarvey, Dan. "Voter, Opponent Shocked to See Calgary Liberal MP-Elect Replace Election Flyer on Security Video." CBC News, 2 September 2021. https://www.cbc.ca/news/canada/calgary/calgary-skyview-george-chahal-jag-sahota-election-northeast-1.6185688.

McGrane, David. "Campaigning in Canada during a Pandemic." *Policy Options,* 28 December 2020. https://policyoptions.irpp.org/magazines/december-2020/campaigning-in-canada-during-a-pandemic/.

Meisel, John. *The Canadian General Election of 1957.* Toronto: University of Toronto Press, 1957.

Mishler, William, and Harold D. Clarke. "Political Participation in Canada." In *Canadian Politics in the 1990s,* 3rd ed., edited by Michael S. Whittington and Glen Williams, 130–50. Scarborough, ON: Nelson Canada, 1990.

Morden, Michael. *Real House Lives: Former Members of Parliament on How to Reclaim Democratic Leadership.* Victoria: Friesen Press, 2020.

Moss, Neil. "Supporters Irked as Parties Eschew Competition amid Tight Deadline to Fill Candidate Slots." *Hill Times,* 18 August 2021, 1.

Nakhaie, M. Reza. "Electoral Participation in Municipal, Provincial and Federal Elections in Canada." *Canadian Journal of Political Science* 39, 2 (2006): 363–90.

NetNewsLedger. "New Liberal Ad: Justin Trudeau's Quebec Team." NetNewsLedger.com, 2 September 2021. https://www.netnewsledger.com/2021/09/02/new-liberal-ad-justin-trudeaus-quebec-team/.

Pal, Michael, and Sujit Choudhry. "Constituency Boundaries in Canada." In *Election,* edited by Heather MacIvor, 87–105. Toronto: Emond Montgomery, 2009.

Patel, Raisa. "'I've Never Seen So Much Division.'" *Toronto Star,* 1 September 2021, A7.

Patten, Steven. "Databases, Microtargeting, and the Permanent Campaign: A Threat to Democracy?" In *Permanent Campaigning in Canada,* edited by Alex Marland, Thierry Giasson, and Anna Lennox Esselment, 47–64. Vancouver: UBC Press, 2017.

Rana, Abbas. "Aspiring Liberal Candidates for Don Valley East Campaigning by Phones and Social Media." *Hill Times,* 26 April 2021, 1.

–. "National Liberal Campaign Director Ishmael Advises Candidates to Rent Campaign Offices for Two Months: Liberal Sources." *Hill Times,* 26 July 2021, 1.

–. "O'Toole Conservatives Missed Winning Government by 98,740 Votes in 42 Ridings: *Hill Times* Analysis." *Hill Times,* 18 October 2021, 1.

–. "Some Potential Liberal and Conservative Candidates in Unheld Ridings Concerned Nominations Won't Be Done before Next Election Call." *Hill Times,* 1 February 2021, 1.

Raycraft, Richard. "Green Party Candidate in Quebec Attacks Leader Annamie Paul in Facebook Post." CBC News, 3 September 2021. https://www.cbc.ca/news/politics/green-party-candidate-1.6164558.

Raynauld, Vincent, and Dany Renauld. "Political Advertisers." In *Inside the Campaign: Managing Elections in Canada,* edited by Alex Marland and Thierry Giasson, 173–84. Vancouver: UBC Press, 2020.

Reynolds, Christopher. "Grappling with How to Press the Virtual Flesh, Parties Gear Up for Election Showdown." CTV News, 9 May 2021. https://www.ctvnews.ca/politics/grappling-with-how-to-press-the-virtual-flesh-parties-gear-up-for-election-showdown-1.5420259.

Robbins-Kanter, Jacob. "Undisciplined Constituency Campaign Behaviour in Canadian Federal Elections." *Canadian Journal of Political Science,* published online 13 May 2022. https://doi.org/10.1017/S0008423922000282.

Robertson, Dylan. "Six Feet of Separation: How to Campaign under COVID." *Winnipeg Free Press,* 23 August 2021, 1.

Roy, Jason, and Christopher Alcantara. "The Candidate Effect: Does the Local Candidate Matter?" *Journal of Elections, Public Opinion and Parties* 25, 2 (2014): 195–214.

Ryckewaert, Laura. "Zoom Meet-Ups and Chat Groups: The Unusual First Term of Parliament's Class of 2019." *Hill Times,* 14 July 2021, 1.

Sayers, Anthony M. *Parties, Candidates, and Constituency Campaigns in Canadian Elections.* Vancouver: UBC Press, 1998.

Sevi, Semra, Marco Mendoza Aviña, and André Blais. "Reassessing Local Candidate Effects." *Canadian Journal of Political Science.* Forthcoming.

Statistics Canada. "Canada and Canada (Table)." Census profile, 2016 census. Statistics Canada Catalogue no. 98-316-X2016001, released 29 November 2017. https://www12.statcan.gc.ca/census-recensement/2016/dp-pd/prof/index.cfm?Lang=E.

Stefanovich, Olivia, Christina Romualdo, and David Thurton. "Some NDP Members Call on Party to Stop Clawing Back Campaign Rebate Cash." *CBC News,* 10 April 2021. https://www.cbc.ca/news/politics/federal-ndp-finances-elections-canada-rebates-decision-1.5979926.

Stevens, Benjamin Allen, Md Mujahedul Islam, Roosmarijn de Geus, Jonah Goldberg, John R. McAndrews, Alex Mierke-Zatwarnicki, Peter John Loewen, and Daniel Rubenson. "Local Candidate Effects in Canadian Elections." *Canadian Journal of Political Science* 52, 1 (2019): 83–96.

Stoodley, Sarah. "The Twists of Campaigning in a Newfoundland and Labrador Election Hit by Pandemic Chaos." *Policy Options,* 26 May 2021. https://policyoptions.irpp.org/magazines/may-2021/the-twists-of-campaigning-in-a-newfoundland-and-labrador-election-hit-by-pandemic-chaos/.

Tasker, John Paul. "Conservative Candidate Banishes Campaign Volunteers Who Were at Trudeau Rally." *CBC News,* 28 August 2021. https://www.cbc.ca/news/politics/conservative-candidate-trudeau-rally-1.6156959.

Thibedeau, Hannah. "Conservatives Say Their 'Virtual' Campaign Strategy Is Paying Off Already." *CBC News,* 27 August 2021. https://www.cbc.ca/news/politics/otoole-conservative-election-virtual-campaign-town-hall-pandemic-1.6154822.

Thibedeau, Hannah, and John Paul Tasker. "Conservative Post-Election Report Says O'Toole Was 'Over-Managed' during the Campaign." *CBC News,* 27 January 2022. https://www.cbc.ca/news/politics/otoole-post-election-report-1.6329961.

Thomas, Paul E.J., and Michael Morden. *Party Favours: How Federal Election Candidates Are Chosen.* Toronto: Samara Centre for Democracy, 2019. https://www.samaracanada.com/docs/default-source/reports/party-favours-by-the-samara-centre-for-democracy.pdf.

Tolley, Erin. *Framed: Media and the Coverage of Race in Canadian Politics.* Vancouver: UBC Press, 2016.

–. "Who You Know: Local Party Presidents and Minority Candidate Emergence." *Electoral Studies* 58 (2019): 70–79.

Turcotte, André. "Under New Management: Market Intelligence and the Conservative Party's Resurrection." In *Political Marketing in Canada,* edited by Alex Marland, Thierry Giasson, and Jennifer Lees-Marshment, 76–90. Vancouver: UBC Press, 2012.

Wagner, Angelia. "LGBTQ Perspectives on Political Candidacy in Canada." In *Queering Representation: LGBTQ People and Electoral Politics in Canada,* edited by Manon Tremblay, 259–78. Vancouver: UBC Press, 2019.

Walsh, Marieke. "Liberal Party Triggers 'Electoral Urgency' Rule for Nominations." *Globe and Mail,* 4 June 2021. https://www.theglobeand mail.com/politics/article-liberal-party-triggers-electoral-urgency-rule-for -nominations-2/.

Watters, Haydn. "New Mobile Election Apps Mean Pressure's on for Local Campaigns." CBC News, 13 June 2015. https://www.cbc.ca/news/politics/ new-mobile-election-apps-mean-pressure-s-on-for-local-campaigns-1. 3102068.

Wesley, Jared, and Renze Nauta. "Party Platform Builders." In *Inside the Campaign: Managing Elections in Canada,* edited by Alex Marland and Thierry Giasson, 123–34. Vancouver: UBC Press, 2020.

Westlake, Daniel. "Ready or Not? The Strength of NDP Riding Associations and the Rise and Fall of the NDP." *Canadian Journal of Political Science.* Forthcoming.

Willing, Jon. "Ottawa Centre Debate Tests Eight Candidates on Hyper-Local Issues." *Ottawa Citizen,* 14 September 2021. https://ottawacitizen. com/news/local-news/ottawa-centre-debate-tests-eight-candidates-on -hyper-local-issues.

Wilson, Paul. "Political Staff." In *Inside the Campaign: Managing Elections in Canada,* edited by Alex Marland and Thierry Giasson, 45–57. Vancouver: UBC Press, 2020.

Wiseman, Nelson. "Get Out the Vote – Not: Increasing Effort, Declining Turnout." *Policy Options,* February 2006, 18–23.

Yates, Stéphanie, and John Chenery. "National Campaign Director of Communications." In *Inside the Campaign: Managing Elections in Canada,* edited by Alex Marland and Thierry Giasson, 147–57. Vancouver: UBC Press, 2020.

Zingel, Avery. "N.W.T.'s Conservative Candidate Has Never Visited the Territory, Doesn't Take Calls." CBC News, 4 September 2021. https:// www.cbc.ca/news/canada/north/lea-mollison-nwt-1.6164702.

PART 1
Local Contests and Candidates

1

Election Administration

Holly Ann Garnett

Abstract   What are the dynamics of local election management and administration in Canada? How much responsibility and how much discretion are retained by the central Elections Canada operation versus local electoral officials? How did the COVID-19 pandemic influence this balance between central and local officials? Drawing from theories of electoral integrity and electoral management, including the centralization of electoral management bodies and recent work on electoral officials as "street level bureaucrats," this chapter considers how Elections Canada at the central and local levels responded to the challenges of running an election in 2021. It highlights Canada's highly centralized system that also relies on a vast network of local electoral officials and organizations to deliver some of the most trusted and high-quality elections around the globe.

Résumé   Quelles sont les dynamiques de gestion et d'administration électorales locales au Canada? Quelle part de responsabilités et de choix discrétionnaires incombe aux activités d'Élections Canada par rapport à celle des fonctionnaires électoraux locaux? Comment la pandémie de COVID-19 a-t-elle influencé cet équilibre entre les responsables nationaux et locaux? Prenant appui sur des théories de l'intégrité et de l'administration électorales, dont la centralisation des organismes de gestion électorale, et de récents travaux considérant les responsables électoraux locaux en tant que « fonctionnaires de proximité », ce chapitre examine de quelle façon Élections Canada a su relever, aux niveaux national et local, les défis de la tenue d'une élection en 2021. Il met en évidence le système très centralisé du Canada, qui compte également sur un vaste réseau de fonctionnaires et d'organismes électoraux locaux qui assurent certaines des élections les plus fiables et les plus remarquables au monde.

WHEN AN ELECTION is called in Canada, Elections Canada is tasked with the challenge of organizing it. In as little as thirty-six days, the shortest campaign time frame possible under Canada's election laws, the independent, non-partisan agency organizes the largest mobilization of Canadian citizens across the country. In 2021, it faced additional challenges: the COVID-19 pandemic and the additional safety concerns and constraints that came with these unprecedented conditions.[1] Running an election under pandemic conditions served to highlight the challenges associated generally with running elections in Canada: the highly centralized system also relies on a vast network of local electoral officials and organizations to deliver some of the most trusted and high-quality elections around the globe.[2]

In this chapter I ask, what are the dynamics of centralization in Canadian electoral management and administration? How much responsibility and how much discretion are retained by the central Elections Canada operation versus local electoral officials? And finally, how did the pandemic influence this balance between central and local officials? Drawing from theories of electoral integrity and electoral management, including the centralization of electoral management bodies and recent work on electoral officials as "street level bureaucrats,"[3] I consider how Elections Canada, at both central and local levels, responds to the challenges of running elections.

Although often used interchangeably, the terms "election administration" and "election management" refer to two different things. Election administration refers to the concrete tasks of registering voters and managing a voting process, be that in person, by post, or online. Toby James, for example, refers to it as the front end of the electoral process, when most voters interact with the "nuts and bolts" of running an election.[4] Electoral management, however, refers to a much broader set of institutions; often working behind the scenes to deliver trusted elections throughout the electoral cycle, they coordinate a variety of government agencies, departments, and organizations, and they cooperate with civil social groups, political parties, and candidates.

Around the globe, electoral management bodies are the government agencies and organizations tasked with administering elections.[5]

They can include a variety of bodies, from independent agencies to government departments to special judiciary bodies or some combination thereof. They can be highly centralized, running all activities through one national elections office, or rely on subnational or local bodies to fulfill key electoral tasks, such as creating an electoral register and conducting balloting. We also see differences in the permanence of electoral management institutions around the globe. Although most countries have some form of permanent electoral management body, the local and regional offices are often set up temporarily for each electoral event or make use of employees seconded from other government offices. Of course, added to this mix are the subnational and local election management bodies that might be subject to entirely different sets of rules.

In Canada, we normally think of our independent electoral management body,[6] Elections Canada, headquartered in Gatineau, Quebec, which has been running national-level elections for over 100 years.[7] However, Elections Canada still requires help on the ground. This is where hundreds of local returning officers (ROs) and tens of thousands of poll workers are hired for each election. Although their head office is permanent, these local offices and the returning officers hired to manage electoral processes in the riding are temporary. Returning officers can be engaged before the writs of election are issued, and remain in waiting between elections, but other staff members, offices, and materials are unique to each electoral event. Thus, with little (or no) notice, Elections Canada implements a country-wide system of local election management for each election. With a government that could fall at any moment – particularly in the situation of a minority Parliament – Elections Canada must have this complex system ready, with returning officers in local communities prepared to hire thousands of poll workers and to rent local offices to give Elections Canada an "on the ground" presence whenever word is received.

For such a huge undertaking, notably, these local operations receive little limelight. Perhaps it is because electoral laws and most procedures are debated and decided by Parliament, and Elections Canada serves as an impartial bureaucracy for implementation. Or perhaps Canada's system of electoral management receives little fanfare because of its relatively streamlined process, compared with that of our American neighbours, for example, in which rules that vary state by state and even county by county have led, in recent years, to claims of discrimination and voter suppression.[8] Some notable exceptions to Elections Canada's relatively low profile were the robocall incidents in 2011, in which some voters were misled by rogue actors to the wrong polling stations,[9] and controversies surrounding the educative role of the chief electoral officer (CEO) in the Fair Elections Act of 2014.[10]

Despite these exceptions, Canada's system of electoral management often works under the radar, and even more understudied are those local returning officers who conduct the day-to-day tasks of electoral management. Yet, in recent years, the study of local electoral officials has emerged as a field, outlining their important contribution to delivering high-quality trusted elections. For example, recent studies surveying people who work for election management bodies worldwide has revealed that input in policy making, recruitment practices, job satisfaction, and mitigating levels of stress is key for local election workers to perform at a high level.[11]

The insights of local electoral officials are also crucial for evaluating policies and processes. Electoral officials have unique "inside" knowledge required to evaluate the quality of an election, which is fundamental to improving electoral integrity more broadly.[12] Since most voters will only encounter a poll worker, or perhaps the returning officer, this type of research at the local level can be important for evaluating the successes and shortfalls of electoral management. Research has demonstrated that perceptions of electoral officials can even be important for a voter's overall satisfaction with democracy.[13] For this reason, studies of the decisions made by poll workers and surveys of these local election workers have expanded as an academic endeavour in recent years.[14]

Local returning officers could be considered the quintessential "street level bureaucrats."[15] Research in this area of public administration has noted that local government workers can use a great deal of discretion in their efforts and work with relative autonomy. In some cases, this can even translate into a policy-making role that often stems from decentralized electoral management, such as seen in the

United States[16] or United Kingdom,[17] where local authorities are tasked with running elections. For example, poll workers can decide whom to ask for identification; this can result in discrimination at the polls if they make their decisions based on race and gender.[18] In such cases, the decentralized nature of electoral administration has been noted to be negative for principles of electoral integrity. However, decentralized and autonomous local election management can also allow for innovation and locally targeted practices.[19]

But what about in Canada? Do local officials exercise certain levels of autonomy and discretion, or do they uniformly implement rules and regulations created at the centre? In a country with huge geographic, cultural, and linguistic differences, and in a climate in which global health concerns have affected different communities in different ways, what role do these street-level bureaucrats of electoral management and administration play in the running of elections in Canada?

Local Trends

The breakdown of roles and responsibilities for election administration at each level is encoded in the Canada Elections Act.[20] The hierarchy in Figure 1.1 is useful in considering these roles and how they relate to each other.

Headed by the chief electoral officer (a parliamentary appointment), Elections Canada has a full-time central staff tasked with the implementation of Canada's election laws.[21] Among these personnel are electoral officials who work permanently at the Elections Canada headquarters throughout the electoral cycle (i.e., between elections), and they are responsible for a broad variety of tasks, including offering public education, studying and testing new voting measures (though they must be approved by Parliament before adoption), cooperating with international electoral management bodies, and running by-elections.[22] In other words, they work on the broader management of elections between electoral events.

However, general elections would not be possible without hiring additional personnel at the local level. It is there that some responsibility for electoral administration or the technical tasks of electoral

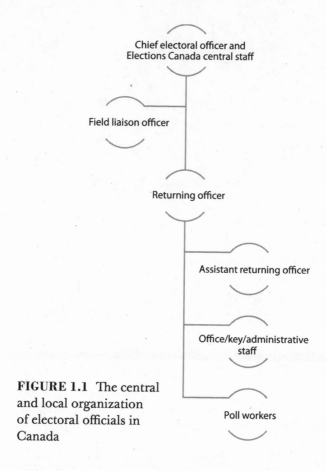

Chief electoral officer and
Elections Canada central staff

Field liaison officer

Returning officer

Assistant returning officer

Office/key/administrative
staff

Poll workers

FIGURE 1.1 The central and local organization of electoral officials in Canada

management is devolved to individuals in the local electoral districts. One returning officer is hired for each electoral district and tasked with the "preparation for and conduct of an election in his or her electoral district."[23] Returning officers are responsible for implementing election law at the local level; identifying spaces for the returning office and polling sites; recruiting, appointing, and training staff; identifying potential issues with the registration list, including where targeted revision might be necessary; and reaching out to target groups. It is in these tasks that the RO can have the most discretion since central Elections Canada staff do not have the on-the-ground knowledge required to engage effectively with staff and facilities in each of the 338 ridings.[24]

However, unlike central Elections Canada staff, returning officers are appointed for a ten-year term but do not work full time between electoral events. Instead, they are paid a small amount between elections to be prepared for electoral events, and they are expected to be ready to work full time when the writs of the election are issued.[25] They are essentially "on hold" until the election is called. Thus, understandably, the position limits the types of individuals who can hold it, for anyone who has a permanent full-time position that cannot be left at a moment's notice is unable to serve in this capacity. Unfortunately, Elections Canada does not release demographic or occupational data on returning officers.

One way that Elections Canada has sought to manage returning officers from headquarters is the development of field liaison officers (FLOs), who officially assist returning officers in the thirty-one geographic regions across Canada.[26] Although every RO is ultimately accountable to Elections Canada's central office, FLOs can act as liaisons and offer additional guidance at the regional level.[27] In the Canada Elections Act, field liaison officers have three responsibilities: to support returning officers, to act as intermediaries between returning officers and the chief electoral officer, and to provide support to returning officers at the request of the CEO.[28]

Their role on the ground is vast, oscillating between electoral management and strictly administrative tasks, and extends beyond the campaign period. Between elections, field liaison officers can be involved in recruiting, training, and assessing returning officers, facilitating communication and information sharing among returning officers in a specific region, and engaging with regional organizations, including the provincial electoral management body (EMB) or local councils.[29] During elections, FLOs can help with regional media requests and advise and coach ROs on a variety of tasks, from budgeting to dealing with issues that arise during the electoral period. In this way, field liaison officers are a means of bridging the central, permanent staff and the local staff, who might not have the same depth of experience in electoral management, particularly if they have been hired recently. In other words, they bridge the noticeable gap between the local, temporary, and potentially newer personnel and the central, permanent, and professional organization.

There are two more devolved sets of employees hired when the writs of election are issued. The first is administrative, key, or office staff.[30] Up to half of these employees can be appointed before the writs, but they are not paid until after the writs.[31] In 2021, Elections Canada listed a variety of positions available, from community relations officers – for example, for electors experiencing homelessness, those with accessibility requirements, youth, or seniors – to technical administrators.[32]

The greatest number of hires at the local level, however, are poll workers and others engaged to work on election day (or in advance polls or post-election counting). Interestingly, the first point of contact for hiring these individuals is stipulated in the Canada Elections Act to be from political parties, which can provide a list of possible names for the returning officer.[33] After a period of seven days, returning officers also look beyond this list for poll workers from the general population. These poll workers, who have a variety of titles and job descriptions, from deputy returning officer to information officer, are responsible for opening polling stations, providing information to electors, ensuring that identities are checked, issuing ballots, counting ballots at the end of the day, and properly storing and transporting election materials. Thus, for election day and advance poll days, this large number of local individuals are those actually implementing election law at the local level.

In Canada, these individuals are provided with clear instructions and not given much decision-making authority, as is the case in some other countries. As mentioned earlier, though, in some jurisdictions, individual poll workers have exercised some discretion in determining who can vote ultimately, as in the case of whose IDs are checked.[34] But there is little mention in media reports or complaints about this happening in Canada. This is likely because of two factors. First, strict and consistent guidelines are issued and training is undertaken uniformly across the country.[35] Second, because of various alternative measures for essential components such as registration (e.g., election day registration) and identification (e.g., vouching), there are few reasons for voters to be turned away at the polls. In this way, the decision-making power of local poll workers, or their direct supervisors, is limited through an already inclusive model of electoral management and election law.

Behind the Scenes

In 2021, the COVID-19 pandemic brought a new set of challenges to election administration in Canada. Although the laws governing elections apply equally across the country, the conditions related to the pandemic and public health measures were not uniform. In this section, I consider three major issues that emerged in the administration of elections during the federal election of 2021: namely, COVID-19 safety procedures, staff and facilities, and the counting of ballots.

The first challenge concerns COVID-19 safety protocols and guidelines. These decisions were made in advance to ensure the safety of electors and electoral officials, including measures such as distancing, hand-sanitizing stations, Plexiglas barriers, single-use pencils, and mandatory mask wearing.[36] Special ballots were encouraged for those who might have been recently exposed to COVID-19 or exhibited symptoms, and it was noted that "electors who have or believe they have COVID-19 and who have not already applied to vote by mail will not be able to vote."[37] There was some controversy surrounding whether poll workers would be required to be vaccinated. Ultimately, because of logistical, recruitment, and time constraints, vaccination was not required.[38]

These guidelines were made at the central level with consultation of public health authorities, and Elections Canada's website explicitly stated that "health and safety measures may vary by province or territory."[39] For example, one mention of variation was the release of entry data for contact tracing.[40] However, though these guidelines were set at the central level, it was the responsibility of local electoral officers to enforce them. Ultimately, there were very few instances of problems with compliance.[41] Notable instances were related to mask wearing and usually dealt with by local security personnel. Thankfully, there were also few mentions in the media following the election of potential COVID-19 exposure, notable cases being exposures at two polling stations in Toronto[42] and at a busy polling station in Kingston.[43] Thus, though health and safety measures were set centrally (even if they required some regional variations), local officials were responsible for implementing the procedures and seeing them followed. There were few reports that this was not achieved in the 2021 election.

The most prevalent challenge related to election administration during the pandemic was that of hiring staff and renting polling locations. There were reports of greater difficulty recruiting local workers. This task is the responsibility of local returning officers. Recruiting election staff can be difficult in ordinary circumstances: it is short-term work (only a few days) for low wages and requires workers to be at polling stations or counting facilities for long shifts (one worker reported being at the polling station for fifteen hours).[44] Although poll workers are paid for training, a 2019 survey of returning officers found the training insufficient for the job.[45] Furthermore, there are few opportunities for long-term career advancement to encourage individuals to become highly skilled election workers. Adding to this was the COVID-19 pandemic, during which hiring was reported to be a significant challenge, perhaps because of health considerations or other pressures related to work or caring responsibilities.[46] A shortage of workers had been experienced in provincial elections under pandemic conditions, notably in Newfoundland and Labrador, where the number of resigning workers contributed to the decision to postpone the election and pivot to an all mail-in election.[47] Ultimately, Elections Canada reported that it had met about 93 percent of its target for workers (or 215,000),[48] less than the estimated 232,000 workers hired in 2019.[49]

Additionally, finding appropriate facilities for polling locations was reported to be a major challenge during the election in 2021.[50] There were obvious pandemic-related reasons for this challenge. First, in some cases, larger locations were sought to allow for better social distancing.[51] Elections Canada officials also reported not being welcomed at some "community centres, churches and schools."[52]

Many school boards decided not to allow polling stations at their schools because of safety concerns. For example, the Toronto Catholic District School Board opted not to have polling stations at its schools.[53] Some provinces chose not to allow polling locations in schools, except in extenuating circumstances, including Manitoba, New Brunswick, and Newfoundland and Labrador.[54] Local school boards were given the authority to make those decisions in other provinces, including Ontario and Alberta.[55] In light of these challenges, local election officials, in coordination with their field liaison officers and Elections Canada's central operations, sought to find larger locations where more polls could be placed within the same polling station.[56] This also resulted in some unconventional polling stations, such as at the IKEA in Winnipeg.[57] Some polling stations were also changed after COVID outbreaks.[58]

There were notable decreases in polling stations in some ridings in the Greater Toronto Area. It was reported that there was more than a 50 percent decrease in polling stations in eleven ridings. Most notable among them was the riding of Toronto Centre, where only fifteen stations were available, whereas in 2019 there had been ninety-one.[59] Ultimately, Elections Canada reported having 14,440 polling stations in 2021, down from 15,484 in 2019.[60] In addition to the lack of polling stations, the changes in locations from where they might "regularly" be located also reportedly confused some voters.[61] They also reported having to travel longer distances to polling stations in some cases.[62]

Some of these shortages in facilities and staff were reported to contribute to the long lineups seen at some polling stations. Yet some of the length was the result of physical distancing and limits to how many people could be in the building. Nonetheless, there were numerous reports of lines well past the close of polling stations across the country.[63] One post-election survey reported that 7 percent of voters reported waiting in line more than an hour.[64] The brunt of the pressure from these lineups was managed by local poll workers, who remained into the night to provide everyone in the line with an opportunity to vote, as per the policy that those who had arrived before the close of the polls could remain to vote.[65]

Other lines sprang up around university campuses, such as at a polling station in Kingston, whose long queues were attributed to many students who needed to register to vote on election day, a more time-consuming process.[66] This could have been one casualty of the decision not to pursue the on-campus voting program used in 2015 and 2019, which allowed students to vote in their home ridings from their campuses. Elections Canada made this decision centrally, not pursuing this program again because of the short notice and pandemic considerations that required staff to be reallocated. Some also questioned whether enough students would be back on campus in time for the program to be useful.[67]

In sum, we can see that recruiting staff and finding locations comprise the major decentralized electoral process in Canada. It is this area where local electoral officials can utilize their on-the-ground knowledge, and Elections Canada's central apparatus remains most dependent on local officials.

Once voting is complete, the task of counting ballots begins. For the case of regular advance and election day ballots, the vote count is a very decentralized process, albeit following strict procedures set out in detail by Elections Canada centrally. Votes are counted in polling stations or other counting facilities by local poll workers, who then call the results in to their returning offices, which then report them to Elections Canada's central office.

However, there is considerable media attention to whether an increase in special ballots, including mail-in ballots, contributes to a longer wait for election results. This system of special ballots in Canada is shared between the central and local levels. At the central level, Elections Canada's new online portal was the focus of special ballot requests.[68] According to Elections Canada's final report on the election, 1,274,447 special ballot kits were issued. For ballots to be counted, they had to arrive before the cut-off on election night. Notably, 90,274 ballots (or approximately 7.1 percent of ballots issued) were returned late and not counted.[69]

In cases in which voters are outside their ridings, special ballots are mailed to a central Elections Canada location. However, most special ballots (approximately 80 percent; see Figure 1.2)

FIGURE 1.2 Special ballots in the 2021 election

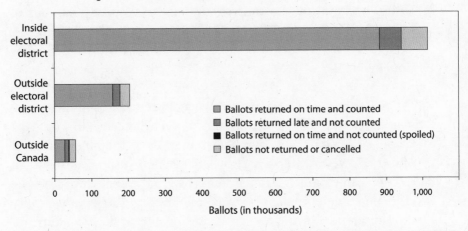

Source: Elections Canada, *Report on the 44th General Election,* Table 3.

Note: "Inside electoral district" refers to "electors voting by mail or at an Elections Canada office from inside their electoral district"; "outside electoral district" refers to "electors absent from their electoral district voting by mail or at a local office, Canadian Forces base or correctional facility"; "outside Canada" refers to "electors living outside Canada voting by mail."

are returned to the local office, either by mail or by hand delivery to the returning office or a polling station. These ballots are verified by local officials before they are counted.[70] Thus, delays that do occur are at the local level.[71] And, unlike at Elections Canada's central location, where ballots can be counted fourteen days ahead of time, local offices can begin the verification and counting process only on election night.

When tallying this volume of physical ballots, human error can happen, and when it does it is largely at the local level. In the federal election of 2021, the only potential problem seriously discussed in the media (at the time of writing) was a typo discovered in a ballot box report in the riding of Chateauguay-Lacolle, leading to a call for a recount.[72] Thus, the only major instance of a contested election because of potential issues with the vote count was the result simply of human error at the local level. Once again, we see that centralized and consistent procedures must be implemented locally both on and after election day; although the procedures in Canada are clearly laid out, the enormity of the task of counting millions of ballots and accounting for human error lies at the local level.

Conclusion

Federal elections in Canada are managed centrally, with decision-making power resting in the hands of Parliament (through the Canada Elections Act) and the discretion of the chief electoral officer. However, they are also administered locally during each election campaign, and this system of central management and decision making relies on local electoral officials. They are given very little discretion in their work regarding the basic procedures of running elections. This helps to retain centralization and consistent application of electoral laws, but it also makes for a precarious system that relies on temporary, potentially less experienced, individuals and local organizations.

The precarity of electoral management in Canada was highlighted by some of the challenges of election management brought on by the COVID-19 pandemic. The pandemic highlighted the challenges of administering elections consistently across such a geographically diverse federal state as Canada. Elections Canada had to negotiate with public health authorities in the provinces and territories to implement safety protocols at a time when these regulations were inconsistent across geography. Likewise, individuals faced local health restrictions, cultures of compliance (e.g., mask wearing), and the inability to access certain facilities.

It is in the logistics of setting up and staffing polling stations that we find the greatest need for local discretion. Local returning officers are responsible for finding staff and locations for polling stations, but they faced significant challenges in 2021 because of the pandemic. In thirty-six days, the mass mobilization had to be achieved, and that task – which could not be completed centrally, requiring on-the-ground know-how – was the first to experience difficulties.

Finally, an increase in the use of special ballots gave local administrators the additional challenge of receiving, verifying, and counting those ballots beyond election night. In 2021, the vast majority of them were sent to local offices, where most of the public focus on the vote count was centred.

This chapter has shown that implementation responsibilities are shared between central and local election officials in Canada, but there are relatively few areas for discretion among local election administrators, except for finding staff and polling locations. As extremely short-term employees under significant time pressures, it is understandable that local electoral officials rely heavily on the central Elections Canada organization. This reliance also contributes to the consistency of electoral administration across the country, such that few anomalies or irregularities were noted in 2021. Yet this leaves little room for experimentation or innovation, potentially stifling the unique contributions of these street-level election administrators and limiting the contribution of local knowledge to election administration in Canada.

Notes

Acknowledgment: With thanks to Madison MacGregor for research assistance.

1 Five provinces and one territory had held general elections since the pandemic was declared: New Brunswick (14 September 2020), British Columbia (24 October 2020), Saskatchewan (26 October 2020), Newfoundland and Labrador (23 March 2021 after postponement), Yukon (12 April 2021), and Nova Scotia (17 August 2021).

2 *National Post,* "Good News."

3 Lipsky, *Street Level Bureaucracy.*

4 James, "Comparative Electoral Management."

5 James et al., "Electoral Management"; Catt et al., *Electoral Management Design.*

6 It is important to note that other bodies, such as the Electoral Boundaries Commission and the Broadcasting Arbitrator, are also involved in the broader tasks of electoral management in Canada.

7 Kingsley, "The Administration of Canada's Independent, Non-Partisan Approach"; Lawlor and Mayrand, "Election Administrators."

8 Pastor, "The US Administration of Elections"; Shanton, *The State and Local Role in Election Administration.*

9 Pal, "Canadian Election Administration on Trial."

10 Fair Elections Act, SC 2014, c 12, https://www.canlii.org/en/ca/laws/ astat/sc-2014-c-12/latest/sc-2014-c-12.html; Williams et al., "An Open Letter on the Fair Elections Act."

11 James, "Better Workers, Better Elections?"

12 Garnett and James, "Measuring Electoral Integrity."

13 Garnett, "On the Front Lines of Democracy."

14 Atkeson et al., "Who Asks for Voter Identification?"; Clark and James, "Poll Workers"; Hall, Monson, and Patterson, "The Human Dimension of Elections."

15 Lipsky, *Street Level Bureaucracy*.

16 Atkeson et al., "A New Barrier to Participation."

17 James, *Elite Statecraft and Electoral Administration;* James, "The Effects of Centralising Electoral Management Board Design."

18 Atkeson et al., "A New Barrier to Participation."

19 James, "The Effects of Centralising Electoral Management Board Design."

20 Canada Elections Act, SC 2000, c 9, https://laws-lois.justice.gc.ca/ eng/acts/e-2.01/.

21 Ibid., s 12 (3).

22 Ibid., s 18.

23 Ibid., pt 3, s 2.

24 Elections Canada, "Returning Officers."

25 Elections Canada, "Tariff of Fees."

26 Elections Canada, "Field Liaison Officers."

27 Ibid.

28 Canada Elections Act, SC 2000, c 9, s 23.

29 Elections Canada, "Field Liaison Officers."

30 These employees are given a variety of names: administrative staff, key staff, and office staff are among the most common. Elections Canada, "Administrative Staff."

31 Canada Elections Act, SC 2000, c 9, s 32 (2).

32 Elections Canada, "Administrative Staff."

33 Canada Elections Act, SC 2000, c 9, s 33 (1).

34 Atkeson et al., "A New Barrier to Participation."

35 The regulations related to the COVID-19 pandemic were one exception in 2021 since each province (and health region) had its own public health guidelines.

36 Elections Canada, "Health and Safety Measures."

37 Elections Canada, "COVID-19 FAQs."

38 Krause, "Elections Canada Recruiting Poll Workers."

39 Elections Canada, "Health and Safety Measures."

40 Elections Canada, "COVID-19 FAQs."

41 Bartko, "Police Respond to Anti-Mask Dispute"; Hristova, "Hamilton Advance Polling Stations Raise Concerns"; Dormer, "Curbside Municipal Voting to Be Available"; Lavoie, "Toronto Police Called."

42 Pagliaro, "Toronto Public Health Warns of Potential COVID-19 Exposures."

43 Mazur, "COVID-19 Case."

44 Alhmidi, "Poll Workers Say Elections Canada Put Them at Risk."

45 See data from 2019 in Elections Canada, "Section 1"; data from 2021 were unavailable at the time of writing.

46 Canadian Press, "Polling Stations Short on Workers."

47 CBC News, "N.L. Election Delayed."

48 Alhmidi, "Poll Workers Say Elections Canada Put Them at Risk."

49 Elections Canada, "The 2019 Federal Election."

50 Patton, "Numerous Ridings in GTA."

51 Ibid.

52 CBC News, "Election-Day Polling Stations Cut."

53 Patton, "Numerous Ridings in GTA"; Rocca, "Canada Election."

54 Young and Mauracher, "Some Provinces Won't Allow Polling Stations in Schools."

55 Ibid.; Campbell, "Schools Are Common Voting Locations."

56 CBC News, "Election-Day Polling Stations Cut."

57 Bernhardt and Grabish, "From Ikea to a Horse-Racing Track."

58 CBC News, "Some Polling Stations in Yellowknife Changed."

59 Patton, "Numerous Ridings in GTA"; CBC News, "Election-Day Polling Stations Cut."

60 Alhmidi, "Poll Workers Say Elections Canada Put Them at Risk."

61 Newcombe, "Vote Where?"

62 Zandbergen, "Fewer Polling Stations"; CBC News, "Election-Day Polling Stations Cut."

63 Rodriguez, "Elections Canada 'Sorry' People Didn't Vote"; Gilmore, "Long Lines Plague Polls."

64 Ipsos, "One in Fourteen (7%) Voters."

65 Canada Elections Act, SC 2000, c 9, s 153 (2).

66 Mazur, "Long Lines at Kingston Polling Stations."

67 CBC News, "Elections Canada Move to Scrap Campus Voting."

68 Bensadoun, "Here's What's Different about This Year's Federal Election."

69 Elections Canada, Report on the 44th General Election.

70 Woolf, "Most Postal Votes to Be Counted by the End of Today."

71 Elections Canada, "FAQs – Counting and Results."
72 Woolf, "'Potential Anomaly' with Ballot Box."

Bibliography

Alhmidi, Maan. "Poll Workers Say Elections Canada Put Them at Risk of Contracting COVID-19." CTV News, 22 September 2021. https://www.ctvnews.ca/politics/federal-election-2021/poll-workers-say-elections-canada-put-them-at-risk-of-contracting-covid-19-1.5595945.

Atkeson, Lonna Rae, Lisa Ann Bryant, Thad Hall, Kyle Saunders, and Michael Alvarez. "A New Barrier to Participation: Heterogeneous Application of Voter Identification Policies." *Electoral Studies* 29, 1 (2010): 66–73. http://www.sciencedirect.com/science/article/pii/S0261379409000912.

Atkeson, Lonna Rae, Yann P. Kerevel, R. Michael Alvarez, and Thad E. Hall. "Who Asks for Voter Identification? Explaining Poll-Worker Discretion." *Journal of Politics* 76, 4 (2014): 944–57. http://www.jstor.org/stable/10.1017/s0022381614000528.

Bartko, Karen. "Police Respond to Anti-Mask Dispute at Edmonton Polling Station." Global News, 20 September 2021. https://globalnews.ca/news/8205087/edmonton-polling-station-mask-dispute/.

Bensadoun, Emerald. "Here's What's Different about This Year's Federal Election in Canada." Global News, 18 August 2021. https://globalnews.ca/news/8122217/key-differences-2021-federal-election/.

Bernhardt, Darren, and Austin Grabish. "From Ikea to a Horse-Racing Track, Winnipeg Polling Stations Look Different This Election." CBC News, 20 September 2021. https://www.cbc.ca/news/canada/manitoba/election-day-2021-manitoba-1.6181603.

Campbell, Taylor. "Schools Are Common Voting Locations. But Maybe Not This Time Out." *London Free Press,* 25 August 2021. https://lfpress.com/news/local-news/where-to-vote-school-polling-stations-may-be-a-no-go-this-election.

Canadian Press. "Polling Stations Short on Workers as COVID-19 Pandemic Hinders Recruitment." Global News, 2 September 2021. https://globalnews.ca/news/8163737/elections-canada-polling-stations-workers/.

Catt, Helena, Andrew Ellis, Michael Maley, Alan Wall, and Peter Wolf. *Electoral Management Design.* Stockholm: International Institute for Democracy and Electoral Assistance, 2014.

CBC News. "Election-Day Polling Stations Cut by More than Half in 11 Greater Toronto Area Ridings." 9 September 2021. https://www.cbc.ca/news/canada/toronto/gta-ridings-polling-stations-federal-election-canada-1.6169830.

–. "Elections Canada Move to Scrap Campus Voting 'Damaging to Our Democracy,' Toronto-Based Group Says." 7 September 2021. https://www.cbc.ca/news/canada/toronto/vote-campus-election-canada-future-majority-federal-1.6166873.

–. "N.L. Election Delayed for Nearly Half the Province Due to COVID-19." 11 February 2021. https://www.cbc.ca/news/canada/newfoundland-labrador/election-nl-staffing-shortages-1.5909976.

–. "Some Polling Stations in Yellowknife Changed amid COVID-19 Outbreak." 18 September 2021. https://www.cbc.ca/news/canada/north/some-polling-stations-changed-yellowknife-covid-outbreak-1.6181392.

Clark, Alistair, and Toby S. James. "Poll Workers." In *Election Watchdogs: Transparency, Accountability and Integrity,* edited by Pippa Norris and Alessandro Nai, 144–65. New York: Oxford University Press, 2017.

Dormer, Dave. "Curbside Municipal Voting to Be Available for Calgarians Who Refuse to Wear a Mask." CTV News (Calgary), 14 September 2021. https://calgary.ctvnews.ca/curbside-municipal-voting-to-be-available-for-calgarians-who-refuse-to-wear-a-mask-1.5585524.

Elections Canada. "The 2019 Federal Election by the Numbers." N.d. https://www.elections.ca/content.aspx?section=med&dir=bkg&document=num&lang=e.

–. "Administrative Staff in Local Elections Canada Offices." N.d. https://www.elections.ca/content.aspx?section=emp&dir=eco&document=index&lang=e.

–. "COVID-19 FAQs." N.d., accessed 23 September 2021. https://elections.ca/content2.aspx?section=faq&document=faqcov&lang=e.

–. "FAQs – Counting and Results." N.d., accessed 23 September 2021. https://www.elections.ca/content2.aspx?section=faq&document=faqcore&lang=e#que1.

–. "Field Liaison Officers." N.d. https://www.elections.ca/content.aspx?section=emp&dir=flo&document=index&lang=e.

–. "Health and Safety Measures." N.d., accessed 23 September 2021. https://elections.ca/content2.aspx?section=secure&document=index&lang=e.

–. *Report on the 44th General Election of September 20, 2021.* https://www.elections.ca/content.aspx?section=res&dir=rep/off/sta_ge44&document=index&lang=e.

–. "Returning Officers." N.d. https://www.elections.ca/content.aspx?section=emp&dir=dsro&document=index&lang=e.

–. "Section 1: Conduct of the Electoral Event." N.d. https://www.elections.ca/content.aspx?section=res&dir=rec/eval/pes2019/rop&document=p3&lang=e.

–. "Tariff of Fees – Reference Table." N.d. https://www.elections.ca/content. aspx?section=emp&dir=rem&document=index&lang=e.

Garnett, Holly Ann. "On the Front Lines of Democracy: Perceptions of Electoral Officials and Democratic Elections." *Democratization* 26, 8 (2019): 1399–418. https://doi.org/10.1080/13510347.2019.1641797.

Garnett, Holly Ann, and Toby S. James. "Measuring Electoral Integrity: Using Practitioner Knowledge to Assess Elections." *Journal of Elections, Public Opinion and Parties* 31, 3 (2020): 1–20. https://doi.org/10.1080/17457289.2020.1824186.

Gilmore, Rachel. "Long Lines Plague Polls across the Country as Voters Try to Cast Their Ballots." Global News, 21 September 2021. https://globalnews.ca/news/8206594/canada-election-line-polls-vote-wait/.

Hall, Thad E., J. Quin Monson, and Kelly D. Patterson. "The Human Dimension of Elections: How Poll Workers Shape Public Confidence in Elections." *Political Research Quarterly* 62, 3 (2009): 507–22. http://journals.sagepub.com/doi/abs/10.1177/1065912908324870.

Hristova, Bobby. "Hamilton Advance Polling Stations Raise Concerns, Offer Convenience for Voters." CBC News, 12 September 2021. https://www.cbc.ca/news/canada/hamilton/advance-polling-station-1.6173223.

Ipsos. "One in Fourteen (7%) Voters Say They Waited More than an Hour to Vote." 27 September 2021. https://www.ipsos.com/en-ca/news-polls/one-in-fourteen-voters-say-they-waited-more-than-an-hour-to-vote.

James, Toby S. "Better Workers, Better Elections? Electoral Management Body Workforces and Electoral Integrity Worldwide." *International Political Science Review* 40, 3 (2019): 370–90. https://doi.org/10.1177/0192512119829516.

–. *Comparative Electoral Management: Performance, Networks and Instruments.* London: Routledge, 2020.

–. "The Effects of Centralising Electoral Management Board Design." *Policy Studies* 38, 2 (2016): 130–48. https://doi.org/10.1080/01442872.2016.1213802.

–. *Elite Statecraft and Electoral Administration: Bending the Rules of the Game?* Houndmills, UK: Palgrave Macmillan, 2012.

James, Toby S., Holly Ann Garnett, Leontine Loeber, and Carolien van Ham. "Electoral Management and the Organisational Determinants of Electoral Integrity: Introduction." *International Political Science Review* 40, 3 (2019): 295–312. https://doi.org/10.1177/0192512119828206.

Kingsley, Jean-Pierre. "The Administration of Canada's Independent, Non-Partisan Approach." *Election Law Journal* 3, 3 (2004): 406–11.

Krause, Laura. "Elections Canada Recruiting Poll Workers for Federal Election – Vaccinated or Not." *CityNews,* 22 August 2021. https://montreal. citynews.ca/2021/08/22/elections-canada-poll-workers-vaccinated-not/.

Lavoie, Joanna. "Toronto Police Called after Couple Refuses to Mask Up at East York Polling Station." *Toronto Star,* 20 September 2021. https:// www.thestar.com/local-toronto-east-york/news/2021/09/20/toronto -police-called-after-couple-refuses-to-mask-up-at-east-york-polling -station.html?li_source=LI&li_medium=star_web_ymbii.

Lawlor, Andrea, and Marc Mayrand. "Election Administrators." In *Inside the Campaign: Managing Elections in Canada,* edited by Alex Marland and Thierry Giasson, 31–43. Vancouver: UBC Press, 2020.

Lipsky, Michael. *Street Level Bureaucracy: Dilemmas of the Individual in Public Services.* New York: Russell Sage Foundation, 1980. http://www.jstor.org/ stable/10.7758/9781610447713.

Mazur, Alexandra. "COVID-19 Case Linked to One of Kingston's Busiest Polling Stations." Global News, 23 September 2021. https://globalnews. ca/news/8216218/covid-19-kingston-busiest-polling-stations/.

–. "Long Lines at Kingston Polling Stations Due to High Unregistered Voter Turnout: Elections Canada." Global News, 22 September 2021. https://globalnews.ca/news/8212274/lines-kingston-polling-unregistered- voters/.

National Post. "Good News: Canada's 2015 Federal Election Ranked among the World's Best in Terms of Electoral Integrity." 31 March 2016. https:// nationalpost.com/opinion/good-news-canadas-2015-federal-election -ranked-among-the-worlds-best-in-terms-of-electoral-integrity.

Newcombe, Darryl. "Vote Where? Fewer Polling Stations in London, Ont. Threatens Turnout on Election Day." CTV News (London), 20 September 2021. https://london.ctvnews.ca/vote-where-fewer-polling-stations-in -london-ont-threatens-turnout-on-election-day-1.5579864.

Pagliaro, Jennifer. "Toronto Public Health Warns of Potential COVID-19 Exposures at Two Elections Canada Polling Stations." *Toronto Star,* 30 September 2021. https://www.thestar.com/news/gta/2021/09/30/toronto -public-health-warns-of-potential-covid-19-exposures-at-two-elections -canada-polling-stations.html.

Pal, Michael. "Canadian Election Administration on Trial: 'Robocalls,' Opitz and Disputed Elections in the Courts." *King's Law Journal* 28, 2 (2017): 324–42. https://doi.org/10.1080/09615768.2017.1351662.

Pastor, Robert A. "The US Administration of Elections: Decentralized to the Point of Being Dysfunctional." In *Electoral Management Design,* edited by Alan Wall, Andrew Ellis, Ayman Ayoub, Carl W. Dundas, Joram Rukambe, and Sara Staino, 273–76. Stockholm: International Institute for Democracy and Electoral Assistance, 2006.

Patton, Jessica. "Numerous Ridings in GTA See Significant Drop in Polling Stations for Upcoming Election." Global News, 10 September 2021. https://globalnews.ca/news/8180892/gta-polling-locations-elections -canada-decrease-covid/.

Rocca, Ryan. "Canada Election: TCDSB Trustees Vote against Allowing Polling Stations in Schools." Global News, 31 August 2021. https:// globalnews.ca/news/8157355/tcdsb-votes-against-allowing-polling -stations-in-schools/.

Rodriguez, Jeremiah. "Elections Canada 'Sorry' People Didn't Vote Because of Long Lineups." CTV News, 21 September 2021. https://www.ctvnews. ca/politics/federal-election-2021/elections-canada-sorry-people-didn-t -vote-because-of-long-lineups-1.5594728.

Shanton, Karen L. *The State and Local Role in Election Administration: Duties and Structures.* Congressional Research Service, 2019. https://fas.org/sgp/ crs/misc/R45549.pdf.

Williams, Melissa, Yasmin Dawood, Maxwell Cameron, Monique Deveaux, Genevieve Fuji Johnson, and Patti Lenard. "An Open Letter on the Fair Elections Act." *Globe and Mail,* 23 April 2014. http://www.theglobeand mail.com/opinion/an-open-letter-from-academics-on-bill-c-23/article 18114166/?page=all.

Woolf, Marie. "Most Postal Votes to Be Counted by the End of Today: Elections Canada." *Ottawa Citizen,* 22 September 2021. https://ottawa citizen.com/pmn/news-pmn/canada-news-pmn/most-postal-votes-to-be -counted-by-the-end-of-today-elections-canada/wcm/84a316cb-36b2 -499f-a1ac-39240a2305d2.

–. "'Potential Anomaly' with Ballot Box Leads to Recount in Châteauguay-Lacolle Riding." Global News, 28 September 2021. https://globalnews. ca/news/8227794/canada-election-chateauguay-lacolle-recount-2021/.

Young, Leslie, and Jamie Mauracher. "Some Provinces Won't Allow Polling Stations in Schools This Federal Election." Global News, 19 August 2021. https://globalnews.ca/news/8126265/election-school-poll-stations/.

Zandbergen, Rebecca. "Fewer Polling Stations Means You May Be Travelling Farther to Vote." CBC News (London), 9 September 2021. https:// www.cbc.ca/news/canada/london/fewer-polling-stations-means-you -may-be-travelling-farther-to-vote-1.6169261.

2

Motivations for Federal Candidacy

Angelia Wagner

Abstract Canadians have several reasons for wanting to become elected representatives. The most common motivations are the opportunity to influence government decision making, make a contribution to their communities, and promote their values. Interviews with Canadians who have run, or who might run, for elected office further reveal that individuals are attracted to a political career at a specific level of government because of an interest in that government's policy domains and/or a rejection of politics at another level of government. Analysis of candidate biographies published during the federal election in 2021 demonstrates that motivations to run can vary by gender and race.

Résumé Les Canadiens souhaitent se faire élire pour diverses raisons. Les motivations les plus courantes sont la possibilité d'influencer le processus décisionnel du gouvernement, de servir leurs collectivités, et de promouvoir leurs valeurs. Des entrevues effectuées auprès de Canadiens qui se sont présentés à des élections, ou qui prévoient le faire, révèlent un intérêt envers une carrière politique à des paliers gouvernementaux précis, en raison de l'intérêt suscité par certains domaines stratégiques du gouvernement ou du rejet de politiques issues d'un autre palier. L'analyse des biographies des candidats publiées au cours de l'élection fédérale de 2021 démontre que les motivations des candidats peuvent varier en fonction de leur genre et de leur groupe ethnique.

IN CANADA'S REPRESENTATIVE democracy, citizens delegate their political power to a small group of elected representatives who govern on their behalf. But this system of governance works only if enough individuals are willing to become representatives. And it works best when a large number of Canadians from all walks of life decide to run for elected office, giving voters a strong slate of candidates from which to choose the country's political leaders. Politicians with diverse life experiences are better positioned to identify, understand, and address issues affecting Canadians.[1] In this chapter, I explore motivations for political candidacy in Canada in two ways. First, why are some individuals interested in federal office holding, and how might their reasons differ from those of individuals who express interest in municipal or provincial office holding? To answer this question, I interviewed 101 individuals between February 2016 and December 2017 about the pros and cons of candidacy at all three levels of government. Second, which reasons did candidates give publicly for their decision to run in the federal election of 2021, and how did these reasons differ by social background? This analysis draws from data in candidate biographies published on campaign websites. The recent federal election afforded an opportunity to compare motivations by social group because of the large number of women, Indigenous, racialized, and queer individuals who ran. The two data sets enable us to better understand the allure of federal office for different types of Canadians.

Political ambition is central to the process of candidate emergence. Considering the sacrifices necessary not only to seek but also to hold elected office, individuals must be strongly motivated to become involved in the governing process. Politics is demanding. People really have to want to do the job to put up with the countless hours, constant scrutiny, online abuse, and never-ending pressures that are the lot of politicians. These drawbacks are likely why many individuals possess nascent ambition, or "the embryonic or potential interest in office seeking that precedes the actual decision to enter a specific political contest,"[2] but do not end up taking the leap. Admittedly, many people run for office in each election. But limited diversity in candidates' social characteristics raises concerns about the quality of political leadership on offer. White, heterosexual men hold a majority of seats in the House of Commons, and as a consequence public policy often reflects their priorities.[3] A strong democracy in Canada does not just need people to run for office – it also needs more diverse individuals to do so, especially in winnable seats.

White, heterosexual men's dominance of political institutions means that whatever we think we know about why people run for elected office is based primarily upon research on this social group and on Americans in particular. Research on the Canadian context – including Indigenous, racialized, and queer people – is more limited. In the American-dominated literature on candidacy, motivations are either intrinsic or extrinsic. Intrinsic motivations refer "to doing an activity for itself and for the pleasure and satisfaction derived from participation,"[4] and they include a desire for job contentment, self-development, sociability, recognition and publicity, autonomy, interesting work, helping others, and learning new things. Extrinsic motivations relate to external factors such as financial benefits, job security, work-life balance, policy making, dissatisfaction with incumbents, and position and power over others. However, few people seek elected office for just one reason. Individuals possess a variety of intrinsic and extrinsic reasons, but savvy candidates admit only to altruistic motives: "When politicians talk about their motives for pursuing a political career, they rarely mention their narrow private interests such as desire for power, prestige, and remuneration. Instead, they refer to their devotion to the people, their commitment to the nation's interests, and a strong sense of mission and responsibility."[5] Because politicians seek to control the public narrative about their candidacy, in this chapter I can only explore publicly expressed motivations for running for elected office.

Although all candidates possess intrinsic and extrinsic motivations, research on women and racial minorities tends to focus on the barriers that keep them out of politics and less on their reasons for jumping over those obstacles to get involved. When scholars do explore motivations, they eschew this classification in favour of other theoretical frameworks. Scholars of gender draw from the concept of stereotypes. Women run to achieve communal, power, and independent goals. Associated with female stereotypes, communal goals include caring for and working with others and serving the community, whereas power goals, associated with male stereotypes, include power, recognition, self-promotion, conflict, and competition. Gender-neutral independent goals include achievement.[6] One American study found that men were more attracted to power goals and women to communal goals.[7] However, a different study found that some women are inspired to run for both communal and power goals: although most women who ran in the US midterm elections in 2018 did so to have an impact on public policy (communal), some women were strongly motivated by negative emotions of threat, anger, and urgency caused by the Trump presidency (power).[8]

Racial stereotypes further influence how women publicly explain their candidacy.[9] Interviews with Texan women from diverse racial backgrounds between 2007 and 2009 reveal that white women strive to conform to gender stereotypes that they should be timid, claiming that their candidacies stem from other people's prodding and not their own ambitions.[10] In contrast, Black women publicly own their ambitions because this narrative conforms to the stereotype of the strong Black woman.[11] Communal goals spur many racialized individuals – but especially racialized women – to become candidates for elected office. Black women see office holding as a continuation of their community and social movement activism and as an opportunity to redress racial injustices.[12]

Despite the importance of motivation, scholars tend to ignore the reasons that people feel compelled to run for elected office in favour of understanding which individuals enter the political fray and how far up the political ladder they go. Researchers routinely compare the levels of political ambition expressed by women and men. Women's lesser ambition is attributed to social, structural, and institutional factors that make politics less hospitable, and thus less desirable, to women. Scholars are especially preoccupied with progressive ambition.[13] They not only assume but also clearly want individuals to move from elected office at a lower level of government to elected office at a higher level of government. The goal is to ensure diversity among elected representatives in national office. Yet studies demonstrate that many individuals exhibit static ambition, serving only at one level of government and not attempting to progress to a higher office for various reasons.[14] Scholarly interest in progressive ambition means that we do not know why people are drawn to one level of government over another. The limited research on motivations often focuses on understanding why people choose to become candidates in general rather than candidates for federal, provincial, or municipal office.

Politicians' tendency toward static ambition suggests two hypotheses. First, individuals are attracted to municipal, provincial, or federal office for specific reasons. The ability to influence public policy is a key motivation for many would-be politicians, but the desire to effect change in a specific policy area would make one office more valuable than another. The Constitution delegates responsibilities between the federal and provincial governments, making each one supreme in specific policy domains. Second, individuals run for the level of government that most interests them if personal, political, and electoral conditions are right. Individuals target another level of government only if conditions are more favourable and that level of government deals in some way with the policy domain of interest. Research suggests that women are more drawn to local government than state/provincial or national government because they are more interested in local issues.[15] Limited research on race/ethnicity precludes the formation of a hypothesis regarding why racialized individuals might be drawn to different levels of government. My purpose in this chapter is to offer some insights into the little-understood Canadian context to guide future research in the area.

Local Trends

To understand why some individuals run for federal office over provincial or municipal office, I draw from data on 101 individuals interviewed for a larger research project on political candidacy in Canada.[16] Participants included fifty-one women, forty-six men, and four non-binary individuals, as well as forty-eight racialized and fifty queer individuals. Two-thirds (70.3 percent) of participants had been members of a federal political party, with 25.7 percent affiliated with a left-wing party such as the New Democratic Party, 21.8 percent with a centrist party such as the Liberal Party, and 16.8 percent with a right-wing party such as the Conservative Party. Although respondents came from all ten provinces and two of the three territories, the largest number came from the populous provinces of Alberta (27.7 percent) and Ontario (24.8 percent). This uneven recruitment means that local trends in candidacy cannot be identified. Another limitation of this study is its reliance on candidate-reported information. I can only explore variations in individuals' publicly expressed motivations rather than their actual motivations. Still, many participants opted to keep their identities confidential, enabling them to be (more) frank about their motivations.

During the interviews, participants were asked a series of questions about candidacy, but in this section, I focus on their answers to a question about whether they had thought about running for a particular level of government and why. The interview results suggest that government preference can be understood in three ways: attraction, aversion, or indifference. Federal office is attractive to some individuals because of its prestige, power, and policy domains. MPs deal with issues of national importance and have greater resources at their disposal, giving them opportunities to help people in their ridings as well as across the country and around the world. The federal government's constitutional responsibility for international relations makes it particularly appealing to individuals focused on global issues rather than national ones. Given the federal government's power and resources, MPs often enjoy greater social standing in their communities than their provincial or municipal counterparts. Some people run federally because of their prior professional experience, such as political staffers.[17] Other individuals choose to run for federal office because they are averse or indifferent to provincial or municipal politics. Some strongly dislike the character of provincial politics in their areas, whereas others see local government as limited in scope, capacity, and importance.

Attraction, aversion, and indifference help to explain why individuals eschew federal politics in favour of provincial or municipal politics. Provincial government is appealing to some because it has constitutional responsibility for education and health care, and the provincial legislature is located closer to their homes. Municipal politics is attractive because of its influence on people's daily lives. Local government is responsible for everything from industrial parks, commercial projects, and housing developments to recreational facilities and arts and culture. In contrast, federal government can be a turnoff because backbench MPs have few opportunities for meaningful impact on public policy.[18] Decision-making power resides mainly with the prime minister and cabinet. Some individuals believe that they can have a greater impact at the provincial or municipal level precisely because of the smaller scope of each government. To them, making a difference matters more than prestige.

But how do publicly expressed motivations for candidacy differ by gender?[19] With some exceptions, women and men participants generally offered the same reasons for why they were attracted to running for office at a specific level of government. Women were as likely as men to cite policy interests as a key motivation. This gendered pattern held regardless of whether the preferred level of government was federal, provincial, or municipal. Men were more likely than women to be motivated by a general passion for federal politics. No one claimed a passion for provincial or municipal politics as a motivation.

Both women and men were drawn to municipal politics because of its non-partisan nature in most parts of the country, but others rejected local government because of the perceived minutiae of its tasks. They preferred the big-picture nature of provincial and federal policy making. "I know that municipal politics has important work that happens, but it's just not what sparks that interest in me in the same way that [politics] provincially or federally does," said a white woman active in right-wing parties who had not run for elected office at the time of the interview. "There's more money being spent, there's issues that are pretty significant when it comes to the direction that the province is taking, more so than just day-to-day life.

That is what interests me most at this point." Although women and men shared an interest in big-picture politics, they preferred different ones: women preferred provincial politics, whereas men were more drawn to federal politics.

Regardless of a government's responsibilities, women and men were equally likely to cite the ability to have an impact as a reason for choosing to run for a specific level of government – but only for municipal or provincial office. No one opted for federal politics from a belief that they could make a difference at that level. A racialized woman who ran to become a school board trustee noted that decisions made by local politicians can affect people's day-to-day lives: "If your lights are out, if your garbage is not being picked up, you have the most direct impact. And as you get further higher up in terms of government, the direct impact of the individual person is further away. You don't see the direct impact of those policies necessarily." Even if federal politicians can influence national or international issues, their work will not have much of a direct impact on citizens. "I like doing things that will have an effect in your community, whether it's little micro-grant projects or whether it is working within the education system," said a white man who ran unsuccessfully for municipal office and was considering a provincial bid one day, "whereas federally they spend a lot of time debating about things like foreign affairs and trade agreements that maybe you don't see a lot of the effect it has, at least locally." The desire to have an impact is key for candidates: it was the second most publicly expressed motivation for government selection behind policy domain.

Women and men might be attracted to federal politics for the same reasons, but they are turned off by different ones. Although few in number, women were the only ones to reject a federal candidacy because the House of Commons is too far away from their homes. All three women lived in western Canada and thought that the commute to Ottawa would be too time consuming. These travel calculations conformed to gendered expectations that women seek political offices that enable them to combine family responsibilities and political activities.[20] Men were more likely to cite party politics and lack of opportunity as reasons to forgo a career in federal politics. Women and men were equally likely to be turned off by how politics is practised in their province or municipality.

As with gender, few discernible differences were found among research participants by race or ethnicity. The only notable difference was that racialized people were almost twice as likely as white people to exhibit a stronger preference for federal government because of policy domain. For example, an Indigenous woman ran for a seat in the House of Commons because the federal government has constitutional responsibility for Indigenous peoples, and an Asian man ran for federal office because of an interest in national economic policy. Some racialized individuals were most keen on national office because the federal government deals with immigration, security, and human rights.

Racialized people were as likely as white people to claim a strong passion for federal politics, to be drawn to provincial and municipal government because they could have an impact at those levels, and to value the work of provincial politics. "I think for me the biggest issues are ones that affect lower-income or middle-class families," said a Southeast Asian woman who considered running for municipal office, "and so things like affordable transportation [and] affordable housing are all issues that I think the municipal government plays a really big part in." Yet racialized people were the only ones to reject municipal government because of its more limited scope. No racialized person cited the federal government's larger scope as a reason to run for federal office. As for rejecting a level of government, racialized people were as turned off as white individuals by the nature of provincial politics, but only white people were deterred by the nature of municipal politics. Racialized women were slightly more likely than white women to discount a federal career because of the distance between their home communities and the House of Commons. However, the limited number of individuals who provided reasons for selecting federal, provincial, or municipal office makes it difficult to offer firm conclusions about preferences by gender, race, or ethnicity, though this study points to possible avenues of research.

Behind the Scenes

To investigate further why individuals are drawn to federal office, in this section I analyze the English-language biographies of candidates who ran for the Conservatives, Greens, Liberals, and New Democrats during the federal election of 2021.[21] Bloc Québécois candidates were excluded because they did not issue English-language biographies. Incumbents were excluded based upon the assumption that they would likely focus on their track records in office. Biographies typically convey information about a candidate's policy positions, qualifications, and personal history.[22] Canadian parties control the messages that candidates convey to voters, including vetting their biographies, but candidates do have some leeway to highlight specific issues within the party platform perceived to be important to local voters. However, the promotional purpose of candidate biographies means that they are more likely to be influenced by social desirability than the interviews. I therefore explore potential differences in publicly expressed candidacy motivations during the federal election of 2021.

Biographies were obtained from party and candidate websites. Although some of these profiles followed a common party template, some candidates had independent websites, used a template from a previous election, created their own content, or repurposed their nomination campaign websites. More than 1,300 candidates ran for the four parties, yet a large number did not operate their own websites or post biographies on party websites. Several Liberal candidates relied on a generic statement provided by the party in which they only had to insert their names. These biographies were excluded because they did not contain information about the candidates. Each original biography was coded for mentions of why the candidate was running for office, with explanations grouped into broad themes. Of the 161 candidates who offered explicit reasons for why they were running, 84 were Greens, 40 were Conservatives, 19 were Liberals, and 18 were New Democrats. The following conclusions thus reflect more of the views of individuals who ran for the Greens and Conservatives than of those who ran for the Liberals and New Democrats. With this caveat in mind, I present an overview of federal candidacy motivations before offering an intersectional analysis focused on gender and race or ethnicity.

In line with the interview results, challengers most often cited a desire to address specific policy areas as the motivation behind their candidacies. That sixty-nine challengers (42.9 percent) claimed a desire to address issues such as the economy and the environment is hardly surprising since voters might consider party platforms when deciding how to vote. Candidates' pronouncements tended to be generic, professing an interest in improving the economy, addressing environmental issues, or building relationships with Indigenous peoples. Candidates did not offer many details. They cited policy domains rather than specific proposals.

The second most publicly expressed reason for running was a desire to give back to the community. Forty candidates (24.8 percent) presented themselves as having a public service orientation: their only concern was about using their talents to improve their communities and not to pursue political careers for their own gain. Racialized Conservative candidates were the most explicit in making this appeal. For example, Leslyn Lewis, who won the Haldimand-Norfolk riding for the Conservatives, insisted that she was "not a career politician. She feels that she has been given much by this great country, and by her hardworking parents before her. She wants her children to inherit an even better Canada than the one that has given her so much." Several candidates combined issue and public service appeals, vowing to contribute their skills and expertise to advance specific agendas.

Twenty-nine candidates (18 percent) were keen to promote their political and/or personal values. Many candidates insisted that Canadians would be better served with their party in government and that they wanted to help promote their party's values. Others simply wanted to provide strong voices. Promoting their political values was especially important to Green candidates, many of whom no doubt knew that they would not be elected. Honoré-Mercier candidate Bianca Deltorto-Russell said that she "has always had a passion to inspire others to make small changes to their lives to aid in the fight against climate change. This motivated her to become a candidate as she is looking for a larger platform to spread her Green values." Challengers for other political parties were more likely to speak of values in general than to frame them explicitly as Conservative, Liberal, or NDP values.

Twenty-four candidates (14.9 percent) decided to run out of a desire to improve the quality of political representation in their ridings and/or in Ottawa. Some candidates disagreed with the values, goals, and/or actions of the other political parties. They variously depicted the incumbent as incompetent, unethical, ineffective, indifferent, or unresponsive. "After years of neglect and having our emails, phone calls and concerns ignored by the Liberal incumbent, Scarborough Southwest deserves better," said Conservative candidate Mohsin Bhuiyan, who decided to put his name forward after receiving encouragement from family members and friends but did not win. Other candidates took a positive approach, focusing on the strong leadership that they could offer. Michelle Bowman, who campaigned unsuccessfully for the Greens in Guelph, decided to run because she "believes we need ethical, everyday people to become more involved in politics to enhance our quality of life and stabilize the climate." Only a few candidates cited other reasons for running, such as having prior experience with politics, being inspired by a new party leader, and being in a position to run. Only Green candidates claimed that providing voters with more partisan choices was why they ran.

To explore potential differences in motivation by a person's social characteristics, I coded candidates' gender and racial identities by examining their biographies and photographs. Of the 161 candidates, 88 were men, 72 were women, and 1 identified as non-binary; 121 were white; and 40 were racialized. Indigenous people were included in the racialized category because of the small number of non-white candidates in the sample, but I acknowledge that Indigenous people do not view themselves as ethnic minorities.

Reconfiguring the categories on an intersectional basis, 64 candidates were white men (38 Greens, 17 Conservatives, 5 Liberals, and 4 New Democrats), 56 were white women (33 Greens, 12 Conservatives, 6 Liberals, and 5 New Democrats), 24 were racialized men (8 Conservatives, 6 Liberals, 5 Greens, and 5 New Democrats), 16 were racialized women (8 Greens, 3 Conservatives, 3 New

Democrats, and 2 Liberals), and 1 was a non-binary white person (New Democrat). The non-binary results are not reported below because of the extremely limited sample. A demographic comparison of candidates whose biographies were and were not included in the data set reveals that, for all four parties, white women and racialized women were generally present in equal proportions in both groups. In contrast, white men were far less likely to have their biographies included in the analysis, whereas the opposite was true for racialized men for all parties but the Greens, in which white men were over-represented and racialized men were under-represented. These results suggest that conclusions about women's motivations can be generalized, whereas those about men's motivations need to be treated with caution.

An intersectional analysis revealed a complex picture regarding why different types of individuals publicly claimed to be running in the federal election of 2021. The only reason consistently offered by all four groups was policy. Racialized women (50 percent) were only slightly more likely than white women (46.4 percent), racialized men (45.8 percent), and white men (40.6 percent) to point to public policy as a key motivation for their candidacies. Regardless of gender or race, challengers were keen to convince voters that they wanted to pursue solutions to important issues. Yet men were twice more likely than women to cite a public service motivation. One-third of both racialized men (33.3 percent) and white men (32.8 percent) told voters that they wanted to make contributions to their communities compared with one-sixth of white women (16.1 percent) and racialized women (12.5 percent). One possible explanation for this gender difference could be men's greater confidence in their qualifications and abilities compared with women,[23] and thus men more than women might possess a greater belief that they have something to offer. Why racialized women were less inclined than white women to publicly proclaim a public service orientation is not clear, especially considering the strong volunteer and activist backgrounds of many racialized women candidates.[24]

Yet racialized candidates were not shy about telling voters that they wanted to promote their political and/or personal values.

One-quarter of racialized women (25 percent) cited their values as a key motivation for running compared with about one-fifth of racialized men (20.8 percent) and white men (18.8 percent) and less than one-fifth of white women (14.3 percent). Racialized candidates were as likely as white candidates to craft their appeals in broad terms, positioning their values as beneficial for the whole community. Ahmed Yousef, who ran unsuccessfully for the Liberals in Pitt Meadows–Maple Ridge, referred to his time as a municipal councillor as proof that "the interests of his constituents come first and that he is committed to putting principles above politics." Michael Chang, who did not end up winning the Langley-Aldergrove riding, said that he was "delighted to be standing with the NDP in this election and for the opportunity to take his guiding principles to Ottawa and start making a difference at the federal level." White candidates also referred to either general or partisan values but did so less often than racialized candidates.

One final racial difference in terms of motivation related to voter choice. Only white candidates said that their candidacies were inspired, at least in part, by a desire to provide voters with a greater range of partisan choices. All five were candidates for the Green Party, which faced recruitment difficulties because of internal party strife related to Annamie Paul's leadership. The party did not end up fielding a full slate of 338 candidates in the snap election, and many individuals who ran for the party were white. Whether greater candidate diversity would have seen racialized individuals cite partisan choice as a motivation is unknown.

The most revealing intersectional finding related to political representation. Women and racialized candidates were more likely than white male candidates to publicly express a desire to improve the quality of political representation as a reason for running for elected office. Less than 10 percent of white men cited this motivation compared with 16.7 percent of racialized men, 19.6 percent of white women, and 25 percent of racialized women. Considering that men have long dominated Canadian political institutions, it is not surprising that they expressed the least desire to improve political leadership, but racialized men's greater interest in doing so could be attributed to their under-representation in Canadian politics. Racialized men can live up to the masculine expectations of political leadership, but they cannot embody its (white) racial norms. White women can achieve the latter, whereas racialized women can embody neither. Considering how vigorously the masculine boundaries of political representation have been defended as more women win elected office,[25] it is not surprising that women as a group – and racialized women in particular – wanted to see reforms. In short, the more candidates deviated from the white, male norms of political representation, the more they told voters that they wanted to improve the quality of representation.

As for the role of partisanship, Green candidates drove many of the intersectional findings, likely because their biographies comprised half of the data set. But some partisan differences did emerge among the white candidates. White women and white men running for the Greens were three times more likely than their Conservative counterparts to publicly express a desire to influence policy, not surprising considering their party's strong desire to tackle environmental issues. Green Party white men were twice more likely than Conservative Party white men to publicly proclaim a desire to contribute to their communities, but both groups of white men were equally likely to cite a desire to promote their political values. Green Party white women were twice more likely than Conservative Party white women to seek better political representation. The lack of partisan differences among racialized candidates was likely a function of the small number of individuals in those categories.

Conclusion

By investigating candidacy preferences, I have demonstrated in this chapter that Canadians who consider running for elected office have strong ideas about where they would like to serve as elected representatives and that this choice is based upon a variety of motivations. Aspiring politicians from all walks of life want the chance to advance specific issues, make a difference in their communities, promote their values, and improve the quality of political representation. The top motivation – policy making – is a key factor for which level of government a candidate prefers. Many individuals run federally because they want to work on issues that fall within the federal government's constitutionally determined policy domains. Candidates' attraction to a specific level of government often comes down to an assessment of each level's ability to meet their policy goals while offering an agreeable (or at least manageable) working environment. Political opportunities also matter. Women often need to be recruited to run, whereas men are typically self-starters. Once ready to run, a person might not want to wait until the next federal election a few years away and thus jump into the current year's municipal election. Or a person might receive greater party, human, and financial resources to run for provincial rather than federal office. Some individuals believe that they need to acquire the necessary experience and expertise in governance at the municipal or provincial level before making a bid for federal office. These findings support my contention that, in Canada at least, static ambition is as prevalent among candidates as progressive ambition. In light of this finding, party officials and activists need to better understand why different types of Canadians are drawn to federal, provincial, or municipal office to improve efforts to attract a more diverse range of individuals to run at each level. Understanding why Indigenous women are attracted to provincial politics, for example, would enable organizations such as Equal Voice to tailor recruitment appeals to the needs and interests of this group of potential candidates.

As for the candidate biographies, an intersectional analysis showed few major differences in publicly expressed motivations based upon gender and race. The communal goal of policy making was the most publicly expressed motivation for both women and men as well as racialized and white people. Candidates of all social backgrounds were keen to have an influence on government policy. Surprisingly, men were more likely than women to publicly express the communal motivation of making a difference in their communities, a reason for running that aligns more with female stereotypes than with male stereotypes.[26] This finding might reflect the small but growing tendency of male politicians to claim feminine traits seen as positive for political leaders.[27] Racialized people were more likely than white people to assert publicly the motive of power to promote values, but their appeals were not usually framed in competitive terms that one would expect with such a motive. Racialized people and white women were more likely than white men to express public dissatisfaction with incumbents and a desire to improve the quality of political representation. That white men rarely cited this motive of power is not surprising considering that their social group established the nature and practice of political representation in Canada. These findings reveal a complex set of reasons that individuals choose to become candidates. Understanding why they run for elected office, and for which level of government, can help parties in their recruitment efforts and ensure that voters have a stronger slate of candidates from which to choose on election day.

Notes

1 Young, *Inclusion and Democracy.*
2 Fox and Lawless, "To Run or Not to Run for Office," 643.
3 Newman and White, *Women, Politics, and Public Policy.*
4 Pedersen, "Committed to the Public Interest?," 888.
5 Beniers and Dur, "Politicians' Motivation," 29.
6 Schneider et al., "Power, Conflict, and Community."
7 Ibid.
8 Dittmar, "Urgency and Ambition."
9 Ibid.; Frederick, "Bringing Narrative In"; Frederick, "'Who Better to Do It than Me!'"
10 Frederick, "Bringing Narrative In"; Frederick, "'Who Better to Do It than Me!'"
11 Ibid.
12 Ibid.
13 See Coffé, "Women Stay Local"; Johnson, Oppenheimer, and Selin, "The House as a Stepping Stone"; and Sieberer and Müller, "Aiming Higher."
14 Einstein et al., "Do Mayors Run for Higher Office?"; Johnson, Oppenheimer, and Selin, "The House as a Stepping Stone."
15 Coffé, "Women Stay Local"; Trimble, "Politics Where We Live."
16 For details about the project's methodology, see Wagner, "Avoiding the Spotlight."
17 Snagovsky and Kirby, "Political Staff."

18 Loat and MacMillan, *Tragedy in the Commons*.

19 A complex gender analysis is not possible because of the limited number of research participants who identified as non-binary and who discussed their government preferences.

20 Trimble, "Politics Where We Live."

21 Campaign biographies cited throughout this section were gathered from party websites, and most of these were taken down in the weeks after an election. Because the web pages are no longer accessible, links have not been provided but copies are on file with the author.

22 Schneider, "Gender-Based Strategies on Candidate Websites."

23 Fox and Lawless, "Gendered Perceptions and Political Candidacies"; Thomas, "The Complexity Conundrum."

24 Frederick, "Bringing Narrative In"; Frederick, "'Who Better to Do It than Me!'"

25 Duerst-Lahti and Kelly, "On Governance, Leadership, and Gender"; Gidengil and Everitt, "Filtering the Female"; Gidengil and Everitt, "Metaphors and Misrepresentation"; Gidengil and Everitt, "Talking Tough."

26 Schneider et al., "Power, Conflict, and Community."

27 Langer, "The Politicization of Private Persona."

Bibliography

Beniers, Klaas J., and Robert Dur. "Politicians' Motivation, Political Culture, and Electoral Competition." *International Tax and Public Finance* 14, 1 (2007): 29–54.

Coffé, Hilde. "Women Stay Local, Men Go National and Global? Gender Differences in Political Interest." *Sex Roles* 69, 5–6 (2013): 323–38.

Dittmar, Kelly. "Urgency and Ambition: The Influence of Political Environment and Emotion in Spurring US Women's Candidacies in 2018." *European Journal of Politics and Gender* 3, 1 (2020): 143–60.

Duerst-Lahti, Georgia, and Rita Mae Kelly. "On Governance, Leadership, and Gender." In *Gender Power, Leadership, and Governance,* edited by Georgia Duerst-Lahti and Rita Mae Kelly, 11–37. Ann Arbor: University of Michigan Press, 1995.

Einstein, Katherine Levine, David M. Glick, Maxwell Palmer, and Robert J. Pressel. "Do Mayors Run for Higher Office? New Evidence on Progressive Ambition." *American Politics Research* 48, 1 (2020): 197–221.

Fox, Richard L., and Jennifer L. Lawless. "Gendered Perceptions and Political Candidacies: A Central Barrier to Women's Equality in Electoral Politics." *American Journal of Political Science* 55, 1 (2011): 59–73.

–. "To Run or Not to Run for Office: Explaining Nascent Political Ambition." *American Journal of Political Science* 49, 3 (2005): 642–59.

Frederick, Angela Howard. "Bringing Narrative In: Race-Gender Storytelling, Political Ambition, and Women's Paths to Public Office." *Journal of Women, Politics and Policy* 34, 2 (2013): 113–37.

–. "'Who Better to Do It than Me!' Race, Gender, and the Deciding to Run Accounts of Political Women in Texas." *Qualitative Sociology* 37, 3 (2014): 301–21.

Gidengil, Elisabeth, and Joanna Everitt. "Filtering the Female: Television News Coverage of the 1993 Canadian Leaders' Debates." *Women and Politics* 21, 4 (2000): 105–31.

–. "Metaphors and Misrepresentation: Gendered Mediation in News Coverage of the 1993 Canadian Leaders' Debates." *Harvard International Journal of Press/Politics* 4, 1 (1999): 48–65.

–. "Talking Tough: Gender and Reported Speech in Campaign News Coverage." *Political Communication* 20, 3 (2003): 209–32.

Johnson, Gbemende, Bruce I. Oppenheimer, and Jennifer L. Selin. "The House as a Stepping Stone to the Senate: Why Do So Few African American House Members Run?" *American Journal of Political Science* 56, 2 (2012): 387–99.

Langer, Ana Inés. "The Politicization of Private Persona: Exceptional Leaders or the New Rule? The Case of the United Kingdom and the Blair Effect." *International Journal of Press/Politics* 15, 1 (2010): 60–76.

Loat, Alison, and Michael MacMillan. *Tragedy in the Commons: Former Members of Parliament Speak Out about Canada's Failing Democracy.* Toronto: Vintage Canada, 2014.

Newman, Jacquetta, and Linda A. White. *Women, Politics, and Public Policy: The Political Struggles of Canadian Women.* Oxford: Oxford University Press, 2006.

Pedersen, Lene Holm. "Committed to the Public Interest? Motivation and Behavioural Outcomes among Local Councillors." *Public Administration* 92, 4 (2013): 886–901.

Schneider, Monica C. "Gender-Based Strategies on Candidate Websites." *Journal of Political Marketing* 13, 4 (2014): 264–90.

Schneider, Monica C., Mirya R. Holman, Amanda B. Diekman, and Thomas McAndrew. "Power, Conflict, and Community: How Gendered Views of Political Power Influence Women's Political Ambition." *Political Psychology* 37, 4 (2016): 515–31.

Sieberer, Ulrich, and Wolfgang C. Müller. "Aiming Higher: The Consequences of Progressive Ambition among MPs in European Parliaments." *European Political Science Review* 9, 1 (2017): 27–50.

Snagovsky, Feodor, and Matthew Kirby. "Political Staff and the Gendered Division of Political Labour in Canada." *Parliamentary Affairs* 72, 3 (2019): 616–37.

Thomas, Melanee. "The Complexity Conundrum: Why Hasn't the Gender Gap in Subjective Political Competence Closed?" *Canadian Journal of Political Science* 45, 2 (2012): 337–58.

Trimble, Linda. "Politics Where We Live: Women and Cities." In *Canadian Metropolitics: Governing Our Cities,* edited by James Lightbody, 92–114. Toronto: Copp Clark, 1995.

Wagner, Angelia. "Avoiding the Spotlight: Public Scrutiny, Moral Regulation, and LGBTQ Candidate Deterrence." *Politics, Groups, and Identities* 9, 3 (2021): 502–18.

Young, Iris Marion. *Inclusion and Democracy.* Oxford: Oxford University Press, 2000.

3

Local Nominations

Anna Lennox Esselment and Matthew Bondy

Abstract   Local nomination contests are how grassroots party members select their candidates to compete in a general election. This traditional role has evolved to be a shared responsibility between the central party and the party on the ground. This chapter examines the development of central party involvement in and oversight of nomination races and argues that recent trends showing Canadian political parties' penchant for safeguarding incumbent MPs from nomination challengers and appointing candidates in lieu of holding nomination races threaten the health of local party associations. Insights drawn from the Conservative nomination race in 2021 in Kitchener–Conestoga show that, where open and contested nominations occur, the local electoral district association is an enthusiastic contributor to the goals of the party. Vigorous vetting processes green-light different types of nomination candidates who in turn embrace diverging contest strategies; the result can engage citizens in a vibrant contest. Parties are still left with the challenges of recruiting a diverse group of individuals to run in nomination races and a social media environment that can be hostile to that end.

Résumé   Les courses à l'investiture permettent aux membres de l'association de circonscription d'un parti de sélectionner le candidat qui représentera la formation lors de l'élection générale. Ce processus traditionnel a évolué en une responsabilité partagée entre les partis centraux et les associations locales de circonscription. Ce chapitre examine l'évolution de la participation des partis centraux et de leur suivi des courses à l'investiture locale. De plus, il soutient que la propension actuelle des partis politiques canadiens à protéger les députés en poste des autres candidats et à nommer des candidats au lieu de tenir des courses à l'investiture menace la santé des associations locales de parti. Les observations tirées de la course à l'investiture des conservateurs dans la circonscription de Kitchener–Conestoga en 2021 démontrent que lorsque les mises en candidature sont ouvertes et contestées, l'association de circonscription locale contribue avec enthousiasme aux objectifs du parti. Des processus de sélection vigoureux favorisent différents types de candidats qui à leur tour adopteront des stratégies diverses, ce qui peut entraîner une course dynamique susceptible d'engager les citoyens. Le défi de recruter un groupe diversifié de candidats à l'investiture incombe toujours aux partis, qui doivent composer avec un environnement de médias sociaux souvent hostile à cette fin.

THE ABILITY OF CITIZENS to choose their representatives freely is at the core of liberal democratic systems. In an election, the vast majority of candidates have been selected by their respective political parties through local nomination contests – in the past three decades, over 99 percent of Members of Parliament (MPs) ran under a party label.[1] These internal nomination races can vary from the highly competitive to the uncontested. They can attract thousands of new members to the party or be relatively small affairs, such as in a riding with a flailing electoral district association (EDA) and little chance of the party winning the seat or where a nominee lacks challengers. Nonetheless, the consistency in Canada's history of nominating candidates is that, until recently, nominations have been the domain of the party's local constituency associations.[2]

Scholars of political parties in Canada have settled on the "stratarchical" model as the best depiction of party organizations today.[3] Described as franchise-type organizations, parties have mutually interdependent national and local dimensions.[4] Like a business franchise, the national party is largely responsible for determining policy positions, brand development, communications, and campaign direction. The local level is primarily in charge of selecting candidates and providing logistical ground support in an election.[5] Put differently, each level or "stratum" of the party, in theory, has principal authority over certain responsibilities. Interdependence, however, suggests that these jurisdictions are not mutually exclusive, and in practice the degree to which the local party association has more or less control over nomination processes can vary.[6]

This prerogative of candidate selection at the local level has endured in Canada despite changes in party types and systems. In the nineteenth century, party organizations began as small groups of local notables who had been elected to Parliament, through selections in their home constituencies, typically as representatives of one of the two major parties. In Canada's first party system, the parliamentary caucus was the party – its members chose the leader, and the party itself was mostly held together through an elaborate system of patronage. But even in this early period, the tradition of choosing candidates locally through various ad hoc processes became well established, eventually settling on a pattern in which interested partisans from across the riding would come together to discuss the merits of various community members who had put their names forward for consideration.[7] In some cases, these meetings would simply confirm a candidate already well known in the constituency. In other instances, several potential nominees would put their names forward, and rounds of voting would take place until one person emerged as the victor. These early exercises established and legitimized the process of bringing together local party members to select their candidate.[8]

As Canada's parties and the systems in which they operated progressed over time, these initial jurisdictional responsibilities did not endure as owned exclusively by either level. In the first part of the twentieth century, for example, regional cleavages witnessed the appearance of new, regionally based parties, such as the Progressives and Social Credit, that aspired to compete against party stalwarts at the federal level. The Liberals and Conservatives managed the era by having powerful regional ministers dominate the party organizations in their regions, knitting together electoral support by articulating regional interests to cabinet, and working to broker regional interests at the national level.[9] When the parties occupied the opposition benches, occasionally they relied on provincial party machines to deliver slates of candidates to carry the party label, especially when electoral support in any particular province was weak. Local nomination practices established in the first party system were challenged by regional party bosses who wanted increased control over who stood as candidates in their particular provinces. The need to ensure meaningful participation of party activists at election time prevented the centralized takeover of candidate selection, but national-level interest in who stood for office was piqued.

Over the second half of the twentieth century, party organizations continued to evolve, which contributed to an erosion of the largely national and local responsibilities within the party. Parties developed grassroots wings in which partisans and activists could take out formal memberships and be involved in increasingly institutionalized internal party processes and activities.[10] Should party members have policy ideas that they wanted to advance to the national level for consideration, mechanisms for doing so were now in place. National conventions, for example, were regular events by the end of the 1920s,[11] and these major party gatherings included the consideration of policy resolutions from local electoral district associations even if most of them never made it into campaign platforms. Party leadership selection became more inclusive in the late 1960s by expanding the number of party members who could be involved in choosing (or ousting) a leader, further diminishing the influence of the party caucus.[12]

Legislative changes to the Canada Elections Act in the early 1970s in turn opened the door to more central party oversight of local affairs. As an element of campaign finance reform, modifications to the Elections Act permitted the printing of party labels on ballots, beginning with the federal election of 1972. Although this has been helpful to prospective voters, whoever is chosen as a party's candidate must now, by statute, be officially approved by a designated party official, normally the leader. Local constituencies can still make selections through their nomination races, but the winning candidates are assured their positions only once the party leader or appointed agent signs off. As a consequence, and much like the regional party bosses in the 1930s, the central party is naturally interested in the potential crop of candidates whom the leader ultimately has to approve and, alongside local associations, now regularly engages in the recruitment of potential nominees.[13] The requirement of approval also means that the national level can step in to appoint a riding's candidate, bypassing a local nomination contest altogether. This can be used as a stopgap measure if a constituency has been unable to mount a successful nomination race, the party has a star candidate whom it wants to run in a certain riding (see Chapters 4 and 5 of this volume), or the central party wants to ensure a broader representation of candidates.[14] These powers of appointment were used sparingly at first, but that is no longer the case; the result can be tension between grassroots members and the central party.

The national level can also impose certain conditions on an electoral district association before it can hold a nomination race, such as conducting a formal search to entice more diverse candidates.[15] What is more, parties can protect existing Members of Parliament from divisive nomination races, but often they make demands of their incumbents before doing so, such as raising a certain amount of money, knocking on a set number of doors, or making a minimum number of phone calls to potential voters.[16] National parties also control when a nomination will take place, how long the race will be, and even who can or cannot run.[17] These levers have been used to undermine local efforts, particularly if there is a certain individual whom the central party wants nominated.

The interconnections between national and local levels of party organizations reflect the stratarchical model. Although generally the central party has authority over policy decisions, the party brand, strategic communications, and campaign direction, there is clear interest and even a degree of control exerted in local nomination races, traditionally the purview of the constituency association. A recent report by the Samara Centre for Democracy has emphasized increased centralization of local nomination processes and undemocratic practices by parties in their candidate nominations.[18] In the next section, we explore these findings and apply them to trends in local nominations for the Canadian federal election of 2021.

Local Trends

Leadership races and local nomination contests are normally when party memberships swell. To win a nomination, a contestant must earn the support of grassroots members in the riding, bring in hundreds (and sometimes thousands) of new party members, or achieve both. With some exceptions, only party members in the riding can participate in a local race, and where a race has multiple contestants the need to find one's own cache of dedicated supporters is critical to a successful outcome.

This portrayal suggests that most local competitions are vibrant affairs full of eager participants in a party's democratic process, but on the ground the reality can be much different. Recent trends show that only a handful of nomination contests actually involve a competition among two or more nominees. The tendency of parties to put nomination rules in place that protect incumbent representatives from facing any internal challenge is often why. In 2019, Liberal MPs had to meet certain requirements in order to avoid an open nomination. Fundraising, phone calling, door knocking, and participating in voter contact "days of action" were a few of the expectations that incumbents had to meet in order to secure their ridings.[19] In advance of the election in 2021 – held in the midst of the COVID-19 pandemic – the nomination rules for incumbents in the three main parties were scaled down but still required MPs to raise small amounts of funding to protect their seats.[20] The penchant of parties to protect their incumbents can induce a range of reactions among local party members. On the one hand, the practice facilitates a focus on general campaign readiness, which saves the MP from a distracting nomination fight that can exhaust resources in advance of an election; on the other hand, there are instances when party supporters or other interested groups want to replace certain MPs. This was exemplified in 2021 by Campaign Life Coalition's attempt to force a vote on an amendment to the Conservative Party's constitution that would allow a plurality of an EDA board or its membership to overrule a party leader's decision to safeguard sitting MPs from nomination challenges.[21] The coalition's proposed amendment was rejected for consideration at the Conservative Party's policy convention in March, leaving decisions about this aspect of local nominations with the party leader and national council.

The scarcity of competitive nomination contests – only 17 percent according to the Samara Centre report[22] – is also the result of an increasing preference among parties to appoint candidates in open ridings. Appointing candidates in ridings, and bypassing nomination contests entirely, puts an additional squeeze on the EDA's traditional role in selecting preferred nominees. Appointments can cause consternation among grassroots members as well as those who had planned to contest, or were in the process of vying for, the candidacy.[23] Valuable time and resources spent by potential nominees to prepare for the race, plan their get-out-the-vote strategies, and fundraise from family members and friends are upended when a party ultimately steps in with appointments. In rare instances, party appointments can detrimentally affect MPs themselves. On the cusp of the election in 2021, for example, Bloc Québécois leader Yves-François Blanchet replaced Terrebonne MP Michel Boudrias by appointing Nathalie Sinclair-Desgagné in his place. The Bloc Québécois justified the move by noting that Boudrias had not met the conditions set out by the central party in order to preserve his federal election candidacy.[24] He ran as an independent instead but was soundly defeated by Sinclair-Desgagné.

Of the elections scrutinized by the Samara Centre,[25] three could be considered "snap" elections, and minority Parliaments can affect the degree to which parties can prepare in advance for an unexpected election, naturally resulting in an increased number of appointed candidates. In fact, most parties have rules in their constitutions that permit accelerated appointments of candidates in this scenario, even before an election has been called. The Liberal Party, for example, empowers its National Campaign Committee with flexible control over the party's nomination process in order to accommodate different election cycle effects.[26] The "electoral urgency" rule falls under this umbrella, and its invocation has been described as "routine" by party officials.[27] The Conservative Party has a similar practice, but it can be triggered only once a general election is officially under way. Nevertheless, the trend toward appointing rather than holding nomination contests for candidates, particularly when it is a minority Parliament, raises concerns about the health of the party's local democratic processes. As the Samara Centre report also points out, associated practices by the central party to curb nomination races include shortening the length of the contests, changing the rules regarding membership in the party, and even retroactively closing a nomination race in order to disadvantage certain nominees. Although to some degree expedient, each of these actions can demoralize grassroots members and nomination participants.

A second trend is the desire of local ridings to recruit a large and diverse set of candidates either to contest nominations or to be considered by the party for appointments. Although it is a stated priority of almost all parties, increasing the number of women and Indigenous people, Black people, and other racialized minorities to stand for nomination can be challenging. This is also true for other equity-seeking groups, including people who belong to the LGBTQ2S+ community, who are disabled, or who are otherwise marginalized. Proximity to an election can be a factor here. When an early election call is imminent, parties sometimes scramble to fill their remaining open seats, and the diversity of candidates becomes less important than fielding an entire slate. In early August 2021, for example, the Conservative Party had over thirty ridings without candidates; the central party sent an email to all of its supporters inviting those interested in being candidates to come forward for consideration.[28] Local EDAs in the Liberal, New Democratic, and Green Parties must demonstrate to the central party that they have made efforts to recruit potential nominees from under-represented groups before a nomination race can officially begin.[29] The demographic mix of some ridings can facilitate this task more easily than that of others. In some cases, a visible minority nominee effectively activates the ethnic community in the riding, and the nomination is won handily. In other cases, there is a dearth of racialized minorities who step forward to contest the nomination, and parties must work harder to entice their participation.

A party's power of appointment is a tool that can be used in favour of selecting candidates from diverse backgrounds, but evidence shows that, ironically, diversity is more assured in a contested nomination.[30] The election of 2021 boasted the highest number of visible minority candidates,[31] but researchers have found that many Indigenous and racialized candidates run in unwinnable ridings and are provided with less financial support than their white counterparts.[32] Increasing diversity among those elected to Parliament is jeopardized as a result.

Women nominees must likewise be sought by EDAs. Although the number of women and gender-diverse individuals who participated in the election in 2021 peaked,[33] the Samara Centre's research demonstrates that parties appoint women at a rate only slightly higher than when women win local nomination contests. When women do seek nomination, they tend to win the race almost as often as their male counterparts.[34] What is more, scholars have demonstrated that Canadians are as willing to vote for female candidates as male candidates in a general election.[35] Over the past twenty years, the number of seats won by female candidates has increased but appears to have plateaued at approximately 30 percent. Clearly, more women need to be recruited to run, and researchers have found several effects that can assist with this goal, such as having a female president of a party riding association, women who serve on local riding executives, women who hold positions in the national executive of the party, and longer nomination races that occur earlier in the electoral cycle.[36]

Encouraging women, and particularly members of LGBTQ2S+ communities, to contest nominations is complicated by a third trend beyond the control of either the local or the central party. Women candidates are more likely to be the recipients of online harassment and trolling (e.g., "toxic tweets") on the campaign trail, and potential nominees who are women, who identify with LGBTQ2S+ orientations, or who are non-white are increasingly aware that they will have to contend with virtual hostility in their bids for election and while holding office.[37] Preparing for the unpleasant digital political environment in which they will be operating can develop into a real barrier for these groups, and research has found that female non-candidates (potential nominees) in particular tend to raise the issue of online harassment more often than those already selected as candidates.[38]

Behind the Scenes

The trends set out above might be of little surprise to readers. News reports leading up to elections often expose the processes, challenges, and outcomes of local nomination races. But there are two aspects of nominations about which we know much less: first is the vetting process that all potential nominees must undergo before the party permits them to run,[39] and second – when a competitive race does occur – are the strategies that nominees use to win the contest and be declared the party's candidate. The insights set out below are based upon a real experience of vying for the open and contested local Conservative Party nomination in the Kitchener–Conestoga EDA for the election in 2021. Participating in the race demonstrated that local riding associations are not just window dressing for the national party. They are engaged with, and serious partners of, the central party to unearth and green-light the best potential nominees; contestants who pass muster must then consider various tactics to conduct a successful mini-campaign in order to emerge triumphant as the chosen candidate.

Contemporary political parties undertake a vetting process for all nomination applicants with a view to assessing their strengths and weaknesses.[40] The process also serves to identify potential vulnerabilities in terms of a candidate's record of behaviour, reputation, previous public statements, or personal affiliations. The ultimate goal of the vetting process is to field candidates who have serviceable political qualities and no politically prohibitive personal attributes or experiences.

Parties mainly review candidates' qualities by proactively replicating the work that competing parties will likely undertake in their opposition research to discredit the successfully nominated candidate in the context of the general election.[41] By "getting ahead" of such attempts through strong vetting, parties can choose either to prohibit a nomination applicant from contesting a nomination or to "de-risk" the candidate by developing mitigation strategies to minimize the political risk of any potentially controversial issue.

In the Conservative Party, both the EDA and the national party organization are involved in vetting each candidate. The depth and rigour of vetting can differ significantly between parties and between electoral districts, mostly because of a mix of factors, including the availability of resources and personnel to engage in the process, the competitiveness of the party, the number of nomination contests under way, and the honesty of the potential nominee. Kevin

Vuong, the Liberal Party candidate in Spadina–Fort York in the election in 2021, chose to hold back the fact that a criminal charge had been withdrawn against him several years earlier. That piece of information was revealed during the latter part of the campaign, and the party was forced to drop him as its candidate. This sort of embarrassment is exactly what good vetting should catch, but nominees do hide information. An NDP insider tells the story of a vetting interview with an aspiring candidate that ended with the party operative reportedly warning "now, if I find out that you have not told me something in your past that could do damage to the leader or the party, I guarantee you that I will ensure that you pay for it for the rest of your life. Are we clear?"[42]

Not every vetting interview ends with a threat from the party, but the campaign does want a full accounting of the individuals interested in running. Nomination applicants – referred to as such until they successfully pass through the vetting process with local and national approval, at which point they become nomination candidates – provide full application packages to local EDAs as a first step. The nomination package seeks to identify both ideological leanings and civil society affiliations so that party officials can evaluate the socio-economic and ideological aspects of the applicant.

Equally as important, however, the nomination package requires extensive financial and legal vetting. Credit scores are commonly considered to be reasonable proxies for personal reliability and financial health and included in the list of information requirements in the package. Also commonly required are police background checks, personal references, and attestations of support for party policy.

When a Conservative nomination applicant submits the application package on time and in full to the EDA, it is immediately shared with the national party apparatus through the party's regional organizer, responsible for the oversight of a number of EDAs in geographically defined regions (e.g., southwestern Ontario or northeastern Manitoba). This ensures that the national party has full visibility of all nomination applicants in all ridings. Regional organizers are hired through the national party structure to ensure alignment with national priorities, considered key to winning elections.

Applicants then move to vetting conversations with their local EDA's candidate nominations committee (CNC), typically comprising the chair and several other committee members who expressed interest in serving in this capacity to the full EDA board of directors and whose service on the committee was voted on and ratified by the board. Their role is to facilitate the process of receiving applications, ensuring their full completion, and interviewing applicants for political qualities and risks. Ultimately, this committee recommends nomination applicants to the national party structure for approval, thus ensuring their entry into the nomination contest, or in more rare instances the committee recommends that particularly problematic candidates not be approved to contest the nomination.

Vetting can involve several interviews with party officials, but in the Conservative Party just one interview is required between the applicant and the CNC, though the national party's regional organizer for the area typically participates as an observer. This speaks to the power of local EDAs to conduct their own candidate recruitment and vetting and provides a valuable sensing function to the national party, which can use these observer opportunities to develop an internal gauge of applicant quality within the national party network.

Applicant interviews typically last for one hour, with each member of the committee taking the opportunity to ask one or more questions of the applicant. The questions are formulated by the CNC prior to the interview, with national party input through the regional organizer. In the Kitchener–Conestoga vetting process, questions ranged from those that probed ideological leanings, to those that confirmed the presence or absence of reputational risks, to those designed to gauge the applicant's commitment to the party's "grassroots," meaning the power of local EDAs. In this way, both candidate recruitment and vetting are expressions of the power of EDAs or party grassroots volunteers and opportunities for EDAs to express stronger support for candidates committed to the party's grassroots political power as opposed to those who might instead state ideology and commitment to the party's leader as their first political loyalties.

At the conclusion of a nomination applicant interview, the nomination committee votes on whether to let the candidate proceed to the national party level for final review and sign-off by the party leader. This is the apex of the exercise of EDA power to select and vet nomination applicants. It is rare for CNCs to prevent candidates from proceeding to the national level for sign-off. Despite the penchant for appointing candidates, there seems to be keen interest in a robust, multi-candidate nomination contest as an expression of the health of the grassroots of the party, and therefore its own relevance, and that of the EDA, to the political process. There are occasions when vetting committees vote against allowing candidates to proceed, but the instances are rarely reported publicly.[43]

After the vetting process is complete, contestants are generally free to begin organizing their nomination campaigns. Nominees can be motivated by a range of objectives (see Chapter 2 of this volume). For most, the objective is to secure the nomination and be the official candidate for the party in the riding – they have, in other words, political career ambitions. Some candidates, however, run to raise awareness of an issue, such as environmentalism or reproductive rights, others run because they are committed to an ideological perspective, and still others join a nomination race simply to have the experience, perhaps as a test run in advance of a more serious bid later.

In the Kitchener–Conestoga nomination contest, two different strategies were employed by the candidates, whose primary objective was to win the nomination. The first we refer to as the "front-runner" strategy and the second as the "activist" strategy.

A front-runner strategy is usually employed by a party insider vying for the nomination.[44] The strategy is designed to present the nomination candidate as the clear favourite of the party, making it relatively easy to secure the endorsements of a number of local influencers, including local politicians, business leaders, and community organizers. The key value proposition of such candidates is their electability in a general campaign. They tend to have name recognition in their communities, for example through business, non-profit, or political leadership, including membership in the party. Sometimes the name recognition is not their own but that of prominent family connections. They have strong personal networks on which they can rely for fundraising and for securing new party members. They are generally motivated by career ambition, a sense of duty to serve, personal loyalty to the party, or all three. Often the front-runner has been encouraged to run by the party's senior leadership and thus expects to enjoy the support of party brass. Front-runner candidates fit the mould of desirable candidates who reflect well on the party and its leader – they demonstrate that the party is attracting strong candidates and planning to perform well in the general election. These nominees are also generally low risk; they willingly fall in line with strategic messages and campaign commitments, are good communicators, are less likely to embarrass the party with indiscretions or campaign missteps, will not burden resources, and are dependable for managing local issues.

But even when there is a strong front-runner candidate, the means of securing victory is still through either a majority or a plurality of votes in the local race. Although front-runners might find it easier to fundraise than their activist counterparts, money is useful only to a certain extent – setting up websites, printing campaign materials, travelling in the riding for certain party events, and hosting get-togethers are some examples. But these efforts must be converted into new party memberships and used to convince both new and pre-existing party members to lend their support. The value proposition communicated by front-runner candidates is often that they are palatable to the community at large and therefore have superior "electability"; nevertheless, their blunt ideological edges can impede the recruitment of hundreds of new party members and be uninspiring for existing party members. Consequently, the activist nomination strategy can usurp the approach applied by front-runners.

The activist strategy can be used by insurgent nominees[45] and is designed to leverage motivated networks of activists and activist groups to ensure that a more ideological or issue-oriented individual is nominated. These groups can be associated with strong heartfelt political positions but also share connections in other ways (e.g., farmers, churchgoers, certain ethnic backgrounds, environmentalists, or parents who home-school their children). The strategy here is to defeat the front-runner candidate through a grassroots campaign that possesses two key ingredients: superior motivation and more human resources.

Motivation is generated by highly engaged individuals who want to see their deeply held views, issues, or communities represented by a potential Member of Parliament (see Chapter 2 of this volume). These individuals can be, but are not necessarily, partisan. What they do embrace is the opportunity for political influence; when an occasion to hold sway over an outcome presents itself, these tightly knit groups can be activated swiftly. Human resources are derived from the sheer number of members and followers from various networks that correlate with the activist nominee's ideological leanings, policy perspectives, or community background. Once triggered, these groups can overwhelm local EDAs with memberships channelled to support their activist nominees and upset the strategic efforts of front-runners. This has occurred numerous times across Canada, particularly in urban ridings where a racialized community seeks political representation.[46] But we also see it in suburban and rural ridings where the margins of victory are slimmer but where the activist candidates and the strength of their support were underestimated. In Kitchener–Conestoga, the triggering issue of parental rights in the provision of public education provided a powerful organizational advantage to the activist nominee.[47]

Conclusion

Being inside a local nomination race reveals internal organizational party machinery in which levers of control and management oscillate between central and local levels. Nomination contests can either invite or discourage broader citizen participation depending on the vagaries of the larger electoral imperative. Preparing to fight an election campaign has many elements, but one of the most important is a slate of candidates who represent the party label. From the beginning of Canada's party system, partisans in local ridings have been involved in choosing their candidates. This eventually led to the development of processes, rules, and regulations formalizing how citizens could vie for a party's candidacy.

In this chapter, we found that nomination contests demonstrate the organizational interdependence of the local and central strata of parties. Many EDAs are heavily involved in the process of candidate selection, and we expect that this is particularly true in ridings normally competitive between two or more parties. The Conservative Kitchener–Conestoga EDA has a strong hand in recruitment and vetting as part of executing a competitive nomination race, and this can be attributed partly to how narrowly (1 percent or less) the Conservative candidate has either won or lost in the past several general elections. Where a seat is in a party's grasp, an EDA might be more likely to play a robust role in the selection procedure; where the party's chances are diminished, or the EDA itself is anemic, the local level might welcome the central party's intervention. We have learned here that, competitiveness of the riding aside, the central party closely monitors and engages with what is happening on the ground. The central party also recruits and vets, but its real power is its ability to set the rules for each nomination contest, including whether to protect incumbents from challengers or circumvent the process entirely by appointing candidates to specific ridings. The central party can also step in where irregularities are found in a nomination vote – often this can be to the benefit of the riding association if it faces pressure to legitimize the competition. To greater and lesser degrees, the interest of the central party in local contests can create tension with EDAs, but retreat by one level or the other in this particular arena is unlikely; particularly where we see healthy riding associations, there is an obvious vibrancy created by nomination races.

This does not overshadow the trends identified above. The bypassing of nomination races in favour of direct appointments by the leader is concerning. Of the seven Parliaments elected since 2004, five have produced minority governments. Minority Parliaments put all parties on an election footing and increase the likelihood of accelerated election readiness and the prospect of appointed candidates. If Canadians prefer minority Parliaments, then the trend of protecting incumbents and permitting appointments of party candidates will continue. This can undermine the relevance of EDAs. Likewise, recruiting a diverse set of Canadians to run remains difficult. This is a Herculean effort and not just because trust in political parties is on the wane. Contemporary political environments are ripe with deterrents; they are more partisan and more polarized, and female politicians are more exposed to trolling and other online harassments that render the job less palatable by the day.

Finally, the Kitchener–Conestoga riding gives us an inside look at the strategies employed by two nomination candidates in the race to be the Conservative Party's standard bearer. The party insider used a front-runner strategy that came up short when the insurgent nominee activated a parents' rights network to clinch membership support. In many respects, the cut and thrust among candidates in general campaigns is as applicable to the mini-contests held at the local level. On election day, the Liberals barely hung on to the Kitchener–Conestoga riding; the competitiveness of the EDA suggests that local Conservative Party members will soon re-engage in a fight for the nomination.

Notes

1 Thomas and Morden, *Party Favours.*
2 Rahat, "Candidate Selection."
3 Cross, "Understanding Power-Sharing within Political Parties."
4 Carty, "Parties as Franchise Systems"; Carty and Cross, "Can Stratarchically Organized Parties Be Democratic?"
5 Cross, "The Importance of Local Party Activity"; Carty and Eagles, *Politics Is Local.*
6 Carty and Cross, "Can Stratarchically Organized Parties Be Democratic?"
7 Carty and Erickson, "Canadian Nomination in Canada's National Political Parties," 101.
8 Ibid.; Siegfried, *The Race Question in Canada.*
9 Carty and Erickson, "Canadian Nomination in Canada's National Political Parties," 101; Carty, Cross, and Young, *Rebuilding Canadian Party Politics.*
10 Whitaker, *The Government Party.*
11 Courtney, *Do Conventions Matter?,* 6.

12 Ibid.
13 Bittner and Koop, *Parties, Elections, and the Future of Canadian Politics.*
14 Sayers, *Parties, Candidates, and Constituency Campaigns.*
15 Pruysers and Cross, "Candidate Selection in Canada."
16 Rana, "Liberals Consulting MPs, Party Base."
17 Thomas and Morden, *Party Favours.*
18 Ibid.
19 Rana, "Potential Candidates in Four Winnable Liberal Ridings."
20 Rana, "Conservative Party Finalize Nomination Rules."
21 Rana, "Anti-Abortion Group."
22 Thomas and Morden, *Party Favours.*
23 Rana, "Backroom Handling of Potential Liberal Nomination."
24 Canadian Press, "As Bloc Prepares for Federal Election, Infighting Grows."
25 Thomas and Morden, *Party Favours.*
26 Liberal Party of Canada, Constitution of the Liberal Party of Canada, s 5 (G, 29).
27 Walsh, "Liberal Party Triggers 'Electoral Urgency' Rule."
28 Boutilier, "Conservatives Email Supporters in Search of Candidates."
29 Patel, "Candidate Diversity Is High on the Agenda."
30 Thomas and Morden, *Party Favours.*
31 Johnson et al., "A New Dataset on the Demographics."
32 Helmer, "'We're Not Having Our Voices Heard.'"
33 Dunham, "Highest Percentage Ever of Female and Gender-Diverse Candidates."
34 Cross, "The Importance of Local Party Activity."
35 Goodyear-Grant, "Who Votes for Women Candidates and Why?"
36 Cross and Pruysers, "The Local Determinants of Representation"; Cheng and Tavits, "Informal Influences in Selecting Female Political Candidates"; Pruysers et al., "Candidate Selection Rules and Democratic Outcomes."
37 Wagner, "Tolerating the Trolls?"
38 Ibid., 9.
39 But see Marland and DeCillia, "Reputation and Brand Management by Political Parties."
40 Marland, "Vetting of Election Candidates by Political Parties."
41 Harris, "How the Parties Screen a Candidate's Past."
42 Sears, "How Should Party Leaders Manage Loony and Craven Candidates?"
43 Ibid.

44   Sayers, *Parties, Candidates, and Constituency Campaigns*, 76–78.
45   Ibid., 73.
46   Offman, "Federal Liberals Cultivate Mandarin Powerhouse in GTA."
47   Pierre, "Why We Cannot Support Matt Bondy."

Bibliography

Bittner, Amanda, and Royce Koop. *Parties, Elections, and the Future of Canadian Politics*. Vancouver: UBC Press, 2013.

Boutilier, Alex. "Conservatives Email Supporters in Search of Candidates Ahead of Election Call." 14 August 2021. https://www.thestar.com/politics/federal/2021/08/14/conservatives-email-supporters-in-search-of-candidates-ahead-of-federal-election-call.html.

Canadian Press. "As Bloc Prepares for Federal Election, Infighting Grows Over Candidate Selection Process." 8 August 2021. https://montreal.ctvnews.ca/as-bloc-prepares-for-federal-election-infighting-grows-over-candidate-selection-process-1.5539197.

Carty, R. Kenneth. "Parties as Franchise Systems: The Stratarchical Organizational Imperative." *Party Politics* 10, 1 (2004): 5–24. https://doi.org/10.1177/1354068804039118.

Carty, R. Kenneth, and William Cross. "Can Stratarchically Organized Parties Be Democratic? The Canadian Case." *Journal of Elections, Public Opinion and Parties* 16, 2 (2006): 93–114. https://doi.org/10.1080/13689880600715912.

Carty, R. Kenneth, William Cross, and Lisa Young. *Rebuilding Canadian Party Politics*. Vancouver: UBC Press, 2000.

Carty, R. Kenneth, and Munroe Eagles. *Politics Is Local: National Politics at the Grassroots*. Don Mills, ON: Oxford University Press, 1999.

Carty, R. Kenneth, and Lynda Erickson. "Canadian Nomination in Canada's National Political Parties." In *Canadian Political Parties: Leaders, Candidates and Organizations,* edited by Herman Bakvis, 95–189. Toronto: Dundurn Press, 1991.

Cheng, Christine, and Margit Tavits. "Informal Influences in Selecting Female Political Candidates." *Political Research Quarterly* 64, 2 (2011): 460–71.

Courtney, John C. *Do Conventions Matter? Choosing National Party Leaders in Canada*. Montreal and Kingston: McGill-Queen's University Press, 1995.

Cross, William. "The Importance of Local Party Activity in Understanding Canadian Politics: Winning from the Ground Up in the 2015 Federal Election: Presidential Address to the Canadian Political Science Association Calgary, 31 May 2016." *Canadian Journal of Political Science* 49, 4 (2016): 601–20. https://doi.org/10.1017/S0008423916000962.

–. "Understanding Power-Sharing within Political Parties: Stratarchy as Mutual Interdependence between the Party in the Centre and the Party on the Ground." *Government and Opposition* 53, 2 (2016): 205–30.

Cross, William, and Scott Pruysers. "The Local Determinants of Representation: Party Constituency Associations, Candidate Nomination and Gender." *Canadian Journal of Political Science* 52, 3 (2019): 557–74.

Dunham, Jackie. "Highest Percentage Ever of Female and Gender-Diverse Candidates Running in This Election." CTV News, 2 September 2021. https://www.ctvnews.ca/politics/federal-election-2021/highest-percentage-ever-of-female-and-gender-diverse-candidates-running-in-this-election-1.5570913.

Goodyear-Grant, Elizabeth. "Who Votes for Women Candidates and Why? Evidence from Recent Canadian Elections." In *Voting Behaviour in Canada,* edited by Cameron D. Anderson and Laura B. Stephenson, 43–64. Vancouver: UBC Press, 2010.

Harris, Kathleen. "How the Parties Screen a Candidate's Past to Dodge – or Deploy – Campaign Gaffes." CBC News, 8 September 2019. https://www.cbc.ca/news/politics/election-campaign-vetting-candidates-1.5271740.

Helmer, Aedan. "'We're Not Having Our Voices Heard or Our Issues Prioritized': Researchers Say Diverse Candidates Disproportionately Underfunded." *Ottawa Citizen,* 18 September 2021. https://ottawacitizen.com/news/were-not-having-our-voices-heard-or-our-issues-prioritized-researchers-say-diverse-candidates-disproportionately-underfunded.

Johnson, Anna, Erin Tolley, Melanee Thomas, and Marc André Bodet. "A New Dataset on the Demographics of Canadian Federal Election Candidates." *Canadian Journal of Political Science* 54, 3 (2021): 717–25. https://doi.org/10.1017/S0008423921000391.

Liberal Party of Canada. "The Constitution of the Liberal Party of Canada." Amended 11 April 2021. https://liberal.ca/wp-content/uploads/sites/292/2021/04/The-Constitution-of-the-Liberal-Party-of-Canada.pdf.

Marland, Alex. "Vetting of Election Candidates by Political Parties: Centralization of Candidate Selection in Canada." *American Review of Canadian Studies* 51, 4 (2021): 573–91. https://doi.org/10.1080/02722011.2021.1986558.

Marland, Alex, and Brooks DeCillia. "Reputation and Brand Management by Political Parties: Party Vetting of Election Candidates in Canada." *Journal of Nonprofit and Public Sector Marketing* 32, 4 (2020): 342–63. https://doi.org/10.1080/10495142.2020.1798857.

Offman, C. "Federal Liberals Cultivate Mandarin Powerhouse in GTA." *Globe and Mail*, 18 August 2014. https://www.theglobeandmail.com/news/politics/federal-liberals-cultivate-mandarin-powerhouse-in-gta/article20104666/.

Patel, Raisa. "Candidate Diversity Is High on the Agenda as Canada's Political Parties Prepare for a Federal Election." *Toronto Star,* 13 July 2021. https://www.thestar.com/politics/federal/2021/07/13/candidate-diversity-is-high-on-the-agenda-as-canadas-political-parties-prepare-for-a-federal-election.html.

Pierre, Teresa. "Why We Cannot Support Matt Bondy, Part 1." *Parents as First Educators* (blog), 18 February 2021. https://www.pafe.ca/blog.

Pruysers, Scott, and William Cross. "Candidate Selection in Canada: Local Autonomy, Centralization, and Competing Democratic Norms." *American Behavioral Scientist* 60, 7 (2016): 781–98. https://doi.org/10.1177/0002764216632820.

Pruysers, Scott, William Cross, Anika Gauja, and Gideon Rahat. "Candidate Selection Rules and Democratic Outcomes: The Impact of Parties on Women's Representation." In *Organizing Representation: Political Parties, Participation, and Power,* edited by Susan Scarrow, Paul Webb, and Thomas Poguntke, 208–33. Oxford: Oxford University Press, 2017.

Rahat, Gideon. "Candidate Selection: The Choice before the Choice." *Journal of Democracy* 18, 1 (2007): 157–70. https://doi.org/10.1353/jod.2007.0014.

Rana, Abbas. "Anti-Abortion Group Wants Conservatives to Give Riding Associations Power to Fire MPs, to Veto Leadership's Call on Nomination Contests." *Hill Times,* 9 March 2021. https://www.hilltimes.com/2021/03/09/campaign-life-coalition-wants-riding-associations-empowered-to-veto-leaderships-decisions-about-nomination-elections-and-to-fire-mps/287702.

–. "Backroom Handling of Potential Liberal Nomination in Kanata–Carleton Causing Fissures in Riding, Say Riding Association Members and Potential Candidates." *Hill Times,* 4 August 2021. https://www.hilltimes.com/2021/08/04/backroom-handling-of-potential-liberal-nomination-in-kanata-carleton-causing-fissures-in-riding-say-riding-association-members-and-potential-candidates/310120.

–. "Conservative Party Finalize Nomination Rules for Its 217 Unheld Ridings." *Hill Times,* 27 September 2020. https://www.hilltimes.com/2020/09/27/conservative-party-finalize-nomination-rules-for-its-217-unheld-ridings/265540.

—. "Liberals Consulting MPs, Party Base on Nomination Rules for Next Election." *Hill Times*, 11 May 2020. https://www.hilltimes.com/2020/05/11/ liberals-consulting-mps-party-base-on-nomination-rules-for-the-next -election-spokesperson-caley/247476.

—. "Potential Candidates in Four Winnable Liberal Ridings Eagerly Awaiting Timeline for Nomination Contests." *Hill Times*, 8 March 2021. https:// www.hilltimes.com/2021/03/08/potential-candidates-in-four-winnable -liberal-ridings-eagerly-awaiting-timeline-for-nomination-contests/ 286989.

Sayers, Anthony M. *Parties, Candidates, and Constituency Campaigns in Canadian Elections*. Vancouver: UBC Press, 1999.

Sears, Robin V. "How Should Party Leaders Manage Loony and Craven Candidates?" *Toronto Star*, 5 September 2021. https://www.thestar.com/ opinion/contributors/2021/09/05/how-should-party-leaders-manage -loony-and-craven-candidates.html.

Siegfried, André. *The Race Question in Canada*. Toronto: McClelland and Stewart, [1906] 1966.

Thomas, Paul E.J., and Michael Morden. *Party Favours: How Federal Election Candidates Are Chosen*. Toronto: Samara Centre for Democracy, 2019. https://www.samaracanada.com/docs/default-source/reports/party -favours-by-the-samara-centre-for-democracy.pdf.

Wagner, Angelia. "Tolerating the Trolls? Gendered Perceptions of Online Harassment of Politicians in Canada." *Feminist Media Studies*. Published ahead of print, 8 April 2020. https://doi.org/10.1080/14680777.2020. 1749691.

Walsh, Marieke. "Liberal Party Triggers 'Electoral Urgency' Rule for Nominations." *Globe and Mail*, 4 June 2021. https://www.theglobeandmail. com/politics/article-liberal-party-triggers-electoral-urgency-rule-for -nominations-2/.

Whitaker, Reginald. *The Government Party: Organizing and Financing the Liberal Party of Canada, 1930–1958*. Toronto: University of Toronto Press, 1997.

4

Recruitment of Star Candidates

Cristine de Clercy

Abstract   The nomination of star candidates – defined here as neophyte party outsiders who possess an attractive reputation or significant public profile – is a relatively common but largely unstudied practice in Canadian federal elections. Identifying eighty-three star candidates representing five different parties, the analysis in this chapter finds that most star candidates in the 2021 election represented the Liberal and Conservative Parties, represented rural as well as urban ridings, and were concentrated in Ontario, Quebec, and British Columbia. About 18 percent of this group won their races and entered the House of Commons. Focusing on one local campaign case of a successful star candidate suggests that building a strong personal brand is key and that it takes stars to make stars: strong campaign support from established party veterans and the party leader is a crucial ingredient for success.

Résumé   La nomination de candidats vedettes – définis ici comme les nouvelles recrues d'un parti qui jouissent d'une excellente réputation ou d'un profil public considérable – est une pratique relativement courante dans les élections fédérales canadiennes, mais peu étudiée. L'analyse dans ce chapitre a révélé que, lors des élections de 2021, les quatre-vingt-trois candidats vedettes issus de cinq partis différents étaient majoritairement affiliés aux partis Libéral et Conservateur, se sont présentés à la fois dans des circonscriptions rurales et urbaines, et étaient concentrés en Ontario, au Québec, et en Colombie-Britannique. Environ 18 pourcent d'entre eux ont réussi à se faire élire à la Chambre des communes. L'étude d'une campagne locale fructueuse d'un candidat vedette semble indiquer que la création d'une marque personnelle solide est essentielle et qu'il faut des champions pour créer des vedettes. En d'autres mots, le soutien de vétérans et du chef d'un parti établi est un ingrédient crucial du succès.

THIS CHAPTER EXPLORES the recruitment of "star" candidates by Canadian political parties to run in local election campaigns and probes how such candidates frame and communicate their identities or brands to win votes. Building upon the extant literature within Canadian political science, I define star candidates here as people who have (or are thought to have) an attractive reputation or a significant public profile that extends beyond their local communities. I focus on the people recruited to join political parties as new candidates to clarify how many people, and the sorts of people, parties seek from beyond their own loyal members. These stars are new entrants to formal competitive politics, though they might possess some minor or historical attachment to a party organization. Their outsider status and relative inexperience on the campaign trail differentiate them from "loyal soldiers," insider candidates who represent local and national party structures and comprise a reliable source of election candidates.

The star candidate recruitment track in federal politics is clearly evident when we consider the political paths of some past national leaders. For example, Pierre Elliott Trudeau was one of the "three wise men" from Quebec recruited by then Liberal prime minister Lester Pearson to run in the election of 1965. In another example, Canada's first female prime minister, Kim Campbell, recounts in her autobiography that, as a young academic teaching at the University of British Columbia, she mentioned to a party organizer that she might like to go into politics in the future. She was advised that, "if you want to run for politics, don't get involved in a party. Become a star."[1] She followed that advice, devoting her energies to building an admirable legal reputation. Recruited by the British Columbia Social Credit party to run in 1983, she won a seat in 1986. Then she ran for Brian Mulroney's Progressive Conservatives in the federal election of 1988 and was elected. Five years later Campbell was chosen to lead the party and was sworn in as Canada's first woman prime minister in 1993.

The recruitment of star candidates from beyond a party's existing membership is a common practice. This is partly because there is a perennial challenge in recruiting capable new candidates to carry the party banner since the existing pool of loyal party candidates diminishes constantly because of illness, retirement, scandal, and death. All major political parties recruit star candidates.[2] These high-profile individuals attract the attention of parties for having built fine reputations from their professional career accomplishments in areas beyond formal politics, such as law, banking, scientific research, athletics, or the arts. They bring new ideas, broad experiences, and fresh perspectives into the political "bubble" of Ottawa and can revitalize tired party leadership groups.

There are other important considerations that parties face when recruiting outside candidates. On the one hand, star recruits can be popular with voters who value independence and believe that excessive party discipline undermines representative government. On the other, because they are connected to the party by thinner bonds than those binding loyal partisans, sometimes stars are quicker to leave the party when party discipline becomes too onerous or better opportunities appear on the horizon. The list of rookie MPs who have crossed the floor of the House of Commons to sit with other parties early in their careers includes several star recruits, such as businesswoman Belinda Stronach and more recently former Green MP Jenica Atwin, who left the Greens to sit with the Liberals.[3]

In the following section, I review the literature to help establish my approach in this study. Then, to focus on the star candidates running for office in the election in 2021, I present and summarize an original data set containing detailed information about this group of candidates. In the next section, I deeply explore the local campaign context of an exemplar star candidate, Arielle Kayabaga, who won the London West riding for the Liberals in 2021. Focusing on one local campaign case study of a successful star candidate emphasizes that building a strong personal brand is key and that it takes stars to make stars: strong campaign support from established, high-profile party veterans and the party leader is a crucial ingredient for success.

Although in some countries, such as the United States, it is acceptable for politicians to project an image of wealth and success, in Canada modesty, humility, and self-deprecation are thought to resonate better with the electorate and media. Perhaps this explains why there is much more study of celebrity politicians among American, British, and Dutch analysts. There is a thoughtful literature exploring the phenomenon of celebrity politicians, defined in line with John Street's understanding of "an elected politician (or nominated candidate) whose background is in entertainment, show business, or sport, and who trades on this background (by virtue of the skill acquired, the popularity achieved or the images associated)."[4] These studies share some similar themes. For example, celebrity as political capital derives from fame, dramaturgy, and personality marketing in the non-political sphere rather than by democratic election, representation, and accountability.[5] Analysts describe with concern how modern image handlers create media campaigns that treat the electorate as fans and thus seriously diminish democracy.[6] And there is widespread agreement that in our time mass communication and an "entertainment culture" have merged with "high-culture" star power. This is a lot more potent than electoral power.[7]

Within the past two decades, a few Canadian studies have focused closely on star candidates. This literature can be divided into two sorts of treatment: studies that focus on how celebrity candidates are brought into the political process and those that consider why parties seek such representatives. Concerning how star candidates are recruited, some researchers focus on the use of direct appointment processes that bypass traditional local selection contests. Royce Koop and Amanda Bittner examine how candidates are "parachuted" into constituencies by party leaders keen to recruit specific representatives, such as women candidates. Focusing on the Liberal Party from 1993 to 2008, they find that candidates appointed to represent ridings are more likely to hold "high-profile" legislative roles than locally nominated candidates chosen by regular party processes.[8] As well, Canadian political parties can ensure the selection of a star candidate favoured by the party leadership by compromising normal recruitment processes. For example, parties might open nominations suddenly, with little warning, and then provide little time for nomination paperwork to be filed by new entrants to give the advantage to a star nominee.[9]

With respect to understanding why political parties seek to nom-inate star candidates, several explanations are proposed in the lit-erature.[10] In the case of the Liberal Party's nomination process during the 1993 and 1997 federal campaigns, party strategists used unilateral appointments to nominate star candidates along with women candidates and to avoid potentially divisive and embar-rassing nomination battles that such nominations can spark. Miriam Koene concludes that the appointment process was used to build more diverse and representative candidate pools, goals clearly valued by Liberal strategists.[11] Anthony Sayers finds that high-profile candidates are successful in competitive and impermeable associations and that run nominations that exhibit limited democ-racy. As well, there are lower-profile, locally notable candidates who tend to emerge within cadre-style parties such as the Liberals and Conservatives when there is a contested nomination in a competi-tive district.[12]

Interestingly, the delineation of the difference between a high-profile or star candidate and a lower-profile or locally notable candidate is vague and subjective in existing studies.[13] The identi-fication of star candidates and celebrity candidates is inherently a subjective exercise: the adjudication of whether candidates possess a larger than normal public profile often relies on their presence in media reporting. Given that Canada is a large, heterogeneous country with two official languages and regionally based media markets, in my approach in this study it is far too restrictive to define a star candidate as a person whose celebrity is widely known across the country. There are few people who possess widespread and unequivocal Wayne Gretzky–style fame in the Canadian con-text, as other analysts note.[14] In fact, most celebrities in Canada are people who have achieved prominence within a province or region, who excel in a single discipline (e.g., trombone or triathlon), or who are well known within a particular professional network, such as law, medicine, or finance. This study is a first effort to examine the profiles and success of Canadian star candidates in some recent federal elections. To this end, I collected biographical information about candidates nominated by the main political parties. Then I identified locally notable candidates and from that pool extracted those politicians whose profiles extended beyond their specific constituencies. In part, I relied on media reporting in local and regional media markets as well as national outlets to help identify candidates whose reputations have attracted media attention and comment. In this way, I aimed to find new party recruits who possessed public profiles that stood out in comparison with those of their peers, who might well be extremely competent but not especially well-known individuals. As discussed above, there is no single objective indicator in the literature of an individual's reputational or star power; most analyses employ several loose indicators to identify political candidates with unusually expansive reputations. For example, in his discussion of what delineates celebrity politicians, Street suggests those who "engage with the world of popular culture" in ways that generally revolve around mediated activity are celebrity politicians.[15] So, though all high-profile candidates are also locally notable candidates, not all of the latter are also the former.

Some analysts point to the modern urban environment as a factor encouraging the fielding of star candidates. The complex character of urban ridings attracts high-profile candidates who can successfully address the social environment and encourages parties to nominate urban candidates as spokespersons to address the issues that arise in a national campaign. Furthermore, if elected, then such candidates can be appealing cabinet choices for prime ministers eager to represent such views.[16]

The motivation to recruit star candidates to ensure more diverse representation often stems from a party's interest in marketing itself to key categories of voters. The growing literature on political branding locates the recruitment of star candidates in the desire to promulgate a certain kind of image. In his book on the subject, Alex Marland observes that modern nomination processes select candidates who are virtuous "brand ambassadors," ushering in preferred candidates and shutting out undesirable ones.[17] Because "the public wants a government to look and feel like them in some way," recruiting preferred candidates is one way to connect voters to a party's brand.[18] In short, the branding literature explains star candidate recruitment as an explicit effort to attract certain segments of voters along with the positive reinforcement of a specific kind of image desired by a party.

In light of arguments that parties recruit star candidates and offer some of them preferential access to the nomination process, and that modern parties deliberately target brand ambassadors, or "brandidates," to help reify the core political message, certainly one expects to find a substantial number of such candidacies in each Canadian election.[19]

Local Trends

In the federal election of 2021, the major parties recruited some star outsiders to contest seats despite some of the risks and difficulties that sometimes result from such candidacies. This activity generates several questions about the local campaign dynamic. How prevalent were star nominations in 2021? Were some regions of Canada more likely to feature star candidates than others? Were stars generally able to win their local contests, or did their novice and outsider status put them at a disadvantage when competing with political veterans or long-serving "loyal soldier" party candidates?

To answer these questions, I collected information about candidates in the election. I collected biographical information about candidates nominated by the main political parties, and from that data set I then identified locally notable candidates and sought to identify those politicians whose profiles extended beyond their specific constituencies. In examining which of the federal candidates in 2021 fit the star candidate profile, I consulted news stories, party nomination statements, social media posts, and personal biographical statements authored by candidates. Initially, 109 nominees representing the Liberal, Conservative, New Democratic, Green, Bloc Québécois, and People's Parties fit the parameters of star candidates. Closer scrutiny revealed that some within this group had prior experience running as partisan candidates in earlier provincial and federal elections or had held such offices in the past. Because this sort of candidate is not a true political neophyte, I further filtered the group of 109 political nominees to remove those who had run or served previously in partisan politics. This filtering is a key step because part of my focus in this chapter, as discussed above, is on how parties recruit new people into their organizations. Focusing directly on neophyte politicians who did not belong formally to party organizations prior to their bid for federal office in 2021, I also removed from the star candidate group a few who had served as political staffers and contested local ridings in 2021, because such candidates possessed solid party ties despite not having run for office officially. Therefore, in my view, they are classified more accurately as internal, "loyal soldier" candidates rather than outsider, neophyte political stars.

At the same time, because most municipal-level and school board elections in Canada do not feature candidates who run as representatives of political parties, and because municipal office often serves as a training ground for people interested in pursuing a legislative career at the provincial or federal level, I chose to include star candidates who had served (or were serving) in local governments or on band councils or school boards. As well, I included people who had worked or were working as public administrators for bureaucracies at the local, provincial, territorial, or federal level. Within these parameters, I found eighty-three candidates who met the criteria for being neophyte political stars running for public office in the federal election of 2021. Interestingly, about 37 percent of the group had run for, or been elected to, a municipal public office.

Examining this pool of eighty-three star candidates offered a unique chance to gain deep insight into the local and regional dynamics of star candidate contests. This was a group of talented, intriguing, and diverse candidates, such as Green Party candidate Maryem Tollar, a Juno-nominated Arabic singer who ran in the Toronto Danforth riding; Avi Lewis, a filmmaker and activist who stood for the NDP in West Vancouver–Sunshine Coast–Sea to Sky Country; the popular broadcaster Frank Cavallaro running for the Conservative Party in Mont-Royal; and Liberal Party nominee Shirley Robinson, who served as a Cross Lake band councillor and contested the Manitoba riding of Churchill–Keewatinook Aski.

With respect to identifying where star candidates ran for office, I found fifteen in British Columbia, four in Alberta, one in

Saskatchewan, one in Manitoba, forty-two in Ontario, eighteen in Quebec, one in New Brunswick, one in Newfoundland and Labrador, one in Prince Edward Island, none in Nova Scotia, and among the territories one in Yukon. There was a significant number of stars running in British Columbia in 2021. Also, clearly, Ontario and Quebec are key locales for star candidacies. This makes sense because these two populous provinces contain 199 of the 338 (or about 59 percent) federal ridings. Ontario alone contained more than half of the star candidate population that I identified, so it is particularly well populated with political stars in my search results.

To understand further the geographical representation of the star candidates, I allocated the ridings among three categories based upon their boundary maps: rural, suburban, and urban.[20] About 55 percent of the star candidates represented rural ridings, about 40 percent urban ridings, and 5 percent suburban ridings. The number of star candidates in rural ridings is surprising because the literature discussed above suggests that stars are found in more heavily populated urban areas. Yet this study's broader approach to defining star candidates as those who have achieved regional or network-based fame clearly allows more people outside urban media markets to be classified as star candidates.

In terms of which parties nominated the largest portions of this group of star candidates, the Liberals nominated thirty-four of the eighty-three stars discussed here (41 percent), the Conservatives nominated twenty-three stars (28 percent), the New Democrats accounted for sixteen stars (19 percent), the Bloc Québécois ran five stars (7 percent), the Greens nominated two stars (2 percent), and the People's Party fielded three stars (about 4 percent). In the election of 2015, the Trudeau Liberals accentuated their efforts to recruit new, talented outsiders, so I expected much the same from Team Trudeau in 2021. However, the Conservatives nominated more star candidates in 2021 than was expected.[21]

Finally, I examined how this group fared on voting day. How many high-profile political neophytes actually won their ridings? Table 4.1 summarizes the candidates' success in winning their ridings by party affiliation. Of the eighty-three candidates identified

TABLE 4.1 Summary of star candidates' win/loss pattern by party affiliation in 2021

Party	Won	Lost
Bloc Québécois	0	5
Conservative Party	3	20
Green Party	0	2
Liberal Party	11	23
New Democratic Party	1	15
People's Party	0	3

here, only fifteen won their seats, for a rate of success in the election of about 18 percent. In other words, not even one in five of the star candidates was a winner; more than 80 percent of this group went down to defeat. So, though some star candidates do go on to represent their fellow Canadians in the House of Commons, for most of them their attractive public profiles alone are not enough to win them power.

This survey of the characteristics of a group of eighty-three star candidates reveals some similarities, such as the frequency of experience in municipal government, along with some large differences, such as the relative dominance of Liberal and Conservative star candidates within the group and the relatively slim probability of election.

Behind the Scenes

To take a deeper look into how star candidates enter formal politics, connect with existing partisan networks, and communicate their personal brands to compete in local campaigns, I now focus on a case study of Arielle Kayabaga. She contested and won the federal riding of London West as a first-time Liberal candidate in 2021. Establishing her brand as a leading voice for Black Canadians, women, marginalized citizens, youth, and immigrants helped Kayabaga to distinguish herself among a field of viable nominees. Her brand is rooted in her personal journey, so it is worth exploring her experiences to help explain how she became a star candidate and won a seat in the House of Commons in 2021.

When she was a child, Kayabaga and her family left the country of Burundi because of the long civil war between the Hutu and Tutsi groups that broke out in the wake of a genocide in 1993. After emigrating to Canada, the Kayabaga family lived in Montreal for a year before settling in London, Ontario, in 2002. Since her first language is French, Kayabaga attended École secondaire Gabriel-Dumont beginning in 2003 and graduated in 2008. London has a small but tightly knit francophone community. Kayabaga was active in la Fédération de la jeunesse franco-ontarienne and later worked as a freelance interpreter and a bilingual services project coordinator for the City of London.

In 2009, she enrolled at Carleton University, graduating four years later with a Bachelor of Arts in Political Science, including a minor in African Studies.[22] Kayabaga gained some experience in government while working briefly as a caucus services assistant for the Liberal Research Bureau in Ottawa, and she was one of twenty-nine young Canadians selected to participate at the United Nations Framework Convention on Climate Change in Cancun, Mexico. From the fall of 2016 to February 2018, Kayabaga worked as a cultural liaison/settlement worker for the Conseil scolaire catholique Providence, providing language, cultural, and diversity supports to students.[23]

In 2018, when she was twenty-seven years old and a single mother of one child, Kayabaga announced her candidacy for Ward 13 in the municipal election in London. This ward is in the city's core and includes immigrant, racialized, and marginalized communities along with a substantial small business community. In this election, the city used a new ranked ballot system. Proponents of the new system hoped that it would provide a way for people from less represented groups to attain public office. The only woman in a field of eight candidates, Kayabaga was an early leader in the contest, unseating the incumbent after eight rounds of vote counting and taking office with about 49 percent of the eligible votes cast. The first Black woman ever elected to London City Council, she chaired the city's Corporate Services Committee and served on the Standing Committee on Municipal Finance.[24] In 2020, Kayabaga received the Pillar Community Leadership Award for her work in building a more equitable London. Her national profile was certainly enhanced when *Chatelaine* named her one of "33 Black Canadians Making Change Now."[25] During her two years in office, she made it a point to support strongly social services, public and affordable housing, anti-racism work, and downtown investments. Her efforts to promote diversity and inclusion attracted considerable positive attention in the community.

In March 2021, Kayabaga announced that she planned to seek the Liberal nomination in the federal riding of London West, just a day after the popular Liberal incumbent, Kate Young, announced that she would not run for re-election.[26] In her statement, Kayabaga pointed to the COVID-19 pandemic and how the public health crisis had disproportionately affected Indigenous people, Black people, and other people of colour and reduced women's participation in the workforce. Those voices are needed in government, Kayabaga said, explaining her decision to seek a seat in the federal election, expected in the fall, even though she had about eighteen months left in her municipal term.[27] The timing of the two announcements can be interpreted as a signal that the Liberals had successfully recruited Kayabaga to contest the nomination and that the federal party in Ottawa was interested in her candidacy.

The riding of London West offered several advantages to the rookie councillor. First, a portion of her municipal ward overlapped the federal riding, so Kayabaga could rely on mobilizing some of the enthusiastic supporters who had elected her to municipal office. Second, London West is a traditional Liberal stronghold. In the fifty-three years from 1968 to 2021, the Liberals had represented the riding for thirty-seven years or 70 percent of the period.[28] Third, incumbent Kate Young was a well-liked MP who had represented the riding since 2015. She won that contest and then the contest in 2019, with more than 40 percent of the ballots cast each time. So the Liberal Party's constituency reputation generally was positive, and the on-the-ground local party organization was active. Fourth, the riding was the only one in the London area where no incumbent was running again, so a new candidate would not displace a sitting MP. And fifth, the riding is home to a small but active French-language community, and several schools offer French-language contexts, helpful given Kayabaga's emphasis on her Franco-Ontarian identity.

One local issue captured public attention a few months later, in late May 2021. The francophone Catholic school board announced that it had removed a popular principal from his position at Monseigneur-Bruyère high school after video surfaced on social media of him in two incidents in 2019 wearing a crude wig fashioned from the hair cuttings of a Black student. A spokesperson for Black Lives Matter London said that the video raised all kinds of red flags and criticized the school board for not acting immediately despite receiving a petition from concerned students.[29] Reacting to news of the firing, Kayabaga stated to the media that ten years earlier she had attended Monseigneur-Bruyère high school in north London but had transferred to another institution before graduation because of a climate of racism at the school.[30] The events surrounding the firing of the principal sparked much community discussion about respect and racism within the Franco-Ontarian and London communities for several months and influenced local political discourse in the summer.

The community discussion about anti-racism was important politically in part because the issue of racism dominated Canadian and international media headlines in the summer of 2021. For example, on 27 May, the Tk'emlúps te Secwépemc First Nation announced that it had located the remains of 215 children in unmarked graves at the site of the former Kamloops Indian Residential School. The story attracted considerable attention across Canada and internationally. In the wake of this tragic news, many other First Nations and activists pressed provincial and federal politicians, and some religious orders that helped to run the schools, to produce attendance records and investigate how these children and many others buried at the sites of former residential schools died.[31] As a consequence of these searing events, discussion of the problem of racism permeated local and national political contexts over the summer months and remained topical when the formal campaign period began in mid-August. In this milieu, Kayabaga's significant community profile as one of the main London spokespersons for working toward equality and ending racism was important.

The Liberal riding organization held a nomination contest on 12 August, three days before the election was formally announced. Kayabaga won the nomination over rivals Afeez Ajibowu and Zeba Hashmi. Matching the colour that had been used for her municipal election signs, Kayabaga used bright yellow for her personal brand in the federal election campaign, regularly wearing yellow clothing and jewellery. Her brand centred on a core message: as a single mother, city councillor, and community activist, she strove to embody the qualities of a new type of political leader – progressive, resilient, and optimistic. Her campaign literature and social media feeds reflected this branding. Although some local Liberals noted that her campaign lawn signs – depicting Kayabaga seated in a bright yellow jacket – did not follow the party's standard candidate package parameters, emphasizing her independence and her personal political brand might well have helped her to win more votes because, as the campaign wore on, Liberal leader Justin Trudeau faced increasing criticism for calling an unnecessary election.[32] So distancing herself somewhat from him by emphasizing her brand and her record in local politics probably was a positive strategy.

Several well-known municipal figures lent their support to Kayabaga at the outset. For example, Councillors Mohammed Salih and Jesse Helmer communicated their enthusiasm for her candidacy, along with Chair of the London Police Board Susan Toth and Huron University political science professor Jennifer Mustapha. Also, several esteemed provincial politicians visited the riding or voiced support for her candidacy, including Mitzie Hunter, Member of the Provincial Parliament for Scarborough–Guildwood.

Kayabaga's team was generally well staffed and coordinated during the local campaign. In comparison with the Conservative and New Democrat rivals, the Liberal team made frequent and effective use of social media outlets such as Twitter and Facebook to document her door-knocking efforts. As well, the campaign's media outreach emphasized the number of well-known local politicians, along with a truly impressive list of federal politicians and strategists, who supported her candidacy. For example, the former incumbent MP, Kate Young, issued a tweet congratulating Kayabaga on winning the party nomination the day of that vote and consistently supported her candidacy throughout the campaign. Such support is not necessarily assured in the context of London federal ridings. Young was featured canvassing with the candidate in London West in several posts, and Kayabaga thanked her for the support and pledged to follow in her footsteps. This endorsement was invaluable in terms of welcoming Kayabaga into the federal Liberal organization in London West and clearly signalled to loyal partisans and Young's followers to give their support to the Liberal nominee, a new and therefore somewhat unfamiliar political recruit.

Support from the national campaign was clearly evident when, eleven days before the vote, London media reported that Kayabaga's campaign manager, Devin Munro, had stepped down "for personal reasons" and been replaced immediately by Zachary Caldwell, the director of parliamentary affairs for Minister of National Defence Harjit Sajjan.[33] Previously, Munro was in charge of Young's successful campaigns and knew the riding intimately. The seamless transfer of campaign responsibilities to a cabinet minister's trusted staffer was evidence of the Liberal Party's commitment to get Kayabaga elected in London West. As well, representing the federal national campaign, former cabinet minister Catherine McKenna, and several sitting cabinet ministers, including Omar Alghabra and Ahmed Hussein, joined Kayabaga to canvass her riding during the thirty-six-day formal campaign period. Similar supportive visits were also made by a handful of staffers for cabinet ministers, including Patty Hajdu and Sajjan.[34] As election day neared and London West was seen to be a riding in play, it was visited by NDP leader Jagmeet Singh, Conservative Party leader Erin O'Toole, People's Party leader Maxime Bernier, and Prime Minister Justin Trudeau, who arrived three days before the vote to support his rookie Liberal standard bearer.

On election day, Kayabaga won the contest, collecting 36.9 percent of the votes cast, and bested her nearest challenger, a

Conservative, by 3,035 votes. This was a solid margin of victory, though not in line with her predecessor's performances in 2015 and 2019. The vote results suggest that the race was relatively competitive, probably made so by the open contest and Kayabaga's status as a political outsider. The impressive array of local, regional, and national notables who visited London West during the short campaign underscores an important lesson about electing star candidates: it takes stars to make stars. In other words, a broad assortment of high-profile, reputable local politicians, cabinet members, and national strategists worked diligently to ensure that the new Liberal Party star recruit was well supported and well advised in her first bid to win federal office.

Conclusion

There are clear incentives for the main political parties to seek high-profile, neophyte outsiders and recruit them as candidates, particularly if they help to reify the party's brand and carry its messages during formal elections. From locating and then examining the cohort of eighty-three star candidates whom I identified in the election of 2021, it is clear that the Liberal and Conservative Parties nominate the most star candidates, and they tend to be heavily concentrated in ridings in the larger, populous provinces of Quebec, Ontario, and British Columbia. Interestingly, and contrary to a view within the extant literature that star candidates are affiliated with urban ridings, in this election there were slightly more star candidates representing rural areas compared with urban areas. Finally, in terms of how successful star candidates are overall, I found that just over 18 percent of the cohort under study here managed to win their seats and join the ranks of incoming rookie MPs in 2021.

In an exemplary case of a star candidate, Arielle Kayabaga's rise to prominence owed much to her work in championing a clear set of causes: namely, addressing racism, helping new immigrants, representing youth, and empowering women. Kayabaga used her initial win at the municipal level to raise her profile regionally and nationally, and she was recruited successfully to run by the Liberals. After she won a competitive nomination vote, her campaign clearly benefited from local support by London's political community along with a significant investment of scarce campaign resources by senior members of Trudeau's cabinet and campaign team. In the case of Kayabaga, her significant public profile as a community activist and anti-racism advocate and her effective personal brand captured the attention of key party strategists, who then worked to ensure that she would be successful in a competitive but winnable riding.

In sum, the candidacies of professionally successful, well-regarded political outsiders in the federal election of 2021 were found in every major party and in most provinces to a greater or lesser extent. Star candidates were well represented in rural ridings as well as in urban ones. Simply being a star and winning a nomination, however, are not a sure path to becoming an MP: only 18 percent of the star candidates studied here went on to enter the House of Commons. Despite some of the risks and difficulties that sometimes accompany such candidacies, star candidates play an important role in enriching, rejuvenating, and diversifying the pool of elected political elites.

Notes

Acknowledgments: My sincere thanks to Western University undergraduate student research interns Alec Mazurek and Mateo Larrazabal, as well as PhD student Daniel Monsannef, for research assistance.

1   Campbell, *Time and Chance,* 26.
2   Gatehouse, "Why Canada's Federal Parties Still Shoot for the Stars."
3   de Clercy, "The Risks and Rewards."
4   Street, "Celebrity Politicians," 437.
5   't Hart and Tindall, "Leadership by the Famous," 2.
6   Weiskel, "From Sidekick to Sideshow"; Wright, *Star Power.*
7   't Hart and Tindall, "Leadership by the Famous."
8   Koop and Bittner, "Parachuted into Parliament."
9   Pruysers and Cross, "Candidate Selection in Canada." See also Chapter 3 of this volume.
10 For extended discussions of why parties seek to recruit star candidates and why they desire specific sorts of political representatives, see Carty, Eagles, and Sayers, "Candidates and Local Campaigns"; Koene,

"Targeted Representation?"; Koop and Bittner, "Parachuted into Parliament"; Street, "Celebrity Politicians"; and 't Hart and Kindall, "Leadership by the Famous."

11 Koene, "Targeted Representation?," 76.
12 Sayers, *Parties, Candidates, and Constituency Campaigns.*
13 Carty, Eagles, and Sayers, "Candidates and Local Campaigns," 621–22.
14 See Carty, Eagles, and Sayers, "Candidates and Local Campaigns," 622–23, on the issue of a candidate who possesses a national profile versus "some public profile"; see also Sayers, *Parties, Candidates, and Constituency Campaigns,* 53.
15 Street, "Celebrity Politicians," 437.
16 Sayers and de Groot, "Urban Style."
17 Marland, *Brand Command;* see also Marland and Wagner, "Scripted Messengers."
18 Lees-Marshment, "The Impact of Market Research," 95.
19 Kaneva and Klemmer, "The Rise of Brandidates?"
20 In some cases, ridings contained a mixture of rural and urban territories, such as Moose Jaw–Lake Centre–Lanigan, so in these cases I allocated the riding to one of the categories based upon the predominant distribution of rural, suburban, or urban voters within the riding.
21 de Clercy and Monsannef, "Star Candidate Recruitment," 11.
22 De Bono, "Meet London's Council."
23 Kayabaga, "Arielle Kayabaga: LinkedIn."
24 City of London, "City Council."
25 Bero et al., "Keep Listening."
26 Kayabaga, "#LdnOnt, I'm committed to this community."
27 Stacey, "'Strong Voice.'"
28 These are my calculations.
29 CBC News, "Ontario Principal Removed."
30 Ibid.
31 Pruden and Hager, "Anthropologist Explains."
32 Stone, Walsh, and Curry, "Trudeau Says No Regrets for Election Call."
33 Needles, "Internal Shift."
34 Ibid.

Bibliography

Bero, Tayo, Bee Quammie, Alicia Cox Thomson, and Kyrell Grant. "Keep Listening: 33 Black Canadians Making Change Now." *Chatelaine,* 20 August 2020. https://www.chatelaine.com/living/trailblazers/black -canadians-making-change-now/.

Campbell, Kim. *Time and Chance: The Political Memoirs of Canada's First Woman Prime Minister.* Toronto: McClelland-Bantam, 1996.

Carty, R. Kenneth, D. Munroe Eagles, and Anthony Sayers. "Candidates and Local Campaigns: Are There Just Four Canadian Types?" *Party Politics* 9, 5 (2003): 619–36.

CBC News. "Ontario Principal Removed after Twice Wearing Hair of Black Student Like a Wig." 29 May 2021. https://www.cbc.ca/news/canada/london/ontario-principal-removed-hair-black-student-1.6045755.

City of London. "City Council: Councillor Arielle Kayabaga, Ward 13." 2021. https://london.ca/government/council-civic-administration/city-council/councillor-arielle-kayabaga.

De Bono, Norman. "Meet London's Council Newcomers." *London Free Press,* 24 October 2018. https://lfpress.com/news/local-news/meet-londons-council-newcomers.

de Clercy, Cristine. "The Risks and Rewards of Star Candidate Recruitment in Canadian Federal Elections." *Policy Options,* 16 September 2021. https://policyoptions.irpp.org/magazines/septembe-2021/the-risks-and-rewards-of-star-candidate-recruitment-in-canadian-federal-elections/.

de Clercy, Cristine, and Daniel Monsannef. "Star Candidate Recruitment in Three Canadian Elections." Forthcoming.

Gatehouse, Jonathan. "Why Canada's Federal Parties Still Shoot for the Stars." CBC News, 15 September 2019. https://www.cbc.ca/news/politics/star-candidates-federal-election-1.5277467.

Kaneva, Nadia, and Austin Klemmer. "The Rise of Brandidates? A Cultural Perspective on Political Candidate Brands in Postmodern Consumer Democracies." *Journal of Customer Behaviour* 15, 3 (2016): 299–313.

Kayabaga, Arielle. "Arielle Kayabaga: LinkedIn Profile." LinkedIn, 2021. https://www.linkedin.com/in/ariellekayabaga/?originalSubdomain=ca.

–. "#LdnOnt, I'm committed to this community." Twitter, 19 March 2021, 8:04 a.m. https://twitter.com/KayabagaArielle/status/1372926908317437962.

Koene, Miriam. "Targeted Representation? An Analysis of the Appointment of Liberal Candidates in the 1993 and 1997 Federal Elections." *Past Imperfect* 7 (1998): 55–86.

Koop, Royce, and Amanda Bittner. "Parachuted into Parliament: Candidate Nomination, Appointed Candidates, and Legislative Roles in Canada." *Journal of Elections, Public Opinion and Parties* 21, 4 (2011): 431–52.

Lees-Marshment, Jennifer. "The Impact of Market Research on Political Leadership and Practitioners' Perspectives." In *Political Marketing in Canada,* edited by Alex Marland, Thierry Giasson, and Jennifer Lees-Marshment, 91–106. Vancouver: UBC Press, 2016.

Marland, Alex. *Brand Command: Canadian Politics and Democracy in the Age of Message Control.* Vancouver: UBC Press, 2016.

Marland, Alex, and Angelia Wagner. "Scripted Messengers: How Party Discipline and Branding Turn Election Candidates and Legislators into Brand Ambassadors." *Journal of Political Marketing* 12, 1–2 (2020): 54–73.

Needles, Craig. "Internal Shift for Kayabaga Campaign Shakes Up London West Race." Blackburn News, 9 September 2021. https://black-burnnews.com/london/london-news/2021/09/09/internal-shift-kayabaga-campaign-shakes-london-west-race/.

Pruden, Jana C., and Mike Hager. "Anthropologist Explains How She Concluded 200 Children Were Buried at the Kamloops Residential School." *Globe and Mail,* 15 July 2021. https://www.theglobeandmail.com/canada/article-kamloops-residential-school-unmarked-graves-discovery-update/.

Pruysers, Scott, and William Cross. "Candidate Selection in Canada: Local Autonomy, Centralization, and Competing Democratic Norms." *American Behavioral Scientist* 60, 7 (2016): 781–98.

Sayers, Anthony M. *Parties, Candidates, and Constituency Campaigns in Canadian Elections.* Vancouver: UBC Press, 1999.

Sayers, Anthony M., and David de Groot. "Urban Style: The Local Politics of Cabinet." Paper presented at the Annual Conference of the Canadian Political Science Association, University of Manitoba, 3 June 2004.

Stacey, Megan. "'Strong Voice': First-Term City Councillor Details London West MP Ambitions." *London Free Press,* 19 March 2021. https://lfpress.com/news/local-news/first-term-city-councillor-eyes-just-vacated-london-west-mp-seat.

Stone, Laura, Marieke Walsh, and Bill Curry. "Trudeau Says No Regrets for Election Call during Pandemic; O'Toole Pitches a 'Changed' Conservative Party." *Globe and Mail,* 10 September 2021. https://www.theglobeandmail.com/politics/article-trudeau-says-no-regrets-for-election-call-during-the-pandemic-otoole/.

Street, John. "Celebrity Politicians: Popular Culture and Political Representation." *British Journal of Politics and International Relations* 6, 4 (2004): 435–52.

't Hart, Paul, and Karen Tindall. "Leadership by the Famous: Celebrity as Political Capital." In *Dispersed Democratic Leadership: Origins, Dynamics, and Implications,* edited by John Kane, Haig Patapan, and Paul 't Hart, 255–78. Oxford: Oxford University Press, 2009.

Weiskel, Timothy C. "From Sidekick to Sideshow – Celebrity, Entertainment, and the Politics of Distraction: Why Americans Are 'Sleepwalking toward the End of the Earth.'" *American Behavioral Scientist* 49, 3 (2005): 393–409.

Wright, Lauren A. *Star Power: American Democracy in the Age of the Celebrity Candidate*. New York: Routledge, 2020.

5

Ministerial Incumbency

J.P. Lewis

Abstract   After party leaders, ministers are the best-known candidates on the campaign trail. The incumbent minister is a star candidate defending a seat that the government clearly wants to retain. However, the defence of a minister's riding can be complicated by the record of the government, the issues related to the portfolio, and the amount of time that the minister can spend in the riding because of departmental responsibilities or national campaign activities. This chapter analyzes the role of the ministerial incumbent in the local campaign.

Résumé   Après les chefs de parti, les ministres sont les candidats les plus connus d'une campagne électorale. Un ministre en poste représente un candidat vedette qui défend un siège que le gouvernement veut manifestement conserver. Toutefois, le maintien de la circonscription d'un ministre peut se compliquer en raison du bilan de son gouvernement, d'enjeux liés à son ministère, et du temps que le ministre peut consacrer à sa circonscription, souvent dicté par ses responsabilités ministérielles et ses activités au sein de la campagne nationale. Ce chapitre analyse le rôle de ministres en poste au sein des campagnes locales.

FOR MANY OBSERVERS, it makes sense that incumbents have an advantage in local election campaigns. An incumbent candidate has numerous strengths: years, possibly decades, of time in public life to build up name recognition and local reputation; prior connections to and secured resources of the local riding association to help organize the election campaign; political capital and connections throughout the community because of both substantive and ceremonial constituency work; and, most notably in the mind of the voter, membership in a successful and likely major political party. Since the incumbent is a standard bearer for a traditional party, there is greater media attention and the possibility of riding on a popular party's or leader's coattails to victory. Just as the spoils go to the victor, so too they generally go to the victor seeking re-election. Yet the evaluation of an incumbent can depend heavily on whether the incumbent is a member of a governing or non-governing party and on the role that the incumbent plays in that party.

Not all incumbents are equal. Some have more parliamentary experience than others, some serve in safe ridings for their parties, and some hold senior positions within their parties. After party leaders, the most exclusive group are ministerial incumbents – sitting cabinet ministers who are part of the government and run for re-election in the constituencies that they represent. Federal cabinet ministers in Canada are the most visible politicians in the political system, and historically these cabinet ministers have been responsible not only for governing but also for electioneering in the regions of the country that they represent.

In the decades following Confederation, cabinet ministers were key cogs in the country's patronage system, and parties relied on them to maintain electoral support across Canada.[1] Ministers kept tabs on who received favours from the government and who returned those favours at election time. The minister-run electoral patronage system was at the heart of re-election plans for both the Conservatives and the Liberals. Although the patronage system gradually subsided from mainstream Canadian politics, the role of ministers in campaigns persisted. Powerful ministers such as C.D. Howe ("minister of everything" from 1935 to 1957) and Paul Martin

Jr. (finance minister from 1993 to 2002) were national political stars of election campaigns. Yet, as the centralization of communications in electoral campaigns has followed the trend of a concentration of power with the prime minister and that office, the role of ministers in local campaigns has been less predictable.

The presence of a minister as a candidate in a local campaign is especially significant in Canada. An experienced ministerial incumbent stands in stark contrast to the high level of amateurism in Canadian elections because of the high rate of candidate turnover.[2] Higher rates of turnover of MPs in elections result in new representatives with little or no parliamentary or political experience, and this has an impact on the quality of candidates that parties field in elections. In political research experiments, strong candidates – a category in which most ministers would fall – have been found to increase a party's vote share.[3] Additionally, research outside Canada has found that certain ministerial portfolios hold electoral advantages.[4] Although there might be external factors clearly out of a candidate's control, there are attributes or characteristics that a local candidate (and an incumbent for that matter) can bring to an election campaign; being a "star candidate" is one such attribute, and this is often ascribed to ministers. The star candidate umbrella can apply to candidates described as high profile, local notable, or party insider.[5] However, when a political star competes in a campaign, it can complicate the general understanding of how incumbency traditionally works in Canada.

Candidate quality aside, incumbents do perform better than non-incumbents in Canadian elections. Canadian researchers have studied the impact of incumbency at all election levels – municipal, provincial, and federal – and found that incumbents enjoy an increased vote share compared with their challengers. Using a data set of forty parliamentary elections from 1867 to 2008, a recent study found that incumbents had a 9.4 percent to 11.2 percent greater probability of winning than non-incumbents.[6] Some research has gone beyond incumbency and considered the role of candidate quality. One study found that the presence of a "strong local candidate," such as a star candidate or minister, can provide on average a 10 percent increase at the polls depending on individual-level factors, including how informed the voter is.[7]

The depiction of flexible partisans as volatile Canadian voters has been central to research on voter behaviour and, consequently, less assurance that incumbents are safe from challengers.[8] The Canadian electoral climate has been defined by its volatility, with one report putting the turnover rate for federal elections at 40 percent.[9] Even with inherently unreliable flexible voters, local factors can assist ministerial incumbents. In elections that resulted in a change of government, usually between 50 percent and 90 percent of ministers nevertheless won their bids for re-election. In Canadian elections, the local candidate is often heavily dependent on the leader and party for success. In one study, the local candidate was part of "decisive consideration" for only 5 percent of voters.[10] In another, it amounted to only a 3 percent difference, but it can be significant in very close elections, such as most of those in Canada since 2000.[11] This suggests that, when the local candidate is someone of note, such as a sitting minister, that person might be given more weight by voters. Factors beyond a local candidate's control – such as the economic and fiscal performance of the party in power – can be major challenges or opportunities for re-election.

Local Trends

Cabinet ministers are almost constantly in campaign mode. The evolution of governments to be continuously pushing branded messages through ministerial announcements has shaped how ministerial incumbents are seen on the campaign trail.[12] Even as governments have continued to focus their communications on the prime minister, ministers still play a major role in delivering government and party messages outside the traditional campaign. Ministers are star players in the government's brand since they make spending and program announcements in ridings across the country. Ministers can be assembled in "B" or "C" tours across the country that support the leader's tour, whereby ministers visit key ridings and battlegrounds when the leader is busy elsewhere. Tours can be organized around thematic units of ministerial and star candidates based upon policy or platform areas. During the campaign in 2021, Minister of the Environment Jonathan Wilkinson and Minister of Employment Carla Qualtrough led announcements on banning American thermal coal, Minister of Finance Chrystia Freeland was deployed outside her Toronto-area riding to campaign for the Liberals (see Appendix), and Minister of Public Safety Bill Blair became the main spokesperson criticizing the Conservative Party gun policy.[13]

In twenty-first-century Canadian politics, ministers have become visible campaigners outside the formal campaign period as the phenomenon of permanent campaigning has become entrenched. The collision of governing and campaigning is significant when considering the role of ministers in the local campaign. Ministers are the faces and voices of government spending announcements that can accelerate in frequency as election calls approach.[14] In the days leading up to the campaign in 2021, Ministers Ahmed Hussen, Catherine McKenna, and Marc Miller all visited Nunavut for government-related announcements for the North.[15] A few days after Parliament was dissolved, Minister of Diversity and Inclusion Bardish Chagger announced federal funding for a number of anti-racism projects.[16]

Spending announcements before and during a campaign are held in targeted ridings and can take place in ministers' ridings or neighbouring ridings in their provinces or regions. Ministers have to campaign for their own re-election as well as the re-election of their government and assume a double duty that most other candidates do not have to assume. For major announcements, they might travel across the country to be on hand for the ceremonies and support their fellow party members. For example, in 2021, Minister of Health Patty Hajdu was on hand for the launch of the Liberal candidate's campaign in her neighbouring riding of Northern Ontario.[17] A flurry of public events reminding voters of the millions of federal dollars pouring into their communities provides content for ministers' channels of communication, both traditional (householder letters) and modern (social media) (see Appendix). Ministers become the jet-setting stars during these highly scripted – and increasingly cynical – forays of political communication.

The ministerial incumbent is a special case in itself. Unlike their backbench colleagues fighting to retain their seats in Parliament, members of cabinet are literally the government. Following the dissolution of Parliament, they remain ministers until a new cabinet is sworn in, and this gives them elevated status during the campaign and can lead to the double duty of both governing and campaigning. As members of the government, ministers bring both the power of the position and the risk of being the faces of government decisions. During campaigns, ministers assume the role of incumbents "plus." High-profile ministerial incumbents usually must conduct a shadow leader's tour (the B tour) during which they visit key targeted ridings that the prime minister cannot visit. As well, ministers can play the role of campaign attack dogs, "going low" on opposition candidates or leaders and keeping their leaders out of the nastier aspects of campaigning, as when Minister Freeland led negative attacks on Conservative leader O'Toole during the campaign in 2021 with tweets questioning his position on health care.[18] Ministerial incumbents' ridings can become the targets of other parties. During the campaign in 2021, Bloc Québécois leader Yves-François Blanchet rallied in Minister of National Revenue Diane Lebouthillier's riding in the Gaspé region.[19]

A minister's actions during a campaign can depend on several factors. Incumbency advantages can be affected by the context of the campaign and the state of the incumbent government and party. Well-known ministers who might benefit during some elections because of better access to resources, name recognition, and visibility can be punished if voters turn the contest into a referendum on the government's record. Campaign activities vary according to the nature of the competitiveness of the minister's riding. The riding can be competitive simply because it was contested in past elections. The minister might have been a candidate who won a surprising victory during an election in which the party won seats in parts of the country where it normally loses. Not only would this scenario keep the minister working on the local campaign in the riding, but also it could bring in more resources from party headquarters since the party would not want to lose the seat.

External factors that affect the minister's responsibilities can pull the minister off the campaign trail and back into portfolio matters. Once the election writs have been issued, the caretaker convention takes effect.[20] Under that convention, ministerial activity continues but is exercised with restraint. Government activity should be limited to matters that are "routine, or non-controversial, or urgent and in the public interest, or reversible by a new government without undue cost or disruption, or agreed to by opposition parties."[21] Depending on external events, ministers may be hauled back into their departmental duties. During the campaign in 2021, the refugee crisis in Afghanistan resulting from the withdrawal of international troops brought Minister of Immigration Marco Mendicino back into ministerial activity.[22] The complexity of the crisis also brought Deputy Prime Minister Chrystia Freeland, Minister of International Development Karina Gould, and Minister of Defence Harjit Sajjan into their ministerial caretaker roles to address the situation.[23]

Unexpected political developments can change the trajectory of a minister's campaign. During the campaign in 2019 – when it was revealed that Justin Trudeau had worn blackface on multiple occasions in the past – cabinet ministers were called in to show public support for their leader. Although Minister Amarjeet Sohi said that he was "disheartened and disappointed," he tweeted support for his leader as a "champion of diversity and inclusion."[24] For ministers in need of help mid-campaign, support can come from staff outside the local team. "Wartime generals," including campaign managers and strategists, can be distributed to ridings where the need for assistance has been identified. The movement of personnel and financial resources across the levels of government and the country has become common.[25] The support can come from beyond just the federal party. Political staff are known to be "loaned" between provincial and federal parties.[26]

Beyond appearing at events, away from the spotlight, ministers are regularly involved in planning and leading the national campaign. In 2021, Minister Mélanie Joly and former minister Navdeep

Bains were the campaign co-chairs, with Ministers Harjit Sajjan (British Columbia) and Ahmed Hussen (Ontario) leading their respective provincial campaigns.[27] Such responsibilities can take ministers away from the tasks involved in defending their seats in local campaigns and reflect the double duties that a minister faces.

However, the centralization of power and the control of government communications by the Prime Minister's Office have curtailed the ability of ministers to show off their political chops on the campaign trail.[28] In the campaign in 2021, ministerial photo-ops became less frequent since the Liberal Party ran a leader-centred campaign in the middle of a pandemic. Freeland joined Trudeau to play soccer with children at a soccer dome in Hamilton, but such high-profile ministerial events were few and far between.[29]

Behind the Scenes

This section is based upon confidential, semi-structured interviews with six campaign managers and ministers to provide behind-the-scenes insights into a local campaign for a ministerial incumbent. On the front lines, the local campaigns of ministerial incumbents might seem to be similar to other incumbent campaigns, but their membership in the government and their elevated status in the party affect a number of variables behind the scenes. The ministerial incumbent has advantages over backbench incumbents but is faced as well with additional unpredictable factors that can hurt or help the bid for re-election. For governments up in the pre-campaign polls and on their way to holding on to power, the campaign for a minister can include low levels of stress in the riding and a more active role in the places where the party sees expansion. For governments in competitive races or down in the polls, the campaigns for ministers can be fights for their political lives played out more on the national stage since the possible downfall of once powerful ministers draws the attention of local and national media.

Ministers can easily be drawn out of their local campaign activities. Campaign managers play major gatekeeping roles for ministerial incumbents because there can be tasks that need attention in Ottawa or calls from party headquarters to help out on the regional or national campaign (relatedly, see Chapters 7 and 8 of this volume). Above all else, though, ministerial incumbents have the same goal as non-ministerial incumbents to defend their seats and return to the nation's capital to represent their ridings and, hopefully, continue their careers in cabinet.

Ministers do not have to expend as much effort introducing themselves to electors as other candidates. As representatives of the government, ministers can become lightning rods for opposition to government policies. National interest groups and third parties can target ministers in their own ridings during the campaign even though the issues are not local. Ministers also remain in their positions during the campaign even as they focus on retaining their seats. Although there are advantages to being a ministerial incumbent during an election, many challenges are present as well.

As one minister noted, "the party does not want ministers to lose their seat[s]." The loss of a minister's seat can be symbolic of a government's waning popularity, and the significance of this is not lost on those working behind the scenes. Ministerial incumbents get more attention and support from party headquarters than non-ministerial incumbents, and campaign headquarters might reallocate resources and staff. When a candidate is clearly going to win or lose the campaign, the party does not want to have "people sitting around" and moves staff to where help is needed. Ministerial incumbents have access to political staff who can volunteer after hours. Ministers have more staff than backbenchers, and the majority of ministers' staff end up taking leave and working on the campaigns. As well, in many cases, their volunteers have more experience having served on previous successful campaigns.

Along with tangible resources such as money and staff, since ministers are closer to the centre of power in the party, generally they have greater access to information and are less out of the loop than challengers or even backbench incumbents. One minister noted about the resource advantage of ministerial incumbents that "[your] team tends to be stronger ... [if you've had] volunteer[s] over the years since the last campaign." The advantages of an incumbent minister can make a loss more puzzling than that of a backbencher. Ministers have the resources of the government to aid them in costing initiatives well in advance of policy rollouts. As members of cabinet, they are privy to exclusive information that gives them greater insights for discussion and debate of policy issues. All of these factors can provide a major information advantage for ministerial incumbents out on local campaign trails.

Regardless of the attention that their portfolios can give ministers, local campaigns matter, as one campaign manager noted: "[Voters] don't care if you are the minister of X and made X policy – they want to know what you did for the constituency ... [Y]ou can be a great minister and a lousy MP." Another campaign manager noted that "I don't know if [visiting another riding] makes a big difference – it makes a difference when the prime minister comes to town but [maybe not] ministers." This insight from a veteran party actor suggests the contradictions of using ministers as campaign props in ridings other than their own.

One of the most difficult tasks for the campaign manager is to keep the minister "riding focused." Political staff struggle before the writ is dropped with bureaucratic staff to ensure that the minister has time for constituency work. Once the writ drops, this struggle continues, but scheduling conflicts are between bureaucratic staff and campaign workers. As mentioned earlier, the caretaker convention requires ministers to continue with their ministerial responsibilities throughout the campaign.

It is key for ministerial campaign personnel to work closely with bureaucratic staff to protect their candidate from too much ministerial work. During the campaign, ministers will be asked to stay in the loop with the work in their departments and to maintain communication with their respective deputy ministers. A minister noted that "you're always a minister, and you always have what's going on [in the department] in your mind." As one campaign manager noted, "the clerk's office makes sure you aren't [m]aking major decisions or announcements ... [Y]ou don't want to be in your [ministerial office], you want to be out on the hustings." In snap elections, in which government business might not yet have reached a natural end, there might be more government work on a minister's desk than during a planned or expected election. Projects and initiatives can be close to hitting full stride.

Ministerial staff will take a strong position with party head-quarters that ministerial candidates in competitive ridings cannot leave those ridings for lengthy tours and that any support for neighbouring candidates take place during the evening. Ministers can help out in a leadership role for regional races with the goal of "sleeping in their [own] bed[s]" every night.

Ministerial campaign staff work hard to maintain the narrative that the candidate is always close to the riding even if pulled into national campaign events or ministerial affairs. If the minister is out of the riding for any length of time, then the campaign will use radio advertising or other means of communication to keep the minister in the public space of the local campaign. As one campaign manager recalled, "when [the minister] was out of the riding, we upped our radio budget ... to make it seem like ... [the minister was] in the riding." As well, even if a minister spends only an hour of the day door knocking and takes time to visit nearby ridings, the campaign will attempt to present the candidate as remaining in the riding all day. Luckily, to meet all of these scheduling challenges, ministers are accustomed to having their time micro-managed. During the campaign, their schedules must be tightly managed to follow the rhythm of their time governing. Campaign managers work with schedulers step by step to build details of a minister's campaign itinerary.

A minister's schedule depends very much on the context of the campaign. If things are going well in the riding, or if the seat is safe historically, then the minister can be pulled out of the riding to help out in other constituencies. For most ministers, this means travelling to other ridings in their province or region, but for some high-profile, powerful, or popular ministers it can involve visiting ridings far away from their own. Ministerial movement is predominantly dictated from the centre. The use of ministers in other ridings should come as no surprise. Ministers are in the news more often, get recognized in crowds, and can help their party teammates. Bringing out high-profile ministers can get a reaction in a local race. A minister who visits a riding is more for the media and campaign volunteers than for average voters. On motivating the local campaign team, one interviewee mentioned, "the day we had [the minister] in the riding they had many more volunteers out door-knocking." The opposite dynamic can take place as well; a minister might have visits to the riding from the leader or other ministers if it is one that the party desperately wants to retain.

Senior ministers can be involved in the national campaign and the leader's campaign as they stay connected through conference and video calls. Ministers can weigh in on whether or not the campaign should shift resources or priorities. Before a campaign starts, ministers might be involved in the recruitment of candidates. As the campaign nears, ministers might be approached to discuss policy and platform ideas.

Ministers need to strike a balance between undertaking high-level campaign activities that reach beyond their ridings and still being present in their own ridings. The absence of ministers will be noted, and they should not be kept from local campaign activities such as canvassing and candidates' debates. The presence of a minister might not make a difference, yet pulling a minister from the riding might hurt the chances of re-election there. As one interview participant explained, "[the average voter] may not be aware of all the high-profile media appearances of a minister; they want to speak to their local representative." This perspective challenges somewhat the media and public attention given to front-bench candidates. If a minister appears to be disconnected from the riding or missed a local all-candidates forum, then it could have negative consequences for support.

Ministers can be valuable to national campaigns. They have expertise in their portfolio areas to deliver on certain policy announcements and can therefore be used as spokespeople across the country on specific platform planks. As one campaign manager suggested, "if you have ministers that have some ability to deliver messages to the media, strategically you may want to rely on them more and pull them off [local] campaign activities to do that." An announcement about health-care spending could see the health minister headlining the campaign events for that day. Another campaign manager suggested that, "for the message of the day, the minister was there to answer about the nuts and bolts [of the policy announcement]."

Inevitably, by the end of the local campaign, a ministerial incumbent's fortune might be similar to that of a non-ministerial incumbent – at the whim of any national momentum that creates coattails or brooms for incumbents. Whether their ministerial position makes a difference in the local campaign is difficult to assess from election to election. Strong campaign managers, disciplined ministers, and non-eventual campaigns for their portfolio responsibilities can all influence the result.

Conclusion

On election night, the fate of a minister becomes a key part of the story of results. Alongside network reports on the formation of the government and the standings of the parties are the fates of the best-known candidates across the country – cabinet ministers. In the same group as party leaders and familiar political faces, ministers' races are considered among those to watch. With the extra attention of national pundits and political watchers, it is easy to overlook that ministerial incumbents are also Members of Parliament who seek to hold on to their seats just like their parliamentary colleagues. Ministers must compete in the rough and tumble and unpredictability of the local campaign, just as every other incumbent does. However, just because they face the common challenges of local campaigns, ministers are not normal candidates in defending their ridings. With access to more information, staff, and money, ministers have an advantage going into local campaigns. As the faces of the party seeking to hold on to government, ministers need to hold their seats, and losses can be an embarrassment even during a successful national election.

In addition to the advantages of being a ministerial incumbent are a number of disadvantages, including being a larger target of opposition from organized groups outside the riding. This negative attention can neutralize any advantage that the minister might have in the local campaign. Ministerial responsibilities or requests from party headquarters can also be major distractions from local campaigns. The powerful, nationally focused minister thrust into the environment of local campaigning is a notable juxtaposition. The Ottawa Press Gallery, the front benches of the House of Commons, and the responsibilities in billion-dollar departments are traded for knocking on doors, charming local media, and debating with unelected, amateur politicians. Ministers in local campaigns rely on their campaign managers, their personal brands, and – depending on their particular riding and portfolio – the fortune of the national campaign. For the weeks during which ministers are on the campaign trail, they share many similarities with their candidate colleagues across the country. However, there is no escaping the fact that they are incumbents "plus."

Notes

1 Bakvis, *Regional Ministers*.
2 Atkinson and Docherty, "Moving Right Along."
3 Roy and Alcantara, *Winning and Keeping Power in Canadian Politics*.
4 Martin, "Policy, Office and Votes."
5 Sayers, *Parties, Candidates, and Constituency Campaigns;* see also Chapter 4 of this volume on star candidates.
6 Kendall and Rekkas, "Incumbency Advantages in the Canadian Parliament."
7 Roy and Alcantara, "The Candidate Effect."
8 Clarke et al., *Absent Mandate;* Atkinson and Docherty, "Moving Right Along"; Moncrief, "Terminating the Provincial Career."
9 Matland and Studlar, "Determinants of Legislative Turnover."
10 Blais et al., "Does the Local Candidate Matter?"
11 Loewen, "Do Local Candidates Even Matter to Voters?"
12 Radford, "$9.8M Announced to Spur Sask. Crop Research in 2021"; Saba, "From TIFF to the Calgary Stampede."
13 Gyramati, "Liberals in Delta Promise Export Ban"; Jarvis, "Freeland Promises 'Truly Massive' Investment"; McParland, "If Justin Trudeau Can't Have Your Love, He'll Settle for Fear."
14 Thompson, "For Harper's Ministers, Pictures Are Worth Millions."
15 Larocque, "Nunavut Doesn't Need a Parade of Federal Cabinet Ministers."

16 Goldenberg, "Federal Funding Announced for Anti-Racism Projects."
17 Haughton, "Bruno in Favour of Vaccine Passports."
18 Burke, "Twitter Adds 'Manipulated' Warning Label."
19 Pinkerton, "Party Leaders Go into Attack Mode."
20 Turnbull and Booth, "Public Servants."
21 Government of Canada, "Guidelines on the Conduct of Ministers."
22 Corbella, "Did Trudeau's Words about Accepting 20,000 Afghan Refugees Help Cause Kabul 'Chaos'?"
23 Glavin, "Canada's Help Was a Shell Game."
24 Stone, Blaze Baum, and Ha, "Liberal Candidates Stand by Trudeau."
25 Pruysers, "Two Political Worlds?"
26 Esselment, "Fighting Elections."
27 Levitz, "The Liberals Are Betting Big."
28 *Globe and Mail,* "Corralling His Ministers Is a Misstep for Harper."
29 Van Dongen, "Justin Trudeau Visits Hamilton Again."

Bibliography

Atkinson, Michael, and David Docherty. "Moving Right Along: The Roots of Amateurism in the Canadian House of Commons." *Canadian Journal of Political Science* 25, 2 (1992): 295–318.

Bakvis, Herman. *Regional Ministers: Power and Influence in the Canadian Cabinet.* Toronto: University of Toronto Press, 1991.

Blais, André, Elisabeth Gidengil, Agnieszka Dobrzynska, Neil Nevitte, and Richard Nadeau. "Does the Local Candidate Matter? Candidate Effects in the Canadian Election of 2000." *Canadian Journal of Political Science* 36, 3 (2003): 657–64.

Burke, Ashley. "Twitter Adds 'Manipulated' Warning Label to Tweet from Liberal Candidate Chrystia Freeland." CBC News, 23 August 2021. https://www.cbc.ca/news/politics/twitter-labels-freeland-tweet-manipulated-media-1.6149734.

Clarke, Harold D., Jane Jenson, Lawrence LeDuc, and Jon H. Pammett. *Absent Mandate: Canadian Electoral Politics in an Age of Restructuring.* Toronto: University of Toronto Press, 2019.

Corbella, Licia. "Did Trudeau's Words about Accepting 20,000 Afghan Refugees Help Cause Kabul 'Chaos'?" *Calgary Herald,* 28 August 2021. https://calgaryherald.com/opinion/columnists/corbella-did-trudeaus-words-about-accepting-20000-afghan-refugees-help-cause-kabul-chaos.

Esselment, Anna Lennox. "Fighting Elections: Cross-Level Political Party Integration in Ontario." *Canadian Journal of Political Science* 43, 4 (2010): 871–92.

Glavin, Terry. "Canada's Help Was a Shell Game." *National Post,* 2 September 2021. https://nationalpost.com/opinion/terry-glavin-canadas-help-for-stranded-afghans-is-little-more-than-a-shell-game.

Globe and Mail. "Corralling His Ministers Is a Misstep for Harper." 18 March 2006. https://www.theglobeandmail.com/opinion/corralling-his-ministers-is-a-misstep-for-harper/article1328576/.

Goldenberg, Joel. "Federal Funding Announced for Anti-Racism Projects." *Suburban,* 19 August 2021. https://www.thesuburban.com/news/city_news/federal-funding-announced-for-anti-racism-projects/article_f3d16b34-50de-56d1-ac68-123ad58c087c.html.

Government of Canada. "Guidelines on the Conduct of Ministers, Ministers of State, Exempt Staff and Public Servants during an Election." August 2021. https://www.canada.ca/en/privy-council/services/publications/guidelines-conduct-ministers-state-exempt-staff-public-servants-election.html.

Gyramati, Sandor. "Liberals in Delta Promise Export Ban on Thermal Coal." *Delta Optimist,* 30 August 2021. https://www.delta-optimist.com/canadavotes2021/local-news/liberals-in-delta-promise-export-ban-on-thermal-coal-4266228.

Haughton, Jay. "Bruno in Favour of Vaccine Passports." *Dryden Now,* 28 August 2021. https://www.drydennow.com/articles/bruno-in-favour-of-vaccine-passports.

Jarvis, Anne. "Freeland Promises 'Truly Massive' Investment in Green Economy, Including EV Production in Windsor." *Windsor Star,* 2 September 2021. https://windsorstar.com/news/local-news/freeland-promises-truly-massive-investment-in-green-economy-including-ev-production-in-windsor.

Kendall, Chad, and Marie Rekkas. "Incumbency Advantages in the Canadian Parliament." *Canadian Journal of Economics* 45, 4 (2012): 1560–85.

Larocque, Corey. "Nunavut Doesn't Need a Parade of Federal Cabinet Ministers." *Nunatsiaq News,* 6 August 2021. https://nunatsiaq.com/stories/article/nunavut-doesnt-need-a-parade-of-federal-cabinet-ministers/.

Levitz, Stephanie. "The Liberals Are Betting Big that They Can Win a Majority. Here's How They Plan to Do It." *Toronto Star,* 17 August 2021. https://www.thestar.com/politics/federal-election/2021/08/17/the-liberals-are-betting-big-that-they-can-win-a-majority-heres-how-they-plan-to-do-it.html.

Loewen, Peter. "Do Local Candidates Even Matter to Voters?" *Ottawa Citizen,* 18 September 2015. https://ottawacitizen.com/news/politics/loewen-do-local-candidates-even-matter-to-voters.

Martin, Shane. "Policy, Office and Votes: The Electoral Value of Ministerial Office." *British Journal of Political Science* 46 (2014): 281–96.

Matland, Richard E., and Donley T. Studlar. "Determinants of Legislative Turnover: A Cross-National Analysis." *British Journal of Political Science* 34, 1 (2004): 87–108.

McParland, Kelly. "If Justin Trudeau Can't Have Your Love, He'll Settle for Fear." *National Post,* 6 September 2021. https://nationalpost.com/opinion/kelly-mcparland-if-justin-trudeau-cant-have-your-love-hell-settle-for-fear.

Moncrief, Gary F. "Terminating the Provincial Career: Retirement and Electoral Defeat in Canadian Provincial Legislatures, 1960–1997." *Canadian Journal of Political Science* 31, 2 (1998): 359–72.

Pinkerton, Charlie. "Party Leaders Go into Attack Mode One Week from Election Day." iPolitics, 13 September 2021. https://www.ipolitics.ca/news/party-leaders-go-into-attack-mode-one-week-from-election-day.

Pruysers, Scott. "Two Political Worlds? Multi-Level Campaign Integration in Canadian Constituencies." *Regional and Federal Studies* 25, 2 (2015): 165–82.

Radford, Evan. "$9.8M Announced to Spur Sask. Crop Research in 2021." *Toronto Star,* 12 January 2021. https://www.thestar.com/news/canada/2021/01/12/98m-announced-to-spur-sask-crop-research-in-2021.html.

Roy, Jason, and Christopher Alcantara. "The Candidate Effect: Does the Local Candidate Matter?" *Journal of Elections, Public Opinion and Parties* 25, 2 (2015): 195–214.

–. *Winning and Keeping Power in Canadian Politics.* Toronto: University of Toronto Press, 2020.

Saba, Rosa. "From TIFF to the Calgary Stampede – Feds Talk Details of $700-Million Funding to Help Arts, Culture and Sports Recover from COVID-19." *Toronto Star,* 28 June 2021. https://www.thestar.com/business/2021/06/28/from-tiff-to-the-calgary-stampede-feds-talk-details-of-700-million-funding-to-help-arts-culture-and-sportrecover-from-covid-19.html.

Sayers, Anthony M. *Parties, Candidates, and Constituency Campaigns in Canadian Elections.* Vancouver: UBC Press, 1998.

Stone, Laura, Kathryn Blaze Baum, and Tu Thanh Ha. "Liberal Candidates Stand by Trudeau, Despite Revelations." *Globe and Mail,* 20 September 2019, A9.

Thompson, Elizabeth. "For Harper's Ministers, Pictures Are Worth Millions: Spending Records." iPolitics, 19 February 2015. https://www.ipolitics.ca/

news/for-harper-government-pictures-are-worth-millions-ministerial
-spending-records.

Turnbull, Lori, and Donald Booth. "Public Servants." In *Inside the Campaign: Managing Elections in Canada,* edited by Alex Marland and Thierry Giasson, 59–70. Vancouver: UBC Press, 2020.

Van Dongen, Matthew. "Justin Trudeau Visits Hamilton Again as Federal Election Campaign Enters Home Stretch." *Toronto Star,* 10 September 2021. https://www.thestar.com/ths/news/hamilton-region/2021/09/10/hamilton-justin-trudeau-federal-election.html?itm_source=parsely-api.

6

Personalization of Local Candidates

*Mireille Lalancette and Vincent Raynauld,
with Anthony Ozorai*

Abstract   This chapter explores the dynamics of political personalization in local political campaigns. Political personalization can be
defined as the process of emphasizing politicians' identity attributes, qualities,
histories, accomplishments, and private lives in voter outreach and campaign
communication. It can shape all facets of online and offline electioneering,
especially at the national level, where party leaders embody political parties'
values and orientations. The chapter takes an in-depth look at Liberal Party
of Canada candidate Martin Francoeur in Trois-Rivières (Quebec) during the
federal election of 2021. It offers insights into how a local candidate navigates
political personalization between national instructions and local expectations
and realities. The chapter shows that, though centralized party leadership
provides guidance and materials for the campaign, there is leeway for local
candidates to present and promote themselves to local audiences. The practices of national leaders inspire and influence local dynamics of political
personalization. This is especially the case on social media platforms, where
personal dimensions of the candidates, including their experience and ties
to the community, hold more importance. Although personalization at the
local level is adapted to national standards, there is flexibility for local candidates who want to tailor their appeal to their personal and professional
identities.

Résumé   Ce chapitre explore la dynamique de la personnalisation politique dans les campagnes politiques locales. La personnalisation
politique peut être définie comme le processus consistant à mettre en avant
les attributs identitaires, les qualités et l'histoire des acteurs politiques, leurs
réalisations et leurs vies privées dans le cadre de la sensibilisation des électeurs et de la communication de campagne. Elle façonne toutes les facettes
de la propagande électorale en ligne et hors ligne, en particulier au niveau
national où les chefs de parti incarnent les valeurs et les orientations des partis

politiques. Ce chapitre examine en profondeur le candidat du Parti libéral du Canada Martin Francoeur à Trois-Rivières (Québec) lors des élections fédérales canadiennes de 2021. Il offre un aperçu de la manière dont un candidat local navigue dans la personnalisation politique entre les instructions au niveau national et les attentes et réalités locales. Ce chapitre montre que si la direction centrale du parti fournit des orientations et du matériel pour la campagne, elle offre une marge de manœuvre aux candidats locaux pour se présenter et se promouvoir auprès des publics locaux. Les pratiques des leaders nationaux inspirent et influencent les dynamiques locales de personnalisation politique. C'est notamment le cas sur les plateformes de médias sociaux où les dimensions personnelles des candidats, notamment leur expérience et leurs liens avec la communauté, prennent plus d'importance. Si la personnalisation au niveau local est adaptée aux normes nationales, elle offre une certaine flexibilité aux candidats locaux qui souhaitent adapter leur appel à leur identité personnelle et professionnelle.

THE WRIT HAS DROPPED. Electoral signs are peppered throughout neighbourhoods. Photographs of local candidates shaking hands, making ceremonial first pitches at local league baseball games, or flipping burgers at community events pervade news media coverage and social media feeds. Candidates are hard at work convincing voters that they should be elected and given mandates to represent them. With the support of their national party leaders and apparatus, they deploy all efforts necessary to win voters' hearts, minds, and – most importantly – votes. The process of highlighting politicians' socio-demographic backgrounds (e.g., race, sex/gender, Indigeneity); identity attributes, qualities, and histories; professional profiles and accomplishments; as well as private lives in voter outreach and campaign communication is known as personalization.[1] There is often particular focus on party leaders since they embody their parties' broader values, policy orientations, and objectives. This is not a new phenomenon. Individuals have always played an oversized role in politics. However, the evolution of the dynamics of news media coverage and the central role played by identity-centric media platforms in political processes over the past few decades have increased the importance of personalization in political life. Furthermore, politicians have adapted their approach to self-presentation and communication to the formats and function-alities of dominant media channels. Personalization is fuelled by different social, political, and economic factors.[2] Of particular importance in this chapter is the process of mediatization.[3] It can be defined as the ways in which political players internalize the logics governing the mass media environment and adapt their communication and engagement practices to exploit them best. These dynamics manifest themselves in four key areas of politics: parliamentary work, internal party democracy, media relations, and electoral campaigning.

Both media and political institutions follow broadly accepted rules to provide buzzworthy content and garner public attention. Political parties turn to specialized campaign workers to develop and strategically broadcast politicians' public images in ways responding to audience expectations and the media's pressures to communicate. During an electoral race, they leverage old and new forms of voter outreach – from publishing ads in community newspapers to posting updates on social media – to find and lock in public support. As traditional and digital media are more intertwined than ever,[4] separating what political appeal is intended for which media channel and which audience is challenging. In many ways, the logics governing politicking on traditional media now apply to digital media.[5]

In this chapter, we zero in on dynamics of personalization in local campaigns during Canadian federal elections. Why take an interest in political image management strategies online and offline? The horse-race coverage of campaign politics – which tends to emphasize polls providing insights into the state of the electoral race and individual candidates' performances – creates favourable conditions for the public to pay closer attention to candidates' personal and professional characteristics instead of their parties or their policy offerings.[6] Throughout a local campaign, candidates and their teams spend time and resources on political image management to frame themselves as ready and able to take on the roles and responsibilities of elected office. While projecting this image, they also need to fuel their closeness to the public by presenting themselves as approachable, relatable, and friendly. These efforts are driven by their knowledge and understanding of which personal and professional attributes local voters find desirable in a candidate, including honesty, intelligence, sincerity, trustworthiness,[7] and experience.[8] In many ways, political affiliation and the particularities of the socio-geographical area where the candidate is running for office impact how the candidate crafts and rolls out the public image. For example, candidates are regularly featured with members of their families to showcase their trustworthiness and reliability. They are also shown interacting with those in the high-tech industry to convey their openness to innovation, their forward thinking, and their intelligence. Candidates who want to portray themselves as open and inclusive regularly emphasize their connection to and engagement with citizens of all walks of life, from children to members of minority/marginalized communities to elderly and racialized voters. They carefully choose which events they take part in throughout an electoral campaign, aware that horseback riding or golfing could be perceived as elitist and out of reach for some segments of the electorate, whereas team sports such as baseball, football, and hockey can help them to connect with the interests of a broader swath of society. Since visual media platforms comprise a central feature of the mediascape, photos and videos are at the forefront of non-stop political campaigning strategies[9] and help to humanize politicians in the eyes of voters (see Appendix for examples). Whereas some elements of candidates' identities can bolster their visibility among and connection with the public, others – including gender, sexual orientation, and ethnicity – can be barriers because of existing perceptions within the electorate. In many ways, personalization is not a universal experience.[10]

These techniques of communication are informed by norms of political communication tied to dynamics of personalization, including individualization, intimization, celebritization, and digitalization, which affect how politicians present themselves and convey their positions and ideas. Conversely, these dynamics influence how voters perceive them and make sense of their performances. Individualization can be viewed as the process through which individual politicians are positioned as integral to political communication appeals. It essentially challenges the dominance of political parties and collective political identity in political processes. Intimization refers to the ways in which politicians leverage elements of their private lives to construct their public images and connect with the electorate on a more personal level. Celebritization can be defined as blurring the line between politics and popular culture. In other words, politicians turn to the codes of celebrity culture to construct their public political appeal. Finally, digitalization refers to the reshaping of social, political, and personal life around digital media. For example, identity-centric social media platforms – including Facebook, Instagram, Twitter, Snapchat, and TikTok – push politicians to adopt more personal and informal forms of communication and engagement adapted to the functionalities of these platforms.

In this context, candidates' personal and professional character traits, identity attributes, and histories – more broadly referred to as their "ethos" in this chapter – become shortcuts for members of the public to familiarize themselves with and understand politics. Using storytelling techniques, candidates roll out narratives highlighting strategically aspects of their identities that can help them to foster personal connections with voters. These narratives can be built with wide-ranging themes, including past personal or professional achievements or failures and character traits such as honesty, integrity, or authenticity. Personalized storytelling can affect all aspects of a political campaign. For example, it can be used by campaign communication teams to brand political opponents negatively or by journalistic organizations to discuss, contextualize, and offer commentary on political news stories. This affects how citizens perceive and understand political information and, by extension, make up their minds about which candidates to support on election day.[11]

As mentioned, party leaders generally command most of the traditional and social media attention during elections since they are the national representatives of their parties' values and programs. This centralization of campaign communication[12] poses significant challenges to local candidates who want to have unique voices.[13] Research shows that party discipline prevents more individualized forms of communication. Indeed, local representatives of political parties essentially serve as brand ambassadors who are unable to stray from or counter the party leader's image and message.[14]

This discussion leads to important questions still being explored by scholars in Canada and abroad. How can local candidates highlight their personalities and accomplishments to promote their candidacies yet embody the party's centralized brand in the context of campaign communication? How can they promote themselves without outshining the party leader? How do partisan and regional differences affect how candidates present themselves to the public? More importantly, how do local candidates develop and operationalize their strategies of political personalization online and offline during a campaign?

Local Trends

Studies of political personalization during elections in Canada and internationally have taken – for the most part – an interest in party leaders and candidates with high name recognition (see, in this volume, Chapter 4 on star candidates). A comparatively smaller volume of academic work has explored how local candidates present themselves on social media and infuse personal elements into their candidacies and relationships with their parties, policy issues, and electors. The following pages profile five conclusions of these studies.

First, an extensive analysis of local candidates' digital campaigning practices in seventeen countries[15] during the European electoral campaigns in 2009 shows that personalization is often based upon a candidate's professional ethos. Candidates generally provide few insights into their personal lives. They prefer to highlight their achievements in wide-ranging professional areas, including politics (especially for incumbent candidates), social engagement, business, or the arts. The authors conclude that there is still a clear separation between politics and personal life at the local level. Another study,[16] which compared tactics of personalization used by US representatives and UK parliamentarians, found that most of them tend to emphasize their reception of and reaction to public demands as well as their ability to manage them in their constituent communication activities. Their public communication efforts also regularly highlight their knowledge of political and policy issues, their experience, their presence in the communities that they represent, and their effectiveness as elected officials.

Second, research on political personalization during the provincial election in Quebec in 2012[17] found that candidates' electioneering activities often included many elements of their personalities. For instance, they provided insights into their political careers and accomplishments (when applicable), non-political management responsibilities, education (e.g., qualifications, diplomas, competencies), and support for political and policy causes. Candidates' more personal characteristics, including age, family situation (e.g., wife, husband, or partner, children and grandchildren, brothers and sisters), hobbies, place of birth, and place of residence were often important components of their public images. Building upon the work of other scholars who have taken an interest in the Canadian context, it can be argued that candidates tend to give greater emphasis to the more professional dimensions of their identities and aspects of their personal profiles.

These findings are consistent with those of similar studies.[18] They demonstrate that personality, skills, and political and policy pledges are three core elements of persuasive contemporary campaign communication. Aspects of candidates' personal lives are not at centre stage. However, their biographies can give electors glimpses of their personal identities deemed important by the centralized party leadership. Character and competence are two categories of a leader's personality traits in relation to public image. Specific traits include leadership, honesty, trustworthiness, compassion, familiarity with political and policy issues, intelligence, empathy, and the ability to inspire.[19]

Third, another core element of a local candidate's public image[20] is the importance given to rootedness or anchoring in the electoral district that the candidate seeks to represent. Candidates frequently mention their ties to communities, such as by highlighting that they were born and raised in specific neighbourhoods or have been living and working in particular localities. They also put forth their support for and involvement in local organizations and causes or their connections with influential and well-known community leaders. In many ways, this allows them to showcase their familiarity with and understanding of issues that matter to the communities. Furthermore, it enables them to manage their reputations and develop strong bonds with some segments of the electorate. Finally, being perceived as rooted in the community helps a candidate to infuse coherence and authenticity in the campaign.

These tactics of political personalization at the local level are in line with processes of candidate selection managed by local party organizations through electoral district associations.[21] As discussed in Chapter 3 of this volume, when local party members vote for and select a nominee, generally they favour high-profile or well-known candidates with strong bonds with the grassroots. They also tend to have strong networks in local communities (e.g., personal, political, economic). These networks allow for the public image to be shaped in ways that are coherent with local political demands and expectations. The image can also be tweaked to satisfy the party brand as dictated by the party leader and centralized party organization. This explains why local businesspeople (e.g., presidents and chief executive officers of companies, managers), media personalities (e.g., journalists, commentators), and other celebrities (e.g., professional athletes, community organizers, artists) are recruited by political parties to run for office in specific communities. They have strong name recognition, which demands less publicity and marketing effort to introduce them to voters, develop their political images, and frame their candidacies.

Fourth, three Canadian studies[22] have shown how political personalization plays a central role in social media politicking, especially on visual-centric platforms such as Instagram. An analysis of Justin Trudeau's Instagram activities during his first year as prime minister of Canada found that visual and textual content was used to showcase Trudeau as a positive and approachable politician. Many photos shared on his personal Instagram feed depicted him interacting with citizens in large crowds, including during visits to businesses and cultural celebrations. Captions were used to reinforce his closeness with constituents, his work ethic, and his family life. This combination of images and captions enabled Trudeau to reinforce seven traits of his political leadership: innovation, positivity, national unity, diversity, reassurance, dialogue, and relatability.[23] His digital storytelling approach put forth theme-based visual narratives generally rooted in his personal attributes. Much of the Instagram content reviewed in the Canadian studies[24] showed him fulfilling his ministerial responsibilities and reasserting the importance of inclusiveness and progressive values. As party leader and vanguard social media user, Trudeau has influenced how other Canadian party leaders and candidates are turning to social media for personal identity construction, especially in local politics.

Fifth, research indicates that political personalization in local campaigns can lead members of the public to focus more on individual politicians and less on political parties, political and policy issues, and institutions. Furthermore, it is fuelling interest in politicians' private lives since non-political traits have gained importance in influencing how voters evaluate political candidacies. Strategies of communication centred on depicting political actors as both "virtuous experts" and "close to the people" help to boost politicians' credibility and authenticity. These strategies revolve around three aspects of a candidate's profile: personality, political and professional skills, and commitment to specific political and policy issues.[25] These elements can be used simultaneously when developing the public image of a candidate, both online and offline.

Behind the Scenes

In this section, we look at the personalization campaign of Martin Francoeur, the Liberal candidate in the hotly contested riding of Trois-Rivières in Quebec. We draw from the participant observations of one of the authors and from a review of the candidate's social media activities. Prior to winning the Liberal nomination, Francoeur was a journalist and editorialist for twenty-seven years at the local daily newspaper, *Le Nouvelliste,* well known among the local population. In many ways, this positioned him as a star candidate. Francoeur faced three other candidates with high profiles in the Trois-Rivières community: René Villemure, an ethician who ran for the Bloc Québécois; Yves Lévesque, the former mayor of Trois-Rivières and former Conservative Party nominee; and Adis Simidzija, the New Democratic Party candidate and well-known community worker. Villemure was declared the winner of the electoral contest by fewer than 100 votes following a judicial recount,[26] and Francoeur ranked third.

It was not the first time that Francoeur was courted to run for the Liberals. Minister François-Philippe Champagne, MP of the riding of St-Maurice-Champlain and a close friend of Francoeur, had asked him to run three times before he agreed in 2021. Prior to becoming a candidate, Francoeur had discussions with influential members of the federal Liberals in Quebec, including Pablo Rodriguez and Mélanie Joly. They insisted on his participation in the electoral race, stating how important it was for the region and the party.

Francoeur could be seen as an ideal candidate for the Liberals. On the one hand, he was a well-known local public figure who had an informed understanding of political and policy matters of importance to the Trois-Rivières community. He had covered current political events extensively during his years at Le Nouvelliste and, to some degree, could be seen as part of the local political elite. Being a journalist, he also possessed communication skills transferable to the political realm. The Liberals liked the fact that he was a person of conviction who could mobilize citizens for or against community projects. On the other hand, Francoeur had strong ties to the region since he was born and raised in Trois-Rivières, and after his law studies at McGill University he returned to Trois-Rivières to work for Le Nouvelliste. All of these elements made him easy to promote locally. His candidacy was in line with the principles of local candidate recruitment discussed earlier.[27]

How were principles of political personalization leveraged by Francoeur's team during the campaign? What role did the party play in helping to promote his candidacy and shape his narrative? Soon after the writ dropped, Francoeur executed a communication campaign relying heavily on his professional ethos. His career in journalism coupled with his standing in the Trois-Rivières

FIGURE 6.1 Candidates René Villemure of the Bloc Québécois and Martin Francoeur of the Liberal Party crossing paths while posting signs in Trois-Rivières

Source: Martin Francoeur's Instagram account.

community allowed him to present himself as someone credible and ready for elected office. Although his team planned several outreach efforts to showcase his qualities, many were developed at the last minute because of unforeseen circumstances. In the early days of the campaign, Francoeur crossed paths with Villemure, the Bloc Québécois candidate, while putting up campaign signs. Francoeur's social media organizer took a picture of the encounter and shared it on Francoeur's social media feeds to portray the candidate as respectful and cordial toward his political opponent (see Figure 6.1). On top of being one of his most popular posts during the campaign, it helped Francoeur to garner positive coverage from local news media outlets.

Members of his communication team thought that it was important to portray Francoeur in a positive light both online and offline. As the campaign became more negative at the national level, with party leaders levelling attacks at each other, his team doubled down and remained positive until and after election day. Justin Trudeau and other star Liberal candidates, such as Mélanie Joly, were used as models when creating and sharing posts on Francoeur's social media feeds. His team used similar visuals to replicate the Liberal Party's values of multiculturalism, multi-generationalism, and family interests but adapted them to the reality of the Trois-Rivières riding. For instance, photographs of Francoeur interacting with elderly citizens at the Service d'accueil des nouveaux arrivants, an organization welcoming immigrants to the Trois-Rivières region, were posted on Instagram. His commitment to working on reconciliation with Indigenous peoples was showcased in Instagram posts showing Francoeur visiting the Centre d'amitié autochthone de Trois-Rivières and interacting with local Indigenous leaders of the centre. Expressing his sadness about the difficulties of following through with reconciliation with Indigenous communities in an Instagram post helped him to portray himself as the only candidate who took the time to meet local Indigenous stakeholders in Trois-Rivières. Finally, Francoeur shared a picture of himself taking part in a public march for women's safety to showcase his support for another important segment of the local electorate. His social media organizer noted that these posts and accompanying captions were inspired by Trudeau's approach to social media politicking. Reproducing how the party leader projected his power and qualities was seen as a way to repackage the party philosophy for local messaging and outreach, and being coherent with how the national party was going about political campaigning was important to the local team.

Francoeur emulated Trudeau's social media aesthetics to convey the image of an open and hard-working candidate dedicated to the well-being of the local population. These qualities were presented using a wide range of content, including visuals, texts, and videos. Vox populi was also shared through social media to give a more interactional dimension to his campaign communications and share carefully selected citizen perspectives on the candidate. Much like Trudeau, Francoeur posted to Instagram pictures featuring him smiling, conversing with citizens of all ages, delivering speeches, or engaging with other candidates during campaign events. In Instagram posts in which he was shown in one-on-one meetings with community leaders, he had an open body posture, was listening attentively to his interlocutors, and was taking notes in a notebook. These visuals framed him engaging with and learning from members of the community.

To design potent political messages, Francoeur's team was provided with the Green Fly application by the Liberal Party. It gave the team access to pre-packaged infographics and banners that could be used for building messages for local audiences. The technology allowed the team to personalize his voter outreach efforts while staying true to the party's broader campaign philosophy. This application was used mostly when creating Instagram stories. However, Francoeur's social media organizer leveraged Instagram's distinct properties when sharing posts targeting specific local audiences. One important aspect was portraying the candidate as having a comprehensive and up-to-date understanding of local issues. Francoeur wanted to be perceived as a *hyper-local* candidate. His modest origins from Bas-du-Cap, a poorer and neglected section of Trois-Rivières, were used as a symbol of social mobility. This enabled him to present himself as being aware of the struggles affecting many residents. More broadly, the approach replicated many facets of Trudeau's strategy on social media. The importance of Francoeur's rootedness in the community was aligned with principles of political personalization at the local level discussed previously.[28]

The Liberal candidate raised several localized issues throughout the campaign. Among them was developing a better housing environment for seniors near the St-Maurice River, engaging in more positive and productive ways with local Indigenous peoples and other minority and marginalized communities, and providing a more welcoming environment for immigrants. Francoeur threw his support behind regional development initiatives that contributed to the development of the city. For example, he pledged to support the development of the Port of Trois-Rivières and the Notre-Dame-du-Cap sanctuary, a significant religious tourist attraction. He also declared his support for funding the Institut de recherche sur l'hydrogène at the Université du Québec à Trois-Rivières (Figure 6.2) and its mission to research renewable energy.

A broader analysis of Francoeur's social media activities throughout the campaign offers findings in line with those of studies that

FIGURE 6.2 Candidate Martin Francoeur promoting new environmental approaches during the 2021 electoral campaign with the Institut de recherche sur l'hydrogène at the Université du Québec à Trois-Rivières

Source: Martin Francoeur's Instagram account.

have examined Trudeau's uses of social media for politicking.[29] Instagram posts often featured Francoeur expressing positive emotions that helped to humanize the candidate and put forth identity cues valued by many voters, including approachability, relatability, and empathy. He presented himself as someone who cared about regional issues and all segments of the Trois-Rivières community, from young families to elderly voters and businesspeople. On certain occasions, he opened up and offered insights into his private life, including his relationship with his same-sex partner. Some social media posts showed Francoeur and his partner canvassing Trois-Rivières neighbourhoods and conversing with citizens. This was in line with broader Liberal values and campaign messages. His personal life[30] was leveraged not to highlight qualities or competencies but to humanize Francoeur in the eyes of his supporters and the public in ways that could help him to expand his appeal and his base of support.

Pictures of local events featuring star Liberal candidates and ministers – including Trudeau, Champagne, Joly, and Steven

FIGURE 6.3 Candidates Martin Francoeur and Mélanie Joly in discussion in Trois-Rivières during her visit to the electoral district

Source: Martin Francoeur's Instagram account.

Guilbeault (Figure 6.3) and the crowds that they drew to the city – were also shared on Instagram. This allowed Francoeur to present himself as a candidate with broad and indefectible support within the Liberal Party. To some degree, it gave the sense that he was on the path to electoral success, particularly given that party leaders rarely make time during electoral campaigns to visit ridings perceived as unwinnable. He was presented not only as a regional leader but also as a competent candidate who could play an instrumental role on the national stage.

Early in the campaign, Francoeur's past professional activities were used by his opponents to delegitimize his public image. For example, some of his work as a *Le Nouvelliste* editorialist was evoked to attack his candidacy given that two of his articles were highly critical of Liberal Party members. One discussed the We Charity scandal and portrayed Trudeau in a negative way, whereas the other took interest in Freeland's international free-trade position, and both were used to present Francoeur as inauthentic and incoherent since he was now seeking office under the Liberal banner and its leader. In the heat of the campaign and to counter the narrative, his team pointed out that Trudeau had been cleared of any wrongdoing and that no charges had been filed.[31] In many ways, these attacks can be seen as the downside of local fame: Trudeau's past activities were used against Francoeur. This highlights that political personalization can be used to undermine a candidate. Some Liberal Party members questioned whether such editorials could derail a local campaign and lead a candidate to leave the electoral race. The party had vetted most of Francoeur's journalistic work prior to the election. As a whole, his work for *Le Nouvelliste* showed that Francoeur had a sound critical mind, was able to take into account all opinions, could foster constructive debates, and, from a broader perspective, constituted an asset for the Liberals. However, it was determined that some of his editorials focusing on narrow issues could be used to delegitimize his candidacy. The party was more worried about traditional media coverage of his previous work in *Le Nouvelliste* and tried to control the message and see whether other editorials could damage the candidate's reputation. Indeed, traditional media play an important role in the day-to-day dynamics of the electoral campaign.

Principles of political personalization at the local level were informed by the broader Liberal values and philosophy in a centralized fashion. Trudeau[32] and other star candidates' social media practices were replicated by Francoeur in order to stay on message. Although he was able to infuse personal and professional elements into his campaign communications, he still followed the Liberal model of political personalization that enabled him to put forth a message that did not clash with other local candidates' messages and the party leader's national campaign.

Conclusion

This chapter has highlighted how national strategies of political personalization are borrowed and implemented at the local level in order to emphasize specific candidate characteristics in line with the national political campaign. These characteristics also tend to be valued by the electorate when assessing politicians. The ethos of a local candidate is as important as that of a national candidate. As mentioned earlier, the ethos is related to the image management practices used by party leaders and candidates in local races. Much scholarly research indicates that local candidates tend to put forth a more professional ethos in their voter outreach and campaign communication.[33] However, they still offer insights into some aspects of their personal lives, including sports and hobbies, religion, as well as marital and family status.[34] The local candidate whom we studied followed this blueprint for political personalization. For the most part, the strategies of personalization used to shape his approach to local campaigning both online and offline focused on his professional profile. He was presented as a candidate with deep ties to the Trois-Rivières region and knowledgeable about local institutions as well as political and policy matters.

Martin Francoeur's approach to personalization was deeply rooted in the Liberal Party approach to messaging and political campaigning. Although party discipline and the ideas put forward in the electoral platform were important, much leeway was given to campaign communication at the local level. Francoeur and his team could choose the issues to discuss in their local voter outreach efforts and how to present them as long as they fit the party's overall philosophy. His social media posts were sometimes approved by party officials, but they were never censored. The Liberal Party philosophy was presented in positive ways and with a twist to suit Francoeur's public image in the Trois-Rivières region. From the start, the candidate and his communication staff wanted to engage in a positive campaign and stay clear of political attacks on opponents. Over the course of the campaign, the team noticed that the national campaign turned negative – especially when polls tightened – but locally the candidate stayed the course with positive messaging. He did so by following Trudeau's and other star candidates' lead. Indeed, those candidates deployed largely positive social media-based political voter outreach and engagement.

From a broader perspective, there was a standardization of personalization strategies used during the campaign in order to convey targeted messages, make the candidates politically appealing and electable, display their insider status, and show their connections with voters at the local level. Inspired by the party leader, Francoeur turned to still images and textual content on Instagram – and other social media platforms such as Twitter – to showcase in a positive and constructive fashion his personality and commitment to voters.[35] His professional profile and qualities were integral elements of all his public communication efforts.

By shedding light on how political personalization is operationalized at the local level, we have explored aspects of political campaigning that deserve more attention in the scholarly literature. There are standardized ways in which candidate personalization is done, such as by emphasizing certain qualities of the candidate, making visible certain actions during the day-to-day campaign, and showing his deep roots in local communities. Some research[36] shows that these strategies are used independently of party affiliation and type of political campaign. Local candidates and their teams have some freedom when personalizing their public images and selecting the political and policy issues at the core of their local messages. However, they still need to deal with local news media organizations and community-based social media users that can affect – at any time – this narrative and force politicians to rethink both their images and their messages. Building upon the case study presented in this chapter, it would be of interest to conduct comparative analyses of how political personalization is used by candidates who compete in specific local political contexts across Canada. Indeed, regional, partisan, cultural, and linguistic factors are likely to affect how it manifests itself in voter outreach and engagement. Furthermore, it would be of interest to expand the understanding of how candidates' socio-demographic profiles can affect their ability to connect with members of the public, especially for candidates from minority or marginalized communities.

Notes

1 Corner and Pels, *Media and the Restyling of Politics;* Van Zoonen, "The Personal, the Political and the Popular."
2 See Carty, "Parties as Franchise Systems."
3 Strömbäck and Van Aelst, "Why Political Parties Adapt to the Media."
4 Chadwick, *The Hybrid Media System.*

5 Strömbäck, "Four Phases of Mediatization."
6 King, "Do Leaders' Personalities Really Matter?"; Bittner, *Platform or Personality?*
7 King, "Do Leaders' Personalities Really Matter?"; Bittner, *Platform or Personality?*
8 Arbour, *Candidate-Centered Campaigns.*
9 For Canadian examples, see Lalancette and Raynauld, "Politicking and Visual Framing on Instagram"; Lalancette and Raynauld, "The Power of Political Image"; Lalancette and Tourigny-Koné, "*24 Seven* Video-style"; and Remillard, Bertrand, and Fisher, "The Visually Viral Prime Minister."
10 Arnesen, Duell, and Johannesson, "Do Citizens Make Inferences?"
11 McGregor, Lawrence, and Cardona, "Personalization, Gender and Social Media."
12 Marland, "Strategic Management of Media Relations."
13 Lewis, Lalancette, and Raynauld, "Cabinet Solidarity in an Age of Social Media."
14 Marland and Wagner, "Scripted Messengers."
15 Hermans and Vergeer, "Personalization in E-Campaigning."
16 Stanyer, "Elected Representatives."
17 Lalancette, "Les 'web-mises en scène' des candidats."
18 For example, see the work of Arbour, *Candidate-Centered Campaigns.*
19 Bittner, *Platform or Personality?*
20 Lalancette, "Les 'web-mises en scène' des candidats."
21 Pruysers and Cross, "Candidate Selection in Canada."
22 Lalancette and Raynauld, "Politicking and Visual Framing on Instagram"; Lalancette and Raynauld, "The Power of Political Image"; Raynauld and Lalancette, "Pictures, Filters, and Politics."
23 King, "Do Leaders' Personalities Really Matter?"
24 Lalancette and Raynauld, "Politicking and Visual Framing on Instagram"; Lalancette and Raynauld, "The Power of Political Image"; Raynauld and Lalancette, "Pictures, Filters, and Politics."
25 Arbour, *Candidate-Centered Campaigns.*
26 Houle, "Trois-Rivières."
27 Pruysers and Cross, "Candidate Selection in Canada."
28 Koop and Marland, "Insiders and Outsiders"; Lalancette, "Les 'web-mises en scène' des candidats."
29 Lalancette and Raynauld, "Politicking and Visual Framing on Instagram"; Lalancette and Raynauld, "The Power of Political Image"; Raynauld and Lalancette, "Pictures, Filters, and Politics."

30 His partner welcomed Radio-Canada's request to profile candidates' spouses. The portrait painted by the journalist was fair, and he was treated as any other spouse featured in the article. There was not any LGBTQ claim or advocacy.

31 Dion, *Trudeau III Report*.

32 Lalancette and Raynauld, "Politicking and Visual Framing on Instagram"; Lalancette and Raynauld, "The Power of Political Image"; Raynauld and Lalancette, "Pictures, Filters, and Politics."

33 Hermans and Vergeer, "Personalization in E-Campaigning."

34 Ibid.

35 Lalancette and Raynauld, "The Power of Political Image."

36 Lalancette, "Les 'web-mises en scène' des candidats."

Bibliography

Arbour, Brian. *Candidate-Centered Campaigns: Political Messages, Winning Personalities, and Personal Appeals*. New York: Palgrave Macmillan, 2014.

Arnesen, Sveinung, Dominik Duell, and Mikael Poul Johannesson. "Do Citizens Make Inferences from Political Candidate Characteristics When Aiming for Substantive Representation?" *Electoral Studies* 57 (2019): 46–60.

Bittner, Amanda. *Platform or Personality? The Role of Party Leaders in Elections*. Oxford: Oxford University Press, 2011.

Carty, Roland Kenneth. "Parties as Franchise Systems: The Stratarchical Organizational Imperative." *Party Politics* 10, 1 (2004): 5–24.

Chadwick, Andrew. *The Hybrid Media System: Politics and Power*. Oxford: Oxford University Press, 2017.

Corner, John, and Dick Pels. *Media and the Restyling of Politics: Consumerism, Celebrity and Cynicism*. London: SAGE, 2003.

Dion, Mario. *Trudeau III Report 2021*. Ottawa: Office of the Conflict of Interest and Ethics Commissioner, Parliament of Canada, 2021. https://ciec-ccie.parl.gc.ca/en/publications/Documents/InvestigationReports/Trudeau%20III%20Report.pdf.

Hermans, Liesbeth, and Maurice Vergeer. "Personalization in E-Campaigning: A Cross-National Comparison of Personalization Strategies Used on Candidate Websites of 17 Countries in EP Elections 2009." *New Media Society* 15, 1 (2013): 72–92.

Houle, Sébastien. "Trois-Rivières: Courte victoire de Villemure, Lévesque évoque un recomptage." *Le Nouvelliste,* 22 septembre 2021. https://www.lenouvelliste.ca/2021/09/22/trois-rivieres-courte-victoire-de-villemure-levesque-evoque-un-recomptage-24792da8475f123a1c5541550af38eca.

King, Anthony. "Do Leaders' Personalities Really Matter?" In *Leaders' Personalities and the Outcomes of Democratic Elections,* edited by Anthony King, 1–43. Oxford: Oxford University Press, 2002.

Koop, Royce, and Alex Marland. "Insiders and Outsiders: Presentation of Self on Canadian Parliamentary Websites and Newsletters." *Policy and Internet* 4, 3–4 (2012): 112–35.

Lalancette, Mireille. "Les 'web-mises en scène' des candidats aux élections québécoises de 2012: Entre discrétion et confession." *Politique et sociétés* 37, 2 (2018): 47–81.

Lalancette, Mireille, and Vincent Raynauld. "Politicking and Visual Framing on Instagram: A Look at the Portrayal of the Leadership of Canada's Justin Trudeau." *Canadian Studies* 89 (2020): 257–90.

–. "The Power of Political Image: Justin Trudeau, Instagram, and Celebrity Politics." *American Behavioral Scientist* 63, 7 (2019): 888–924.

Lalancette, Mireille, and Sofia Tourigny-Koné. "*24 Seven* Videostyle: Blurring the Lines and Building Strong Leadership." In *Permanent Campaigning in Canada,* edited by Alex Marland, Thierry Giasson, and Anna Lennox Esselment, 259–77. Vancouver: UBC Press, 2017.

Lewis, J.P., Mireille Lalancette, and Vincent Raynauld. "Cabinet Solidarity in an Age of Social Media: A Case Study of Twitter Use by Member of Parliament Carolyn Bennett." In *What's Trending in Canadian Politics? Understanding Transformations in Power, Media, and the Public Sphere,* edited by Mireille Lalancette, Vincent Raynauld, and Erin Crandall, 170–93. Vancouver: UBC Press, 2019.

Marland, Alex. "Strategic Management of Media Relations: Communications Centralization and Spin in the Government of Canada." *Canadian Public Policy* 43, 1 (2017): 36–49.

Marland, Alex, and Angelia Wagner. "Scripted Messengers: How Party Discipline and Branding Turn Election Candidates and Legislators into Brand Ambassadors." *Journal of Political Marketing* 19, 1–2 (2020): 54–73.

McGregor, Shannon C., Regina G. Lawrence, and Arielle Cardona. "Personalization, Gender and Social Media: Gubernatorial Candidates' Social Media Strategies." *Information, Communication and Society* 20, 2 (2017): 264–83.

Pruysers, Scott, and William Cross. "Candidate Selection in Canada: Local Autonomy, Centralization, and Competing Democratic Norms." *American Behavioral Scientist* 60, 7 (2016): 781–98.

Raynauld, Vincent, and Mireille Lalancette. "Pictures, Filters, and Politics: Instagram's Role in Political Image-Making and Storytelling in Canada." *Visual Communication Quarterly* 28, 4 (2021): 212–26.

Remillard, Chaseten, Lindsey M. Bertrand, and Alina Fisher. "The Visually Viral Prime Minister: Justin Trudeau, Selfies, and Instagram." In *Power Shift? Political Leadership and Social Media,* edited by Richard Davis and David Taras, 49–62. London: Routledge, 2020.

Stanyer, James. "Elected Representatives, Online Self-Presentation and the Personal Vote: Party, Personality and Webstyles in the United States and United Kingdom." *Information, Community and Society* 11, 3 (2008): 414–32.

Strömbäck, Jesper. "Four Phases of Mediatization: An Analysis of the Mediatization of Politics." *International Journal of Press/Politics* 13, 3 (2008): 228–46.

Strömbäck, Jesper, and Peter Van Aelst. "Why Political Parties Adapt to the Media: Exploring the Fourth Dimension of Mediatization." *International Communication Gazette* 75, 4 (2013): 341–58.

Van Zoonen, Liesbet. "The Personal, the Political and the Popular: A Women's Guide to Celebrity Politics." *European Journal of Cultural Studies* 9, 3 (2006): 287–301.

PART 2
Campaign Management and Campaigning

7

Regional Campaign Directors

Jared Wesley and Richard Maksymetz

Abstract   Regional campaign directors are the linchpins of modern federal election campaigns in Canada. They connect the national headquarters to dozens of local campaign organizations, and their success in recruiting candidates, relaying intelligence, and coordinating leader's tour stops reflects directly on the party as a whole. In this chapter, we explore the challenges faced by these often faceless and thankless party operatives. Despite the centralization and professionalization of modern party politics, and the intense focus on the national "air war" and local "ground wars," regional campaign directors are responsible for translating broad objectives into measurable gains in ridings across the country.

Résumé   Les directeurs de campagne régionaux sont les clés de voûtes des campagnes électorales fédérales modernes au Canada. Ils relient la cellule de crise nationale à des douzaines d'organisations de campagne locales, et leur succès dans le recrutement de candidats, la transmission de renseignements, et la coordination des arrêts de la tournée des chefs se reflète directement sur le parti dans son ensemble. Dans ce chapitre, nous explorons les défis auxquels sont confrontés ces agents du parti, souvent sans visage et ingrats. Malgré la centralisation et la professionnalisation de la politique moderne du parti, et l'accent mis sur la « guerre des ondes » nationale et les « guerres de terrain » locales, les directeurs de campagne régionaux sont chargés de traduire les grands objectifs en gains mesurables dans les circonscriptions du pays.

REGIONAL CAMPAIGN DIRECTORS fulfill an important intermediary role in modern Canadian campaign organizations. Responsible for connecting the national party headquarters to the hundreds of candidates and thousands of volunteers in the field, they foster crucial linkages between the "air" and "ground" campaigns. They are often in charge of sizable campaign budgets, have substantial control over recruiting candidates and local campaign teams, feed information back to the central party organizers, and have influence over the strategies and tactics deployed in their regions. Without regional campaign directors, national campaigns would lack the local intelligence and coordination necessary to compete in coastto-coast elections. They would struggle to form full slates of credible candidates and organize effective events on the leader's tour. Left to their own devices, local campaigns would be further marginalized from the centre. In short, modern Canadian election campaigns would look very different without regional campaign directors.

These directors go by many names (e.g., regional campaign managers, regional campaign chairs, provincial field directors), and their authority and territory vary from party to party. Some have responsibility for all of Atlantic Canada, for example, whereas others are in charge of the campaign in a particular province or large city. Depending on the party, some regional campaign directors have often worked closely with provincial or party campaign chairs – often current or former MPs and senators appointed by the party leader to serve as spokespeople and rally forces in particular parts of the country. Overall, the role of regional campaign chairs has waxed and waned over time, reflecting broader shifts in the nature of party competition and innovations in communication and transportation.

In the first fifty years of Confederation, party politics in Canada was highly regionalized. Indeed, the country's first nationwide election did not take place until near the turn of the twentieth century. Up to that point, federal elections consisted of a couple hundred local contests without much coordination by central party organizations.[1] In this early atmosphere, party elites recruited local notables to run under their party's banner. In some cases, party leaders undertook this task themselves, supported by a small cadre of well-heeled donors.[2]

Over time, the role of chief recruiter came to be filled by provincial lieutenants. These Members of Parliament, premiers, and provincial legislators served as primary advisers to the leader on matters of importance to their regions while also controlling the flow of patronage to their respective parts of the country. During elections, such regional campaign chairs were the faces of their party for most voters since national leaders were unable (or unwilling) to venture into many parts of Canada.

Regional lieutenants grew in stature from the interwar period through the 1950s. Titans such as Ernest Lapointe, William Lyon Mackenzie King's Quebec lieutenant, assumed key roles as regional ministers when their parties were in government and regional caucus chairs when they were in opposition.[3] Lieutenants also took on leadership roles during federal election campaigns, developing strategy, recruiting candidates, drafting regional policy platforms, and securing and deploying resources. On occasion, national party leaders would lean on premiers to fill the role. Progressive Conservative leaders relied heavily on Ontario premiers John Robarts and Bill Davis during federal campaigns, for instance, just as the federal Liberals depended on the support of Premier Joey Smallwood in Newfoundland and Premier Ross Thatcher in Saskatchewan. Whether given the title of formal lieutenant or not, these regional power brokers played a big role in federal elections.

Communication and transportation networks remained highly regionalized during this early period, allowing the national Conservative and Liberal Parties to run region-specific campaigns against a growing number of regional parties, such as the Cooperative Commonwealth Federation and Social Credit. This changed with the advent of broadcast television and air travel, which focused most of the attention on the leader and encouraged national parties to run Canada-wide campaigns. Beginning in the 1960s, the Progressive Conservatives and Liberals positioned themselves as regional brokerage parties. This meant stitching together broad coalitions of voters across regional divides rather than waging

vastly different campaigns in various parts of the country.[4] This
shift in approach altered the role of regional campaign chairs, whose
responsibility it became to host the leader on tours of their regions
and feed provincial interests into the national strategy. The gradual
separation of provincial and federal party organizations also loosened the ties between federal party leaders and their provincial
counterparts,[5] though activists remained shared between levels.[6]
No longer the sole faces of the party in their home provinces,
regional ministers, caucus chairs, and provincial party leaders faded
into the background somewhat over the twentieth century as federal party leaders grew in prominence.

At the same time, national parties began to develop organizational structures outside Parliament.[7] Up to the mid-twentieth
century, the caucus was virtually synonymous with the party. With
the advent of mass party organizations such as the Cooperative
Commonwealth Federation and Social Credit, all parties began
building national associations consisting of non-politicians – mostly
volunteers, members, and some paid staff. Regional representation became embedded in these new organizations with the election
or appointment of regional vice-presidents and heads of provincial/
territorial associations. Between federal elections, these individuals
helped to develop party policy and recruit members and donors.
During elections, they were led by a regional campaign chair –
typically a high-ranking politician or an established party figure
– in executing the party's "ground game" by recruiting candidates,
raising money, and marshalling volunteers. The national campaign
became increasingly professionalized and centralized around the
leader over this period, however, reducing the role of regional
campaign chairs in developing and executing the much more visible
"air war" on television.[8]

In the closing decades of the twentieth century, the prominence
of regional campaign directors as leading figures in the national
campaign team declined for a variety of interrelated reasons. The
continued consolidation of power in the leaders' office eliminated
the regional fiefdoms that characterized earlier periods in Canadian
history. By the turn of the twenty-first century, political parties had
come to resemble franchise organizations, with significant control

wielded by the central headquarters and regional/local organizers reduced to executing strategies developed by national party officials.[9] At the same time, the growing professionalization of the campaign team elevated the importance of pollsters and marketing specialists relative to regional network builders and power brokers. The shift from regional brokerage toward non-geographic forms of voter segmentation lessened the need to rely on regional expertise or framing.

As with the demise of regional ministers over the same period, the relegation of regional campaign directors resulted in parties assuming an hourglass shape, with power concentrated at the top in the leader's office and central party headquarters and resources concentrated at the bottom among members, donors, volunteers, and voters.[10] Central party organizations could now work directly with lower parts of the organizational hierarchy to raise money, recruit candidates, mobilize volunteers, and develop policy (see Chapter 8 of this volume).[11] Party databases and internal polling gave headquarters more intelligence about local races than regional and district leaders, with the latter becoming increasingly dependent on the national campaign for resources and information.[12] Indeed, internal polling is closely guarded, and regional campaign directors are seldom given direct access to it. Regional lieutenants and campaign directors, once integral to the party's success, have been gradually squeezed out of the middle. Nonetheless, they remain an important conduit for the two-way flow of messages from the headquarters to the ground and vice versa.

Rather than developing strategy and taking a leadership role in the campaign in their parts of the country, regional directors today tend to implement the national strategy as developed by the central party organization and feed information back to the top about how well the local groups are meeting the targets set by the centre. These targets can include reaching candidate or fundraising quotas or obtaining attitudinal data from door-to-door canvassing. Regional directors play a key organizational role in the overall success of the party. Particularly in close elections, in which control of Parliament rests on a handful of battleground constituencies, regional directors are integral in persuading accessible voters and getting out the vote.[13]

Local Trends

During an election campaign, the regional campaign director has three principal responsibilities: first, to ensure that the party has a full slate of credible, vetted candidates across the region; second, to act as a conduit for communication between the local campaign organizations and the central party headquarters; and third, to help design, organize, and orchestrate regional stops by the leader's tour.

Regional campaign directors lead efforts to recruit, vet, and on occasion replace their parties' candidates for office (see also in this volume Chapter 3 on candidate nomination processes). This work spills into the writ period, especially in the case of snap elections like the one in 2021. When the writs were dropped on 15 August, no party had a full slate of candidates. Of the major national parties, the Conservatives led the way with 90 percent of their candidates in place, followed by the Liberals (84 percent), New Democrats (62 percent), and Greens (41 percent). The Bloc Québécois had candidates in all but three ridings in Quebec.[14] Recruiting candidates and getting them onto the ballot occupy most of the regional director's attention for the first two weeks of the campaign leading up to the nomination deadline.

The regional campaign director's work has significant implications for the party's image. Having a full slate of candidates is an indication of the health of the political party in a given region. A great local candidate can add a few percentage points to the popular vote, above and beyond the central campaign. A poor local candidate can drag down a regional or national campaign, pulling the party off message to address local controversies. Thus, regional campaign directors are responsible not only for identifying people willing to carry the party banner but also for ensuring that those people will not cause embarrassment to the party because of their previous affiliations, social media posts, or other evidence of an unsavoury past. "Bozo eruptions" can result in parties stripping certain candidates of their nominations, provided that the timing of the controversies is prior to the mid-campaign nomination deadline. Researchers in the central campaign headquarters often will dig up dirt on their opponents, reserving disclosure of any harmful revelations until the point at which their rivals cannot remove the party label from a damaged candidate. Nine candidates were removed from their parties' slates during the campaign in 2019 – from each of the top four parties. In 2021, this number decreased to five, including one Liberal and one Conservative, both because of allegations of sexual misconduct; another Conservative over Islamophobic tweets; and two New Democrats whose online comments were deemed anti-Semitic by NDP officials. In all of these cases, the parties were unable to replace their candidates before the election.

This is why regional campaign directors work closely with local electoral district associations (EDAs) and campaign managers to recruit and vet quality candidates for party nomination contests. The regional campaign director plays various roles depending on the specific riding in play. This is where pre-writ seat triage becomes important,[15] helping the party to identify which type of candidate to recruit.[16] In a riding where the party has a willing and popular incumbent, the process is typically straightforward; as Anna Lennox Esselment and Matthew Bondy note in Chapter 3 of this volume, such a nomination is seldom contested. In a winnable riding where there is no incumbent, the regional campaign director works with the EDA to find a star candidate or local notable – someone with name recognition in the community and a strong fundraising network. For these reasons, successful politicians at other levels of government are prime targets for recruitment. When the Liberal Party looked to build support in the Prairies in 2015, for example, it recruited former Members of Legislative Assemblies and municipal councillors. Ten of the twelve Liberals elected in the region had this sort of background. The leader's office is often directly involved in cajoling these politicians into joining the party ticket. In areas where a party has been strong historically – such as the Conservatives in western Canada or the Liberals in central and eastern Canada – the regional campaign director can play a role in coordinating a longer-term, "farm team" approach to developing federal candidates. This involves encouraging up-and-coming politicians to run in local or provincial elections as a precursor to seeking the federal nomination.

The second tier of ridings is often the most difficult type for regional campaign directors to fill – those that are marginally within reach of victory for the party. These ridings are typically identified by polls and previous election results that suggest the party is within 5 to 9 percentage points of the frontrunner. These seats are out of reach unless a sudden local controversy or national wave of support propels the party's candidate past the favoured opponent. Local notables and star candidates are unlikely to put their names forward for the party's nomination given the risk involved. Regional campaign directors and local EDAs often struggle to find strong candidates as a result.

The final tier of ridings – the non-winnable seats – involves a different type of recruitment. Rather than looking for stars, the focus shifts to avoiding embarrassment. Strong vetting will ensure that these stopgap candidates have clean financial and criminal records as well as pristine digital footprints on social media. Central party organizers offer some help in scrubbing social media accounts. As important as having a full slate is to the national image of the party, there is little that the central campaign can or will do to assist with the candidate recruitment process in these difficult ridings. With spending caps and donation limits, campaign resources are limited. Parties spend most on winnable ridings, leaving regional and local campaigns to support marginal and unwinnable seats to the best of their ability. This is particularly true since per-vote subsidies (funds provided to parties based upon how many votes they receive) have been eliminated, which used to give central party organizers some incentive to build support in traditionally unwinnable regions.

Beyond candidate recruitment, regional campaign directors serve as key intermediaries between local and national campaigns. In Chapter 8 (of this volume) on campaign managers, Royce Koop and Anthony Sayers refer to this as "managing outward." A big part of this involves tracking resources, including monitoring the revenues and expenditures of local EDAs. On occasion, EDAs can encounter challenges in raising funds to support the local candidate; in others, they might be reluctant to spend funds on a parachute candidate or someone whom they think will fare poorly in the general election, preferring to preserve the war chest for another campaign. Although some parties, such as the Liberals, have developed databases that allow central party organizers to track the finances of EDAs, historically this role fell to regional campaign directors who conveyed local financial information to the central party and then carried out a central directive to spend or raise more. At times, such conversations would involve incentives and disincentives for compliance. Leader's tour stops could be raised in the negotiations. EDAs typically bristle at this sort of control, viewing it as meddling from Ottawa. As discussed below, regional campaign directors encounter similar push back when they broach other resource issues, including the distribution of volunteers in the closing weeks of the campaign.

Regional campaign directors play a limited role in defining the shape of the national strategy. Designed at the centre, regional campaigns tend to be distinguished by unique expressions of policy priorities by leading political personalities. Although some parties title portions of their platforms after specific regions – such as the Conservatives' "Contract with Quebec" in 2021 – regional campaigns are based most often upon different issue clusters.[17] The environmental planks of party platforms are likely to receive more attention in British Columbia and Quebec, for instance, and parties might emphasize seniors' issues to a greater extent in Atlantic Canada, where the median age of the population is higher. During the writ period, the regional campaign director and local candidates feed those priorities that they hear at doorsteps into central decision making. Combined with public opinion data, this intelligence helps the policy and communication teams to adjust messaging as necessary.

A well-functioning national campaign engages the various regional directors in this sort of strategizing. Without an integrated approach, parties can risk highlighting priorities in one part of the country that turn off voters in another part. Sometimes this can be intentional, particularly when a party is looking to shore up support in one region while downgrading its prospects in another region. At other times, heightened inter-regional tensions might be unavoidable or unintended. The Conservative Party's decision to embrace carbon pricing as part of its platform in 2021 signalled its willingness to trade the support of some of its massive anti-tax base in western Canada for an opportunity to gain traction in seat-rich Ontario.[18] In the same campaign, the NDP's pledge to end subsidies to oil and gas companies played to its environmentalist base while alienating many supporters in oil-producing provinces such as Alberta and Saskatchewan.[19] Announcements of these policy promises are made in regions where they are popular, with other parts of the platform being highlighted in different parts of the country. As a result, regional campaigns seldom feature great debates between two or more parties about the same issue. Instead, the campaigns resemble ships passing in the night, each emphasizing its unique sets of priorities while trying to avoid being drawn into conflict over another party's preferred issues.[20] The Conservatives wanted to avoid talking about their environmental platform in the West in 2021, for instance, hoping to keep attention focused on things such as economic development.

This is where the leader's tour becomes so important. Regional campaign directors have considerable responsibility for working with the leader's advance team to identify ideal locations for the staging of events. On the ground, the regional director often drives the advance team around in search of venues that align with the chosen messaging – in terms of both backdrop and guests' affinity for the party. This alignment is crucial. Confrontations between Trudeau and violent protesters at various campaign stops illustrate the importance of staging and security. They can also help the party to avoid embarrassment. When the NDP held a campaign event in 2021 with First Nations chiefs from northern Manitoba, the party failed to anticipate that the chiefs would use the opportunity to endorse publicly an Indigenous Liberal candidate instead of the New Democratic candidate. In-depth work by the regional campaign director can help the leader to avoid such gaffes.

Once the location is set, the regional campaign director is charged with filling the location with supportive audience members. This involves calling local campaign teams to send volunteers to attend rally events or to serve as background extras in main street photo ops (e.g., as customers in restaurants). Convincing local campaign managers and volunteers that their time is better spent boosting the leader's tour stop than door knocking can be a hard sell. But it is a necessary part of the campaign given that the national headquarters has neither the time nor the contacts to set up the regional events themselves.

Behind the Scenes

In analyzing the federal election of 2021, we spoke to two or three regional campaign directors on a weekly basis over the course of the campaign. Most were Liberals, though we had off-the-record conversations with New Democratic and Conservative officials periodically as well.

The election in 2021 posed a series of challenges for the Liberal Party in all three areas of the regional campaign director's responsibility. In terms of candidate recruitment, the party had to fill fifty-four vacancies in the first two weeks of the campaign. Many of them were in rural parts of western Canada, where the party's prospects for success were the most limited. The Conservative Party encountered similar challenges in Quebec and parts of urban Ontario. Recruiting stopgap candidates for these seats required local organizers and the regional campaign director to identify and convince quality candidates to stand for nomination, hold nomination contests, vet each potential candidate, and then secure the 150 signatures necessary to get the name of the candidate on the general election ballot. Crucially, the collection of signatures cannot occur until the candidate is nominated by the party. This creates immense pressure on the regional director and local EDAs to expedite their internal party selection processes. Once the nominee is chosen, volunteers and paid party employees begin securing signatures. This involves far more than sending out mass emails or making calls through the voters list. Collecting signatures often entails cajoling close friends and family members or standing out front of small-town grocery stores to ask residents to sign nomination papers. The pitch often takes the form of "we know that you likely won't vote for our candidate, but we hope that you think it's important that they have the ability to run."

The election in 2021 revealed the important role played by regional campaign directors in distributing resources among local campaigns and from party headquarters to the regions. This was particularly important in the closing days of the campaign when decisions must be made about which seats remain winnable and which do not. These resources include funds, advertising, and – perhaps most importantly – volunteers. Throughout most of the campaign, most parties keep a disproportionate number of people in the National Capital Region to support their headquarters. People who stay behind to staff ministers' offices are asked to moonlight as volunteers, for instance, working alongside the hundreds of paid staff. In the final week of the campaign, after advance polls close, the party must decide where to send these volunteers. This involves triaging ridings on both a national basis and a regional basis, determining which local campaigns are best positioned to capitalize on a last-minute, get-out-the-vote surge. Regional campaign directors are critical to this triage process. They must judge which of the various ridings in their regions are the most competitive and which ones should go without additional support, whether because they are coasting to victory or because they are unable to close the gaps with their leading opponents. In the case of the former, the regional campaign director requests party headquarters to send volunteers and make targeted ad buys. In the case of the latter, the regional campaign director must initiate difficult conversations with local campaign managers, trying to convince them to release some of their resources to support their counterparts in tighter races.

These dynamics played out for the Liberals in three regions in 2021. In eastern Ontario, local organizers made the pitch to secure more resources to support incumbent Neil Ellis in the Bay of Quinte riding. Ellis had held the seat since 2015, though the Conservatives had closed the gap to less than 3 percentage points in 2019. Internal polls and door step intelligence suggested that in 2021 the race was close. A similar set of developments arose in

Kanata–Carleton, where Jenna Sudds was trying to retain the seat for the Liberals following the retirement of incumbent MP Karen McCrimmon. In the end, Sudds received an influx of volunteers to help in the closing days of the campaign. Ellis did not. Sudds went on to win by just over 1,000 votes (3 percentage points), whereas Ellis lost by 3,000 votes (5 percentage points).

Meanwhile, in Winnipeg, the Liberals had to decide whether to redistribute volunteers from the campaigns supporting their four incumbent MPs to the team of Doug Eylofson, contesting the potential swing riding of Charleswood–St. James–Assiniboia–Headingley. Given the historically tight nature of elections in Winnipeg, some of the four incumbents had found themselves on the opposite side of these negotiations earlier in their careers. All had a good sense of the value of volunteers in the closing days of a campaign. Ultimately, meaningful resource shifts did not occur. Eylofson lost by 460 votes, raising questions about whether additional volunteers would have been enough to push him ahead of his Conservative opponent.

Farther west, the Liberals encountered a third triage dilemma. Early in the campaign, they had identified a pair of winnable ridings in Alberta's capital city: Edmonton Centre and Edmonton Mill Woods. In the former, Randy Boissonnault was trying to win back the riding that he had lost to Conservative MP James Cummings. In the latter, Councillor Ben Henderson was trying to win back the riding that Conservative Tim Uppal had claimed from the Liberals in 2019. Both races were close but featured very different dynamics. In Edmonton Centre, a three-way race was emerging. The New Democrats had surged more than 30 percent in the last week of the campaign following the declaration of a public health emergency in Alberta that elevated the prominence of the provincial NDP opposition. Edmonton Mill Woods was a two-way race, with Henderson challenged to overcome a perceived disadvantage because he had never lived in the riding. The regional campaign director played the role of arbiter between these campaigns as each asked for volunteers from other Edmonton-area campaigns and central headquarters. There was no consensus, which left each campaign to contest the closing week without a significant shift of resources. Boissonnault emerged victorious by just over 600 votes, whereas Henderson lost by about 1,500 votes.

Turning to the leader's tour, there can be miscommunication or tension between national campaign organizers and their regional counterparts. The story of Liberal George Chahal's candidacy in Calgary Skyview in 2021 is illustrative. Historically, Conservative parties have dominated the northeast corner of Calgary. The Liberals broke a long drought with Darshan Kang's surprise victory in 2015. Winning the seat was not materially important to the Trudeau Liberals in terms of forming the government that year, but it was symbolically important for the governing party to have caucus representation from one of western Canada's largest cities. The Conservatives took back the seat in 2019, with Jag Sahota winning over half of the popular vote. This set the stage for a rubber match in 2021 between Sahota and Chahal, a sitting member of Calgary City Council. The regional campaign director would play a crucial intermediary role in connecting the national campaign to the local organization, particularly when it came to organizing a stop on the leader's tour.

At the outset of the campaign, the Liberal Party identified a handful of winnable seats in urban Alberta in 2021, and Calgary Skyview was one of them. For this reason, the leader's tour was scheduled to make a stop in Chahal's riding in the second week of the campaign. The outdoor event, if held under Alberta's COVID-19 protocols at the time, could have involved an unlimited number of people. Unknown to local rally organizers, the central Liberal campaign had set a nationwide policy for events, limiting them to 100 people. The result was that up to 400 supporters were turned away from the event, creating understandable disappointment and frustration among Calgary Liberals. Although the mainstream, English-language media did not pick up on the story, the misstep featured prominently in the Punjabi press for a number of days. Letters to the editor and calls to radio shows were full of questions for the Liberal campaign, asking why the Liberal Party appeared to turn a sizable public rally into an exclusive engagement with the prime minister and 100 of Chahal's closest family members and friends. The blowback concerned local officials, who feared that the loss of votes could cost them a tight election.

After the event, the regional campaign director conveyed the potential impact on Liberal fortunes in the riding. Understandably focused on upcoming events, the central campaign left it up to the regional director and local officials to rebuild trust and morale. Numerous calls were made to Liberal supporters to clarify the context of the situation and to encourage them to remain on board with the campaign. In the end, the effort was enough to carry Chahal to a 3,000 vote (or 7 percentage point) victory. As with the campaigns in eastern Ontario, Winnipeg, and Edmonton, the actions of regional campaign directors were highly influential in determining the outcomes of tight races. In close elections like that in 2021, these efforts can even determine the balance of power in Parliament.

Conclusion

Canadian political parties have become increasingly centralized and professionalized over the past number of decades. As a result, the "air war" gets the lion's share of attention by observers of Canadian elections. This primary focus is not necessarily misplaced. Nationwide campaigns throughout modern Canadian history have been far more important to the overall outcomes of elections. Most media and academic attention remains focused on party leaders and the machinations of those in the central party headquarters in Ottawa. Today elections are won or lost on the strength of political marketing, including the management of voter identification databases (see Chapter 11 of this volume for a discussion on this issue) and the microtargeting of individual Canadians by experts in each party's headquarters. In contrast, many of the most important resources – particularly volunteers – are managed at the local level. Grassroots organizers, led by constituency campaign managers, run the "ground war." They support local candidates by fundraising, sign canvassing, door knocking, and executing get-out-the-vote drives. Although many of Canada's seats are relatively safe for incumbents and parties that fare well historically in certain regions, a strong local campaign can help to tip the scales in tight races.

Local candidates and campaigns matter the most in marginal seats, where a five-point gap between candidates could well be overcome with a dynamic local politician or an extraordinary get-out-the-vote campaign. In close national contests, like those in 2019 and 2021, these local campaigns can decide which party forms the government.

Often lost in this air/ground dichotomy, regional campaign directors help to transform the national strategy into local tactics. Without their knowledge, experience, credibility, and networks, parties would lack the ability to mount competitive nationwide campaigns. Regional campaign directors fill vacancies in the campaign slate, act as conduits of intelligence from the centre to the peripheries of the party, and help to orchestrate the leader's tour stops. They often find themselves caught in the middle, at times acting as arbiters of local disputes and coordinators of efforts within their regions. At other times, they are forced to mend relationships harmed by the friction that comes from running a single national campaign through 338 local organizations. At all times, they are responsible for maintaining morale and keeping lines of communication open between constituencies and the centre. As centralized and professionalized as modern campaigns have become, and as much as national elections are contested on hundreds of individual battlegrounds across the country, it is important to remember the important role played by regional campaign directors. As the election of 2021 demonstrated, their performance can be pivotal to the success of individual candidates and the party as a whole.

Thus, despite being out of the limelight, the regional campaign director plays an integral role in Canadian elections. Over time, the role of a regional campaign director has evolved to resemble that of a film producer. Both are intermediaries who connect the central organization to the people at work on the front lines. Just as a producer must execute the studio's vision with the resources provided, so too a regional campaign director must connect the party's national campaign office with the politicians and volunteers on the ground. Each film in production features a different cast and crew, as does each regional campaign. Every production, like every region, has its own storylines and dynamics. Although the studio might attempt to package and market the film in the most favourable light, if the quality of the production is poor, then it will reflect poorly on the entire organization. Casting is as important as assembling a full and competent campaign slate, just as staging a scene is as important as organizing a leader's tour stop or photo-op. Executive producers, like national campaign managers, often get most of the credit or blame. But they rely heavily on their producers – regional campaign directors – to get the job done.

Notes

1   Ames, "The Organization of Political Parties in Canada."
2   Carty, Cross, and Young, *Rebuilding Canadian Party Politics.*
3   Bakvis, *Regional Ministers.*
4   Carty, "Brokerage Parties, Brokerage Politics."
5   Rayside, "Federalism and the Party System."
6   Esselment, "Fighting Elections."
7   Azoulay, "The Evolution of Party Organisation in Canada."
8   Carty, "Brokerage Parties, Brokerage Politics."
9   Carty, "Parties as Franchise Systems."
10 Savoie, *Democracy in Canada;* Ie, "Representation and Ministerial Influence on Cabinet Committees."
11 Coletto, Jansen, and Young, "Stratarchical Party Organization."
12 Turcotte, "Under New Management."
13 Flanagan, *Winning Power.*
14 Turnbull, "Candidate Nominations."
15 Flanagan, *Winning Power.*
16 Carty, Eagles, and Sayers, "Candidates and Local Campaigns."
17 Yakabuski, "Erin O'Toole Makes Subtle Gains in Quebec."
18 Bakx, "How Conservatives Came Around to Supporting a Carbon Tax."
19 Serebrin, "Singh Focuses on Environment in Montreal."
20 Riker, "Heresthetic and Rhetoric in the Spatial Model."

Bibliography

Ames, Herbert B. "The Organization of Political Parties in Canada." *Proceedings of the American Political Science Association* 8 (1911): 181–88.
Azoulay, Dan. "The Evolution of Party Organisation in Canada since 1900." *Journal of Commonwealth and Comparative Politics* 33, 2 (1995): 185–208.

Bakvis, Herman. *Regional Ministers: Power and Influence in the Canadian Cabinet.* Toronto: University of Toronto Press, 1991.

Bakx, Kyle. "How Conservatives Came Around to Supporting a Carbon Tax – and Whether It's Here to Stay." CBC News, 31 August 2021. https://www.cbc.ca/news/business/bakx-o-toole-conservatives-carbon-policy-1.6158942.

Carty, R. Kenneth. "Brokerage Parties, Brokerage Politics." In *Parties and Party Systems: Structure and Context,* edited by Richard Johnston and Campbell Sharman, 13–29. Vancouver: UBC Press, 2015.

–. "Parties as Franchise Systems: The Stratarchical Organizational Imperative." *Party Politics* 10, 1 (2004): 5–24.

Carty, R. Kenneth, William Cross, and Lisa Young. *Rebuilding Canadian Party Politics.* Vancouver: UBC Press, 2000.

Carty, R. Kenneth, D. Monroe Eagles, and Anthony Sayers. "Candidates and Local Campaigns: Are There Just Four Canadian Types?" *Party Politics* 9, 5 (2003): 619–36.

Coletto, David, Harold J. Jansen, and Lisa Young. "Stratarchical Party Organization and Party Finance in Canada." *Canadian Journal of Political Science* 44, 1 (2011): 111–36.

Esselment, Anna Lennox. "Fighting Elections: Cross-Level Political Party Integration in Ontario." *Canadian Journal of Political Science* 43, 4 (2010): 871–92.

Flanagan, Tom. *Winning Power: Canadian Campaigning in the Twenty-First Century.* Montreal and Kingston: McGill-Queen's University Press, 2014.

Ie, Kenny William. "Representation and Ministerial Influence on Cabinet Committees in Canada." *Canadian Journal of Political Science* 54, 3 (2021): 615–36.

Rayside, David M. "Federalism and the Party System: Provincial and Federal Liberals in the Province of Quebec." *Canadian Journal of Political Science* 11, 3 (1978): 499–528.

Riker, William H. "Heresthetic and Rhetoric in the Spatial Model." In *Advances in the Spatial Theory of Voting,* edited by James M. Enelow and Melvin J. Hinich, 46–65. Cambridge: Cambridge University Press, 1990.

Savoie, Donald J. *Democracy in Canada: The Disintegration of Our Institutions.* Montreal and Kingston: McGill-Queen's University Press, 2019.

Serebrin, Jacob. "Singh Focuses on Environment in Montreal, as NDP Runs 'Targeted' Quebec Campaign." *Globe and Mail,* 23 August 2021. https://www.theglobeandmail.com/politics/article-ndp-leader-jagmeet-singh-to-end-oil-gas-subsidies-if-elected/.

Turcotte, André. "Under New Management: Market Intelligence and the Conservative Party's Resurrection." In *Political Marketing in Canada,* edited by Alex Marland, Thierry Giasson, and Jennifer Lees-Marshment, 76–90. Vancouver: UBC Press, 2012.

Turnbull, Sarah. "Candidate Nominations: Where the Parties Stand on Day 1 of the Campaign." CTV News, 15 August 2021. https://www.ctvnews.ca/politics/candidate-nominations-where-the-parties-stand-on-day-1-of-the-campaign-1.5548142.

Yakabuski, Konrad. "Erin O'Toole Makes Subtle Gains in Quebec as Anybody-but-Conservative Sentiment Fades." *Globe and Mail,* 30 August 2021. https://www.theglobeandmail.com/opinion/article-subtle-signs-the-ground-is-shifting-in-quebec-again/.

8

Campaign Managers in Constituency Campaigns

Royce Koop and Anthony M. Sayers

Abstract   There is a substantial literature on Canadian political parties in the constituencies, particularly related to local members, constituency associations, and candidates. But much less is known about the actual structure and behaviour of constituency campaigns in Canadian elections. We address this gap through an in-depth examination of the roles and functions of campaign managers. These actors are situated within relatively recent changes related to digital technology that have altered their roles, as seen in the federal election campaign of 2021. Our central theoretical contribution is that campaign managers' tasks fall into three categories: managing the local campaign team (managing downward), managing the candidate (managing upward), and managing relations with the central campaign (managing outward). The experiences of these grassroots actors differ both in the challenges that they face in each category and in how they confront those challenges.

Résumé   Il existe une abondante documentation sur les partis politiques canadiens dans les circonscriptions, particulièrement en ce qui concerne le membership local, les associations de circonscription, et les candidats. Cependant, on en sait beaucoup moins sur la structure et les actions menées au sein des circonscriptions lors des élections canadiennes. Nous pallions cette lacune en examinant en profondeur les rôles et les fonctions des directeurs de campagne. De récents changements liés aux technologies numériques ont modifié le rôle de ces acteurs, comme l'a démontré la campagne électorale fédérale de 2021. Notre principale contribution théorique pose que les tâches des directeurs de campagne sont réparties en trois catégories : la gestion de l'équipe de campagne locale (gestion descendante), la gestion du candidat (gestion ascendante), et la gestion des relations avec la campagne centrale (gestion externe). L'expérience de ces acteurs de terrain se distingue par les défis particuliers auxquels ils font face et la manière dont ils les relèvent.

THE COMPARATIVE LITERATURE on political campaign officials tends to focus on professionalization, with the development of campaign managers and campaign professionals as a class of political actors who can exist largely independently of political parties.[1] This perspective derives mainly from the United States (but not entirely[2]), reflecting its role as an early adopter of now widely used campaign techniques.[3] Although local campaign techniques and functions have not changed significantly, there is growing emphasis on best practices, knowledge of which is increasingly available to campaign managers in developed democracies.[4] Yet little is known about how the managers of Canadian constituency campaigns are located within this broader context. We reanalyze existing research through a manager-centric lens and add information gleaned from structured interviews with current managers to begin filling this analytical gap.

Campaign managers in contemporary elections perform many of the same activities as their predecessors but in ways reshaped by continuously evolving digital technologies.[5] The national campaigns of Canadian parties have vested interests in the success of local managers and sometimes intervene in local campaigns, though these campaigns – with some exceptions – are still largely left on their own.[6] The national campaign uses party funds to prioritize certain local campaigns over others, and strong constituency associations redistribute funds to help the party as a whole.[7] Fundamentally, however, Canadian parties still are organized along the lines of the franchise bargain outlined by R. Kenneth Carty, so local campaign managers are entrusted to organize their campaigns in response to distinct local needs, and they do so largely unmolested by the wider party.[8]

One result of this continuity in local campaign practices is that other aspects of constituency politics have been emphasized in the literature on Canadian parties, including constituency associations, party members, candidate nominations, and the personalization of candidates in Canadian elections.[9] The structure of local campaigns and the personnel who staff them, in contrast, have not been studied as often or as rigorously. Anthony Sayers's ethnographic account of constituency campaigns in the election of 1988, published prior to more recent changes in communication technology, suggests one approach.[10] Constituency campaign teams, according to Sayers, can be viewed as a series of concentric circles surrounding the candidate. Those circles, beginning with the one closest to the candidate, are the inner circle, secondary workers, and sympathizers. The campaign manager is the most important member of the candidate's inner circle or, as Paul Wilson in Chapter 9 of this volume refers to it, "the core group of key people who provide the most commitment and anchor the campaign." The functions of the role flow from the position relative to both the candidate and others who contribute to the functioning of the campaign.

Campaign managers can be described in two ways: who they are and what they do in their role. Differences in these two respects are generally attributable to two influences. First, the nature of the constituency shapes the role of the local manager. Second, the nature of the party shapes who takes on the role and what they do, sometimes directly and sometimes indirectly through an intermediary nomination contest. The local structures and traditions of the Liberal and Conservative Parties are different from those of the New Democratic Party, and this has consequences for the managers.

Campaign managers are generally selected by candidates, but the local party association might have some input into the selection or even decide on behalf of the candidate. In the Liberal and Conservative Parties, the tradition is for candidates in competitive seats to select their own campaign staff, and these recruits (like the candidates themselves) might have little if any recent connection to the parties. These candidates often opt for friends, colleagues, and others with whom they have direct relationships, and the local party generally does not interfere in these decisions. Often team members have worked with the candidate during the prior nomination race and are likely to share the same economic and social backgrounds as the candidate. However, when the local party is strong and the candidate is relatively inexperienced, members of the local constituency association can play a role in selecting a manager.[11] Even our small number of interviews conducted for this chapter illustrates diversity in how campaign managers are selected: one was the candidate's relative, two were experienced local campaigners hired by the candidates, and one was hired by the local constituency association's campaign committee with the consent of the candidate.

Things are starkly different in the mass-style NDP, in which campaign managers are generally chosen not by the candidates but by local party officials. Indeed, a manager is often selected prior to a local nomination process; the candidate then enters a pre-existing campaign structure that already includes a manager. Campaign staff are selected in generally competitive processes in which both experience and expertise are prioritized. Managers in NDP campaigns, like candidates, often have long records of service to the party.[12] We have observed that division in the NDP is more commonly ideological than in the Liberal and Conservative Parties, so the manager is likely to derive from the same ideological camp as the successful nomination candidate.

Sayers quotes a campaign manager from the federal election in 1988 who provided the following description of the job: "[The manager] guides the entire campaign, helps develop and ensures its strategic direction, acts as the peak organizer, and oversees important functional elements of the campaign such as media relations, the candidate's schedule, [and] spending ... with the final say on most things."[13] Campaign managers often perform these roles with little guidance or supervision. The role is to manage the myriad campaign activities so that candidates are free to knock on doors and otherwise campaign. A key goal is to persuade the candidate to be out of the office and leave administrative duties to others.

The functions performed by a campaign manager are shaped by the nature of the constituency as well as the strength of the local party and campaign. Managers must adapt activities to the unique idiosyncrasies of the ridings. A campaign in a dense urban riding will differ substantially from one in a dispersed suburban riding, which in turn will differ greatly from one in a far-flung rural constituency. Although Liberal and Conservative candidates often choose managers with whom they have previous relationships, a candidate also considers whether potential campaign staff have roots in and familiarity with the riding, precisely so that they can successfully adapt the campaign to local needs.

The role taken on by a campaign manager is further shaped by local conditions in urban centres close to national media in which star candidates often run.[14] The activities associated with these high-profile campaigns are starkly different from those in ridings distant from the nodal urban campaigns that drive the election narrative. The functions of campaign managers are also shaped by the strength of the local party and campaign. Constituency campaigns vary widely with respect to the resources – particularly volunteers and funds – available.[15] Some campaigns, notably those of the Liberal and Conservative Parties, are flush with contributions but lack volunteers.[16] These campaigns must grapple with an absence of labour and try to compensate with spending. A well-funded, professional campaign sometimes provides the campaign manager with a salary.[17]

Other campaigns might have the opposite problem: few funds but a formidable army of volunteers. Still others lack both: in these stopgap campaigns, managers take on multiple roles to make up for an absence of workers. Sometimes they must become a jack-of-all-trades, doing any work that must be done to ensure the success of the campaign. In contrast, a well-funded campaign in which all major specialist roles are filled allows the manager to focus on high-level responsibilities rather than on the grunt work of the campaign.

Local Trends

Constituency campaigning in Canadian elections is parochial in the sense that the fundamental goals of the campaign – introducing the candidate to voters, canvassing, get-out-the-vote (GOTV) activities – have not changed in some time. That said, some of the methods used to pursue those goals have changed largely because of the availability of continuously evolving digital communication technology, and it is important to identify these local trends and how they have changed the role of campaign managers. As in the past, the development and adoption of innovative campaign technologies at the grassroots level have reshaped the activities of both the campaign manager and the constituency party organization.

The first trend is the increasing use of funds to pay firms and consultants for work traditionally performed by party volunteers. Campaign managers have always relied on volunteers to perform the fundamental tasks of Canadian constituency campaigns, but managing those volunteers – especially drop-ins – is challenging, and often campaigns struggle to find enough helpers. In recent elections, we have observed managers attempting to identify areas where capital (often derived from transfers from the national campaign or other constituency campaigns) can be used to hire firms and consultants to play key roles that plug the holes left by a lack of volunteers.[18]

There are several examples. Local campaigns sometimes hire polling firms to supplement the local canvass by identifying supporters ahead of time, allowing the campaign to target those supporters to host lawn signs or for GOTV activities. Phone banks are also used to assist in GOTV activities since sending robocalls is an affordable way of reminding supporters to vote. Furthermore, local campaigns sometimes hire private firms – or small businesses run by entrepreneurial residents with a pick-up truck and hammer – who can deliver lawn and highway signs, maintain and replace them throughout the campaign, and take them down at the conclusion of the campaign.[19] The advantage is that campaigns can avoid the need for significant coordination of labour, but this comes at a price. Campaigns can also hire local firms to conduct a canvass or distribute literature in mailboxes, avoiding the need to coordinate volunteers to do so.

The second trend changing the role of Canadian constituency campaign managers is the adoption of new canvassing techniques in response to evolving technologies (see Chapters 10 and 11 of this volume). All of the major parties have adapted apps for canvassers' smartphones to identify more easily residents of the homes that they are visiting and whether they have previously expressed support for or opposition to the party.[20] More importantly, they allow for uploading and monitoring data collected during the canvassing that can be assessed by both the local and the national campaigns.[21]

Campaigns have adopted these changes in both structure and strategy to varying degrees depending on the financial resources available. The result has been a change in the job descriptions of some campaign managers, with responsibilities shifting from managing large groups of volunteers to managing contracts with independent service providers. The result has been that the role has almost certainly become less exhausting for many. Furthermore, these professional relationships often flow across multiple campaigns, so managers can simply contact reliable contractors to provide these services instead of investing significant energy in amassing and organizing armies of volunteers.

The election campaign in 2021 was distinctive in that many local campaign techniques had to be adapted to ensure compliance with relevant public health orders that limited public interactions to stem the spread of COVID-19. Campaign managers were often concerned about COVID and volunteers on their teams and implemented precautions to limit interactions while still being free to campaign. In some ridings, this necessitated a renewed emphasis on communication and advertising via social media.[22] In others, the physical address of the campaign office was not published, and canvassers were instructed to keep a clear distance from people while knocking on doors.[23]

Behind the Scenes

Managers heavily shape the character of local campaigning in Canada. We have observed many Canadian constituency campaigns and spoken with hundreds of people who have volunteered in these campaigns. We draw from this experience, as well as from four original semi-structured interviews with party campaign managers from the federal elections in 2021, 2019, and 2015, to provide a behind-the-scenes perspective on the role and work of these crucial actors in Canadian constituency campaigns.

Following the insights of scholars who emphasize the multi-dimensional character of management, we identify three central challenges facing local campaigns: managing the local campaign, managing the candidate, and managing relations with the national campaign.[24] Managers differ in both extent and manner when responding to these challenges. Some deal extensively with the national campaign and others not at all. Some are more heavily involved in district or regional politics. Resources and local contexts also shape how they conceive of their role. For example, some find themselves flush with cash and managing a team of paid coordinators overseeing hundreds of volunteers, whereas others have little money and only a handful of volunteers. Moreover, how managers respond when confronted with the multiplicity of demands and options embedded in campaigning is shaped by their backgrounds and experiences in politics and beyond.

Although the functions performed by campaign managers can vary substantially, often what they have in common are long hours of work during the campaign. Most anticipate full-time work and then are surprised to discover that they are working fourteen-hour days. One manager whom we interviewed was assured that the role would be only a part-time job, so he arranged his employment to work twenty hours a week. Once the campaign began, however, he was alarmed to discover that he was working a full-time job in politics in addition to his other job.

The first challenge for campaign managers is managing downward, the most important and demanding function. The campaign team and its resources must be garnered, organized, and mobilized to focus on central goals that will help the candidate to get elected. Constituency campaign teams consist of both secondary workers and sympathizers who perform a range of both specialized and non-specialized roles. Some campaigns have several specialists who manage teams of their own. They include sign chairs who oversee the distribution and maintenance of signs, field captains who take the lead in canvassing efforts, and office managers who ensure that the campaign office works well and efficiently. Although some campaign managers try to manage only these specialists, many are drawn into managing non-specialized volunteers, especially those who drop in to help.

The presence of several specialists who report to the manager and direct teams of volunteers is a sign of a professional campaign. In such a campaign, managers delegate tasks to these specialists and do not involve themselves in the day-to-day minutiae of the campaign, instead taking a broad strategic view of activities and focusing on managing the candidate and the national campaign. In some cases, these specialized employees are hired by the manager prior to the campaign and paid a salary. One campaign manager identified this recruitment as his most important function prior to the campaign. When asked what advice he would provide to new campaign managers, he referred to these specialists: "Bring on good people. Hire the best possible people." He also revealed that he felt guilty during the campaign because he had hired and delegated so well that he had little to do in the office while his volunteers were out working.

In a rural campaign, the manager must also grapple with conducting it potentially in many communities across a great distance. In such a situation, specialization includes knowledge of the distinct local politics of communities in a large rural district. Managers often rely on local specialists who take on several jobs in their communities, from leafleting to delivering signs to canvassing. Managers stay in regular contact with these specialists, and candidates work directly with them while visiting the different communities of the riding.

Where there is a reliable team of specialists managing volunteers, campaign managers emphasize the importance of regular and open communication. This usually consists of meetings each day during which issues and problems in each of the specialized areas of the campaign are addressed, with the added benefit of making members feel as if they are part of a well-functioning team. One manager met with his team every morning of the campaign in the office but generally did not include the candidate since there seemed to be little point in drowning him in the administrative details of the campaign. Another recalled that volunteers loved to stay in the campaign office visiting late into the evening, but eventually he had to evict them so that he would have time to consult with what he called the "small core group" of his campaign team.

Most functioning campaigns have such specialists, but they might not be paid. Where there is no expertise, the campaign manager might end up taking on some or even most of these tasks. One noted that he had to take on some responsibility for planning volunteer activities throughout the campaign, including dispatching drop-in volunteers who simply showed up at the campaign office. Directing even a modestly sized team of volunteers can easily consume a manager's time. In another situation, a campaign manager decided to hire only a part-time assistant to operate the campaign office, with the result that he had to answer telephone calls or greet visitors to the office whenever the assistant was busy. In campaigns not well staffed, the manager can even end up performing tasks normally reserved for volunteers. Managers might wish to drop leaflets or help to canvass to build team spirit or lead by example, but it is problematic if these activities take them away from the more specialized functions that they are meant to perform.

All serious campaigns include volunteers who perform indispensable tasks, whether they are only a handful of friends and family members or an army of grassroots activists (see Chapter 9 of this volume). A particularly pressing issue confronting campaign managers is how to coordinate volunteers who do not show up regularly. The chaotic nature of constituency campaigns is the result of this inconsistency: volunteers who do what they can and often show up unannounced and unpredictably. The campaign needs either to reject these offers or to be flexible and imaginative enough to find ways to bring volunteers into the campaign and, even better, make sound use of their time and skills. "It's a logistical headache," one manager complained, referring to drop-in volunteers. "You always have to be prepared for people to come in." The worst outcome is not to have anything ready for a willing volunteer to do; the person will be disappointed, and the campaign loses a potential helper.

Volunteers, far from all being casual drop-ins, are sometimes hardened partisans committed to the party and engaged in both federal and provincial campaigns.[25] But even for these highly mobilized volunteers, a manager must provide benefits to sustain their engagement beyond whatever drew them to the campaign. Most campaign managers report that keeping spirits high is an important aspect of the job, and they must thank volunteers and build a sense of community in the campaign. Occasional pizza in the evening at the campaign office can help. And the campaign can buy gift cards for local drive-thru restaurants so that volunteers can grab lunch on the go rather than returning to the campaign office, a particularly important initiative on election day when constituency campaigns are focused on GOTV activities and time is precious.

The second challenge that campaign managers confront is to manage upward, which means managing the candidate. The candidate is the crucial public figure in the constituency campaign, so the time and effort of the candidate must be used wisely. Generally, this role falls to the manager but can also be filled by other members of the candidate's inner circle.

It sometimes surprises outsiders that the need to keep candidates productively engaged in the campaign is a central goal for managers. The first way in which they do so is by keeping candidates focused on what they are able to accomplish. The classic example that several campaign managers relayed to us is of candidates who enjoy hanging out at the campaign office chatting with volunteers. Since there are no votes to be found in the campaign office, managers must push candidates out the door and schedule them to be canvassing or increasing name recognition by campaigning throughout the riding. "Candidates need to be out on the doorsteps," asserted one manager, and he saw it as his role to ensure that his candidate was out in the community. The relatively high turnover rate of MPs in Canada means that many candidates have virtually no experience running for office or in constituency campaigns; one consequence is that candidates often rely heavily on their campaign managers to direct them.[26] Some candidates are easily directed; others are not.

Just as campaign managers must direct candidates to what is important, so too it is necessary to direct them away from what is not important in the campaign. Candidates running for public office are exposed to a variety of information that can be deflating. Managers try to dissuade candidates from focusing on national polls or bad news stories, especially negative stories in local newspapers or, worst of all, angry comments on social media. "Let's get outside," one campaign manager recalled telling his candidate after some critical comments on social media surfaced. "You don't need to be reading that stuff."

As candidates knock on doors, shake hands, and build name recognition throughout the constituencies, campaign managers try to ensure that candidates make no mistakes that could lead to embarrassing press coverage. In doing so, they use insights from others in the community. When one candidate, for example, visited an event at a local gurdwara (a place of assembly and worship for Sikhs), his manager encouraged him to focus on positive themes such as family and the success of the local Sikh community. The candidate took the advice offered and was received warmly. His opponent, in contrast, launched a partisan attack, which many in attendance thought was distasteful given the event and the venue. In this case, the campaign manager's sense was that his candidate might have made the same mistake without his guidance. Another manager spent time observing the candidate's interactions with voters so that he could provide suggestions for improvement, emphasizing some themes over others.

A recurring theme when discussing managing upward is the importance of knowing the candidates well enough to shape campaigns that make use of their strengths while managing activities with which they might struggle. Little wonder that many candidates select friends, colleagues, and family members as their campaign managers. Sometimes candidates are bored by their parties' policy platforms and never-ending arguments about policy, so their managers must encourage them to be sufficiently informed to be able to talk about them on the doorstep. At other times, candidates do not enjoy shaking hands or undertaking other aspects of local campaigning, so their managers must gently push them toward doing so and provide encouragement. Some candidates do not meet their canvassing targets, so managers must find ways to get them to move faster from doorstep to doorstep, even if doing so is awkward for them. More frequently, candidates run themselves ragged during the campaign, and some campaign managers intervene and insist that the candidates take a day off to recuperate. This was especially the case in the gruelling election campaign in 2015, one of the longest in Canadian history.

In all cases, the goal of managing upward is to engender trust between the campaign manager and the candidate, which provides the basis for the campaign to function smoothly. Candidates must be able to trust their managers and accept criticism. Candidates who trust that the administrative aspects of their campaigns are well managed are free to focus on reaching out to constituents during the campaign. At the same time, managers must be willing to intervene with candidates when necessary and believe that their views will be both heard and respected. Tension between these two actors can lead to critical problems for the campaign.

The third challenge that campaign managers confront is managing the relationship with the national campaign (managing outward). Constituency campaigns can benefit from the national campaign in the form of money or other resources, such as volunteers, as national campaign coordinators sometimes direct volunteers from one riding to another if it is determined that it can be won with additional effort. Local campaign officials can also benefit from the guidance of experienced campaign professionals, especially if local officials are relatively inexperienced.

Most campaign managers report satisfaction with the national campaign. In 2021, the national Conservative Party campaign hosted a weekly call during which it would discuss internal polling and messaging that could be helpful to those campaigning at the grassroots level. The party also offered regular remote training sessions that became parts of many managers' work during the campaign. One manager had contact information for people in the national campaign whom he could contact depending on the nature of the question, from communication to voter software to general campaign advice.

Campaign managers at the grassroots level typically are assigned a provincial or regional representative of the national campaign (described in Chapter 7 of this volume) responsible for interfacing with the constituency campaigns within the region. The national campaign tends to leave local officials alone if things are going well but can provide services if asked for them. One local manager reported that the national campaign had identified his as a "targeted riding" that the party could win, which meant that he benefited from additional attention and resources. Yet sometimes national officials intervene if local officials are having difficulties. If constituency campaigns are not meeting targets for canvassing, then a national official will be in contact to encourage volunteers to move more quickly when door knocking. The campaign manager will bear the brunt of this hectoring and must contemplate whether to or how to implement the national campaign's guidance.

Friction between the constituency campaign and the national campaign can develop if the latter or the party leader performs poorly, leading to the impression that the local candidate is being dragged down. Indeed, the sense that local efforts are being damaged by a poorly performing national campaign is one of the perennial dynamics of Canadian electoral politics, and this appeared in the election campaign of 2021.[27] In these situations, managing outward can become a significant challenge for campaign managers. For the most part, their first loyalty is to the candidates and the constituency campaigns. This means that, when the interests of the national campaign and those of the local campaign appear to diverge, the manager will side with and protect the interests of the latter. One campaign manager, for example, refused to distribute flyers sent from the national campaign, arguing that they did not reflect the competitive reality of the riding. Instead, he had his own flyers made up that he thought addressed local concerns. Others simply ignored advice from the national campaign. But local campaign managers are not generally or reflexively belligerent toward the national campaign, recognizing that one of their roles is to act as intermediaries between the two campaigns for the overall benefit of the local campaign.

Conclusion

The structures of political parties and elections in Canada place campaign managers at the centre of retail politics. Whereas the public sees candidates, both the candidates and the local campaign apparatus that supports them are shaped and guided by campaign managers. Furthermore, these actors mediate between the constituency campaign and the national campaign, a crucial relationship given Canada's vast and diverse geography as well as its single-member plurality electoral system. Despite their centrality to electoral politics in Canada, there has been very little direct scholarly attention paid to local campaign managers.

Driven by changing technology, local campaign management is evolving in terms of both activities and relationships across several dimensions. This is true with respect to campaign managers' relationships with the local campaign team, the candidate, and the national campaign. These managers must adapt to a constantly evolving web of relationships and the need to learn new methods for managing campaign teams and relations with voters either directly or by hiring professional help. Although the goal remains the same – electing the candidate – increasingly it requires a focus on melding successfully digital technologies and techniques with the personal relations (both within and outside the constituency campaign) key to a successful local effort. The challenges that campaign managers face and how they interact with them vary by local context, competitiveness, partisan organizational ethos, and characteristics of the managers themselves.

Notes

1 For example, see Farrell, Kolodny, and Medvic, "Parties and Campaign Professionals," and Plasser, "Parties' Diminishing Relevance."
2 See Gillies and Coletto, "Political Strategists in Canada."
3 Plasser and Plasser, *Global Political Campaigning*.
4 For example, Gerber and Green, *Get Out the Vote!*
5 See, for example, Belfry Munroe and Munroe, "Constituency Campaigning in the Age of Data."
6 Koop, "Constituency Campaigning in the 2015 Federal Election."
7 For example, Carty and Young, "The Local Underpinnings of Electoral Competition," and Currie-Wood, "The National Growth of a Regional Party."

8   Carty, "The Politics of Tecumseh Corners."
9   On constituency associations, see Koop, "Party Constituency Associations." On candidate nomination, see Pruysers and Cross, "Candidate Selection in Canada." And on candidate personalization, see Cross and Young, "Personalization of Campaigns in an SMP System."
10 Sayers, *Parties, Candidates, and Constituency Campaigns.*
11 Ibid., Chapter 5.
12 Ibid., Chapter 5.
13 Ibid., 69.
14 Ibid., Chapter 5.
15 For example, Eagles, "The Effectiveness of Local Campaign Spending."
16 See, for example, Currie-Wood, "The National Growth of a Regional Party."
17 Belfry Munroe and Munroe, "Constituency Campaigning in the Age of Data," 150.
18 For example, Koop, "Constituency Campaigning in the 2015 Federal Election."
19 Vandalism of election signs, which arose as an issue in the campaign in 2021, necessitates maintenance throughout the campaign. See, for example, Gyarmati, "Delta Candidate Qualtrough."
20 See, for example, Belfry Munroe and Munroe, "Constituency Campaigning in the Age of Data."
21 See Tumilty, "In a Tight Race."
22 See Pursaga, "Playing Politics in the Time of COVID."
23 See Robertson, "Six Feet of Separation."
24 For an example of this scholarly treatment of managers, see O'Toole, Meier, and Nicholson-Crotty, "Managing Upward, Downward and Outward."
25 For example, Esselment, "Fighting Elections," 877, and Koop, *Grassroots Liberals,* Chapter 4.
26 On turnover among Canadian MPs, see, for example, Kerby and Blidook, "It's Not You, It's Me."
27 For example, MacCharles, Boutilier, and Patel, "'Justin Trudeau Does Not Do Shakeups.'"

Bibliography

Belfry Munroe, Kaija, and H.D. Munroe. "Constituency Campaigning in the Age of Data." *Canadian Journal of Political Science* 51, 1 (2018): 135–54.

Carty, R. Kenneth. "The Politics of Tecumseh Corners: Canadian Political Parties as Franchise Organizations." *Canadian Journal of Political Science* 35, 4 (2002): 723–45.

Carty, R. Kenneth, and Lisa Young. "The Local Underpinnings of Electoral Competition in Canada, 1979–2008." *Canadian Political Science Review* 6, 2–3 (2012): 227–36.

Cross, William, and Lisa Young. "Personalization of Campaigns in an SMP System: The Canadian Case." *Electoral Studies* 39 (2014): 306–15.

Currie-Wood, Rob. "The National Growth of a Regional Party: Evidence of Linkages between Constituency Associations in the Conservative Party of Canada." *Canadian Journal of Political Science* 53, 3 (2020): 618–37.

Eagles, Munroe. "The Effectiveness of Local Campaign Spending in the 1993 and 1997 Federal Elections in Canada." *Canadian Journal of Political Science* 37, 1 (2004): 117–36.

Esselment, Anna Lennox. "Fighting Elections: Cross-Level Political Party Integration in Ontario." *Canadian Journal of Political Science* 43, 4 (2010): 871–92.

Farrell, David M., Robin Kolodny, and Stephen Medvic. "Parties and Campaign Professionals in a Digital Age: Political Consultants in the United States and Their Counterparts Overseas." *International Journal of Press/Politics* 6, 4 (2001): 11–30.

Gerber, Alan S., and Donald P. Green. *Get Out the Vote! How to Increase Voter Turnout.* Washington, DC: Brookings Institution Press, 2004.

Gillies, Jamie, and David Coletto. "Political Strategists in Canada." In *Political Elites in Canada: Power and Influence in Instantaneous Times,* edited by Alex Marland, Thierry Giasson, and Andrea Lawlor, 168–83. Vancouver: UBC Press, 2018.

Gyarmati, Sandor. "Delta Candidate Qualtrough Says Her Campaign Hit with 'Hateful' Vandalism." *Delta Optimist,* 13 September 2021. https://www.delta-optimist.com/canadavotes2021/local-news/delta-candidate-qualtrough-says-her-campaign-hit-with-hateful-vandalism-4329385.

Kerby, Matthew, and Kelly Blidook. "It's Not You, It's Me: Determinants of Voluntary Legislative Turnover in Canada." *Legislative Studies Quarterly* 36, 4 (2011): 621–43.

Koop, Royce. "Constituency Campaigning in the 2015 Federal Election." In *Canadian Election Analysis: Communication, Strategy, and Democracy,* edited by Alex Marland and Thierry Giasson, 42–43. Vancouver: UBC Press, 2015. https://www.ubcpress.ca/canadianelectionanalysis2015.

–. *Grassroots Liberals: Organizing for Local and National Politics in Canada.* Vancouver: UBC Press, 2011.

–. "Party Constituency Associations and the Service, Policy and Symbolic Responsiveness of Canadian Members of Parliament." *Canadian Journal of Political Science* 45, 2 (2012): 359–78.

MacCharles, Tonda, Alex Boutilier, and Raisa Patel. "'Justin Trudeau Does Not Do Shakeups': Liberals Tell Rattled Candidates to Hold the Course as Campaign Trail Gets Bumpy." *Toronto Star,* 27 August 2021, A3. https://www.thestar.com/politics/federal-election/2021/08/26/justin-trudeau-does-not-do-shakeups-liberals-tell-rattled-candidates-to-hold-the-course-as-campaign-trail-gets-bumpy.html.

O'Toole, Laurence J., Kenneth J. Meier, and Sean Nicholson-Crotty. "Managing Upward, Downward and Outward." *Public Management Review* 7, 1 (2005): 45–68.

Plasser, Fritz. "Parties' Diminishing Relevance for Campaign Professionals." *International Journal of Press/Politics* 6, 4 (2001): 44–59.

Plasser, Fritz, and Gunda Plasser. *Global Political Campaigning: A Worldwide Analysis of Campaign Professionals and Their Practices.* Westport, CT: Praeger, 2002.

Pruysers, Scott, and William Cross. "Candidate Selection in Canada: Local Autonomy, Centralization and Competing Democracy Norms." *American Behavioral Scientist* 60, 7 (2016): 781–98.

Pursaga, Joyanne. "Playing Politics in the Time of COVID: Candidates Forced to Break with Tradition, Focus on Virtual Campaigns." *Winnipeg Free Press,* 16 September 2021. https://www.winnipegfreepress.com/special/federal-election/playing-politics-in-the-time-of-covid-575332292.html.

Robertson, Dylan. "Six Feet of Separation: How to Campaign under COVID." *Winnipeg Free Press,* 23 August 2021. https://www.winnipegfreepress.com/special/federal-election/six-feet-of-separation-how-to-campaign-under-covid-575152662.html.

Sayers, Anthony M. *Parties, Candidates, and Constituency Campaigns in Canadian Elections.* Vancouver: UBC Press, 1999.

Tumilty, Ryan. "In a Tight Race, Boots on the Ground Key to Election Win." *National Post,* 15 September 2021. https://nationalpost.com/news/politics/in-a-tight-race-boots-on-the-ground-key-to-election-win.

9

Local Campaign Workers

Paul Wilson

Abstract   The day-to-day work of individuals on local campaign teams has received little academic attention and is not well understood outside the relatively small circle of party activists serving in the electoral trenches. Based upon interviews with party activists, this chapter documents the activities of these local campaign workers and especially how they go about communicating with voters to increase the candidate's profile and name recognition, canvassing to identify certain and possible supporters, and ultimately getting out their supporters to vote on election day. The chapter also raises questions about whether partisan volunteers are becoming less engaged, whether this is encouraging more reliance on paid staff, and consequently whether parties are relying more on the data-harvesting potential of social media to identify supporters than on local campaigns and with what implications. Overall, a large-scale survey, such as the one last conducted for the 1991 Royal Commission on Electoral Reform and Party Financing, is needed to explore these questions.

Résumé   Le travail quotidien des équipes travaillant dans les campagnes locales est peu documenté et n'est pas bien compris hors du cercle relativement restreint des militants des partis impliqués dans ces campagnes. Prenant appui sur des entrevues réalisées auprès de militants, ce chapitre présente les activités des travailleurs de campagne locale. Plus précisément, il révèle comment ils communiquent avec les électeurs pour faire connaître leur candidat, comment ils approchent les gens pour repérer les partisans sûrs et potentiels, et ultimement comment ils les incitent à aller voter le jour de l'élection. Le chapitre soulève également des questions concernant l'affaiblissement de l'engagement électoral des militants : Cela encourage-t-il une plus grande dépendance à l'égard du personnel rémunéré? Par conséquent, les partis comptent-ils davantage sur le potentiel de collecte de données tirées des médias sociaux pour identifier les partisans que sur les activités de pointage des campagnes locales? Quelles sont les conséquences de ces transformations? Dans l'ensemble, une étude à grande échelle, comme celle qui a été menée dans le cadre de Commission royale sur la réforme électorale et le financement des partis de 1991, est nécessaire pour explorer ces questions.

THE DAY-TO-DAY WORK of individuals on local campaign teams is not well understood outside the relatively small circle of party activists serving in the electoral trenches. Based upon interviews with ten experienced campaign workers about the 2021 federal election, this chapter documents the roles of these local workers to understand better their contribution and significance.

Studies have consistently shown that the identities of local candidates and the efforts of their teams can have small but important impacts on the final votes within their ridings (see the Introduction to this volume). Often the impact can decide the winner in the riding and even the winning party nationally. For example, in the 2019 federal election, which resulted in a minority government, the first- and second-place candidates were separated by less than 5 percent of the vote in 47 of 338 electoral districts overall.[1] In the 2021 election, again resulting in a minority government, thirty-six ridings had a gap of less than 4 percent between the first- and second-place candidates.[2]

Some scholarship, such as R.K. Carty's survey of local party officials for the 1991 Royal Commission on Electoral Reform and Party Financing,[3] has investigated important questions about how campaigns are run on the ground, including the impacts of local party structure and the candidate nomination contest on campaign team formation, competence, and capacity to recruit volunteers.[4] Strong electoral district associations and open, contested nominations are important for enlarging the pool of campaign volunteers,[5] and well-staffed teams of volunteers (increasingly augmented with some paid staff) are essential if the campaign is going to be competitive.[6] Since very few Canadians are members of political parties, and most party members are not very active,[7] moving supporters up the ladder of engagement from taking a lawn sign to contributing money to volunteering with the campaign effort is challenging. People get involved for different reasons. Perhaps they are enthusiastic about the candidate, especially someone who is a star or local notable,[8] or perhaps it is because of their political and policy goals, for social and psychological reasons, or even because of economic motivations.[9] Nor are all campaign workers volunteers. Carty found that serving as a campaign manager was "increasingly becoming a full-time specialized job,"[10] though at the time this was more common for the New Democratic Party.

Full-time political staff also support local campaigns. Although the numbers ebb and flow, over 2,000 political staffers are employed in the offices of Members of Parliament (including party leaders), either on Parliament Hill or in MPs' constituency offices, and a further 750 or so work as political "exempt staff" in ministers' offices.[11] These staffers vary significantly in terms of their political experience and partisan commitment. However, their jobs depend on their MPs – and, for ministerial staff, their parties – getting re-elected. They are therefore highly motivated to work on the campaign. Because they are paid by tax dollars, staff employed by ministers and MPs may not participate in partisan activities while on the public payroll. Therefore, many take unpaid leaves to campaign. They often volunteer in their boss's constituency or are sometimes assigned to work on the central campaign or to help out in their party's targeted ridings. Those who do not take unpaid leave may campaign only outside normal office hours. Staffers generally recognize that supporting the party's campaign effort demonstrates commitment to the team and is unspoken recompense for the privilege of keeping their jobs after the election.

Despite the significant differences in organizational structure among local campaign teams because of party tradition, region, nomination type, relationship to the national party, and competitiveness, their key activities are remarkably similar: identifying supporters and mobilizing voters on election day.[12] However, the practical aspects of how campaign teams work on the ground to accomplish these goals have seldom been explored in a systematic way. There are exceptions, though. Royce Koop's 2011 study contains practical insights into the activities of grassroots Liberal workers, especially examples of "secondary workers" who carry out tasks such as placing lawn signs or negotiating the borrowing of tangible campaign resources from party supporters at a different level of government.[13] Another exception is Kaija Belfry Munroe and H.D. Munroe's 2018 study, which examined how three parties in a single riding gathered and used data during the 2015 election.[14] Overall, however, though the literature occasionally includes practical observations about the work of campaign teams, the work itself is seldom of primary concern.

Therefore, there is a lack of practical knowledge of how local campaign teams operate on the ground. Is it any wonder that, reflecting on his experience as a candidate in the 2015 federal election, journalism professor and former national reporter Allan Thompson wrote that, even though he had decades of experience covering politics, he had "virtually no concept" of what organizing and executing a local campaign involved?[15]

Local Trends

The COVID-19 pandemic presented a challenge for local campaigns. Although restrictions in some areas of the country had loosened from the height of the pandemic, limits on the size of indoor gatherings often continued and meant that campaigns had to adjust to take them into account. Many voters also expected campaign teams to respect social distancing even if it was not legally required, and for political reasons as well as public health reasons many campaigns adjusted their normal practices.

As detailed in Chapter 1 of this volume, Elections Canada experienced particular challenges with election administration in 2021. The agency issued "Campaign Guidance for Canvassing during COVID-19,"[16] which encouraged candidates and campaign workers to keep a two-metre distance from other people, to avoid handshakes and other types of physical contact, to wear masks, and to avoid distributing pamphlets, buttons, and other materials. Although not binding, these guidelines created expectations for how campaign teams ought to behave and implied some level of political risk for parties whose workers did not comply. Elections Canada also issued additional mandatory guidelines for scrutineers working at polling stations on election day. These included wearing a mask at all times (in a neutral colour, not a party colour), always maintaining a two-metre distance from others, including voters and poll workers, and bringing their own pens to sign ballot box seals.[17]

Except for the People's Party of Canada, political parties generally tried to conform – or to appear to conform – to these sorts of pandemic measures. Journalists paid significant attention to whether parties required their candidates to be vaccinated, and the Conservatives in particular were on the defensive because a majority of their candidates would not confirm their vaccination status. This resulted in media coverage of candidates who decided to campaign in non-traditional ways to maintain social distancing. For example, some candidates decided to forgo door-to-door direct voter contact and to focus instead on phone calls, outdoor events, or even mounting a megaphone and speakers on a car.[18]

There was little corresponding coverage, however, of how campaign workers were supporting candidates. In interviews conducted for this chapter, campaign workers discussed different measures that they took while canvassing to meet voters' expectations of social distancing. Some, a Liberal noted, wore masks all the time; a Conservative said that they would stand back from the door and ask permission to remove the mask; another Conservative said that they would put on a mask if the homeowner was wearing one. But all campaign workers interviewed stressed that they stayed at a respectful distance when engaging with potential voters. Conservative campaigns in the Ottawa area produced a blue button, branded with the party logo, that proclaimed "I am double vaxxed." This was both a medical and a political statement assuring residents that the canvassers respected their health and signalling that the campaign was not opposed to vaccination.

The snap election call came in late August 2021 when pandemic restrictions had only recently been relaxed in parts of the country and a fourth wave was looming, forest fires were raging in British Columbia, other parts of the country were experiencing a heat wave, and children had not yet returned to school. All of this might have contributed to voter fatigue generally. In addition, political fatigue was evident among some volunteers. Frequent elections put significant pressure on the pool of party volunteers since the same people tend to get involved at both national and provincial/territorial levels of government. The Nova Scotia election overlapped with the start of the federal campaign, and five other provincial or territorial elections had been held since September 2020 (New Brunswick, British Columbia, Saskatchewan, Newfoundland and Labrador, and Yukon). According to one Liberal campaign manager, volunteer fatigue made campaigning "drastically different" from what it had been in 2019. "The electorate didn't want to hear from us, and volunteers didn't want to hear from us." Volunteers were "burned out" and "exhausted," and as a consequence the campaign had only a quarter of the volunteers that it had in 2019. That campaign manager ended up spending more money on dinners and events to make volunteers feel appreciated: "This was the only way we'd get people out this time." An Ottawa-area Conservative observed the same burnout: because the burden of constant political activity falls to a small number of dedicated people, "even the most ardent volunteers" were tired in 2021 and had trouble getting motivated. The Green Party experience, at least in Kitchener Centre, was different. An experienced Green Party activist with knowledge of the local campaign described a mix of experienced workers from 2019 and newly engaged volunteers and said that there were over 400 volunteers in the riding during the campaign and over 200 on election day alone.

When volunteers are harder to find, some campaigns may start paying not only campaign managers, which has been a trend for several decades,[19] but also workers in other positions. An Atlantic Liberal campaign manager paid an office manager and sign team members, offering them mileage during the campaign and a stipend to take down signs after it. Several Ontario Conservatives confirmed that some ridings were paying canvassers.

Did this decline in campaign volunteer availability and this increase in paid campaign workers result simply from pandemic fatigue, or from too many campaigns in a short period of time, or do they represent longer, more pronounced trends? Belfry Munroe and Munroe found that campaign workers in the 2015 election from all parties had noticed a trend toward fewer volunteers.[20] In 2021, several experienced Conservative campaign staffers said the same thing: volunteers are increasingly hard to find, and local campaigns must make adjustments to attract workers. Their comments might reflect a decline in the Conservative Party's local organizational capacity, though the same problem was also observed in the NDP in 2021.[21] The question deserves further study.

Behind the Scenes

Based upon ten interviews with campaign workers, this section documents typical approaches to how staff are allocated and their key roles. Respondents often stressed that factors such as riding demographics, a campaign's volunteer capacity and experience, financial resources, and the flow of the campaign both nationally and locally could influence how the campaign is run. Yet workers from different parties seem to take a very similar approach. Voter identification through canvassing on doorsteps and get-out-the-vote (GOTV) efforts are the essence of local campaigning for all parties, and it is striking how much they have in common in pursuing these objectives.

A campaign typically revolves around a core group of key people who provide the most commitment and anchor the campaign. One Atlantic Conservative explained how his campaign had two dozen or so volunteers involved at some point, but four or five people who worked more or less full-time hours, either on a paid basis or in the early mornings and evenings/weekends around their normal employment. These people "generate all the activity that makes the campaign look credible and makes the volunteer giving six hours a week useful." Formal titles are not necessarily a good guide to who is carrying the weight. "Titles are free, so give them away" as a reward for volunteer engagement, advised a Liberal organizer. But people's participation is not usually constrained by an organizational chart, because there is so much work to do, so little time to do it, and so much overlap among roles. "Everyone does a little bit of everything," explained another Liberal, so "whether you're in an official role or you're a volunteer everyone kind of has to pull together."

The local campaign manager (whose role is more fully examined in Chapter 8 of this volume) serves as part senior adviser and confidant to the candidate and part senior administrator with overall responsibility for the campaign, directing and coordinating all of the separate pieces. This role includes setting and managing the budget and signing-off on all expenses. One Liberal campaign manager worked with the candidate's official agent to prepare three budgets, each with different spending assumptions depending on when the writ was dropped. The campaign manager also advises on communication strategies and messages and establishes priorities for canvassing and GOTV efforts. The role requires establishing trust and sound working relationships with different people, including the candidate, the local riding association and volunteers, as well as the central campaign headquarters.

If resources permit, then many campaigns will designate an aide to accompany the candidate day to day and act as a combination of executive assistant, driver, coach, and cheerleader. This means accompanying the candidate to all events and activities, knocking on doors, recording data, maintaining the schedule, boosting spirits, reminding the candidate about talking points, and making sure that the candidate pays attention to self-care. A knack for using social media is valuable since it allows the aide to write and upload posts on behalf of the candidate. An important task is making sure a candidate does not take too long at doors – "twenty seconds, tops," a Liberal campaign worker mentioned – and helping to extract the candidate from awkward situations. An NDP worker who had been an aide said that good relational skills are important: "It's got to be someone who can not only do the job but do it well and do it without irritating the candidate." The position involves hard work, stress, diplomacy, and mature judgment yet typically is held by a younger person with little campaign experience but lots of enthusiasm and stamina.

Campaigns often designate a director of communications, though sometimes the function is performed by the campaign manager or deputy campaign manager, especially because advertising costs affect the budget. Although messaging is usually provided by the central party to align with that of the national leader and platform, and to provide consistency across the country, the local campaign communications lead must use judgment in applying national templates to specific situations. A Green Party activist thought that the party's candidates enjoyed significant autonomy for personalized messaging. An NDP adviser, in contrast, believed that his party expected candidates to adhere "fairly rigidly" to the party's overhead messaging. Whereas candidates in target areas and those with well-resourced campaigns with technical capacity might have "a bit more discretion" to refine messaging for local audiences, he thought that the majority of local campaigns would simply use the templates provided by the central party: "It is [insert] picture here, name here, riding name here, and print it off and send it out."

Adopting these central message templates and arranging for printed literature are important since campaigns need a variety of products for distribution at doorsteps and by mail. Digital content, however, is becoming the preferred method of campaign communication, including advertising. As a Liberal campaign manager in Ontario said, "I hate any kind of ad spend that doesn't give us data back." Facebook ads allow a campaign not only to push out messages to voters but also to track voter engagement (how many people clicked on an ad, how many people "liked" it) and even to harvest data for voter identification if voters can be induced to provide details.

For the public, the "sign war" on arterial roads and in residential neighbourhoods is perhaps the most obvious indication of an election campaign (see Chapter 16 of this volume for further information on campaign signage operations). Signs represent a proxy for the campaign team's operational strength, increase name recognition for the candidate, and buoy the partisan enthusiasm of supporters. Typically, a campaign has a crew of volunteers who drive around the riding putting up signs in key areas, delivering signs to supporters who have requested them, and replacing or repairing signs that have been stolen or vandalized.

Anthony Sayers asserts the importance of this activity, arguing that "campaign teams measure their success by how many signs they erect compared to their opponents."[22] However, though the popular perception might be that signs indicate a party's and a candidate's momentum, not all campaign activists share this view. On the contrary, many believe that signs cause more trouble than they are worth and distract campaigns from the more important work of identifying supporters. A Toronto-area Liberal thought that putting up signs is "such a waste of time" and that effort would be better spent knocking on doors. An Ottawa-area Conservative adviser called signs "the biggest pain in the ass in a campaign," and an Atlantic Liberal campaign manager declared that "I hate them a lot." Another Ontario Liberal summarized his perspective on putting up signs: "I hate it because it takes time. It takes resources. It's a lot of trouble. People ask for them. You need to arrange getting them out there. People complain when they don't get them up when they ask for them. Or they do get them, and they didn't ask for them. They get damaged and need to be replaced." At the end of the day, he said, "signs don't vote," and ideally volunteers should focus on identifying voters. However, "the fact that signs exist means you have to compete, and you've got to look like you exist." So he advised deploying them in such a way as to suggest momentum whether it exists or not: erect large signs along arterial roads as soon as the election is called, then save up requests so that halfway through the campaign you can put them up, and "all of a sudden it'll look like we're building momentum across the riding. And then close to election day or on election day put up a ton."

Campaigns often have prospective volunteers walk in – usually fresh-faced political science students – and confidently announce that they are best suited to work on policy. "You laugh at them," said an experienced Conservative campaign operative. Local campaigns have very little leeway to develop policy statements, especially within parties that have a hope of winning, since prime ministers do not want to be saddled with all sorts of uncoordinated and unauthorized promises by candidates.

Someone needs to assist the candidate with learning the party's platform and preparing for debates. But candidates generally strive for efficiency in door knocking and therefore try to avoid lengthy policy discussions on doorsteps. Nor are debates an exercise in informed policy deliberation since, "by and large," a Liberal campaign worker noted, "the people that show up have got their minds made up and are there to support one of the candidates," not to hear an exchange of ideas. As a Liberal campaign manager commented, "there's only so much policy you can do in a campaign, particularly when the platform comes out," though candidates can decide to emphasize or downplay party policies according to public opinion and facts on the ground in their areas or perhaps find ways to apply the policies to local contexts.

Volunteers are the lifeblood of a campaign, and recruiting, training, tasking, and motivating them are vital. Sometimes this work is done by the campaign manager, but if possible campaigns name someone to this role specifically. Ironically, as a Liberal campaign worker mentioned, this is often a "super-junior person" because more senior people want to do more political work. It is a hard job because "you have to go and cajole a bunch of non-politicos into coming out in the first place and then to come out again." This requires a delicate touch with people. However, if volunteers are not managed well, they can diminish the campaign's capacity elsewhere since so many campaign activities are volunteer intensive.

Just as posting signs is designed to boost recognition of the party and the candidate in the riding, so too are other campaign activities. Volunteers are often marshalled to participate in a "burma shave," in which they gather with the candidate along an arterial road to wave campaign signs and cheer to attract attention from passing motorists. This display increases the candidate's personal profile and gives the impression of a fun-loving, positive campaign in the hope that such enthusiasm might be contagious.

"Mainstreeting" is another activity designed to increase attention for the candidate. A contingent of volunteers gathers in an area with concentrated pedestrian traffic to wave signs and button-hole passersby to build the campaign's profile. "You wave your signs until somebody kicks you out or says that you're not allowed to be there, and then you move on to the next one," said an NDP campaigner. Unlike demonstrations along a highway, mainstreeting allows volunteers to ask voters for support, and responses can be collected and entered into the campaign database. This is useful but does not amount to systematic voter identification.

Candidates canvass voters to identify party supporters and subsequently ensure that they vote on election day (see also Chapter 10 of this volume for a more detailed account of local canvassing procedures). These functions – voter ID and GOTV – are the two pillars of local election campaigns, and volunteers are deployed to ensure that they are done most efficiently. Some voters might harbour the illusion that canvassing is a method of public engagement or persuasion. This is no longer its primary purpose, if it ever was. Instead, canvassing has become an exercise in the efficient harvesting of data.

Volunteers are dispatched in pairs or in teams throughout the riding to knock on doors and ask residents whom they intend to vote for and, if supporters, whether they will take lawn signs, volunteer, or donate. Since there are many volunteers but only one candidate, they canvass to increase the candidate's efficiency in reaching voters. "Leapfrogging" is a popular technique in which volunteers knock on doors ahead of the candidate and, if someone is home, keep the resident at the door while the candidate runs up to meet the person.[23] Evenings and weekends are more productive times since more volunteers tend to be available and more people are at home. Door knocking was especially effective during the election in 2021 since, because of the pandemic and late-summer heat, more people were at home, so canvassing resulted in a higher contact rate.

Voter identification can also be done by phone, but some practitioners increasingly view telephone canvassing as a poor substitute for door knocking. "Industrial phone banking no longer works" for voter ID, said one senior Conservative volunteer in Atlantic Canada. "If we got 10 percent pick up, we considered ourselves lucky." Therefore, experts strongly prefer in-person canvassing when campaigns have sufficient resources to do it. "I think any time you can engage with someone face to face, that's preferable," commented an NDP campaigner. "I feel like I can read a person better. You get a sense of their body language and how they're engaging, whether they're being genuine, whether they're just trying to kind of brush you away." Again, the Green Party's experience in Kitchener Centre was different, with an experienced activist saying that phone banking "had a great impact on our ability to ID" and reached supporters not contacted through door knocking.

Voter identification efforts show local campaigns who their supporters are so that they can follow up and encourage them to vote on election day. Because it is the culmination of the entire campaign's effort, "e-day" requires all available workers to be tasked and coordinated properly to contact all identified supporters to ensure that they vote, and to keep contacting them until Elections Canada confirms that they have voted. This operation is a large logistical challenge.

The GOTV manager, ideally someone with experience who can function well under pressure, often recruits people to run home centres or satellite campaign offices in areas throughout the riding, and each home centre acts as a local base of operations for volunteers on election day. Although this can be done out of the main campaign headquarters, district centres keep volunteers closer to the neighbourhoods on which they are focusing. The number of districts depends on the number of volunteers available and on the nature of the riding: an urban community with large apartment complexes needs an approach different from that in a rural area with a spread-out population. One Liberal explained that he prefers a relatively small number of centres – perhaps one in each quarter of the riding – because this allows geographic proximity while tying up as few resources as possible in managing the centres.

The day before the vote, the GOTV manager will prepackage bundles for each home centre. They can include door hangers along with stickers printed with the relevant polling station address and hours, campaign flyers and "don't forget to vote" cards, a copy of Elections Canada rules for the polling station, and an official form signed by the candidate authorizing a volunteer to act as the candidate's representative at the polling station. Several Conservative campaign workers expressed distrust of the party's mobile app and included printed maps in the bundles; by contrast, Liberal campaign workers used virtual maps generated by their app.

When volunteers arrive at the home centre early on e-day, they can pick up door hangers with the poll location affixed and start delivering them to their assigned supporters. Later in the day, volunteers can drop off vote reminder cards and continue door knocking in an effort to get voters to the polls, offering rides if needed. At the same time, the campaign office can make telephone calls to the same supporters to encourage them to vote. If it is a target riding, then perhaps the central campaign will also pay a phone bank to call supporters in the riding.

The key to successful GOTV is collecting and coordinating information from different sources. First, home centre managers record which volunteers are going where in a Google doc (or similar live format) so that the GOTV manager can see in real time which areas have been covered and efficiently route resources as needed. Second, a volunteer, by presenting the candidate's signed representative form, can go to the polling station and collect "bingo sheets." These are lists that Elections Canada officials provide to candidates regularly throughout the day showing who has voted. The volunteer either communicates this information back to the campaign headquarters or enters it into the database directly. This ensures that individuals who have already voted are not contacted again – a nuisance for voters and inefficient for the campaign. Third, canvassing data permit campaigns to target voters according to different degrees of support. Campaigns obviously want to encourage their strongest supporters to vote and probably their likely supporters too. However, campaigns must decide whether to "pull" undecided voters or even "soft opposition," or to retrench and focus only on confirmed supporters. This is a strategic decision that the campaign manager makes in consultation with the central headquarters, whose big-picture perspective and advanced analytical capacity allow it to see and exploit macro-trends as campaigns across the country report their efforts.

As noted, candidates can authorize campaign workers to represent them at polling stations. Doing so permits them to observe voting throughout the day and, after the polls close, to observe the counting of ballots, though they may not interfere with voters and must follow all directions from Elections Canada officials.[24] Ideally, campaigns have at least one representative present at each polling station (up to two are permitted per candidate) throughout the voting and to observe the counting. However, in practice, comprehensive staffing is a challenge because, as a Conservative noted, by the end of election day volunteers are tired and want to attend the hoped-for victory party. Admittedly, "you're never, ever going to make the difference in an election through scrutineering," a Liberal mentioned. But having a presence is important to ensure that there are no "shenanigans" and that the rules are enforced, especially at polls with histories of volatility. Allegations of vote fraud and disputes over access for partisan poll watchers in the 2020 US presidential election underscore how important transparent voting procedures and routine, uncontroversial access for partisan scrutineers are to the integrity of Canada's electoral system.

Conclusion

This chapter has outlined the principal activities of local campaign workers and shown that, regardless of party, campaigns tend to emphasize the same priorities and employ the same techniques to identify their supporters and get out the vote. In a close election, the local campaign organization and the commitment of local party workers, both volunteer and paid, can make the difference between winning and losing the riding. However, the federal election of 2021 suggests that partisan volunteer engagement might be waning and could accelerate the trend toward more paid campaign staff.

At the same time, the data-gathering and analytical capabilities of national party headquarters – especially the Liberal Party – are increasing. If local campaign organizations become less adept at canvassing, and if national parties start to harvest data more and more through social media advertising, then what are the implications for local campaigns and how parties engage voters? It is trite to call for more research. However, it has been thirty years since the last comprehensive survey-based study of local campaign workers. Up-to-date data are surely warranted to address these questions.

Notes

1 Elections Canada, "Table 12."
2 Raj, "How the Race Was Won," A25.
3 Carty, *Canadian Political Parties.*
4 Sayers, *Parties, Candidates, and Constituency Campaigns,* 66.
5 Cross, "The Importance of Local Party Activity," 611.
6 Carty and Eagles, *Politics Is Local,* 122; Sayers, *Parties, Candidates, and Constituency Campaigns,* 8.
7 Cross and Young, "The Contours of Political Party Membership," 431, 440.
8 Sayers, *Parties, Candidates, and Constituency Campaigns,* 87. See also Chapter 4 of this volume.
9 Carty, *Canadian Political Parties,* 173.
10 Carty, *Canadian Political Parties,* 158.
11 Wilson, "The Impact of the COVID-19 Pandemic," 21; Wilson, "The Work of Canadian Political Staffers," 6; Dion, *Annual Report,* 4.
12 Sayers, *Parties, Candidates, and Constituency Campaigns,* 66; Carty and Eagles, *Politics Is Local,* 122.
13 Koop, *Grassroots Liberals,* 125–33.
14 Belfry Munroe and Munroe, "Constituency Campaigning in the Age of Data."
15 Thompson, "Mounting a Local Campaign," 195.
16 Elections Canada, "Campaign Guidance."
17 Elections Canada, "Additional Guidelines."
18 Blewett, "From a Refusal to Door-Knock"; Egan-Elliott, "Less Door-Knocking, More Outdoor Events."
19 Carty, *Canadian Political Parties,* 158.
20 Belfry Munroe and Munroe, "Constituency Campaigning in the Age of Data," 149.
21 Clark, "The NDP Is Strong on TikTok."
22 Sayers, "Electoral Volatility," 8.
23 Stolte, "The Art and Science of Door Knocking in Edmonton."
24 Elections Canada, "Guidelines for Candidates' Representatives."

Bibliography

Belfry Munroe, Kaija, and H.D. Munroe. "Constituency Campaigning in the Age of Data." *Canadian Journal of Political Science* 51, 1 (2018): 135–54.

Blewett, Taylor. "From a Refusal to Door-Knock, to Grab-and-Go Election Signs: Campaigning in the COVID-Era." *Ottawa Citizen,* 21 August 2021. https://ottawacitizen.com/news/politics/election-2021/covid-campaigning-presents-thorny-issues-for-candidates-to-navigate.

Carty, R.K. *Canadian Political Parties in the Constituencies.* Toronto: Dundurn, 1991.

Carty, R. Kenneth, and Munroe Eagles. *Politics Is Local: National Politics at the Grassroots.* Don Mills, ON: Oxford University Press, 2005.

Clark, Campbell. "The NDP Is Strong on TikTok but Weak on the Ground." *Globe and Mail,* 8 October 2021. https://www.theglobeandmail.com/politics/article-the-ndp-strong-on-tiktok-but-weak-on-the-ground/.

Cross, William. "The Importance of Local Party Activity in Understanding Canadian Politics: Winning from the Ground Up in the 2015 Federal Election: Presidential Address to the Canadian Political Science Association Calgary, 31 May 2016." *Canadian Journal of Political Science* 49, 4 (2016): 601–20.

Cross, William, and Lisa Young. "The Contours of Political Party Membership in Canada." *Party Politics* 10, 4 (2004): 427–44.

Dion, Mario. *Annual Report: Conflict of Interest Act.* Ottawa: Office of the Conflict of Interest and Ethics Commissioner, Parliament of Canada, 2021.

Egan-Elliott, Roxanne. "Less Door-Knocking, More Outdoor Events: The Art of Pandemic Campaigning." *Times Colonist* [Victoria], 20 September 2021. https://www.timescolonist.com/federal-election-2019-archive/less-door-knocking-more-outdoor-events-the-art-of-pandemic-campaigning-4692221.

Elections Canada. "Additional Guidelines for Observing Voting Operations at Ordinary and Advance Polling Places." 23 August 2021. https://elections.ca/content.aspx?section=pol&dir=can/gui&document=p1&lang=e.

–. "Campaign Guidance for Canvassing during COVID-19." 21 June 2021. https://www.elections.ca/content.aspx?section=pol&document=index&dir=can/pand&lang=e.

–. "Guidelines for Candidates' Representatives." N.d. https://elections.ca/content.aspx?section=pol&document=p&dir=can/gui&lang=e.

–. "Table 12: List of Candidates by Electoral District and Individual Results." Official Voting Results (Raw Data) for the 43rd General Election, 21 October 2019. https://www.elections.ca/res/rep/off/ovr2019app/51/data_donnees/table_tableau12.csv.

Koop, Royce. *Grassroots Liberals: Organizing for Local and National Politics.* Vancouver: UBC Press, 2011.

Raj, Althia. "How the Race Was Won: The Inside Story of How the Liberals Turned Around Their Faltering Campaign and Won the 2021 Election." *Toronto Star,* 9 October 2021, A22–25.

Sayers, Anthony M. *Parties, Candidates, and Constituency Campaigns in Canadian Elections.* Vancouver: UBC Press, 1999.

–. "Electoral Volatility and Political Party Organization in Canada and Australia." Paper presented at the annual meeting of the Canadian Political Science Association, Saskatoon, 2007. https://cpsa-acsp.ca/papers-2007/Sayers.pdf.

Stolte, Elise. "The Art and Science of Door Knocking in Edmonton." *Edmonton Journal,* 9 April 2011. https://edmontonjournal.com/news/the-art-and-science-of-door-knocking-in-edmonton.

Thompson, Allan. "Mounting a Local Campaign." In *The Canadian Federal Election of 2015,* edited by Jon H. Pammett and Christopher Dornan, 195–224. Toronto: Dundurn, 2016.

Wilson, R. Paul. "The Impact of the COVID-19 Pandemic on Canadian Parliamentary Political Staffers." *Canadian Parliamentary Review* 43, 3 (2020): 20–32.

–. "The Work of Canadian Political Staffers in Parliamentary Caucus Research Offices." *Canadian Public Administration* 63, 3 (2020): 498–521.

10

Voter Canvassing

Jacob Robbins-Kanter

Abstract   Voter canvassing varies substantially from constituency to constituency in terms of its importance, its intensity, and how it is conducted. This chapter draws from eight interviews with local candidates and campaign managers in the context of the federal election of 2021. These interviews demonstrate the nature of variation in canvassing practices and reveal how they have evolved to meet the needs of constituency campaigns and the central party apparatus. The chapter highlights how canvassing activities are shaped by constituency competitiveness, geography, and available resources. Today, as with most aspects of local campaign activity, canvassing has been affected by the rise of digital technologies. Crucially, candidates for the major federal parties increasingly make use of social media platforms, party apps, and other digital tools to gather voter data and efficiently identify their levels of support. The chapter argues that the growth of these technologies has accentuated disparities between local campaigns with modest resources, often affiliated with smaller parties, and resource-rich local campaigns equipped to pursue sophisticated voter identification and mobilization.

Résumé   Le pointage électoral varie considérablement d'une circonscription à l'autre, en termes d'importance, d'intensité, et de la façon dont il est mené. Ce chapitre repose sur huit entrevues avec des candidats locaux et des directeurs de campagne effectuées au cours de l'élection fédérale de 2021. Ces derniers mettent en lumière la variation des pratiques de pointage et comment elles ont évolué pour répondre aux besoins des campagnes locales et du parti central. Les activités de pointage sont profondément façonnées par la compétitivité des circonscriptions, la géographie, et les ressources disponibles à l'échelle locale. Actuellement, le pointage est influencé par l'essor des technologies numériques. Essentiellement, les candidats des principaux partis fédéraux utilisent de plus en plus les plateformes des médias sociaux, les applications mobiles, et d'autres outils numériques pour recueillir des données et identifier efficacement leurs degrés de soutien. Le chapitre soutient que la croissance de ces technologies accentue les disparités entre les campagnes locales ayant des ressources modestes et celles qui sont bien équipées pour faciliter une identification précise et sophistiquée des électeurs.

CANVASSING REFERS TO direct, unmediated, personal contact between voters and campaign workers or candidates. It entails both door knocking and telephone contact. A canvasser seeks to ascertain voters' political leanings, likelihood of voting for the canvasser's party, and willingness to offer other forms of support, such as accepting lawn signs.[1] Using this information, a local campaign can determine its level of political support in the constituency and develop a get-out-the-vote (GOTV) strategy for advance polls and election day. This chapter builds upon Chapter 9's brief discussion of voter canvassing by examining standard and innovative canvassing methods and their implementation during the federal election in 2021. The finding is that the emergence of new canvassing techniques has enhanced the capabilities of resource-rich local campaigns, whereas resource-poor campaigns rely on tools with diminishing utility.

Local campaigns engage in a variety of activities intended to maximize their vote share, but canvassing is usually regarded as their most important function and the core of the ground campaign.[2] First, canvassing is important in terms of the time and resources consumed. A visitor to any local campaign office will quickly note that a large share of the campaign's focus is devoted to coordinating campaign workers and canvassing locations, managing collected data, and canvassing itself.[3] It is a daunting task to speak personally with tens of thousands of voters spread across the electoral district. For the major federal parties, canvassers distribute thousands of campaign leaflets, which represent another substantial campaign expense. Even local campaigns with large numbers of volunteers find that voters can be difficult to reach or unfriendly to canvassers, and more resources are expended to bolster outreach as these problems arise. Second, despite these challenges, local campaigns engage in canvassing because it is viewed as important to their electoral success. Although personal contact occasionally can persuade undecided voters,[4] canvassing is used primarily to identify pre-existing supporters and to ensure that they vote. Accordingly, a major goal of canvassers is to lay the groundwork for an effective GOTV operation. Third, canvassing is important because it provides valuable data for political parties. The information obtained by campaign workers is typically entered into a party database. These data are useful to parties even beyond the formal campaign period since they can be used to send microtargeted messages to voters based upon political preference, occupational sector, geographic location, ethnocultural background, and other features.[5] Moreover, the major parties have developed predictive voting algorithms, which feed on these data and can be used, among other things, to improve future canvassing strategies.[6]

In addition to benefits for parties and candidates, canvassing can be beneficial to voters. It is the only time that many citizens will encounter politicians and campaign workers in person and have the opportunity to express their views directly. Moreover, canvassing generally has positive effects on voter engagement and mobilization. In contrast to the national party, which might seek to suppress voter turnout for those unlikely to vote for it, local canvassers aim to motivate voters and move them to the polls.[7]

Debates about the efficacy of canvassing are embedded within debates about the overall impact of local campaigns on voting intentions. The vast majority of Canadians vote based upon their preferred party and leader rather than the local candidate.[8] However, even if local campaign activity accounts for only 5 or 6 percent of voting intentions, this percentage is sufficient to change the outcomes of many close races. For example, based upon the federal election in 2011, 31 percent of constituencies were so-called battlegrounds, whereas 69 percent were party strongholds.[9] For these marginal contests, an effective canvassing operation plays a major part in the potential electoral impacts of local campaigns.[10]

Canvassing is often referred to as door knocking because it commonly occurs in person at voters' doorsteps. However, phone canvassing is another important way to reach potential voters. To canvass by phone, volunteers and campaign staff rely on lists of electors and structure their interactions around scripted campaign messages. Well-resourced campaigns often have access to automated dialing software that allows them to avoid using personal phone numbers and to enter information directly into the party database. Candidates can also conduct follow-up calls with voters who requested to speak to them directly. Telephone canvassing is thus distinct from the campaign practice of sending automated prerecorded phone messages and facilitates more authentic one-on-one discussions.[11]

Phone canvassing boasts certain advantages: theoretically, canvassers can reach large numbers of voters in a short time, they can speak to voters in distant or remote areas, it is relatively cost effective, and it can be undertaken by campaign workers with mobility challenges or those reluctant to engage in face-to-face interactions. However, a shrinking number of households have landlines, and cellphone numbers can be difficult to obtain. Compared with door canvassing, the mobilizing effect for telephone respondents is typically weaker, the refusal rate is higher, and communication barriers are more pronounced.[12] For example, David Nickerson calculates that phone canvassing is roughly half as effective in increasing voter turnout as door canvassing.[13] However, research has shown that well-trained canvassers, the careful targeting of respondents, and a persuasive script can help to overcome obstacles to effective phone canvassing.[14]

More generally, canvassing in Canada varies substantially based upon local party support and campaign resources. A local campaign with a substantial support base can afford to limit its outreach to sympathetic voters. It might begin the campaign with a long list of likely supporters and calculate, together with the central party, how many confirmed supporters are needed to win the race. In these stronghold ridings, local campaigns likely never need to canvass hostile or indifferent voters. Once they have reached their target number of confirmed supporters, they can be relatively confident of impending election victories. Conversely, local campaigns in uncompetitive ridings possess modest lists of their confirmed supporters and more often canvass voters with unknown political leanings or even those expected to support other parties.

There is considerable variation in canvassing practices depending on campaign resources.[15] Money and volunteers allow local campaigns repeatedly to blanket their supporters with door knocks, pamphlets, and phone calls to ensure that they will make it to the polling stations. They can match specific canvassing teams to certain areas of the electoral district, for example, based upon their familiarity with the neighbourhood or their ethnolinguistic background. Incumbent candidates often have a further advantage in their familiarity with voters and effective canvassing practices since many door-knock continuously between election campaigns (relatedly, see Chapter 5 of this volume). Meanwhile, for local campaigns with minimal resources, the candidates might do most of the canvassing work on their own or draw from the same small group of volunteers. Some candidates continue to work a full-time job or have difficulty taking an unpaid leave of absence. These challenges often result in limited canvassing coverage or effectiveness. For smaller parties, including the Green Party, canvassing efforts and resources converge on target seats, and uncompetitive districts are canvassed minimally.[16]

Although the central party can indicate its preferred canvassing tactics, ultimately it is up to local campaign actors to implement them.[17] Since local campaigns possess varying resources and are staffed largely by volunteers, this implementation can be more difficult than anticipated by the party. Moreover, despite its superior resources, the central party does not always know best when it comes to implementing appropriate canvassing tactics. For example, in 2015, the Liberal Party headquarters mistakenly and repeatedly sent canvassers to empty vacation homes in Whistler, British Columbia, and to politically unfriendly neighbourhoods rather than to higher-density, Liberal-friendly polling divisions.[18]

Along these lines, the central party regularly provides targets for the number of supporters to identify and expects local campaigns to meet them.[19] If these objectives are not met, then a central party worker is likely to follow up with the offending campaign team. Yet the smooth transmission and local implementation of national party directives should not be assumed given that campaign workers have a variety of abilities and motivations (see Chapter 9 of this volume). The candidate and the campaign manager might not always view their interests as aligned with those of the central party. Even if they do, it can be challenging to manage teams of volunteer canvassers. Thus, though the central party can establish canvassing targets, their attainment depends on the dedication and competence of local campaign teams. Canvassing challenges are most pronounced for local campaigns with insufficient resources that might view canvassing targets as overly demanding or unrealistic. In addition, a leader's or party's popularity can vary considerably by region and electoral district.

Nonetheless, technology seemingly has increased the central party's control over local canvassing activities. For the major federal parties, smartphone apps have replaced pen and paper canvassing. Canvassers enter voter data directly into an app, which then uploads the information to party databases.[20] These developments have given the central party greater input into local canvassing decisions since it can view and respond to data in real time. For example, party officials can ask to reroute a canvassing team or even ask that it move to a neighbouring constituency to help a different local campaign.

Local Trends

Across Canada, canvassing goals for local campaigns are largely the same: canvassers aim to identify supporters, recruit volunteers and other forms of support, gather data on voter preferences, and solidify GOTV strategies. However, variation in physical and human geography requires that local campaigns reach these goals using different canvassing practices and strategies. In remote areas, some citizens might be virtually inaccessible to canvassers, so local campaigns must rely on phone canvassing. In other cases, canvassers must travel long distances between homes, which makes their work more physically onerous or time consuming than in densely populated areas. To be sure, urban areas feature their own challenges, which can include the perception of invasiveness when canvassing high-rise dwellings, difficulty obtaining access to these buildings, or facing out-of-date information because voters might have moved elsewhere between election periods.[21] Although population turnover presents an enduring challenge, it can be beneficial to meet new residents, who might become new donors, party enthusiasts, or volunteers.

Altogether, the logistical challenges of reaching voters at their homes are common to urban and rural settings. Faced with these difficulties, local campaigns instead might canvass at shopping centres, local events, or public gathering places. For example, former Liberal MP Adam Vaughan found that many voters in his downtown Toronto constituency did not answer their apartment doors, and his campaign workers had better results canvassing in city parks.[22] Skilled local campaign teams will seek productive ways to meet voters face to face.

The spatial, aesthetic, and other visible features of neighbourhoods can also provide cues to canvassers and inform campaign strategy. In this manner, Vaughan's campaign team witnessed the extent to which residents spent their free time in crowded public spaces. In another case, Brampton East MP Maninder Sidhu determined while canvassing in 2019 that crime was a major concern in his constituency after observing the number of homes that had installed security cameras.[23]

In addition, the challenges posed by inclement weather vary based upon the physical and human geography of the constituency. Door canvassers must adapt to rain, snow, or extreme heat, for example, by confining their activities to high-rise buildings, coffee shops, and other indoor venues. These challenges are more pronounced in rural communities, where weather can derail canvassing plans if there are few indoor alternatives available.

For these reasons, canvassing protocols established by the major federal parties must be adapted to local circumstances.[24] As long as they are making consistent progress and echoing party messages, local campaigns have some leeway to implement their preferred canvassing techniques. This was highly apparent during the federal election in 2021 as the major federal parties implemented some generic COVID-19 canvassing protocols yet allowed campaigns to follow the advice of local public health units.

For door canvassers, campaign leaflets remain a vital tool. They serve as a reminder to party sympathizers of the impending election and help to cement locally tailored messages, even if flyers are quickly sent to the recycling bin. In fact, some canvassing excursions consist simply of leaflet drops in residents' mailboxes or on their doorsteps, without any face-to-face interaction. At times, partisan leaflets have raised ethical concerns and caused tensions between rival campaigns. In recent elections, seemingly inaccurate or sensational leaflets have elicited local controversy.[25] In rare cases, campaigns or candidates have been accused of interfering with leaflet distribution. For example, in 2021, Calgary Skyview Liberal candidate George Chahal was allegedly captured on a doorbell video camera removing a canvassing card that had been placed by his Conservative rival.[26] Regardless of potential controversies, campaign leaflets remain an important element of canvassing strategy. They can be tailored to local concerns, speak to ethnocultural communities, and implement local campaign tactics such as encouraging or discouraging strategic voting.[27]

In recent elections, the largest federal parties have continued to emphasize the importance of canvassing in their campaign training. For example, the Liberal Party's online training hub for volunteers features the following quotation from Justin Trudeau: "Knocking on doors. Making calls. Reaching out to Canadians, one conversation at a time. With your hope and hard work, we'll win the next federal election, community-by-community and block by block."[28]

The major parties' investment in canvassing ensures that it remains a collaborative enterprise. Although canvassing is spearheaded by local campaigns, parties pay close attention and send additional resources, where feasible, to target marginal seats. This assistance can include sending additional campaign workers from central party offices or neighbouring ridings, transferring campaign resources, and arranging visits from high-profile party figures, including the leader. In recent elections, the Conservatives and Liberals have focused intensive efforts on the 905 belt around metropolitan Toronto. For its part, the New Democratic Party has tended to target seats where the party finished in second place in prior elections. For other parties, the most vigorous canvassing occurs in ridings where they hope to make electoral breakthroughs.

Behind the Scenes

During the federal election in 2021, local campaigns explored new canvassing opportunities and faced familiar challenges. To understand current canvassing trends, I conducted eight semi-structured interviews with local campaign representatives. I emailed randomly selected local campaign offices affiliated with Canada's five major parties at their publicly listed email addresses. For this reason, the sample is limited by its exclusion of local campaigns without publicly listed email addresses. After receiving a sufficient number of positive responses, I chose a sample with the aim of including a range of local campaign experiences in terms of party affiliation, campaign resources, and riding geography. Interview participants included one Conservative campaign manager and one candidate, two Liberal campaign managers, two NDP candidates, one Bloc Québécois campaign manager, and one Green Party candidate.

Interview participants suggested that social media platforms present increasingly important venues for gathering voter data. Seven of eight participants contended that their canvassing frequently occurred through social media. For example, in the vast constituency of Labrador, NDP candidate Amy Norman stated that "I consider social media to be a form of canvassing ... [We're] using community groups and message boards on Facebook. It's completely interwoven into the fabrics of our communities."

High-resource campaigns are most able to capitalize on social media as a canvassing venue. Campaign manager Andrew Goodridge (Liberal, Beaches–East York) explained that his team monitored social media activity and recorded voter data in a manner similar to door canvassing. Goodridge contended that voters declare preferences "for certain politics and policies pretty plainly online. And that's information that could be gathered if one were wanting to inform [a] campaign's strategy ... [W]e look at what people are posting online, and we make a judgment about how we think they're going to vote." Conversely, campaigns with limited time to track social media activity during the campaign period can postpone doing so. A Conservative campaign manager in Ontario explained that "in the off season we plan to go there because that data still lives there online. I can go and look at who's interacting on particular issues, and we can harvest that." However, this delay prevents the campaign from using these additional data to inform its election strategy. Based upon these impressions, contemporary canvassing does not necessarily entail live interactions between voters and campaign workers. Instead, local campaigns rely on various social media platforms for traditional canvassing objectives: namely, voter engagement and the identification of voter preferences.

In 2021, other campaigns increased their focus on social media because of the ongoing COVID-19 pandemic. In the constituency of Kanata–Carleton, NDP candidate Melissa Coenraad contended that her campaign respected "people's reluctance to talk, so social media is picking up some of the slack." In Sherbrooke, Conservative candidate Andrea Winters felt uncomfortable with extensive door canvassing during the pandemic and reduced that activity in favour of literature drops, phone canvassing, and social media interaction.

Another recent canvassing innovation is the use of mass text messages sent to voters' cell phones. A Liberal campaign manager stated that "we try to make sure the messages we're sending out seem authentic and ... as natural and human as possible and as coming from the candidate. That's been extremely useful, and I can definitely see us using [text messages] again." However, this technique is limited by the availability of voters' cellphone numbers. Most local campaign representatives interviewed mentioned the unreliability of phone numbers on their voters lists. For example, a Conservative campaign manager in a high-resource Ontario riding stated that the campaign workers knew just 10 percent of their supporters' cellphone numbers. Similarly, Goodridge suggested that "we're really only able to get landlines in Canada because of laws around this, unless you buy [cellphone numbers], and there's only so many available to buy. We have predominantly landlines, and they're of eroding quality." The lack of phone numbers is even more pronounced for smaller parties. Green Party candidate Cynthia Lavictoire (Ville-Marie–Le Sud-Ouest–Île-des-Sœurs) explains that unreliable phone numbers led her campaign to abandon phone canvassing entirely and to emphasize door canvassing instead.

Some local campaigns have more reliable email addresses for supporters than cellphone numbers. Accordingly, social media and email have overtaken phone canvassing as a data-gathering tool for some local campaigns. A Conservative campaign manager spoke favourably of email as a potential canvassing tool with which supporters can be enticed to click on online links, with their responses recorded for the party. This campaign manager further highlighted restrictions on purchasing Canadian cellphone numbers and on uploading numbers to foreign-owned servers as reasons for diminishing returns on phone canvassing, particularly with paid canvassing teams.

Recent elections have also seen the entrenchment of app-based canvassing for the major parties. For example, a Conservative campaign manager stated that the campaign's canvassing efforts were 100 percent app based. Similarly, a Liberal campaign manager explained that smartphone or tablet canvassing is the norm "99 times out of 100." Both campaign managers offered praise for how user friendly their respective apps have become.

However, app-based canvassing is not consistently available outside the Conservative and Liberal Parties. At the time of her interview, Melissa Coenraad's campaign team was using paper canvassing sheets because it found the NDP app to be incomplete and unreliable. Fellow NDP candidate Amy Norman encountered technical difficulties with the app, mostly because of limited cellular service in remote parts of her district. For her part, Cynthia Lavictoire used a mix of pen and paper and the Green Party app, GVOTE. In some cases, volunteers for smaller parties have recorded voice notes on their phones to keep track of voter information after running out of paper, a practice that raises privacy concerns about the storage of data.

Local campaigns also grappled with some familiar challenges, such as ensuring voter data accuracy. Andrea Winters recalled that canvassing data in 2019 overestimated Conservative support in Sherbrooke and assumed that some voters declared their apparent support to canvassers merely out of politeness. Ultimately, these Sherbrooke residents supported other parties or did not vote. Canvasser error compounds the challenge of obtaining accurate data since campaign workers sometimes make subjective judgments on voters' receptivity to their party. Indeed, canvassers rarely ask voters to quantify their support in the terms used by party databases. Along these lines, Andrew Goodridge suggested that canvassers can produce "myopic results that aren't always accurate." Other local campaign representatives agreed that canvassers can emerge with data that are unrepresentative of their interactions with voters.

The potential degradation of voter data constitutes a related concern. A Conservative campaign manager suggested that voter data are perishable because of changing public opinion. From that view, prudent local campaigns can only assume perpetual support from their most committed loyalists and should approach the remainder of residents "from scratch" each election cycle. This is particularly true if a major party has changed its leader since voter commitments can shift based upon leader evaluations. Even voters who declare committed support to canvassers can change their minds during a campaign. In addition, when considering population turnover, or even changing electoral boundaries, the potential for expired or incomplete data is apparent.

Well-resourced local campaigns can compensate for these challenges by canvassing between election periods. This is a particular advantage for incumbents. As Goodridge explained, Beaches–East York MP Nathaniel Erskine-Smith continually door-knocks as part of his MP duties. Erskine-Smith and other MPs can gather ample up-to-date voter data while offering constituency services to residents as a rationale for the visits.

A second long-standing challenge consists of stretching limited campaign resources to meet canvassing objectives. In some cases, this challenge can prevent canvassing altogether, particularly for longshot local candidates. In the riding of Portneuf–Jacques Cartier, Bloc Québécois campaign manager Normand Beauregard stated that his campaign did not engage in any form of canvassing because of limited resources. For her part, Amy Norman faced especially resource-intensive canvassing duties in Labrador. She described her intention to visit all of the major communities in the vast riding, using a combination of car, plane, ferry, and speedboat. Labrador's isolated north coast is inaccessible by car, and Norman was unable to fit campaign signs into "a small Twin Otter plane." Instead, she travelled with collapsible vinyl banners and brochures that could be rolled out to create window signs. Her campaign expended additional resources to translate some campaign materials into Indigenous languages. Meanwhile, in Ontario, a Conservative campaign manager recalled similar challenges in the rural portions of the riding, where it can take five minutes to travel from one door to the next. Consequently, residents of these low-density areas are less likely to receive visits from door canvassers.

Similarly, resource limitations compel local campaigns to prioritize canvassing based upon their geographic areas of strength, which they identify based upon past election results by polling division. Winters explained that this approach allowed her to determine the best use of her limited resources since "reinforcing the strong points is a better strategy than trying to change the weak points." Lavictoire also planned her canvassing based upon poll-by-poll results from the previous election. She preferred to visit ambiguous polls, where the results showed no clear preference for a single party.

A Liberal campaign manager explained that, in a typical campaign, canvassing would begin with the candidate's most likely supporters and then other voters. However, the shorter campaign period in 2021 made this strategy unviable. This campaign manager emphasized the need to "make the best use of your time, which means reaching those most likely to vote and most likely to vote for your candidate." Since Liberal campaigns rank voters on a 1–5 scale, with 1 being most likely to support and 5 being least likely to support, the campaign sought to focus heavily on canvassing voters in the first two tiers. Nonetheless, local campaigns with sufficient resources can reach a wider array of residents, even during a shorter election period. Goodridge noted that the Beaches–East York Liberal campaign benefited from the involvement of forty young people paid to canvass as members of the locally run Young Liberals internship program. Additionally, this campaign team benefited from a relatively dense urban canvassing grid that expedited door knocking.

The value of volunteers and other campaign resources is perhaps most apparent on election day. For example, a Liberal campaign manager explained that the day begins with campaign volunteers who wake up very early to distribute door hangers at the homes of likely supporters "to make sure that when they're leaving for work they see it hanging on their door with their information on where they need to go to vote." Throughout the day, volunteers continue to ensure that every identified supporter has actually voted, with multiple reminders delivered by phone, email, text, and in person. Rides are offered to transport supporters to polling stations, where approved scrutineers are stationed to oversee the vote count.

Conversely, many local campaigns lack the resources for an effective GOTV operation. This obstacle to success can be reflected in the local election results if voters are not effectively moved to the polls. Encouraging supporters to vote in advance polls can help to address this challenge by easing demand and freeing up more resources on election day. As a Conservative campaign manager explained, "the more people vote in advance polls, the easier our job is on election day ... [W]e want to especially get people who have trouble standing in line for a long time, so when canvassing we try to identify accessibility issues. We can ask, 'Do you need a ride?'"

Additional challenges mentioned by local campaign representatives are low canvasser morale, exhaustion, and withdrawal from canvassing duties. These concerns are most pronounced in constituencies with physically demanding canvassing requirements and minimal resources. To boost morale, campaign managers can send canvassers to politically friendly territory, emphasize the social aspect of canvassing, grant them face-to-face time with the local candidate, and generate other forms of volunteer appreciation such as pub nights. A Liberal campaign manager noted that canvasser morale is also aided by candidate involvement in canvassing, the extent of which varies from one candidate to another.

Finally, local campaign representatives offered mixed responses regarding canvassing's importance relative to other campaign activities. Andrea Winters argued that canvassing was less important to her campaign than her frequent appearances on local media, a privilege that most candidates do not enjoy. Other campaign representatives argued that canvassing remains extremely important despite recognizing that it might not make a meaningful difference to the election outcome. For some, the importance of canvassing lies in aiming for the strongest possible election result. Still others are firmly socialized into their parties' canvassing obligations and unlikely to question its necessity. For Melissa Coenraad, the importance of canvassing lies more in voter engagement than in electoral impact. Similarly, according to Cynthia Lavictoire, who has canvassed extensively in longshot constituencies, canvassing is a meaningful and rewarding experience. It bears noting that campaigns often attract citizens who enjoy the challenge of improving voter engagement, discussing political issues, and getting to know their communities in a unique way.

Conclusion

Canvassing remains an indispensable part of a viable local campaign. Across Canada, campaign teams share similar canvassing goals, particularly in obtaining voter data and executing a GOTV strategy. Yet substantial resource discrepancies entail that some do not have the ability to fulfill these objectives. Further variation in constituency geography entails that local campaigns rely on diverse canvassing tools and techniques.

Campaigns with significant resources invest heavily in canvassing. They visit every household in their constituencies, sometimes more than once, and keep sophisticated, up-to-date records with detailed voter information. Some even keep voter data within the campaign team rather than sharing everything with the central party. In contrast, a lack of resources leads some campaigns to skip canvassing altogether. This is undoubtedly the product of a single-member plurality electoral system in which the outcomes in certain districts are foregone conclusions. In terms of geographic diversity, remote and rural constituencies present a particular set of challenges to canvassers. Despite the time, money, and physical demands involved, dedicated campaign workers and candidates continue to visit these communities each election cycle. They are aided in these efforts by phone canvassing and increasingly by online platforms.

Interviews conducted during the federal election of 2021 revealed how local campaigns are exploring new canvassing possibilities in the digital age. Campaign representatives emphasized a shift away from phone canvassing, with its diminishing return on investment, and toward social media. Since most citizens are unaware that their actions on social media are sometimes recorded by political parties, this highlights the need to balance privacy concerns with parties' and local campaigns' desires for rich and plentiful data. Local campaigns for the largest federal parties also rely heavily on app-based canvassing, and some are adopting mass automated text messages as a tactic for voter identification and mobilization.

Constituency campaigns faced familiar challenges in 2021, including ensuring reliable and up-to-date data, using their resources as efficiently as possible, and maintaining morale among canvassers. Alongside these enduring challenges, the core components of canvassing have remained consistent for many decades. Canvassers seek to engage voters, gauge their preferences, sometimes attempt to persuade them, and always keep track of their responses. These aspects of canvassing are unlikely to change, even as new techniques and tools emerge.

Notes

1 Belfry Munroe and Munroe, "Constituency Campaigning in the Age of Data."
2 Carty and Eagles, "Do Local Campaigns Matter?"
3 Thompson, "Mounting a Local Campaign."

4 Arceneaux, "I'm Asking for Your Support."
5 Marland and Giasson, "From Brokerage to Boutique Politics."
6 Bennett, "Data-Driven Elections in Canada."
7 Koop, "Constituency Campaigning in the 2015 Federal Election."
8 For example, Stevens et al., "Local Candidate Effects in Canadian Elections."
9 Bodet, "Strongholds and Battlegrounds," 585.
10 Cross, "The Importance of Local Party Activity."
11 Small and Philpott, "The Independent Candidate."
12 Gerber and Green, "The Effects of Canvassing."
13 Nickerson, "Volunteer Phone Calls Can Increase Turnout," 283.
14 John and Brannan, "How Different Are Telephoning and Canvassing?"; Abrajano et al., "When Campaigns Call, Who Answers?"
15 Sayers, *Parties, Candidates, and Constituency Campaigns.*
16 Thurton, "Annamie Paul Is Leading the Green Party's National Campaign."
17 Richler, *The Candidate.*
18 Belfry Munroe and Munroe, "Constituency Campaigning in the Age of Data."
19 Koop, "Constituency Campaigning in the 2015 Federal Election."
20 Delacourt, *Shopping for Votes.*
21 Sayers, *Parties, Candidates, and Constituency Campaigns.*
22 Adam Vaughan, interview with the author, 12 December 2018.
23 Talbot and McAllister, "Candidates Seek Connection with Voters."
24 Carty and Eagles, *Politics Is Local.*
25 For example, Riedner, "Saroya, Chiang Campaigns."
26 CBC News, "Calgary Police Investigate Liberal MP-Elect George Chahal."
27 Grauer, "Attack Flyers Show Conservative Candidate 'Bleeding' Support."
28 Liberal Party of Canada, "Events."

Bibliography

Abrajano, Marisa, Taylor N. Carlson, Lisa Garcia Bedolla, Stan Oklobdzija, and Shad Turney. "When Campaigns Call, Who Answers? Using Observational Data to Enrich Our Understanding of Phone Mobilization." *Electoral Studies* 64 (2020): 1–11.

Arceneaux, Kevin. "I'm Asking for Your Support: The Effects of Personally Delivered Campaign Messages on Voting Decisions and Opinion Formation." *Quarterly Journal of Political Science* 2, 1 (2007): 43–65.

Belfry Munroe, Kaija, and H.D. Munroe. "Constituency Campaigning in the Age of Data." *Canadian Journal of Political Science* 51, 1 (2018): 135–54.

Bennett, Colin J. "Data-Driven Elections in Canada: What We Might Expect in the 2019 Federal Election Campaign?" In "The Informed Citizens' Guide to Elections: Current Developments in Democracy," edited by Gregory Tardi and Richard Balasko, special issue, *Journal of Parliamentary and Political Law* (2019): 277–90.

Bodet, Marc André. "Strongholds and Battlegrounds: Measuring Party Support Stability in Canada." *Canadian Journal of Political Science* 46, 3 (2013): 575–96.

Carty, R. Kenneth, and Munroe Eagles. "Do Local Campaigns Matter? Campaign Spending, the Local Canvass and Party Support in Canada." *Electoral Studies* 18, 1 (1999): 69–87.

–. *Politics Is Local: National Politics at the Grassroots.* Toronto: Oxford University Press, 2005.

CBC News. "Calgary Police Investigate Liberal MP-Elect George Chahal." 24 September 2021. https://www.cbc.ca/news/canada/calgary/george-chahal-investigation-flyer-1.6188304.

Cross, William. "The Importance of Local Party Activity in Understanding Canadian Politics: Winning from the Ground Up in the 2015 Federal Election: Presidential Address to the Canadian Political Science Association Calgary, 31 May 2016." *Canadian Journal of Political Science* 49, 4 (2016): 601–20.

Delacourt, Susan. *Shopping for Votes: How Politicians Choose Us and We Choose Them.* 2nd ed. Toronto: Douglas and McIntyre, 2016.

Gerber, Alan S., and Donald P. Green. "The Effects of Canvassing, Telephone Calls, and Direct Mail on Voter Turnout: A Field Experiment." *American Political Science Review* 94, 3 (2000): 653–63.

Grauer, Perrin. "Attack Flyers Show Conservative Candidate 'Bleeding' Support Ahead of Burnaby-South Byelection: Singh Campaign." *Toronto Star,* 24 February 2019. https://www.thestar.com/politics/federal/2019/02/24/attack-flyers-show-conservative-candidate-bleeding-support-ahead-of-burnaby-south-byelection-singh-campaign.html.

John, Peter, and Tessa Brannan. "How Different Are Telephoning and Canvassing? Results from a 'Get Out the Vote' Field Experiment in the British 2005 General Election." *British Journal of Political Science* 38, 3 (2008): 565–74.

Koop, Royce. "Constituency Campaigning in the 2015 Federal Election." In *Canadian Election Analysis 2015: Communication, Strategy, and Democ-*

racy, edited by Alex Marland and Thierry Giasson, 42–43. Vancouver: UBC Press, 2015. https://www.ubcpress.ca/canadianelectionanalysis2015.

Liberal Party of Canada. "Events." N.d. https://event.liberal.ca/en/events.

Marland, Alex, and Thierry Giasson. "From Brokerage to Boutique Politics: Political Marketing and the Changing Nature of Party Politics in Canada." In *Canadian Parties in Transition: Recent Trends and New Paths to Research,* 4th ed., edited by Alain-G. Gagnon and Brian Tanguay, 343–63. Toronto: University of Toronto Press, 2017.

Nickerson, David W. "Volunteer Phone Calls Can Increase Turnout: Evidence from Eight Field Experiments." *American Politics Research* 34, 3 (2006): 271–92.

Richler, Noah. *The Candidate: Fear and Loathing on the Campaign Trail.* Toronto: Doubleday, 2016.

Riedner, Heidi. "Saroya, Chiang Campaigns Spar over 'Disturbing' Election Flyer Distributed in Markham." *Toronto Star,* 17 September 2021. https://www.thestar.com/local-markham/news/federal-election/2021/09/17/saroya-chiang-campaigns-spar-over-disturbing-election-flyer-distributed-in-markham.html.

Sayers, Anthony M. *Parties, Candidates, and Constituency Campaigns in Canadian Elections.* Vancouver: UBC Press, 1999.

Small, Tamara A., and Jane Philpott. "The Independent Candidate." In *Inside the Campaign: Managing Elections in Canada,* edited by Alex Marland and Thierry Giasson, 197–206. Vancouver: UBC Press, 2020.

Stevens, Benjamin Allen, Mujahedul Islam, Roosmarijn de Geus, Jonah Goldberg, John R. McAndrews, Alex Mierke-Zatwarnicki, Peter John Loewen, and Daniel Rubenson. "Local Candidate Effects in Canadian Elections." *Canadian Journal of Political Science* 52, 1 (2019): 83–96.

Talbot, Michael, and Mark MacAllister. "Candidates Seek Connection with Voters in Immigrant-Rich Brampton East." *CityNews* [Toronto], 11 October 2019. https://toronto.citynews.ca/2019/10/11/cityvote2019-candidates-seek-connection-with-voters-in-immigrant-rich-brampton-east/.

Thompson, Allan. "Mounting a Local Campaign." In *The Canadian Federal Election of 2015,* edited by Jon Pammett and Christopher Dornan, 195–224. Toronto: Dundurn, 2016.

Thurton, David. "Annamie Paul Is Leading the Green Party's National Campaign – But Hasn't Left Toronto Once." CBC News, 4 September 2021. https://www.cbc.ca/news/politics/annamie-paul-green-party-federal-election-1.6162700.

11

Local Data-Driven Campaigning

Kaija Belfry Munroe and H.D. Munroe

Abstract   Despite continued claims of a big data revolution in Canadian elections, and much discussion of microtargeting, we observed significant variation in the extent to which local campaigns in Charlottetown in 2021 embraced data-driven tactics. Some of these variations resulted from resource constraints, but we also observed skepticism about the supposed superiority of data-driven campaigning. Despite having the capability to adopt the latter, the incumbent Liberal campaign deliberately eschewed such tactics in favour of a more traditional approach made possible in part by the riding's small size and the party's robust local organization. Claims of a big data revolution should not be exaggerated: data can be most useful when they enable campaigns in large rural ridings, or ridings where the party organization is weak, to operate as if they were in a small riding with a robust, well-connected local organization.

Résumé   Malgré plusieurs affirmations indiquant qu'une révolution des mégadonnées et du micro-ciblage dans l'organisation électorale aurait lieu au Canada, nous avons plutôt observé d'importantes variations quant à l'adoption de tactiques axées sur les données dans les campagnes locales de la circonscription de Charlottetown en 2021. Bien que certaines de ces variations soient attribuables à des contraintes de ressources, nous avons également observé un scepticisme quant à la prétendue supériorité des campagnes axées sur les données. Même s'il était possible de les adopter, la campagne libérale a délibérément évité de telles tactiques au profit d'une approche plus traditionnelle rendue possible en partie par la petite taille de la circonscription et par la solide organisation locale du parti. Ainsi, l'hypothèse d'une révolution des mégadonnées dans l'organisation électorale au Canada ne doit pas être exagérée: les données peuvent toutefois s'avérer utiles dans de grandes circonscriptions rurales ou dans des circonscriptions où l'organisation du parti est faible, afin de faire campagne comme s'il s'agissait d'une petite circonscription avec une organisation locale solide et bien connectée.

IN RECENT YEARS, the idea that elections are won by the campaigns with the most data has taken hold among practitioners and academics around the world.[1] Indeed, in the midst of the election that this book covers, a Liberal Party volunteer offered a succinct statement of this perspective in the Canadian context:

> Since the 2005–06 [Canadian federal] election campaign, big data has become a staple feature of the modern campaign. It's used to micro-target voters, mobilize supporters, recruit volunteers and solicit donations. Microtargeting – the identification of key segments of the electorate in swing ridings who might be swayed by a key message or issue – has armed parties with crucial data that informs virtually every facet of their campaigns, including policy, communications and fundraising.[2]

This and many similar assertions about the role of big data in Canadian politics often entail two claims. The first and most obvious claim is one of universality, that all campaigns run by all parties are permeated by nebulously defined data. The second and more subtle claim is one of superiority: the revolutionary modern campaign, with its emphasis on using data to craft influential messages microtargeted at individuals, has replaced an older, less efficient style of campaigning grounded in local knowledge and broad voter outreach. Beneath much of the discourse about data-driven campaigning is an assertion that it is or ought to be universal because it is more efficient and therefore better.

One cannot deny that data have become a significant aspect of election campaigns in Canada, particularly since Barack Obama's successful election in 2008 demonstrated their significance to North America's political elite. The rhetoric of revolutionary change might be overblown, however. There is little empirical evidence behind claims of universality and superiority, particularly in Canada. Our own previous research revealed considerable variations among campaigns in a single riding in the federal election in 2015.[3] We observed similar variations during subsequent fieldwork in 2017 and 2019. In those elections, some campaigns were heavily data driven, others aspired to be, and some ignored data entirely. The persistence of these variations across three elections is strong evidence *against* claims that big data campaigning is universal. They do not tell us much by themselves about whether such campaigning is perceived by political actors as better than alternatives.

The variations that we observed were all the more surprising because all of our fieldwork took place in a riding where, according to the claim of superiority underpinning the rhetoric of data-driven campaigning, such approaches ought to be most useful. We observed campaigns in a geographically large riding with many small, separated communities in which social networks were loose as a result of high levels of population mobility. In such circumstances, we would expect all campaigns to have two strong incentives to embrace the supposed efficiency of data-driven campaigning. The first incentive is a function of scale: the size and population of the riding mean that any campaign will struggle to be equally present in all parts of it, forcing certain areas to be prioritized over others. In principle, campaigns that use data to prioritize their operations can maximize the impact of each hour of volunteer time at the ballot box and thus will fare better than campaigns that cannot do so. The second incentive stems from loose social networks. When fewer people in the riding are likely to know even their neighbours' names, a campaign team is unlikely to be able to draw from deep-rooted local knowledge about their supporters. All of the campaigns that we observed in prior elections had these incentives to embrace the supposed advantages in efficiency of data-driven campaigning. That they did not do so universally suggests that such adoption is easier said than done – or that the incentives are not as strong as the claims of superiority imply.

This led us to wonder whether campaigns use data in smaller ridings such as R.K. Carty's iconic Tecumseh Corners, where the smaller scale diminishes the first of the incentives outlined above.[4]

Are parties in these places adopting data-driven techniques to increase the efficiency of their campaigning? In one such riding, that of Charlottetown, we found that this was not the case. None of the campaigns that we studied was data driven. More interestingly, though, this was not entirely because of resource constraints. Whereas the Green Party and NDP candidates attributed this to various constraints facing their campaigns, the winning Liberal Party team purposely eschewed the data-focused campaign strategies of the national party in favour of time-honoured methods and less intrusive politics. Although Charlottetown, as the smallest (population-wise) urban electoral district in the country, is a unique riding, these findings suggest that we should be skeptical about the role of data at the riding level in Canadian elections. The purported gains in efficiency of data-driven techniques are hard to achieve in the absence of other resources such as people and money. Moreover, some political actors with an abundance of both people and money do not necessarily believe that the expected gains in efficiency from data-driven techniques make them inherently superior to old-school campaigning.

This is in sharp contrast to much of the literature on big data in politics. Scholarly conversations on this topic have coalesced around themes of privacy and surveillance,[5] social media and digital (or hybrid) political marketing,[6] and subversion by foreign powers in cyberspace.[7] One common thread running through these conversations is the idea that, by analyzing troves of data on individuals, political actors can develop ever-more-focused campaign messages whose motivating power grows as their intended audience shrinks. Even as they disagree about the positive or negative consequences of this power, scholars typically seem to accept the premise that data enable a more effective – or at least more efficient – kind of campaign.

Data-driven campaigning is a nebulous concept, however, and much of the literature elides important distinctions among different types and uses of data. The use of data to enable microtargeting of campaign communications is a perennial topic of interest, but as various scholars have noted the use of data in political campaigns is far broader than this specific phenomenon.[8]

Various conceptual frameworks have been used to try to unravel this complex terrain.

Katharine Dommett, for example, applies a framework based upon asking *who* is using data, *what* sources are being used, and *how* data are informing campaign communications.[9] Conversely, Jessica Baldwin-Philippi reduces data-driven campaigning to the meta-practices of targeting and testing.[10] In this chapter, we apply a framework developed in our earlier work that examines whether campaigns perceive data as a resource, how they generate data (integrating known voter data, inferring unknown voter data, and/ or tracking campaign activities), and whether they make decisions based upon the data.[11]

Although Canada's major federal parties have followed different trajectories in their adoption of data-driven campaigning, the federal election in 2015 was the first in which these approaches were deployed at scale by all major parties.[12] During our ethnographic fieldwork in that election, we noted that the main national parties clearly perceived data to be a resource, akin to money or volunteers, and that having more data was good. This perception reflects David Beer's concept of the data imaginary, which includes, *inter alia,* a belief that careful analysis of data can provide decisive advantages.[13] Some scholars have noted, however, that claims about the advantages of data analysis are advanced by people and companies that have strong organizational and financial incentives to promote this belief.[14] As a result, we continued to ask whether local political actors have bought in to this perception of data as a resource rather than assuming that this is the case.

Similar to Dommett,[15] we also wondered where campaigns were getting their data – and what kinds of data they were getting. There are many possible sources of data that might be of interest to political campaigns. In our prior work, we distinguished between campaigns that integrated known data on voters (e.g., combining lists of donors with lists of volunteers and lists of supporters into a single database) and campaigns that used predictive analytics to infer unknown data on voters (e.g., calculating the probability that a given individual will or will not support a given party). Although much is made about the bulk acquisition of data by political campaigns, it might often be exaggerated.[16] Another possible source of data is a campaign's own activities if they are systematically re- corded in a way that makes them amenable to ongoing analysis. Finally, social media and other online advertising platforms offer their own streams of data, some of which can be readily inte- grated with other kinds of data on campaign activities or individ- ual voters.[17]

The vast majority of riding-level campaign organizations in Canada do not have the resources to generate or collect any of these kinds of data at scale; for the most part, they are reliant on data management platforms provided by central party organizations. Those platforms, in turn, can structure how riding-level campaigns operate as well as how they relate to campaign central. After the election in 2015, we wondered whether the power of the platform would serve to centralize Canada's franchise-style parties. This was a major question in our minds as the election of 2021 approached.

In the intervening years, however, the technologies embedded in these platforms have been commodified.[18] Given Canada's prox- imity to the much larger professional election industry in the United States, it is unsurprising that commercial data services originally developed for the American market, such as E-Canvasser or Nation- Builder, are being adopted by Canadian campaigns. Commodification also occurs through the adoption of marketing tools by political elites. The use of algorithms to predict whether a given person is likely to be a supporter is commonly referred to as "lookalike" targeting, for example, because this is the name that Facebook gives to its commercial version of this service.[19] One implication of this proliferation of commercial options is that a riding-level campaign is not necessarily forced to adopt its party's in-house data manage- ment platform – which can alter the balance of power associated with such a platform. Meanwhile, the need to recruit people with the requisite technical skills to use these tools contributes to gen- erational divides among party volunteers and a further shrinking of local party organizations.[20] These trends complicated our expecta- tions of the election in 2021.

Based upon our experiences in the election of 2015, we argued that "data-driven" campaigns did not just believe in the value of data, or invest time and energy in gathering and managing it, but also used the data at their disposal to inform campaign decision making. In US presidential elections, every aspect of a campaign's operations is increasingly subject to ongoing experimentation and analysis.[21] When a campaign lasts for hundreds of days and spans an entire country, there is ample scope for such analysis. In a typical Canadian election, particularly at the riding level, this is far from the case. Furthermore, David Nickerson and Todd Rogers point out that no amount of actionable insight will help a campaign that lacks the capacity to act.[22] Data can make campaign operations more efficient, but this is only worthwhile if the gains in efficiency are greater than the costs of obtaining them. This raises some important questions about the resource trade-offs that underwrite a data-driven campaign, particularly in a Canadian context. Rather than investing hours of volunteer time on data-processing tasks or training with apps and systems, might a campaign be better served simply by investing those hours in some other activity instead? As we headed back into the field in 2021, particularly for a campaign of only thirty-six days, we wanted to know more about how riding campaigns managed this trade-off.

Notwithstanding the point that data can be used to inform a wide variety of campaign decisions, much discussion about the uses of data in politics concerns microtargeting: namely, the use of data on voters to target a campaign's communicative effort at specific individuals. In many respects, scholarly debates about microtargeting are a microcosm of the larger literature on data in campaigns, with a similar mix of hyperbole, skepticism, and concern about what is possible and a similar muddling of concepts. Mathieu Lavigne, for example, defines microtargeting as "the use of voters' personal information by a party to send the right message to the right person."[23] This neatly encapsulates what scholars find interesting about the practice, but it collapses together three different campaign manoeuvres. One is to identify specific individuals. Another is to decide what message to send to them. The third is to actually send the message, which is often much less straight-forward than it might seem. Other scholarship implicitly or explicitly includes the use of a digital medium in the definition.[24] We argue that the distinctions between these steps should not be ignored, nor should the role of "data" be assumed. Analysis of various kinds of data, in various ways, can be involved in any, all, or none of these steps.

The furor over microtargeting, like the larger scholarly conversations about data-driven campaigning, often conflates what is possible with what is actually happening. Blurry conceptual schemas, implicit assumptions, and a scarcity of empirical evidence undermine our ability to understand the actual effects of such practices, an understanding sorely needed. Lavigne operationalizes microtargeting in the election of 2015 as direct contact of a voter by a party with which the voter identifies, on the assumption that *all* voter contact in that election was microtargeted. Unsurprisingly, he finds that being contacted by a party with which one already identified increased one's sense of identification with that party. Lavigne, like many scholars, implicitly assumes microtargeting to mean the use of data analysis to identify prospective voters with whom parties do not already have relationships, but his operationalization equally describes a local campaign team phoning well-known supporters to remind them about election day – a long-standing practice hardly at the forefront of data-driven campaigning. Clearly, large-n studies of this phenomenon need to be anchored in some ground truths.

As we re-entered the field in the election in 2021, we did so with a host of questions about microtargeting. Are riding-level campaigns microtargeting in the sense of singling out specific individuals? If not, why not? If so, how are they picking those people, how do they try to communicate with them, and how successful are campaigns at actually reaching those people with their intended messages? Ultimately, these questions come together in one overarching curiosity: Are all campaigns, even those in small ridings, actually employing data-driven methods such as microtargeting, and if not is this simply for want of other resources or for other reasons?

Local Trends

Charlottetown is an ideal place to look for answers to these questions. Our previous research took place in a riding arguably a "most likely" case for data-driven campaigning, a sprawling urban and rural riding with more than 100,000 people spread across several communities with high levels of mobility and population growth. This combination of geographic extent, population size, and loose social networks resulting from high levels of mobility meant that campaigns faced strong incentives to seek efficiency through data. Charlottetown is radically different. It had a population of only 36,000 people in 2016 in a single urban community of only forty-four square kilometres. Despite being relatively small, however, Charlottetown's population has seen relatively high levels of mobility. In the 2016 census, 43 percent of people reported moving in the previous five years, compared with 35 percent in Canada as a whole. Since the 2016 census, Statistics Canada estimates that the population of Charlottetown and its surrounding area has increased by 12 percent, roughly double the overall rate of growth in Canada's cities.[25] Given this rapid population growth, one might reasonably expect campaigns in Charlottetown to rely on data to supplement local knowledge. Yet the small scale of the riding poses fewer logistical challenges than most ridings. Like any riding, Charlottetown also has its own idiosyncrasies, in particular a traditional style of politics that emphasizes a high level of personal contact and constituency services from sitting MPs. Data on voters' past interactions with a party could well be seen by political actors as a way to meet voters' expectations for highly personalized campaigning.

Did the parties that contested this riding in 2021 perceive data as a campaign resource and systematically gather data to enable techniques such as microtargeting? To find out, we reached out to the campaigns representing all of the parties that participated in the English-language televised leaders' debate in 2021. We were able to secure interviews with the Liberal Party, Green Party, and NDP candidates as well as the Liberal campaign manager. Unfortunately, despite repeated invitations, the Conservative Party campaign did not respond to requests to participate.

As one would expect of an incumbent, the Liberal Party ran a well-organized campaign with significant volunteer resources. The campaign manager (also the electoral district association president) was joined by distinct teams of volunteers who worked the phones, door-knocked with the candidate, put up signs, and distributed leaflets. The entire effort was organized out of campaign headquarters on Charlottetown's main downtown thoroughfare.

The NDP campaign, in contrast, was a candidate-only affair. There were no volunteers save the candidate's family members, and the candidate ran all aspects of the campaign herself. This meant, of course, that she was able to undertake only the bare minimum of attending all candidates' debates and putting up signs at major street intersections. The campaign's $3,000 budget was spent almost entirely on the nomination deposit to Elections Canada ($1,000) and the purchase of the aforementioned signs ($1,500).

The Green Party campaign fell between these two organizational extremes. Faced with fewer volunteers and much less time than expected, the candidate sought to run a campaign that was full featured but smaller in scope. Campaign workers knocked on doors, put up signs, and telephoned supporters throughout the riding; although there was no dedicated volunteer coordinator or campaign manager, the candidate was also able to delegate certain tasks to volunteers (including, e.g., the campaign's social media effort). Although not as well resourced as the incumbent Liberals in terms of money or people, the candidate was supported by a group of experienced and new partisans operating out of highly visible headquarters on a busy roadway.

Behind the Scenes

From our interviews, we sought to understand the extent to which local campaigns in Charlottetown adopted a modern, data-driven approach. The discourse on big data and politics suggests that these practices are (or ought to be) universal because the gains in efficiency that they enable confer electoral advantages. We found that data-driven campaign practices were not universal in this riding and not only because resource constraints made them unachievable for some campaigns; there was a notable degree of skepticism about the supposed superiority of such practices as well.

In Charlottetown, only the Green campaign saw data as a resource akin to money and people. Although a lack of people and time hampered the campaign's attempts to increase its data holdings in that election, the candidate saw much utility in GVOTE, the party's data-management platform, and used it systematically to record data gleaned about voters' partisan preferences and issues of concern during door-to-door canvassing. The system also allowed her to keep track of voters who wanted a candidate follow-up, requested a sign, or sought to volunteer. Most importantly, the stories that the candidate told indicated that she viewed data as a valuable enabler. For instance, when an outbreak of COVID-19 in the community caused the campaign to shut down door canvassing, the candidate was able to use data from past elections to call people in specific polling divisions who had taken lawn signs in the past and ask them if they would put up signs in the current election. This, she explained, allowed the campaign to build visibility in those polling divisions where otherwise it would have been unable to do so.

The Liberal campaign, in contrast, had a very different view. Rather than generating a valuable resource, it perceived the central party's emphasis on data as a threat to its success in the riding. The campaign clearly valued local knowledge, but not necessarily data. It took advantage of knowing its supporters in order to sustain a highly targeted get-out-the-vote (GOTV) operation, for example, and used past electoral results to inform its targeting decisions for door-to-door canvassing. Neither activity is particularly complex, however, and is done as easily with a simple spreadsheet program as with a powerful data management platform such as the Liberal Party's Liberalist. Indeed, despite having considerable volunteer resources available, the campaign deliberately sought to minimize the amount of data collected on voters because the candidate and campaign leadership perceived questioning voters as intrusive and disrespectful.

Whether the NDP candidate saw data as a resource is unclear because she lacked the means to engage with data collection. According to the candidate, the central party required that she pay $700 to get access to the party's data management platform, Populus. This was more than she could afford, so she simply did without it. We note, however, that commercial substitutes such as Nation Builder are available for considerably less ($44 per month), albeit without any data, such as the list of electors. The candidate's focus was entirely on the basic logistics of campaigning, such as getting on the ballot and putting up signs. Even if she perceived data as a valuable resource, a lack of money and time meant that she could do little about it.

The Green campaign mainly generated data from its contact with voters, such as recording their levels of support or hostility on a five-point scale, their issues of concern, and their requests for lawn signs or candidate follow-up calls. This data collection was largely done using printed walksheets, with a commensurate data entry task afterward, rather than with a mobile application. The candidate noted, however, that GVOTE has a mobile-friendly web interface that largely replicates the functions of a dedicated mobile app. Door-to-door or telephone canvassing was not the campaign's only source of data. Its website was integrated with GVOTE, such that information gathered from donations or offers to volunteer on the site would automatically be put into the party's database. The platform was also used to manage the campaign's volunteers and, as a consequence, generated data on those volunteers, though many aspects of the campaign's operations were managed with traditional methods, such as calendars and printed maps on the walls of the headquarters. There was no attempt to integrate data from the campaign's social media efforts, and the candidate's account of the platform suggests that there was no capability for predictive modelling of voters' preferences.

The Liberal campaign manager was explicit about the approach to the campaign: "Our strategy is not data focused; it is candidate focused." In keeping with this approach, the campaign generated very little data. Door-to-door canvassing was always done by the candidate personally, supported by a small group of volunteers, because the candidate believed that, in Prince Edward Island's political culture, voters who interacted only with campaign volunteers would be insulted by the implication that the candidate thought them unworthy of a visit. The candidate was the only person who recorded data on voters' preferences into the party's data platform using the mobile app. As a result, interaction with the candidate was the only way that the campaign added anyone to its list of known supporters. The campaign deliberately avoided other opportunities to do so. For instance, during telephone calls to known supporters, volunteers were not to ask whether people were planning to support their candidate, nor did they record it when people offered unsolicited declarations that they were (or were not) going to do so. This was in part because campaign organizers believed that voters would find such questions intrusive and might vote for an opponent as a result. It was also because the party continued to use paper printouts for phone calling and did not trust that anyone but the candidate could truly gauge voters' intentions. The campaign recorded who had voted in advance polls and on election day using Liberalist but tracked sign requests, offers to volunteer, and information about donors in diverse ways, such as using a Google doc or spreadsheet, rather than with the party-provided data platform. For the most part, the campaign's operations were not integrated and likely had not changed much, from an information management perspective, since the party first won back the riding in 1989.

Interestingly, though we are aware from previous research that the Liberal Party has the capacity to infer voters' preferences through predictive analysis, the Liberal campaign in Charlottetown was unaware of this fact. Although its GOTV volunteers called every person identified in Liberalist as Tier 1 (Liberal) and Tier 2 (Possible Liberal), local campaign leaders understood these identifications to be based upon interactions with the candidate during door-to-door canvassing or past interactions with previous candidates or the central party. If Liberalist continued to use predictive analysis to rank voters during the election in 2021, the campaign in Charlottetown was unaware of this fact.

As mentioned, the NDP candidate had no access to the party's data platform and made no attempt to acquire a commercial alternative. The candidate did very little door knocking because of a recent medical issue, and – though she used her personal email account to manage requests for signs – she made no attempt to record the data for future use. In short, the NDP in Charlottetown did not generate any data.

Although the Green campaign clearly viewed data as a resource and made some attempts to generate data using GVOTE, there is little evidence that it used the data in decision making beyond a few occasions. Campaign workers visited all homes on any street that they walked, rather than employing any form of microtargeting, and picked those streets based upon convenience rather than any analysis of past electoral results or known levels of support. Although the candidate used GVOTE daily to look up who had requested a lawn sign or a candidate follow-up the previous day, the only notable use of data to inform or enable campaign activities came when a COVID-19 outbreak led the campaign to suspend door-to-door canvassing, and past data were used to distribute signs (as described above). According to the candidate, the combination of the short writ period of thirty-six days and a much smaller group of volunteers meant that there was no further attempt at analysis of data. These constraints might not have been the only factors in this decision. Although the candidate valued the insights gleaned from voter data, she expressed skepticism about the utility of microtargeting.

The Liberal campaign relied on experienced judgment rather than data in decision making. The candidate's commitment to doing all door-to-door canvassing in person meant that the extent of canvassing was necessarily limited – though the hard-working candidate ultimately managed to knock on roughly a third of the doors in the riding, no small accomplishment. Rather than being narrowly driven by data analysis, however, the canvassing was directed by an experienced volunteer who weighed past electoral results – emphasizing areas where the candidate had performed badly in the previous election rather than the more common emphasis on areas of strength – and an estimation of the Conservative opponent's most supportive areas, which the candidate visited more than others. Logistical factors also played a role. The campaign tried to get the candidate out in every neighbourhood of the city at least once, ideally either before or after an event in that neighbourhood. Decisions were based upon previous experience, tradition, and the campaign's sense of the culture of the community, distinctly different from microtargeting as described in the literature. The candidate, for instance, purposely knocked on every door of homeowners on the electoral list in every neighbourhood that he visited. Although he was willing to skip the houses of people ineligible to vote, he made a point of knocking on the doors of well-known Conservatives. He considered this a mark of respect for his voters and potential constituents. This was a marked departure from other Liberal campaigns that we have observed, which microtarget voters by knocking only on the doors of people identified in Liberalist as likely or possible supporters. The Liberal campaign in Charlottetown had a much deeper understanding of Canadian voters as flexible partisans who often switch their allegiances. By getting their candidate in front of voters who might do just that, Liberal campaign organizers believed that they could win the riding, which they did ultimately and handily. As a consequence, the campaign considered the data-driven doctrine of the central party to be inferior, rather than superior, to its more traditional approach.

The only Liberal campaign activity that could be said to be data driven or microtargeted was the GOTV operation, in which volunteers used Liberalist to generate telephone lists of supporters who had not yet voted on election day. The campaign was able to do this despite the limited extent of door-to-door canvassing because the local party organization kept records of people's support over multiple elections. These lists were used to call supporters repeatedly until they voted. Although this meets most of the common definitions of data-driven campaigning, it is far from cutting edge. This aspect of the Liberal campaign was run by a volunteer with a decade of experience with the candidate and over thirty years of experience with Liberal campaigns. New technologies such as Liberalist undoubtedly make textbook GOTV operations such as this more efficient, but as with the rest of the campaign the overall approach was to win by respecting voters' privacy rather than by meticulously surveilling their preferences.

Conclusion

Notwithstanding the hype, data-driven campaigning is demonstrably not universal among local campaigns in Canada. There continues to be significant variation in how different campaigns perceive, generate, and use data. Some variation is to be expected because it is imposed by constraints. More surprisingly, the snapshot of Canadian politics that we provide here suggests that at least some political actors are as skeptical as we are about the other implicit assumption of the data imaginary: namely, that data-driven campaigns are superior to more traditional campaigns because they are more efficient. In Charlottetown in 2021, the incumbent Liberals – despite being the party that appears to be the most committed to data-driven politics at the national level – were skeptical of the purported advantages of such practices and deliberately ran a more traditional campaign.

In the first instance, data-driven campaigning is not universal because it is not cost free. To generate, analyze, and act on data require investments of other resources. Across Canada, many campaigns – perhaps a majority of them – look more like the NDP and Green campaigns described in this chapter than the Liberal one. Data on supporters, donors, and volunteers can be an important asset, as the Green campaign's experience with lawn signs or the Liberal campaign's GOTV operation demonstrates. Building up these data requires a prior investment of volunteer time and occasionally money that exceeds the capacity of small or candidate-only campaigns, however. What is more, even when the data are there, analyzing them takes time, and time is always in short supply in any Canadian election. The data platforms provided by central parties try to make it as easy as possible to collect and analyze data, but these platforms can come with other barriers, as with the NDP's fee for access to Populus. Even in one of Canada's smallest ridings, there are notable constraints on the ability of many campaigns to pursue the purported advantages of data-driven politics.

The more interesting finding from our case study is that political actors themselves are skeptical about data-driven campaigning, particularly microtargeting. The central Liberal Party, for example, puts considerable pressure on its riding associations, candidates, and campaigns to collect data on voters during and between elections, presumably because the party has embraced the assumption that data-driven campaigns are superior to alternatives. Possibly in response, previous federal Liberal campaigns that we observed in another riding were highly data driven. The incumbent Liberal candidate in Charlottetown pushed back hard against that pressure, limiting his use of Liberalist to election periods and insisting on identifying supporters personally. As a Member of Parliament, he told us, he uses a separate system for constituency work because he considers his ongoing contacts with constituents between elections as parliamentary business and that any data collected on them should not be used for partisan purposes. His campaign's decision making relied heavily on local knowledge and experience, which other campaigns ignore in favour of data analysis emanating from party headquarters, at times to their detriment. This choice produced consternation in the Liberal Party's central campaign apparatus, leading to phone calls and text messages to local campaign leaders expressing concern that the campaign was not on track to identify the approximately 6,700 supporters that the central party had determined were needed to win. Victory confers absolution of almost any sin, however, and the local campaign's track record of winning doubtless helped to minimize any friction with the central party.

Both the Liberal campaign and the Green campaign explicitly refused to engage in microtargeting in Charlottetown, choosing instead to connect with as many voters as possible. Respondents in these campaigns believed that the pursuit of microtargeting led other campaigns to limit their contacts with voters rather than expand them in the belief that all voters are either supportive or hostile and that it is better to avoid speaking to a voter entirely than to run the risk of activating a hostile voter. Strict adherence to this approach would lead a campaign to contact an ever-diminishing subset of voters in the riding. When a campaign speaks only to known supporters, its universe of voters shrinks rather than expands. Such a strategy would be counterproductive over the long run. The Greens and Liberals in Charlottetown, in contrast, sought to expand their universe, rather than merely identify existing supporters, through broad voter contact efforts minimally, if at all, targeted.

The perception of data as a campaign resource on par with money and volunteers is likely to persist; however, like money and volunteers, whether data confer decisive advantages on any particular campaign will depend on circumstances. Data are perhaps most valuable when they allow campaigns in large, spread-out places to be run as if they were in small places, for example by allowing the Obama campaign to organize volunteers and engage voters across the United States in 2008 and 2012, when this so-called revolution began. In an electoral system like that in Canada, with 338 simultaneous small elections, the advantages of data-driven campaigning are less obvious. In large rural ridings, or in ridings where party organizations are weak or non-existent, data can offer an important substitute for local knowledge and enable increases in efficiency large enough to be worthwhile if not decisive. In smaller, more urban ridings, or in ridings with vibrant, long-standing party organizations, a data-driven campaign cannot automatically confer such advantages – and, indeed, some of the practices associated with this approach can be counterproductive. Scholars and practitioners should remain skeptical of claims that there is a data-driven revolution in campaign affairs in Canada. Instead, it might be that data are most useful when they enable a campaign to simulate the more traditional politics of Tecumseh Corners ... or Charlottetown.

Notes

1 Anstead and Chadwick, "Parties, Election Campaigning and the Internet"; Theviot, *Big Data Electoral.*
2 Perez, "Big Data, Social Media and Political Fundraising Laws."

3 Belfry Munroe and Munroe, "Constituency Campaigning in the Age of Data."

4 Carty, "The Politics of Tecumseh Corners."

5 Bennett and McDonald, "From the Doorstep to the Database"; Bennett, "Data Driven Elections and Political Parties in Canada"; Montigny, Dubois, and Giasson, "On the Edge of Glory."

6 Small and Giasson, "Political Parties."

7 Tenove et al., "Digital Threats to Democratic Elections"; Al-Rawi and Rahman, "Manufacturing Rage."

8 Bennett and Lyon, "Data-Driven Elections."

9 Dommett, "Data-Driven Political Campaigns in Practice."

10 Baldwin-Philippi, "Data Campaigning."

11 Belfry Munroe and Munroe, "Constituency Campaigning in the Age of Data."

12 Patten, "Databases, Microtargeting, and the Permanent Campaign"; Patten, "Data-Driven Microtargeting."

13 Beer, *The Data Gaze.*

14 Simon, "'We Power Democracy.'"

15 Dommett, "Data-Driven Political Campaigns in Practice."

16 Ibid.; Nickerson and Rogers, "Political Campaigns and Big Data."

17 Small and Giasson, "Political Parties."

18 McKelvey and Piebiak, "Porting the Political Campaign"; Simon, "'We Power Democracy.'"

19 Judge and Pal, "Voter Privacy and Big-Data Elections."

20 Montigny, Dubois, and Giasson, "On the Edge of Glory."

21 Nickerson and Rogers, "Political Campaigns and Big Data."

22 Ibid.

23 Lavigne, "Strengthening Ties," P1, citing Patten, "Databases, Micro-targeting, and the Permanent Campaign."

24 Borgesius et al., "Online Political Microtargeting."

25 Statistics Canada, "Table 17-10-0135-01."

Bibliography

Al-Rawi, Ahmed, and Anis Rahman. "Manufacturing Rage: The Russian Internet Research Agency's Political Astroturfing on Social Media." *First Monday,* 16 August 2020. https://doi.org/10.5210/fm.v25i9.10801.

Anstead, Nick, and Andrew Chadwick. "Parties, Election Campaigning and the Internet: Toward a Comparative Institutional Approach." In *The Handbook of Internet Politics,* edited by Andrew Chadwick and Philip N. Howard, 56–71. New York: Routledge, 2010.

Baldwin-Philippi, Jessica. "Data Campaigning: Between Empirics and Assumptions." *Internet Policy Review* 8, 4 (2019). https://policyreview.info/articles/analysis/data-campaigning-between-empirics-and-assumptions.

Beer, David. *The Data Gaze: Capitalism, Power and Perception.* London: SAGE, 2018.

Belfry Munroe, Kaija, and H.D. Munroe. "Constituency Campaigning in the Age of Data." *Canadian Journal of Political Science* 51, 1 (2018): 135–54.

Bennett, Colin. "Data Driven Elections and Political Parties in Canada: Privacy Implications, Privacy Policies and Privacy Obligations." *Canadian Journal of Law and Technology* 16, 2 (2016): 195–226.

Bennett, Colin J., and David Lyon. "Data-Driven Elections: Implications and Challenges for Democratic Societies." *Internet Policy Review* 8, 4 (2019). https://policyreview.info/data-driven-elections.

Bennett, Colin, and Michael McDonald. "From the Doorstep to the Database: Political Parties, Campaigns, and Personal Privacy Protection in Canada." SSRN Scholarly Paper, 1 September 2019. https://papers.ssrn.com/abstract=3516992.

Borgesius, Frederik, J. Zuiderveen, Judith Möller, Sanne Kruikemeier, Ronan Ó Fathaigh, Kristina Irion, Tom Dobber, Balazs Bodo, and Claes de Vreese. "Online Political Microtargeting: Promises and Threats for Democracy." *Utrecht Law Review* 14, 1 (2018): 82–96. https://doi.org/10.18352/ulr.420.

Carty, Roland Kenneth. "The Politics of Tecumseh Corners: Canadian Political Parties as Franchise Organizations." *Canadian Journal of Political Science* 35, 4 (2002): 723–45.

Dommett, Katharine. "Data-Driven Political Campaigns in Practice: Understanding and Regulating Diverse Data-Driven Campaigns." *Internet Policy Review* 8, 4 (2019). https://policyreview.info/articles/analysis/data-driven-political-campaigns-practice-understanding-and-regulating-diverse-data.

Judge, Elizabeth F., and Michael Pal. "Voter Privacy and Big-Data Elections." SSRN Scholarly Paper, 10 December 2020. https://papers.ssrn.com/abstract=3746632.

Lavigne, Mathieu. "Strengthening Ties: The Influence of Microtargeting on Partisan Attitudes and the Vote." *Party Politics,* 23 April 2020. https://doi.org/10.1177/1354068820918387.

McKelvey, Fenwick, and Jill Piebiak. "Porting the Political Campaign: The NationBuilder Platform and the Global Flows of Political Technology." *New Media and Society* 20, 3 (2018): 901–18. https://doi.org/10.1177/1461444816675439.

Montigny, Eric, Philippe R. Dubois, and Thierry Giasson. "On the Edge of Glory (… or Catastrophe): Regulation, Transparency and Party Democracy in Data-Driven Campaigning in Québec." *Internet Policy Review*, 8, 4 (2019). https://policyreview.info/data-driven-elections.

Nickerson, David W., and Todd Rogers. "Political Campaigns and Big Data." *Journal of Economic Perspectives* 28, 2 (2014): 51–74. https://doi.org/10.1257/jep.28.2.51.

Patten, Steve. "Databases, Microtargeting, and the Permanent Campaign: A Threat to Democracy?" In *Permanent Campaigning in Canada,* edited by Alex Marland, Thierry Giasson, and Anna Lennox Esselment, 47–64. Vancouver: UBC Press, 2017.

–. "Data-Driven Microtargeting in the 2015 General Election." In *Canadian Election Analysis: Communication, Strategy, and Democracy,* edited by Alex Marland and Thierry Giasson, 14–15. Vancouver: UBC Press, 2015. https://www.ubcpress.ca/canadianelectionanalysis2015.

Perez, Andrew. "Big Data, Social Media and Political Fundraising Laws Have Transformed Election Campaigns." *Policy Options,* 20 September 2021. https://policyoptions.irpp.org/magazines/septembe-2021/big-data-social-media-and-political-fundraising-laws-have-transformed-election-campaigns/.

Simon, Felix M. "'We Power Democracy': Exploring the Promises of the Political Data Analytics Industry." *Information Society* 35, 3 (2019): 158–69. https://doi.org/10.1080/01972243.2019.1582570.

Small, Tamara A., and Thierry Giasson. "Political Parties: Political Campaigning in the Digital Age." In *Digital Politics in Canada: Promises and Realities,* edited by Tamara A. Small and Harold J. Jansen, 136–58. Toronto: University of Toronto Press, 2020.

Statistics Canada. "Table 17-10-0135-01 Population Estimates, July 1, by Census Metropolitan Area and Census Agglomeration, 2016 Boundaries." https://doi.org/10.25318/1710013501-eng.

Tenove, Chris, Jordan Buffie, Spencer McKay, and David Moscrop. "Digital Threats to Democratic Elections: How Foreign Actors Use Digital Techniques to Undermine Democracy." SSRN Scholarly Paper, 16 January 2018. https://papers.ssrn.com/abstract=3235819.

Theviot, Anais. *Big Data Electoral: Dis-moi qui tu es, je te dirai pour qui voter.* Lormont, France: Le Bord de l'Eau, 2019.

12

Local Party Fundraising

Erin Crandall, with Kody Blois

Abstract   Party fundraising for Canadian elections happens at national and local levels, and both are critical. However, comparatively little is known about how local party candidates and riding associations go about raising the funds that they need to run an effective election campaign, particularly since 2007, when corporate and union donations were banned. Using the riding of Kings–Hants (Nova Scotia) as a case study, this chapter explores differences in party fundraising between national and local levels. At the local level, a candidate-focused, labour-intensive approach to fundraising is important for building connections and strategically leveraging a relatively small number of large donations. In a rural riding, such as Kings–Hants, this candidate-focused approach carries over to all facets of the election campaign, including campaigning on local issues, which can push against the position of the candidate's party.

Résumé   Les campagnes de financement des partis pour les élections canadiennes se déroulant à l'échelle nationale et locale sont essentielles. Néanmoins, on sait très peu de choses sur la façon dont les candidats des partis locaux et les associations de circonscription recueillent les fonds nécessaires au déroulement d'une campagne électorale efficace, surtout depuis que les dons des sociétés et des syndicats ont été interdits en 2007. En utilisant la circonscription de Kings–Hants (Nouvelle-Écosse) comme étude de cas, le présent chapitre explore les différences entre le financement national et local des partis. À l'échelle locale, une approche axée sur les candidats qui requiert une forte main-d'œuvre est importante pour établir des liens et tirer parti stratégiquement d'un nombre relativement faible de dons importants. Dans une circonscription rurale comme celle de Kings–Hants, l'approche axée sur les candidats s'applique à tous les aspects de la campagne électorale, y compris aux enjeux locaux, qui peuvent aller à l'encontre de la position du parti du candidat.

THERE IS NO SINGLE formula for winning a local campaign, but effective fundraising is always key. A party candidate can draw from two pools of funding: money raised by the local party organization and money transferred from the national party. Election regulations, fundraising tools, and party fortunes have meant that a candidate's reliance on either stream has varied over time and across parties. The balance struck between these two sources of funding prompts important questions about the relationship between the national party and the local party candidate. How does local party fundraising differ from that undertaken by the national party? How does fundraising affect the way that a party candidate campaigns? This chapter explores these questions.

The riding of Kings–Hants in Nova Scotia and the experiences of the Liberal candidate for the election in 2021, Kody Blois, are used to provide insights into the challenges and opportunities of fundraising at the local level. We developed this case study over three in-person and remote semi-structured conversations that spanned the immediate lead-up to, middle of, and end of the election campaign. These conversations on fundraising ranged in topic from possible differences between urban and rural ridings, balancing candidate and party messaging, the importance of a candidate-focused fundraising approach, and the unique features of the riding that affect fundraising and campaigning. All information regarding Kings–Hants is drawn from these conversations and the insights of Blois, who has been the Member of Parliament for the riding since 2019 and was re-elected in 2021.

To understand the political terrain of local fundraising in Canadian elections, we turn first to the rules. Canada's modern regulatory regime for parties and elections was introduced in the early 1970s.[1] These reforms to the Canada Elections Act provided political parties with public funding and introduced election spending limits, regulations for the reimbursement of election expenses for parties and candidates, as well as a generous tax credit for political contributions by individuals and corporations.[2] Taken together, these regulations favoured local party fundraising. Electorally competitive local party associations tended to be financially well off, benefiting from the generous (50 percent) reimbursement of candidates' election expenses. In comparison, the national parties received only 22.5 percent reimbursement and often were unable to raise enough funds to spend to their election expense limits.[3]

Election regulations underwent another round of major reforms beginning in 2004 when Liberal prime minister Jean Chrétien introduced contribution limits for corporations, unions, and individuals. Fundraising was further restricted by the Conservative government of Stephen Harper in 2007 when corporate and union contributions were banned altogether and the limit on contributions by individuals to each registered party and its affiliated entities (candidates, nomination contestants, and party associations) was lowered from $5,000 to $1,000. The move to individual donations affected the fundraising strategies of parties at national and local levels differently. In 2000, only 35 percent of donations to the Liberal Party and 45 percent of donations to Liberal candidates came from individuals, whereas these numbers were significantly higher for the Bloc Québécois (74 percent and 82 percent), Canadian Alliance (61 percent and 68 percent), and New Democratic Party (64 percent and 55 percent).[4] The limits for individual donations have been adjusted incrementally in the years since. For 2021, an individual could contribute up to $1,650 to each registered party and another $1,650 in total to the local entities of each registered party.

These reforms limited the sources of fundraising, but the costs of running a campaign have increased as the outsourcing of professional services has become a standard part of modern campaigning. For example, the typical candidate for the Liberals, Conservatives, and New Democrats spent about $66,000 in the federal election of 2015.[5] To offset the loss of available funds created by these regulations, the reforms in 2003 also introduced a publicly funded annual party allowance calculated at a rate of $1.75 for each vote that a party won in the most recent election. This infusion of public funding had a marked effect on the balance between local and national party funding, with an observable trend toward more centralized party financing.[6] This party allowance, however, was short lived. It was discontinued by the Harper Conservative government, with the final payments distributed in 2015, and fundraising in Canadian federal elections now relies entirely on relatively small individual donations.

This reliance on individual donations appears to have centralized party financing further since national parties are best equipped to scale up the types of technologies needed to send out personalized messages targeting potential individual donors.[7] This type of fundraising can also benefit local party associations, though. For example, the Liberal Party's Victory Fund targets small monthly donations split between the national party and a chosen local riding.[8] Nonetheless, this type of approach makes much less sense for local fundraising, which relies on volunteers and, ultimately, the candidate's ability to leverage personal support. Accordingly, targeting larger donations is still an attractive approach for local party fundraising. If a local party candidate can attract fifteen to twenty larger donors ($500 to $1,650 each), then the campaign is on its way to being well financed.

Despite the centralizing effects of more recent regulatory reforms, many Conservative and Liberal candidates are able to finance their own campaigns without relying on transfers from the national parties.[9] NDP candidates historically have been more reliant on transfers from the central party, but even so transfers for the federal election in 2015 amounted to just over 20 percent of a local campaign's funding.[10] This financial balance for the NDP appears to be changing, however. For the federal elections in 2019 and 2021, the party's national office kept 100 percent of all Elections Canada campaign expense reimbursements, money that had previously been transferred to local candidates and riding associations. In comparison, for the federal election in 2021, the Conservatives and Greens committed to transferring their entire reimbursements to the local ridings, and the Liberals indicated that 40 percent would be transferred to the local ridings.[11] The move by the NDP coincided with the party's plan to increase its national campaign budget, highlighting how the fundraising needs of a party can sometimes lead to tensions between national and local campaigns.[12]

The challenges of local fundraising are especially felt by independents, who are only permitted to accept donations during the regulated election campaign period, whereas a local party association – legally named the electoral district association or EDA – can raise money continuously throughout election and non-election years.[13] Thus, candidates with active local party associations have a considerable fundraising advantage since they will receive transfers from their EDAs for their election campaigns.[14] Undoubtedly, MPs running for re-election are the most likely to be motivated and the best able to take advantage of their EDAs' potential for continuous fundraising. An incumbent has a natural self-interest in keeping the EDA active in non-election years in order to be financially well positioned for the next campaign.

How differences in amounts and sources of funding both within and between parties affect how a local party candidate campaigns and the likelihood of winning the riding have been the focus of some scholarly attention. There is now considerable evidence that the strength of the local candidate is a decisive factor that accounts for anywhere between 4 percent and 14 percent of the ballots cast in Canadian elections.[15] And though money alone does not determine the strength of a local campaign, there appears to be an observable correlation between funds raised and election performance at the local level. For example, William Cross found that, in ridings where the Liberal Party won in the election in 2015, the local party associations were more active and had a larger increase in the number of financial contributions compared with those ridings where the Liberal candidate was unsuccessful.[16] The source of money also matters in terms of how a local candidate is likely to campaign. Cross and his collaborators found that, the greater the percentage of income from the national party, the more emphasis candidates will place on the party relative to themselves.[17] Interestingly, the same study found that candidates in rural districts place less emphasis on their parties compared with candidates in urban districts,[18] suggesting that both geography and the source of campaign funding are important for understanding the likelihood that a party candidate will stay on message and follow a party's election script.[19] Taken together, fundraising at the local level is consistent with the expectations of the franchise model of Canadian party organization,[20] giving party candidates considerable autonomy and flexibility to fund and execute their own election campaigns.

Local Trends

The federal election in 2021 posed a number of challenges from a fundraising perspective. Because it came less than two years after the federal election in 2019, parties and local candidates had little time for replenishment of funds or recalibration of tactics. The short period between the elections was made even more challenging when the emergence of the COVID-19 pandemic led parties temporarily to pause some of their fundraising following public criticism.[21] Nonetheless, federal party fundraising numbers in the first three quarters of 2021 were strong and even record breaking for some parties, indicating that parties and donors had adjusted.[22] The first half of 2021 had the Conservative Party continuing its tradition of outpacing the other parties, as it had in fifty-nine of the past sixty-four quarters, raising $5,099,434 from 35,865 individual contributions.[23] This pattern continued into the third quarter (July–September), which encompassed the election campaign period, and saw the Conservatives raise $9,843,840 from 50,185 individual contributions. In contrast, in the third quarter, the Liberals raised $7,648,139 from 57,146 contributions, followed by the New Democrats at $3,994,678 from 33,604 contributions, the Greens at $1,326,696 from 12,364 contributions, and the Bloc Québécois at $1,228,726 from 7,825 contributions.[24]

Although the short period between elections was not unexpected given that the election in 2019 had produced a minority Liberal government, the election in 2021 was unlikely to be greeted warmly for those tasked with financing either a national or a local campaign. Fundraisers faced the enduring challenge of quickly soliciting donations, but this time in the midst of a growing fourth wave of the COVID-19 pandemic, which necessarily foreclosed larger in-person fundraising options at the local level, such as a spaghetti supper.[25]

For fundraisers in Nova Scotia, where a provincial election had just been held on 17 August, the task was all the more daunting given that the two election campaigns overlapped momentarily. The prospect of donor fatigue seemed to be a real concern for campaign fundraisers.

With limited resources at the local level, these fundraising challenges arguably were even more daunting for local party candidates. National party campaign teams have staff whose exclusive focus is fundraising. The automation of these types of fundraising models, though not immune to donor or pandemic fatigue, means that the resource challenges are different from those faced at the local level, where fundraising commonly relies on the party candidate. For example, Kody Blois, the Liberal Party candidate for Kings–Hants, acted as his own fundraising lead for the federal election campaigns in both 2019 and 2021. This meant that he was responsible for calling likely donors and providing personalized follow-up emails with information on how to donate. In his experience, this labour-intensive, candidate-driven strategy is typical, especially in rural ridings. Relying on the candidate for fundraising reflects in part the fact that local riding associations are not as robust as they used to be, and there are simply fewer volunteers willing to commit their time and money. In other words, the age of the "bagmen," when a few well-connected businesspeople were responsible for a large portion of party fundraising, has passed.[26]

Given this personalized approach, focusing on larger donations from a smaller number of supporters makes sense. Small donations are still a part of local fundraising efforts; for example, the Kings–Hants Liberal riding association receives small monthly donations as part of the Liberal Party's Victory Fund that amounted to about $1,400 per month in 2021. However, this approach is not likely to drive local campaign funding. The focus on larger donations for the local campaign becomes apparent when comparing the average donation amounts for the national party and local party entities. From the fourth quarter of 2015 to the second quarter of 2021, the Liberal Party averaged $103 per contribution, compared with an average of $148 for the Conservative Party, whereas the NDP and Green Party each averaged under $90 per donation.[27]

The average donation to party candidates and riding associations is generally higher. For this chapter, we focus on Nova Scotia. From 2015 to 2020, the average donation to Conservative riding associations and candidates was $527, for the Greens it was $426, and for the New Democrats it was $338, all amounts considerably higher than those for the national parties.[28] Local donations to the Liberals in Nova Scotia, however, came in at an average of $108, close to that of the national party. This lower average reflects the high proportion of small donations received by Liberal riding associations in the province, with 79 percent of these donations being $50 or less. The number of individual donations received by Liberal candidates and riding associations (13,863) was more than those of the other parties combined, and contributed to the Liberals' fundraising prowess in the province, raising $1,494,815 over this period, compared with the second-place Conservatives at $528,656. However, though these smaller donations made up most of the Liberals' individual contributions, they amounted to just under 15 percent of the total funds raised. The Liberal Party's donation profile in Nova Scotia helps to illustrate two things: first, the party's fundraising strength in Atlantic Canada;[29] second, how the Liberal Party's Victory Fund program has fostered a different distribution of contribution sizes compared with the other political parties at the local level.

Behind the Scenes

How local conditions affect fundraising is further illustrated by looking at the fundraising efforts of the Liberal Party candidate in the riding of Kings–Hants for the election in 2021. As noted, research suggests that candidates who campaign in rural districts appear to place less emphasis on their party compared with candidates in urban districts.[30] The importance of emphasizing local issues and candidate-framed messages for both campaigning and fundraising was experienced by the Liberal candidate, Kody Blois, who sought re-election in 2021 after one term as the MP for the riding. Like every riding in Canada, Kings–Hants – primarily a rural riding in western Nova Scotia with a large agricultural sector – has its own unique features that influence the local election campaign.

Although the Liberal Party has held the riding since 2003, it is not easily categorized as a Liberal stronghold. From 1997 to 2019, the riding was represented by long-time MP, and former Trudeau cabinet minister, Scott Brison. Notably, he was first elected as a member of the Progressive Conservative Party before crossing over to the Liberal Party in 2003. The riding had generally trended Conservative prior to Brison, and after his switch to the Liberals the Conservative candidate always placed second. Brison's political career spanned some twenty years and two political parties, and his departure prompted the question of whether Kings–Hants had grown into a Liberal-friendly riding or if it was ultimately a Brison riding, and he just happened to be Liberal. The strong performance of the Progressive Conservative Party in the Nova Scotia election in 2021, in which the party captured a surprise majority government in large part thanks to its strength in rural ridings, added a layer of uncertainty in regard to the status of Kings–Hants as a Liberal riding.

Regardless of whether Brison's personal brand was the key contributor to his political success, his popularity in the riding meant that the Liberal riding association was in a strong financial position when he left office. When Blois won the party nomination in 2018, he was in the enviable position of inheriting a comparatively well-off and supportive riding association. Brison's success in fostering personal support in the riding was also a lesson that Blois carried over in terms of his own approach to fundraising and campaigning more generally. Because most voters in Kings–Hants are not dyed-in-the-wool Liberal supporters, it is electorally prudent for a Liberal candidate to focus on local issues rather than national campaign messages. Some supporters might choose to donate to local Liberal candidates because they are part of "Team Trudeau," but there are clear fundraising advantages to emphasizing the local candidate over the national party.

In Blois's experience as the Liberal candidate for Kings–Hants, it is not uncommon for those who make large donations of $1,000 or more to state that they do not view themselves as Liberals. Their willingness to donate stems from the view that the local candidate has prioritized issues of personal concern to them. In a riding that has a large agricultural sector, Blois focused on agriculture throughout his campaign and first term in office, which included serving as a member of the House of Commons Committee on Agriculture and Agri-Food and chair of the Rural Liberal Caucus. When he reached out to potential donors who work in agribusinesses, his focus on agriculture was emphasized and, in many cases, resulted in large donations from individuals who otherwise might not have considered supporting the Liberal Party. The importance of a particular business sector for a local candidate's fundraising is interesting since donations from businesses, corporations, and unions have been banned since 2007. At a strategic level, this appears to be a common-sense approach for party candidates, who need to be aware of their ridings' demographics and how their own backgrounds and values mesh with those who might support their campaigns. Business interests undoubtedly remain tied to some donations, though they are now from individuals rather than directly from businesses themselves. This can raise concerns for some, but given that donations are capped at $1,650 (as of 2021) there seems to be little reason to anticipate that individual donations can create the conditions for undue influence.

As in 2019, this focus on a personalized, local approach to fundraising was largely successful. Over the campaign period, Blois raised $36,679 from eighty-six donors, which averaged about $427 per donation. During the same period, the campaign raised approximately $2,600 from ninety-eight contributions through the Victory Fund program (for an average of about $27), again highlighting the importance of large donations to the local campaign. In total, Blois raised $39,279 from 184 donations. This amount was less than the $48,000 raised in 2019. A drop in donations is not necessarily surprising given that the Liberals lost two of the ten seats that it held in the province prior to the election. However, in Kings–Hants, the Liberal vote share ultimately increased, and the lower fundraising tally might be better explained by two additional factors: COVID-19 and the provincial election. First, the pandemic deeply affected people across Canada and the globe, and the food and beverage industry faced significant economic challenges. For Blois, this meant recognizing that some small business owners who had donated in 2019 were not well positioned to make similar contributions again and choosing not to reach out to them for donations. Second, with the Nova Scotia and federal elections running back to back, some supporters of the Liberal Kings–Hants campaign donated smaller amounts than they had previously because they had already made sizable donations during the provincial election. In other words, donor fatigue was at play. The Liberal campaign for Kings–Hants was successful in raising the funds that it needed for the election, but fundraising was more challenging than it had been in the previous campaign.

The focus on local issues also extended to the campaign more generally. For many voters in Kings–Hants, an issue of top concern was the federal government's continuing order to control the water flow at the Windsor Causeway, which resulted in the draining of the manufactured head pond, Lake Pisiquid.[31] The purpose of the order was to allow more fish to flow through the gated aboiteau system, something long asked for by local Mi'kmaq, fishers, and environmental groups, whereas those against the order raised concerns about the destruction of Lake Pisiquid, the flooding of agricultural lands, and other possible economic impacts.[32] It was a highly visible and politically divisive issue in the riding and one that Blois needed to address during the campaign. Finding that it was a top issue while knocking on doors, he mailed 6,000 postcards to homes in the Windsor area that stated his position on the issue, which partly critiqued the actions of his own government (see Appendix, p. 408). Ultimately, it is difficult to know how this move that prioritized local concerns over party messages affected the final election outcome; however, it does illustrate how a candidate-focused approach to a local election might require adopting a position that departs from that of the party.

Conclusion

In this chapter, we have explored party fundraising at the local level. Looking closely at the rural riding of Kings–Hants in Nova

Scotia, we have shown how the local candidate can be the key driver of fundraising activities in terms of both messaging and the laborious task of soliciting donations. This results in significant differences in fundraising approaches, evident in the average donation amounts between national parties and local party entities. A notable exception is the Liberal Party, for which many donations to riding associations in Nova Scotia are small. Nonetheless, large donations ultimately play a critical role for all local party entities. Whereas national parties can leverage technologies to scale up small donations, the labour-intensive approach of direct outreach at the local level means that focusing on comparatively large donations makes strategic sense. This approach does come with costs. A candidate-focused fundraising strategy is a major commitment during a campaign that already requires significant labour from the local candidate. For Blois, one lesson of the election in 2021 is the potential benefits that can come from having a campaign infrastructure that includes lead campaign volunteers for the different regions of the riding. Like so many features of a local campaign in a rural riding, this objective will require Blois to undertake significant relationship building but can pay dividends if some of the labour of the election campaign can be distributed better among the members of the campaign team. This approach, however, requires a relatively long-term commitment, likely making it difficult to execute for non-incumbents.

This candidate-focused approach can also carry over to the campaign more generally. In a riding like Kings–Hants that does not fit the mould of a party stronghold, the importance of local issues and candidate engagement is understood to be paramount. The intensity of local riding issues might not be felt as strongly in other ridings across the country, which undoubtedly affects how a candidate will choose to fundraise and campaign.[33] For the Liberal Party, which has found its strength in rural ridings weaken dramatically over the past few decades,[34] a focus on local issues might well be the determining factor between a win and a loss in a riding such as Kings–Hants. These differences in local conditions are an important reminder that the riding and candidate are crucial for understanding Canadian elections.

Notes

1 Elections Expenses Act, RSC 1974, 1st Supp, c 51.
2 Young, "Regulating Campaign Finance in Canada."
3 Coletto, Jansen, and Young, "Stratarchical Party Organization," 114; Carty and Eagles, *Politics Is Local.*
4 Young, "Regulating Campaign Finance in Canada," 457.
5 Cross, Currie-Wood, and Pruysers, "Money Talks," 6.
6 Coletto, Jansen, and Young, "Stratarchical Party Organization."
7 Crandall and Roy, "Party Fundraisers"; Marland and Mathews, "'Friend, Can You Chip in $3?'"
8 Liberal Party of Canada, "Fundraising Programs and Donation Forms."
9 Cross and Young, "Personalization of Campaigns in an SMP System," 309.
10 Cross, Currie-Wood, and Pruysers, "Money Talks," 6.
11 Stefanovich, Romualdo, and Thurton, "Some NDP Members Call on Party."
12 Ibid.
13 Small and Philpott, "The Independent Candidate."
14 Coletto and Eagles, "The Impact of Election Finance Reforms."
15 Stevens et al., "Local Candidate Effects in Canadian Elections"; Blais et al., "Does the Local Candidate Matter?"; Roy and Alcantara, "The Candidate Effect."
16 Cross, "The Importance of Local Party Activity," 611. See also Carty and Eagles, "Do Local Campaigns Matter?"
17 Cross, Currie-Wood, and Pruysers, "Money Talks," 8.
18 Ibid.
19 Marland, *Whipped.*
20 Carty, "Parties as Franchise Systems."
21 Patel, "As Governments Struggle with Pandemic Response."
22 Canadian Press, "Federal Liberals, Tories Hit Record Fundraising Marks"; Grenier, "The Q2 Fundraising Numbers Are In!"
23 Grenier, "The Weekly Writ for Nov. 3."
24 Ibid.
25 McGrane, "Campaigning in Canada during a Pandemic."
26 For more on the history and importance of "bagmen" for election fundraising, see Crandall and Roy, "Party Fundraisers," 112–14.
27 Grenier, "The Q2 Fundraising Numbers Are In!"
28 Unlike federal parties, local party associations are only required to report their fundraising to Elections Canada annually, so data, as of the time of writing, were available to 31 December 2020.

29 Grenier, "The Q2 Fundraising Numbers Are In!"
30 Cross, Currie-Wood, and Pruysers, "Money Talks," 8.
31 Ryan, "Windsor Residents."
32 Baxter, "Small Dam, Big Controversy."
33 It is important to acknowledge that this case study of Kings–Hants does not address several other factors that can affect local election fundraising, including demographic features of the candidate and local riding. For example, research indicates that gender and ethnic group differences affect who donates and to which local candidate. Besco and Tolley, "Ethnic Group Differences"; Tolley, Besco, and Sevi, "Who Controls the Purse Strings?"
34 Armstrong, Lucas, and Taylor, "The Urban-Rural Divide"; Wherry, "Two New Solitudes."

Bibliography

Armstrong, David A., Jack Lucas, and Zack Taylor. "The Urban-Rural Divide in Canadian Federal Elections, 1896–2019." *Canadian Journal of Political Science* (2021): 1–23.

Baxter, Joan. "Small Dam, Big Controversy." *Halifax Examiner,* 8 December 2020. https://www.halifaxexaminer.ca/environment/small-dam-big -controversy/.

Besco, Randy, and Erin Tolley. "Ethnic Group Differences in Donations to Electoral Candidates." *Journal of Ethnic and Migration Studies* 48, 5 (2022): 1072–94.

Blais, André, Elisabeth Gidengil, Agnieszka Dobrzynska, Neil Nevitte, and Richard Nadeau. "Does the Local Candidate Matter? Candidate Effects in the Canadian Election of 2000." *Canadian Journal of Political Science* 36, 3 (2003): 657–64.

Canadian Press. "Federal Liberals, Tories Hit Record Fundraising Marks amid Boost in Election Spending." Global News, 29 October 2021. https://globalnews.ca/news/8337311/liberals-tories-fundraising-records -election/.

Carty, R. Kenneth. "Parties as Franchise Systems: The Stratarchical Organizational Imperative." *Party Politics* 10, 1 (2004): 5–24.

Carty, R. Kenneth, and Munroe Eagles. "Do Local Campaigns Matter? Campaign Spending, the Local Canvass and Party Support in Canada." *Electoral Studies* 18, 1 (1999): 69–87.

–. *Politics Is Local: National Politics at the Grassroots.* Don Mills, ON: Oxford University Press, 2005.

Coletto, David, and Munroe Eagles. "The Impact of Election Finance Reforms on Local Party Organization." In *Money, Politics, and Democracy: Canada's Party Finance Reforms,* edited by Lisa Young and Harold J. Jansen, 104–29. Vancouver: UBC Press, 2011.

Coletto, David, Harold J. Jansen, and Lisa Young. "Stratarchical Party Organization and Party Finance in Canada." *Canadian Journal of Political Science* 44, 1 (2011): 111–36.

Crandall, Erin, and Michael Roy. "Party Fundraisers." In *Inside the Campaign: Managing Elections in Canada,* edited by Alex Marland and Thierry Giasson, 111–22. Vancouver: UBC Press, 2019.

Cross, William. "The Importance of Local Party Activity in Understanding Canadian Politics: Winning from the Ground Up in the 2015 Federal Election: Presidential Address to the Canadian Political Science Association Calgary, 31 May 2016." *Canadian Journal of Political Science* 49, 4 (2016): 601–20.

Cross, William P., Rob Currie-Wood, and Scott Pruysers. "Money Talks: Decentralized Personalism and the Sources of Campaign Funding." *Political Geography* 82 (2020): 1–11.

Cross, William, and Lisa Young. "Personalization of Campaigns in an SMP System: The Canadian Case." *Electoral Studies* 39 (2015): 306–15.

Grenier, Éric. "The Q2 Fundraising Numbers Are In!" The Writ, 3 August 2021. https://www.thewrit.ca/p/q2-2021-fundraising.

–. "The Weekly Writ for Nov. 3." The Writ, 3 November 2021. https://www.thewrit.ca/p/the-weekly-writ-for-nov-3.

Liberal Party of Canada. "Fundraising Programs and Donation Forms." https://my.liberal.ca/general/fundraising-programs-and-donation-forms/.

Marland, Alex. *Whipped: Party Discipline in Canada.* Vancouver: UBC Press, 2020.

Marland, Alex, and Maria Mathews. "'Friend, Can You Chip in $3?' Canadian Political Parties' Email Communication and Fundraising." In *Permanent Campaigning in Canada,* edited by Alex Marland, Thierry Giasson, and Anna Lennox Esselment, 87–108. Vancouver: UBC Press, 2017.

McGrane, David. "Campaigning in Canada during a Pandemic." *Policy Options,* 28 December 2020. https://policyoptions.irpp.org/magazines/december-2020/campaigning-in-canada-during-a-pandemic/.

Patel, Raisa. "As Governments Struggle with Pandemic Response, Political Parties Shift Gears on Fundraising." CBC News, 24 March 2020. https://

www.cbc.ca/news/politics/covid-19-coronavirus-pandemic-parties
-fundraising-1.5508111.

Roy, Jason, and Christopher Alcantara. "The Candidate Effect: Does the Local Candidate Matter?" *Journal of Elections, Public Opinion and Parties* 25, 2 (2015): 195–214.

Ryan, Haley. "Windsor Residents Say Federal Order Has Led to Dust Bowl Conditions." CBC News, 27 May 2021. https://www.cbc.ca/news/canada/nova-scotia/windsor-residents-say-federal-order-has-led-to-dust-bowl-conditions-1.6041745.

Small, Tamara A., and Jane Philpott. "The Independent Candidate." In *Inside the Campaign: Managing Elections in Canada,* edited by Alex Marland and Thierry Giasson, 197–206. Vancouver: UBC Press, 2019.

Stefanovich, Olivia, Christina Romualdo, and David Thurton. "Some NDP Members Call on Party to Stop Clawing Back Campaign Rebate Cash." CBC News, 10 April 2021. https://www.cbc.ca/news/politics/federal-ndp-finances-elections-canada-rebates-decision-1.5979926.

Stevens, Benjamin Allen, Md Mujahedul Islam, Roosmarijn de Geus, Jonah Goldberg, John R. McAndrews, Alex Mierke-Zatwarnicki, Peter John Loewen, and Daniel Rubenson. "Local Candidate Effects in Canadian Elections." *Canadian Journal of Political Science* 52, 1 (2019): 83–96.

Tolley, Erin, Randy Besco, and Semra Sevi. "Who Controls the Purse Strings? A Longitudinal Study of Gender and Donations in Canadian Politics." *Politics and Gender* 18, 1 (2022): 244–72.

Wherry, Aaron. "Two New Solitudes – Rural and Urban – Now Define the Canadian Political Landscape." CBC News, 3 October 2021. https://www.cbc.ca/news/politics/2021-election-rural-urban-conservative-liberal-1.6197095.

Young, Lisa. "Regulating Campaign Finance in Canada: Strengths and Weaknesses." *Election Law Journal* 3, 3 (2004): 444–62.

PART 3
Local Communications

13

National-Local Messaging

Stéphanie Yates

Abstract   When campaigning, local candidates must adapt their speeches and commitments to the wishes and demands of their constituents while remaining consistent with the party's electoral platform and, more generally, its brand image. National campaign managers tolerate little dissent in this regard, and they closely monitor local campaigns. To this end, they provide daily talking points and communication materials to feed into local advertising campaigns and field and social media presence. However, star candidates, such as Alexandre Boulerice, deputy leader of the New Democratic Party, have more flexibility to tailor the party's proposed messages to local priorities and even to present their own local and regional commitments. In the Quebec context, several parties have developed the habit of presenting a "Quebec platform" that puts forward specific commitments for the province. This dynamic articulation of messages between national and local levels is not without its tensions. During the campaign in 2021, the issues of pipelines, religious symbols, firearms, and health care sometimes put NDP candidates in a delicate position, forcing them to adopt vague or ambiguous language to navigate these troubled waters.

Résumé   En campagne électorale, les candidats locaux doivent savoir adapter leurs discours et engagements aux souhaits et demandes de leur électorat, tout en affichant une cohérence avec la plateforme électorale du parti et, plus généralement, son image de marque. Les responsables des campagnes nationales tolèrent peu de dissidence sur ce plan, et encadrent de près les campagnes locales. Dans cette perspective, ils leur fournissent des lignes de presse quotidiennes ainsi que du matériel communicationnel servant à alimenter les campagnes publicitaires locales ainsi que la présence sur le terrain et dans les médias sociaux. Les « candidats vedettes », comme Alexandre Boulerice, chef adjoint du Nouveau Parti Démocratique, disposent toutefois d'une plus grande marge de manœuvre pour adapter les messages proposés par le parti en fonction des priorités locales, et même pour présenter leurs propres engagements locaux et régionaux. En contexte québécois, plusieurs partis ont d'ailleurs pris l'habitude de présenter une « plateforme Québec » mettant de l'avant des engagements spécifiques pour la province. Cette dynamique d'articulation des messages entre le national et le local n'est pas sans générer certaines tensions. Lors de la campagne électorale de 2021, la question des pipelines, des symboles religieux, des armes à feu, et de la santé ont ainsi parfois placé les candidats du NDP dans une posture délicate, les contraignant à adopter un langage flou ou ambigu afin de naviguer dans ces eaux troubles.

A CANADIAN FEDERAL election consists of hundreds of localized elections. Although the candidates who run for office in each constituency act as the regional voices for their party's electoral platform, they must also play up their personal electoral commitments. Generally, these local candidates' weight is rather low in regard to voting intentions.[1] Still, by calling attention to key messages, they can help to secure voters and sway the undecided – along with getting out the vote, this is the ultimate goal of local campaigns.[2] When it is a close race, securing but a handful of voters through local campaigning can make the difference in winning a seat.

Ideally, messages crafted for local voters fit naturally into the national campaign framework. Political parties delineate the boundaries within which candidates can tie in local messages. Hence, though local candidates cannot deviate from the party's electoral promises, they are granted space within which to promote commitments that speak more specifically to electors' concerns.[3] One could equate this dynamic to a "franchise model": local candidates leverage a party's brand, yet they have the latitude and autonomy to determine strategically the space that they will grant to the party and its leader in their campaigns.[4] Incumbents may also take advantage of this leeway to showcase their accomplishments from an accountability perspective.

With this flexibility, candidates can respond to local concerns, and such a response remains at the core of representative democracy; indeed, it is a tenet of it, beyond any electoral consideration.[5] From this perspective, local civil society groups urge and expect candidates to take stands on specific issues in their constituencies.[6] From one campaign to the next, there are recurring and persistent concerns, such as local economic development, that are particularly important in rural ridings or those located on the outskirts of major centres. Tailoring the message to segmented audiences' immediate concerns is the basis of political public relations.[7] Indeed, this customized approach is personalized even further with voters' microsegmentation in political marketing.[8]

Local campaign teams put together communication materials and work with tools such as newspaper ads, radio or television spots, signs, leaflets, brochures, and more to get their messages across. Social media platforms such as Twitter are also readily available as means to broadcast locally focused messages.[9] In short, the goal is to reach the optimal synergy level between local and national campaigns. This amalgamation is material – such as common communication tools and volunteers – as well as symbolic; a party's endorsement of a local candidate, for instance, is akin to "royal anointing."[10]

In the Canadian context, though very few studies have examined the effects of highlighting local issues during an election campaign, both on voters and on media coverage, it seems that some candidates are more successful than others at grasping and leveraging local issues while remaining consistent with the national campaign. It would be beneficial electorally.[11]

Unsurprisingly, political parties usually keep tight control of local campaigns' messages and promises. Even though they cannot oversee the details of all local campaigns, they aim, with this high level of centralization, to avoid inconsistencies between the national and local campaigns' respective messaging. Moreover, framing communications according to the party's concerns rather than those of the candidate is also more effective; a party's rhetoric immediately "taps into voters' broader understanding of what their party is" and calls to mind "the positive reputation members of their party have earned over time."[12] Parties are reasonably successful at curbing candidates' inclinations to craft their own messages; centralized decision making and control over messaging remain very strong.[13] A political party will call to order a candidate who veers from core messages. The correction can go as far as revoking the endorsement and appointing a new candidate.

The degree of independence afforded to a local campaign depends mainly on the type of candidate and the nomination process. Hence, as stressed in Chapter 5 of this volume, notable local figures generally have more latitude to insist on their own commitments compared with party insiders who are beholden to the party and naturally prone to run local campaigns that rely on the national campaign, high-profile candidates who are generally integrated as features or components of the national campaign, or stopgap candidates who typically run shadow campaigns in unfavourable constituencies.[14] As well, star candidates who have name recognition pull in support from communities of interest (see Chapter 4 of this volume). Ultimately, only strong figures with charismatic personalities and deep roots in their constituencies can afford to deviate from the messages put forward at the national level.

However, this independence from the national campaign is exceptional, because political parties tend to replace notable local figures with lesser-known candidates.[15] In this context, voters are more interested in the candidate's views on issues presented by party leaders than in the candidate's own propositions. Another noteworthy exception concerns remote ridings, such as communities in the Far North, where external considerations have minimal influence and people's primary concerns have little to do with national political parties' commitments.

In short, to craft a compelling message, local campaign managers should consider several factors: the personal characteristics and professional backgrounds of candidates, the national issue agenda, as well as local priorities. Tensions can arise in this process, especially if a party's fundamental positions do not reflect local constituents' concerns or the candidate's views. In these circumstances, local candidates tend to distance themselves from the national campaign and to disseminate messages that they deem more relevant to their audiences. Candidates might also wish to distance themselves from official party positions and instead focus on the issues that inspired their decisions to enter politics in the first place.

Local Trends

The development of a specific local or regional message is a recurrent dynamic in the Canadian electoral context. In order for these messages to be in line with the national campaign, local teams receive talking points – or scripted messages – on a daily basis. Their mission is to relay the messages in order to amplify them. Local commitments, therefore, must fit into the overall message put forward by the party and, more broadly, be consistent with the party brand and the electoral platform.[16] To promote this coherence, the national campaign provides local teams with various communication tools: visual assets designed for social media or templates for signs and brochures. The national campaign also advises local teams on advertising, media outreach, and social media tactics.[17]

In Quebec, the will of local teams to adapt the national campaign to regional specificities often leads to the release of a given platform for the province. This is particularly useful since significant national promises might not resonate with the electorate in the province. Consider the flagship campaign promises in 2021 of the Liberals and New Democrats on a national ten-dollar-a-day child-care system and universal prescription drug coverage, both of which have already been in place in Quebec for several years.

Regional platforms can also be a means to respond to some critics. That was the case in the campaign in 2021, marked by Premier of Quebec François Legault's call for Quebecers to be wary of federal parties that are too "centralizing" and therefore "dangerous."[18] In this context, the NDP proposed its "Quebec platform." It sought to counter the party's centralizing image by promising "asymmetrical, cooperative and respectful federalism" based upon recognition of the "uniqueness of the Quebec nation."[19] From this perspective, the Quebec platform pledged that all appointees to the Supreme Court would be bilingual; furthermore, an NDP government would choose them based upon a list of candidates preselected by the Quebec government. The party also promised to engage in discussions with Quebec to achieve full cultural sovereignty. Furthermore, NDP candidates in Quebec could fall back on the party's commitment to subjecting businesses under federal jurisdiction to the provincial Charter of the French Language and its promise not to conduct environmental assessments on projects under provincial jurisdiction.

For its part, the Conservative Party presented its "contract" with Quebecers, proposing a "partnership federalism."[20] Hence, Conservative candidates emphasized their leader's promise to give Quebec specific or increased powers, including in immigration, and openness to adopting a single tax return. In both cases, Quebec candidates used these regional platforms to show their party's openness to taking into account the specific interests of their constituents – sometimes arguing that their own efforts had helped the party to develop these particular approaches.

In contrast, the Liberal Party has always favoured a unified approach, arguing that the measures set out in its national platform serve all Canadians, including Quebecers. According to Richard Johnston,[21] this unified approach, especially on the matter of Quebec's autonomy, has served the party very well. However, in the wake of the election in 2019, Prime Minister Justin Trudeau appointed a "Quebec lieutenant" (MP Pablo Rodriguez) in response to the dissatisfaction of several party members and elected officials from Quebec who accused the party of being controlled from Toronto.[22] As head of the ten or so Quebec ministers, the lieutenant played an essential role in ensuring that Quebec's priorities had a place in the electoral platform for the campaign in 2021: for instance, spending on aeronautics, support for tourism and culture, and funding for the electrification of transportation.[23]

Although these regional initiatives highlight how the party's commitments are beneficial for a given segment of the electorate (e.g., Quebec), they do not eliminate the tensions that can emerge between national positions and local issues. The Green Party provided a concrete illustration of this during the campaign in 2021 when it also chose to present a platform specifically dedicated to Quebec voters. However, this was a unilateral initiative of the Quebec branch of the party, presented without the knowledge and approval of the national leadership. Indeed, Quebec Green candidates and their teams threw a spanner into the works by formulating new commitments that did not appear in the national platform, such as fiscal and environmental objectives. Above all, they presented promises that sometimes contradicted national commitments, such as the recognition of Quebec as a nation and of its right to make French its only official language.[24] These positions ran counter to those of leader Annamie Paul[25] and thus further reflected the profound leadership crisis within the party. In the end, this strategy did not pay off, with the Greens obtaining only 1.5 percent of the vote in Quebec.

The campaign in 2021 also showed that tensions can arise between candidates from the same region, such as when Bloc Québécois leader Yves-François Blanchet said that he favoured a planned highway tunnel to ease traffic between Quebec City and its suburbs. Environmentalists strongly criticized this project because of its impact on increasing automobile use and urban sprawl. Given that environmental issues are presented by the Bloc Québécois as core priorities, some candidates expressed their reservations about the project to the media. However, they did so anonymously, thus avoiding direct opposition to their leader.[26]

Several issues in national election campaigns traditionally have led to tensions within parties because of differences in regional perceptions, forcing candidates to do their best in reconciling visions that often are not easily compatible. Among these issues is gun control, traditionally considered a wedge issue,[27] for which clear divisions have always existed between rural and urban areas, with the former generally opposing gun registration and the latter favouring greater control or even a ban on assault weapons and other semi-automatic weapons. Conservative Party leader Stephen Harper's promise during the election campaign in 2011 to abolish the long-gun registry put several Conservative candidates in a difficult position, especially in Quebec,[28] where groups such as Poly-Remembers were strongly opposed to the Conservative measure. In that contest, the Conservatives elected only five MPs in Quebec as Jack Layton's NDP "orange wave" swept the province. The issue of gun control came back to haunt Conservative candidates in the campaign in 2021, with leader Erin O'Toole taking an ambiguous position on maintaining the ban on several assault weapons.[29] Although O'Toole was still relatively unknown and working to build a reassuring and caring image, journalists pressured local Conservative candidates by asking them to clarify the party's position on the issue.

Another example is the exploitation of the oil sands and the construction of pipelines that it underpins, with many Canadians expressing resistance to the development of this energy sector. Tensions over this issue became concrete when Justin Trudeau's Liberal government bought the Trans Mountain Pipeline from Kinder Morgan in 2018 at the cost of $4.4 billion Canadian. At the time, the project was presented as a compromise for Alberta's commitment to join the carbon-trading marketplace, believed to incentivize market agents to decrease their greenhouse gas emissions.[30] In the campaign in 2021, at least one Liberal candidate openly opposed the project, contradicting the party's official position.[31] However, this type of reaction remains exceptional: in the end, and with few exceptions, it appears that tensions over electoral commitments in national platforms and their reception at the regional level rarely lead to open conflict. Candidates are generally loyal to their parties. At least that is the position that they state publicly, trying as best as they can to reconcile local issues with national commitments. Conflicting elements are thus confined primarily to discussions behind closed doors, whether in caucus or in the leader's office.

In the next section, I explore how NDP candidate Alexandre Boulerice's team developed regional and local content during the campaign in 2021, the specific tools that they crafted, and the strategy that they adopted to reach the electorate better. I also address the tension with the national team that sometimes arose in the process.

Behind the Scenes

This section is based upon two interviews with Alexandre Boulerice, held at the outset of the campaign and three days after the election, and upon an interview with Lisa Cerasuolo, Boulerice's communications officer, held three weeks after election day.

The campaign in 2021 was the candidate's fourth in Rosemont, where Boulerice was defeated in 2008 but then won in 2011, 2015, and 2019 with solid majorities. To present local commitments that would be attractive to the electorate of the Rosemont–La Petite-Patrie riding, located in the centre-east of Montreal, the incumbent's team consulted with citizens of the riding before the election. To do so, they asked voters to respond by email to questions presented in their newsletter. They also inserted reply coupons in the MP's bulletin distributed a few times a year to all households in the riding. Furthermore, they used social media – Facebook in particular – to solicit voters' opinions on various subjects. Incumbents have a head start on their political opponents since they can benefit from a team to support them in preparing their campaigns. In the process, they can also leverage the communication channels already established with constituents.

As a result of these exercises, it became clear that the environment was a priority for voters in the riding, along with access to housing and fiscal issues for a better distribution of wealth. In relation to the environment, the idea of protecting the St. Lawrence River by giving it legal status, discussed a year earlier at a party convention, was tested with the electorate ahead of the campaign. During the spring, the candidate and his team visited various parks in the riding, particularly popular in the context of the COVID-19 pandemic, to present the idea and get people to sign a petition in favour of such a commitment. Also, in the months preceding the campaign, a group of ornithologists contacted the MP to inform him of the threat to a wetland belonging to the Montreal-Trudeau International Airport, where a developer was considering building a plant dedicated to producing N95 masks. The team decided to make the protection of this natural environment another electoral commitment; in the middle of the election campaign, Boulerice answered the activists' call in favour of protecting this territory by participating in a demonstration demanding the end of the planned project.[32] During the campaign, the community of Kanesatake, aware of the environmental focus chosen by the Boulerice team, approached the candidate and asked him to take a stand against the Trudeau government's inaction on an illegal dump on the reserve, where traces of highly toxic products were found, including PCBs. The team agreed to this request: it issued and relayed on Twitter a press release denouncing the inaction of the Trudeau government in this matter.[33]

Regional issues thus took precedence over strictly local ones, relatively absent from the campaign. The fact that Boulerice was the deputy leader of the NDP in 2021, and the party's only elected member in Quebec, could explain this focus on regional considerations. Indeed, he could be considered a star candidate, confirmed by the election results: Boulerice garnered 48.6 percent of the vote in his riding, whereas at the Quebec level the party received the support of only 9.8 percent of voters. This special status gives him considerable leeway to decide which will be winning issues in Quebec. The party's leadership had to validate the most important regional positions, which led to tough negotiations, particularly with respect to the commitment to protect the St. Lawrence River and the legal precedent that it set.[34]

As in previous election campaigns, the party hired a Quebec-based advertising agency to craft the campaign communication tools, which notably used focus groups to determine the most effective messages in the province. These professionals proposed a slogan for Quebec, "Oser ensemble," that was slightly different from the national one ("Ready for Better"), directly daring the electorate to vote NDP; this strategy echoed the one adopted in 2011, when the party chose to replace the national motto "Canadian Leadership" with "Let's Work Together" in Quebec.

Despite these efforts to court the Quebec electorate with a specific platform and locally adapted messages, some commentators observed early in the campaign that the NDP appeared to have chosen to let Quebec down to avoid alienating other segments of the electorate.[35] One reason they gave for this assumption was that leader Jagmeet Singh seemed to have ignored the Sherbrooke Declaration. Adopted under Jack Layton's leadership in 2005, this declaration recognized Quebec's specificity and its right to opt out, with full compensation, from federal programs that impinge against its jurisdictions. Not only was this declaration not part of Singh's speeches, but also the NDP's flagship commitments under his leadership included issues of provincial jurisdiction, particularly health care.[36] In addition, pundits pointed to the leader's timid response to his Toronto MP Matthew Green, who had praised a University of Ottawa professor for associating the Quebec government with "white supremacists."[37] In short, it seemed that giving up on Quebec was the price to pay for attracting young voters elsewhere in Canada.

This analysis is not shared by Boulerice. From his perspective, the party has exerted considerable effort in helping Quebec candidates to get elected while allowing them latitude to put forward specific local issues. Although the relationship between the central organization and the local campaigns can be a matter of obvious tension – even in a party like the NDP[38] – from Boulerice's perspective the relationship put trust in the Quebec team. In his view, this gave the Quebec NDP wing a great deal of latitude to shape its approach to the specific needs and expectations of the province, all within the party's boundaries.

Specifically, in the campaign in 2021, the main talking points were discussed during a weekly call with the campaign managers of each district and/or the candidates themselves, though some candidates running in less winnable districts campaigned alone. The talking points were then widely distributed to candidates as well as telephone operators and door-to-door volunteers. During these weekly meetings, the national team also presented and distributed party-provided "shareables," including images, videos, and news articles to use against opponents. The purpose of these meetings was to ensure that all local campaigns were amplifying the same message. Given Boulerice's status as deputy leader, some of his team members also took part in the morning meetings of the Quebec campaign leaders, during which the strategy was adjusted based upon the more immediate news.

The issues discussed at the national level were generally well aligned with the priorities identified at the local or regional level in Quebec – a peculiarity of the campaign in 2021, in which the linkages between national and local messages were natural in the province. However, the tone chosen by the Boulerice team was often more direct and familiar, even more aggressive or punchy, than the press lines suggested by the national campaign. The candidate's team also took the liberty, on some occasions, of engaging in negative campaigning based upon opposition research. They did so, for instance, with the commitment to tax the "ultra-rich." The local team wanted to put a face on these ultra-rich people and thus attacked businessman Stephen Bronfman. The team suggested that the businessman's project of building a baseball stadium on a former industrial site in Montreal (the Peel Bassin) was favoured unfairly by Prime Minister Justin Trudeau because of their long-term friendship. Singh echoed this attack rhetoric at a press conference in Montreal on the subject and committed to building thousands of social housing units on the same site instead of going ahead with the stadium.[39]

This more aggressive approach, sometimes taken up by the leader himself, is characteristic of Boulerice, affectionately known as Angry Boubou. His unique status in Quebec and within the party – one could characterize him as a notable local figure – gives him room to manoeuvre and distance himself from the party's planned press lines. Indeed, in the past, Boulerice has dissented from the official party position. In early 2018, as Israeli forces were bombing the Gaza Strip, he widely relayed a petition calling on the government of Canada to play its role as peacekeeper and condemn the Jewish settlement offensive. Although the NDP leader's office asked him to remove this petition from his website because of the sensitive nature of the subject, the Quebec MP refused to do so. He won his case and presented the petition before the House of Commons in February 2018.[40] From his point of view, this episode shows that, by pushing back and standing his ground, a "star" MP can gain space for freedom from the central party leadership.

With this in mind, throughout the campaign in 2021, Boulerice's team adapted the content provided by the national campaign to reflect his style and priorities better. The team sometimes deviated from the daily scripted message when it was less meaningful in Quebec, as with child care, universal prescription drug coverage, or even the housing crisis. When these issues were on the daily agenda, the local campaign turned to environmental issues, address-ing them from different angles. The health-care issue, very present in the national campaign, was also approached with caution in the province. The Quebec wing of the NDP chose its words carefully when referring to the party's commitments in this domain, insisting on the collaboration that it would establish with Quebec to solve what was presented as a failure of the health-care system to fulfill its mission. This precaution was deemed essential since the party's electoral commitments in this domain encroached on provincial responsibilities; indeed, this centralized approach was often pointed out by some political opponents, in particular the Bloc Québécois.

The fact that the national campaign was less scripted than in previous campaigns facilitated content adaptation by local teams. This situation was attributable mainly to the verification processes for policy-related content on Facebook, which resulted in campaigns losing control over the pace of their publications, with publishing becoming slower. In this context, betting on the daily theme was less relevant. For their part, Boulerice's team chose to deal with several issues on a weekly basis but from different angles.

The social media content prepared by the national campaign was also largely modified – if not outright set aside – because it adapted poorly to the local electorate. To develop their own content, the local team worked with the Quebec advertising agency hired for the campaign. Three people worked to feed Boulerice's social media: the candidate himself for Twitter, his communications director for Facebook, and a field manager for Instagram.

The loss of control over the timing of publishing social media advertising and the high cost of traditional media advertising led the local team to shift their advertising budgets. They focused on direct advertising (door hangers, flyers, text messages on cell-phones), volunteer mobilization (parties, snacks), and field ac-tivities (see Appendix, p. 410). They made this adaptation of communication tools to local realities, each time, without con-sulting the party's central office. Admittedly, Boulerice's team learned to work with their leeway within the party's boundaries over the years. More generally, it appears that in the end, the broad contours established by the NDP's central campaign allowed candidates to navigate relatively easily between the positions taken at the national level and regional considerations.

Despite this overall room for manoeuvring, some issues put local candidates in difficult positions, leading their teams to maintain certain degrees of vagueness and to use a few linguistic contortions. This was the case with the future of the Trans Mountain Pipeline. Continuing the project could cost Canadian taxpayers several billion dollars,[41] and in a context in which the very idea of spending public funds on the oil sands industry was widely contested in Quebec, committing to ending the project would have paid off politically for any candidate in Quebec. However, the NDP thought that it could win two Alberta ridings in 2021, where the provincial NDP was leading in voting intentions. Although many Albertan voters expressed concern about environmental issues, the idea of cancelling Trans Mountain, losing billions of dollars already invested in the project, and turning their backs on the job creation associated with it was not an option. To take such a position was to alienate these voters and thus lose the opportunity to win two additional ridings. So the party took the line that, if it formed the government, it would carefully explore all of the possible options on the table, including expansion of the project. This was a difficult position to defend in Quebec, where, from Boulerice's point of view, the issue fortunately had largely gone under the radar. Boulerice recognizes that his defence would have been weak had the party's opponents chosen to attack him from this angle. He also argues that this is the price to pay for being part of a party rather than running as an independent candidate. Nationally, the pipeline gamble did pay off, with the NDP winning one of the two targeted Alberta ridings.

The NDP's position on the Quebec law respecting the laicism of the state (Bill 21, 2019) has also forced candidates in Quebec to go against the party's official position. The law prohibits government employees in positions of coercive authority and teachers in the public school system from wearing or exposing religious symbols. Although Quebec's population widely supports the law, the NDP advocates freedom of choice to wear religious symbols. The party emphasizes the importance of defending minorities and is concerned about the discrimination that could result from implementing the law. Quebec candidates had to support this position, but they also had to avoid coming across as Ottawa's lead lesson givers.

As always, the issue of guns also pitted urban and rural constituencies against each other in the campaign in 2021. Although the NDP proposed a firm ban on military and assault weapons, its position on handguns was more nuanced. Like the Liberal Party, the NDP delegated the issue to municipal governments, arguing that it was up to them to determine the rules governing the use of handguns in their jurisdictions. Municipalities considered this a false solution, and they jointly asked the federal parties to take responsibility for this issue during the campaign. The NDP persisted in refusing to take a more decisive position on the divisive issue by yet again "passing the buck," this time to the provincial governments. Once again this did not have a decisive impact on the vote in Quebec.

In the end, the budget issue might have had a more significant effect on the outcome of the election. The financial framework proposed by the NDP forced all of its candidates, including those running in Quebec, to defend a vision that was sometimes inconsistent with their perspectives. Although party members, candidates, and MPs worked together to develop the electoral platform, the party's central office imposed the financial framework presented during the campaign. With spending projected to be $214 billion over five years, many pundits questioned the seriousness of the party and its ability to form the government.[42]

Candidates themselves were surprised by the magnitude of the planned spending, in stark contrast to the balanced budget presented during the election campaign of 2015 and the more conservative approach taken in 2019. To offset such spending, the party planned to generate new revenues with a rigorous fight against tax evasion to make the "ultra-rich" pay. However, these measures received mixed reviews. In the end, the press depicted the framework as unrealistic, even jocular. Although all NDP candidates were willing to defend the framework – most were not highly comfortable with it regardless of the magnitude of the proposed spending – the fact remains that the budget's magnitude might have generated some unease with the electorate.

In sum, the campaign of Boulerice during the election in 2021 shows that he benefited from significant leeway in deciding his discourse on issues deemed priorities at local and regional levels. He also had the room to adapt the press lines and other communication tools provided by the party to local realities. However, this latitude did not prevent certain national positions from generating delicate, even tense, situations at the local level to ensure overall coherence.

Conclusion

Candidates must often deal with national positions or engagements that have little resonance in their ridings, and sometimes these positions run squarely counter to the wishes of their constituents. Their capacity to veer away sometimes from the national message depends mainly on their status within the party. National campaign organizers might be open to candidates with some leadership putting forward their own local or regional campaign commitments, following their constituents' demands, and this process is at the core of representative democracy. However, local candidates can do so as long as these local commitments do not conflict with national promises and have little budgetary, judicial, or constitutional impact. Political parties might even agree to provide the resources necessary to highlight these commitments through a regional or local platform dedicated to a specific or culturally defined segment of the electorate, such as Quebec.

However, the party line on key electoral engagements or issues that cut across all ridings remains strong, and candidates must conform to it. This obligation sometimes forces them to take positions inconsistent with the mood or supposed interests of their electors or even with their political convictions. In such contexts, candidates will temper their language or frame issues to minimize any inconsistency. During the election campaign in 2021, NDP candidates in Quebec had to deal with such dynamics on pipelines, religious symbols, firearms, and, to a lesser extent, health-care funding.

Despite the awkward positions in which candidates sometimes find themselves, dissent is rare. Thus, they generally seem to agree to bow to the party's imperatives: as stressed by Alexandre Boulerice, this is the price to pay for being part of a political party rather than running as an independent candidate. That being said, most citizens vote primarily for a party or its leader rather than the local candidate. Thus, they tend to overlook inconsistencies between local and national messages or conflicts between a candidate's positions and the desires of the electorate. These inconsistencies can gain attention, however, if political opponents decide to raise them during electoral debates. However, the targeted candidates can often hide behind vague, hollow, or ambiguous discourses to mask their conflicting positions.

In the end, the leaders' national campaigns weigh much more heavily on voters' choices than local campaigns. During the NDP's campaign in 2021, the party's dubious financial framework likely undermined its credibility in forming the government, coupled with a leader who had difficulty embodying the image of a prime minister in waiting. Nevertheless, efforts by candidates to develop a coherent, specific, and locally relevant message can pay off. As illustrated by Boulerice, long-term constituency work carried out during and between elections coupled with national visibility can contribute to the development of a strong feeling of confidence among electors toward an incumbent candidate. This trust is likely to translate, during subsequent campaigns, into a vote for the candidate first, with the party and its leader becoming less relevant in the decision-making process. Paradoxically, perhaps it is in these situations that voters pay more attention to the articulation of the discourses deployed at national and local levels and that the issues of coherence discussed here might become more salient.

Notes

Acknowledgments: Thank you to Alexandre Boulerice, Member of Parliament for Rosemont–La Petite-Patrie, and Lisa Cerasuolo, communications officer for Rosemont–La Petite-Patrie, for their invaluable input.

1   Steven et al., "Local Candidate Effects in Canadian Elections."
2   Koop, "Constituency Campaigning in the 2015 Federal Election."
3   Baines, "Political Public Relations and Election Campaigning."
4   Cross and Young, "Personalization of Campaigns in an SMP System."
5   Sayers, *Parties, Candidates, and Constituency Campaigns.*
6   Carty and Eagles, *Politics Is Local.*
7   Kiousis and Strömbäck, "Political Public Relations."
8   Lees-Marshment et al., *Political Marketing.*
9   Killin and Small, "All Politics Is Not Local."
10 Maarek, *Campaign Communication and Political Marketing.*
11 Sayers, *Parties, Candidates, and Constituency Campaigns.*
12 Arbour, *Candidate-Centered Campaigns,* 605.
13 Marland, *Brand Command.*
14 Carty, Eagles, and Sayers, "Candidates and Local Campaigns."
15 Maarek, *Campaign Communication and Political Marketing.*
16 Wesley and Nauta, "Party Platform Builders."
17 Yates and Chenery, "National Campaign Director of Communications."
18 Messier, "Un gouvernement minoritaire conservateur est préférable."
19 Nouveau parti démocratique, *Oser ensemble.*
20 Conservative Party of Canada, "Conservative Leader Erin O'Toole Unveils His Contrat."
21 Johnston, "Polarized Pluralism in the Canadian Party System."
22 Bellavance, "Vivement un lieutenant québécois pour Trudeau."
23 Leblanc and Blouin, "Les ministres du Québec s'organisent."
24 Buzzetti, "Le Parti vert, version québécoise."
25 Martin, "L'aile québécoise du Parti vert."
26 Desrosiers and Martin, "Des candidats bloquistes."
27 Dumouchel, Ouellet, and Giasson, "Guns for Votes."
28 TVA Nouvelles, "Jean-Guy Dagenais change son fusil d'épaule."
29 Houdassine, "Erin O'Toole fait volte-face."
30 Prime Minister of Canada, "Trans Mountain Expansion."
31 Gilmore, "Liberal Candidate Opposes Trans Mountain Pipeline."
32 Sébire, "À Montréal, un poumon vert en danger."
33 Nouveau parti démocratique, "Le NPD dénonce la lâcheté des libéraux."
34 Morin-Martel, "Le NPD promet d'accorder un statut juridique."
35 Chouinard, "Le NPD aspire-t-il encore au pouvoir?"
36 Dutrisac, "Le NPD et le Québec."
37 Yakabuski, "Le NPD tourne-t-il le dos au Québec?"
38 On this subject, see Richler, *The Candidate.*

39 Gobeil, "Des logements sociaux."
40 Canada, House of Commons, Petition e-1293 (Israel).
41 Gunton, Joseph, and Dale, *Evaluation of the Trans Mountain Expansion Project.*
42 Buzzetti, "Le tour de magie du NPD."

Bibliography

Arbour, Brian. *Candidate-Centered Campaigns: Political Messages, Winning Personalities, and Personal Appeals.* New York: Palgrave Macmillan, 2014.

Baines, Paul. "Political Public Relations and Election Campaigning." In *Political Public Relations: Principles and Applications,* edited by Jesper Strömbäck and Spiro Kiousis, 115–37. New York: Routledge, 2011.

Bellavance, Joël-Denis. "Vivement un lieutenant québécois pour Trudeau." *La Presse,* 23 April 2018. https://www.lapresse.ca/actualites/politique/politique-canadienne/201804/22/01-5162064-vivement-un-lieutenant-quebecois-pour-trudeau.php.

Buzzetti, Hélène. "Le Parti vert, version québécoise." *L'Actualité,* 14 September 2021. https://lactualite.com/politique/le-parti-vert-version-quebecoise/.

–. "Le tour de magie du NPD." *L'Actualité,* 13 September 2021. https://lactualite.com/politique/le-tour-de-magie-du-npd/.

Canada. House of Commons. Petition e-1293 (Israel). Presented to the House of Commons on 14 February 2018. https://petitions.ourcommons.ca/en/Petition/Details?Petition=e-1293.

Carty, R.K., and Munroe Eagles. *Politics Is Local: National Politics at the Grassroots.* Oxford: Oxford University Press, 2005.

Carty, R. Kenneth, D. Munroe Eagles, and Anthony Sayers. "Candidates and Local Campaigns: Are There Just Four Canadian Types?" *Party Politics* 9, 5 (2003): 619–36.

Chouinard, Stéphanie. "Le NPD aspire-t-il encore au pouvoir?" *L'Actualité,* 15 April 2021. https://lactualite.com/politique/le-npd-aspire-t-il-encore-au-pouvoir/.

Conservative Party of Canada. "Conservative Leader Erin O'Toole Unveils His Contrat avec les Québécois et les Québécoises." 18 August 2021. https://www.conservative.ca/conservative-leader-erin-otoole-unveils-his-contrat-avec-les-quebecois-et-les-quebecoises/.

Cross, William, and Lisa Young. "Personalization of Campaigns in an SMP System: The Canadian Case." *Electoral Studies* 39 (2015): 306–15.

Desrosiers, Sébastien, and Laurence Martin. "Des candidats bloquistes expriment des réserves à l'égard du troisième lien." Radio-Canada, 25

August 2021. https://ici.radio-canada.ca/nouvelle/1819291/bloc
-quebecois-troisieme-lien-critiques-reserves-quebec.

Dumouchel, David, Catherine Ouellet, and Thierry Giasson. "Guns for
Votes: Wedge Politics in the Canadian Multiparty System." *Parliamentary
Affairs,* gsab003 (2021). https://doi.org/10.1093/pa/gsab003.

Dutrisac, Robert. "Le NPD et le Québec: Quantité négligeable." *Le Devoir,*
26 August 2021. https://www.ledevoir.com/opinion/editoriaux/627486/
le-npd-et-le-quebec-quantite-negligeable.

Gilmore, Rachel. "Liberal Candidate Opposes Trans Mountain Pipeline,
Will Ensure Party 'Answers' for It." Global News, 15 September 2021.
https://globalnews.ca/news/8193853/canada-election-trans-mountain
-pipeline-liberal/.

Gobeil, Mathieu. "Des logements sociaux et non du baseball au bassin Peel,
promet le NPD." Radio-Canada, 1 September 2021. https://ici.radio
-canada.ca/nouvelle/1820884/logements-sociaux-baseball-bassin-peel
-montreal-npd-singh-terrains-federaux.

Gunton, Thomas, Chris Joseph, and Daniel Dale. *Evaluation of the Trans
Mountain Expansion Project.* Burnaby, BC: School of Resources and Environmental Management, Simon Fraser University, 2018. http://rem
-main.rem.sfu.ca/papers/gunton/TMX%20CBA%20Report%20final%
20march%2021.pdf.

Houdassine, Ismaël. "Erin O'Toole fait volte-face sur les armes d'assaut."
Radio-Canada, 5 September 2021. https://ici.radio-canada.ca/nouvelle/
1821868/campagne-parti-conservateur-securite-police.

Johnston, Richard. "Polarized Pluralism in the Canadian Party System:
Presidential Address to the Canadian Political Science Association, June
5, 2008." *Canadian Journal of Political Science* 41, 4 (2008): 815–34.

Killin, Julie, and Tamara A. Small. "All Politics Is Not Local: Local Candidate Tweeting in the 2015 Election." In *Canadian Election Analysis:
Communication, Strategy, and Democracy,* edited by Alex Marland and
Thierry Giasson, 44–45. Vancouver: UBC Press, 2015. https://www.
ubcpress.ca/canadianelectionanalysis2015.

Kiousis, Spiro, and Jesper Strömbäck. "Political Public Relations." In *Political Communication,* edited by Carsten Reinemann, 249–67. Handbooks
of Communication Science 18. Boston: De Gruyter Mouton, 2014.

Koop, Royce. "Constituency Campaigning in the 2015 Federal Election."
In *Canadian Election Analysis: Communication, Strategy, and Democracy,*
edited by Alex Marland and Thierry Giasson, 42–43. Vancouver: UBC
Press, 2015. https://www.ubcpress.ca/canadianelectionanalysis2015.

Leblanc, Daniel, and Louis Blouin. "Les ministres du Québec s'organisent pour mettre leur empreinte sur le budget." Radio-Canada, 4 April 2021. https://ici.radio-canada.ca/nouvelle/1781680/budget-federal-ministres -liberaux-quebec-elections.

Lees-Marshment, Jennifer, Brian Conley, Edward Elder, Robin Pettitt, Vincent Raynaud, and André Turcotte, eds. *Political Marketing: Principles and Applications*. 3rd ed. New York: Routledge, 2019.

Maarek, Philippe J. *Campaign Communication and Political Marketing*. Malden, MA: Wiley-Blackwell, 2011.

Marland, Alex. *Brand Command: Canadian Politics and Democracy in the Age of Message Control*. Vancouver: UBC Press, 2016.

Martin, Laurence. "L'aile québécoise du Parti vert en contradiction avec sa cheffe." Radio-Canada, 14 September 2021. https://ici.radio-canada.ca/ nouvelle/1823965/aile-quebecoise-parti-vert-programme-contradiction -avec-cheffe-annamie-paul.

Messier, François. "Un gouvernement minoritaire conservateur est préférable, laisse entendre Legault." Radio-Canada, 9 September 2021. https:// ici.radio-canada.ca/nouvelle/1822840/election-federale-francois-legault -gouvernement-minoritaire.

Morin-Martel, Florence. "Le NPD promet d'accorder un statut juridique au fleuve Saint-Laurent." *La Presse,* 7 September 2021. https://www. lapresse.ca/elections-federales/2021-09-07/le-npd-promet-d-accorder-un -statut-juridique-au-fleuve-saint-laurent.php.

Nouveau parti démocratique. "Le NPD dénonce la lâcheté des libéraux dans le scandale du dépotoire illégal de Kanesatake." News release, 14 September 2021. Posted by Alexandre Boulerice (@alexboulerice), Twitter, 16 September 2021, 8:37 a.m. https://mobile.twitter.com/alex boulerice/status/1438527585294733313/photo/1.

–. *Oser ensemble pour les Québécoises et Québécois*. N.d. https://static1. squarespace.com/static/604facb0c71e7e5b752ee028/t/61323b6a54 63e316084d1413/1630681982275/Plateforme+Québec+NPD+2021.pdf.

Prime Minister of Canada. "Trans Mountain Expansion Will Fund Canada's Future Clean Economy." News release, 18 June 2019. https://pm.gc.ca/ en/news/news-releases/2019/06/18/trans-mountain-expansion-will-fund -canadas-future-clean-economy.

Richler, Noah. *The Candidate: Fear and Loathing on the Campaign Trail*. Toronto: Doubleday Canada, 2016.

Sayers, Anthony M. *Parties, Candidates, and Constituency Campaigns in Canadian Elections*. Vancouver: UBC Press, 1998.

Sébire, Marie. "À Montréal, un poumon vert en danger." *Ricochet,* 13 September 2021. https://ricochet.media/fr/3775/a-montreal-un-poumon-vert -en-danger.

Steven, Benjamin Allen, Md Mujahedul Islam, Roosmarijn de Geus, Jonah Goldberg, John R. McAndrews, Alex Mierke-Zatwarnicki, Peter John Loewen, and Daniel Rubenson. "Local Candidate Effects in Canadian Elections." *Canadian Journal of Political Science* 52, 1 (2019): 83–96.

TVA Nouvelles. "Jean-Guy Dagenais change son fusil d'épaule." 29 March 2011. https://www.tvanouvelles.ca/2011/03/29/jean-guy-dagenais-change -son-fusil-depaule.

Wesley, Jared, and Renze Nauta. "Party Platform Builders." In *Inside the Campaign: Managing Elections in Canada,* edited by Alex Marland and Thierry Giasson, 123–34. Vancouver: UBC Press, 2020.

Yakabuski, Konrad. "Le NPD tourne-t-il le dos au Québec?" *Le Devoir,* 3 April 2021. https://www.ledevoir.com/opinion/chroniques/598154/le -npd-tourne-t-il-le-dos-au-quebec.

Yates, Stéphanie, and John Chenery. "National Campaign Director of Communications." In *Inside the Campaign: Managing Elections in Canada,* edited by Alex Marland and Thierry Giasson, 147–57. Vancouver: UBC Press, 2020.

14

Local News

*Colette Brin, with François Cormier
and Myriam Descarreaux*

Abstract   The idea of local news as a critical need of communities has come into the spotlight with media concentration, shrinking newsrooms, and closures. The vitality of local news has been linked to democratic life in general and elections in particular. Across Canada, there are considerable disparities in local coverage of candidates and issues. In a case study of Quebec City focusing on a television newsroom, we find that in this relatively diverse ecosystem both news organizations and parties are turning to low-cost digital strategies for local communication. The campaign is framed around issues considered to be relevant for citizens and sometimes comes second to other local news.

Résumé   L'idée que les informations locales sont un besoin essentiel des communautés est devenue un problème urgent en raison de la concentration des médias, la réduction des effectifs rédactionnels, et les fermetures. La vitalité des nouvelles locales a été liée à la vie démocratique en général et aux élections en particulier. Au Canada, il existe des disparités considérables dans la couverture locale des candidats et des enjeux. Dans une étude de cas de la ville de Québec axée sur une salle de rédaction télévisuelle, nous constatons que dans cet écosystème relativement diversifié, tant les organismes de presse que les partis se tournent vers des stratégies numériques peu coûteuses pour la communication locale. La campagne s'articule autour de questions considérées comme pertinentes pour les citoyens et passe parfois après d'autres nouvelles locales.

THE BELIEF THAT POLITICS is rarely local,[1] contrary to US Senator Tip O'Neill's famous remark, seems to apply to the media in particular. The evolving structure of the media industry – especially technological changes, all-news national television networks, and corporate concentration – is often cited as a major factor in the decline of local campaigns,[2] contributing to the centralization of power, reduced visibility for Parliament and local parties, and ultimately the weakening of Canadian democracy.[3] As well, studies of media coverage of federal or national elections have long disregarded local campaigns and local news.[4] There is a lack of descriptive and localized studies on the role of media in elections at the constituency level.[5]

Laura Stephenson and colleagues[6] found coverage of the federal election of 2015 to be framed in terms of issues, horse race, and leadership across regional and national newspapers and television, with little variation among provinces, except for the tone of coverage of leaders. As well, in the three cities studied – Vancouver, Toronto, and Montreal – there was scant coverage of local candidates.[7] However, this study focused on the three largest metropolitan centres in Canada, including the two national media hubs of Toronto and Montreal. Other studies suggest that media outlets in less populated areas offer more contrasted and localized coverage compared with national and metropolitan news sources.[8] Moreover, federal elections are covered by French-language media in Quebec somewhat less intensively than provincial elections because of the higher costs as well as presumed lower audience interest, with the exception of Radio-Canada given its legal mandate.[9]

Social media – especially Facebook, Twitter, and YouTube – have played a large role in recent years in election campaigns. Local candidates and organizations use these platforms to reach out to their constituents; social media also serve to create or circulate scandals of varying magnitude, with or without the intervention of journalists.[10] A survey of journalists in Quebec suggests that they maintain a love/hate relationship with social media: most respondents consider them to be "indispensable" in gathering information and contacting sources, but they also report negative impacts of social media platforms on their work, especially in terms of lost advertising revenue for news organizations and the circulation of false or misleading information.[11]

The study of relationships between human communities and the digital environment – that is, data, apparatus, machines, devices, and connected objects – often borrows the vocabulary of ecology. Research on news ecosystems focuses on the interactions between news media, networks, organizations, social groups, and institutions, often to assess or improve the "health" of the ecosystem itself.[12] The vitality of local news media can be related to democratic life more generally, as suggested by a recent American study linking the closure of media outlets and a decline in the number of journalists in a region to lower voter turnout and a lower number of candidates in local elections.[13]

The distinction among local, regional, and national media ecosystems in Canada also requires some clarification. Although in the English-language literature "regional" can refer to large metropolitan areas, provinces, or even groups of provinces and territories,[14] French-language media analysts consider the Montreal-based media serving the province of Quebec as national and media in other parts of the province as regional.[15] From a media production perspective, the term "local" is generally used not only for a geographic territory but also in the economic sense of a market or distribution area defined strategically by the organization or corporation, a preferred or targeted audience based upon a business model.[16] A local media outlet typically serves both urban and semi-urban areas, including one or several federal electoral ridings.

In the past two decades, the transformation of the media landscape has accelerated. Half of Canadian news users (53 percent) and 77 percent of those aged eighteen to twenty-four now turn to digital platforms – social media, search engines, websites, or apps – as their main sources for news.[17] But the most influential news brands remain legacy organizations, including broadcasters, newspapers, and the Canadian Press, which continue to play a major role in federal politics. Despite dwindling advertising revenues, they devote considerable resources to election campaign coverage, are assiduously consumed (especially television news programs and all-news channels), and remain a priority for party strategists.

But the national media have their blind spots. Parliamentary correspondents typically pay scant attention to local and regional issues when covering leaders' tours.[18] The insularity of the Ottawa media bubble is aggravated by the fact that regional newspapers, in particular from the Postmedia chain, have reduced – or eliminated – their press gallery bureaus.[19]

Local media, especially community newspapers and even dailies in mid-sized cities, are considered a secondary source of political news by citizens.[20] For party strategists, they are a low-risk opportunity for visibility, with their smaller newsrooms, less experienced reporters, and positive stories, such as profiles of the candidates, showcasing their positions on local issues and ties to the local community. But in recent years, political parties and candidates have increasingly targeted local audiences – especially party supporters or potential supporters – through social media, particularly Facebook.[21] Hyper-local start-ups and citizen journalism initiatives have attempted to fill the gap left by local media closures.[22]

The role of talk radio in particular has drawn relatively little scholarly attention in studies of election coverage despite the presence and popularity of such programs in local media markets across Canada.[23] Talk radio is a long-standing component of the American right-wing media ecosystem, which some consider to be a much more significant factor in the radicalization of US politics than recent phenomena such as the Cambridge Analytica scandal or Russian hackers and bots.[24] While recognizing differences between the two countries' political, electoral, and media systems, we should not ignore media trends south of the border and their potential influence on Canada.

The scarcity of research on local news media is also found more generally in journalism research. However, with the decline of local "civic-minded" journalism[25] as newsrooms have shrunk and media outlets have closed, and its implications for voter turnout and civic engagement,[26] scholars are raising issues of media localism,[27] news deserts, or news poverty and defining local journalism as a critical need of communities[28] and a policy problem. Several recent publications have offered comparative analyses of local journalism beyond the United States, and to a lesser extent the United Kingdom,

Australia, and Canada, which represent the bulk of previous studies.[29] April Lindgren has tracked closures and service reductions by local news outlets across Canada and raised concerns about the implications for federal elections as investigative, in-depth campaign reporting becomes a rarity: "Many overwhelmed, understaffed newsrooms are often reduced to repurposing press releases and grabbing quotes from politicians' social-media posts."[30] Finally, the COVID-19 pandemic has heightened concerns about the need for independently reported local news and the sustainability of news organizations at the local level.[31]

Since 2019, the Canadian government has begun funding local journalism in underserved communities[32] and has implemented tax benefits for qualifying print and digital written media organizations producing original news content, including coverage of democratic institutions and processes.[33] Some observers have raised concerns that this government aid could compromise editorial independence, whereas others argue that professional roles and values of journalists are sufficiently robust to resist such pressures.[34]

Local Trends

Traditionally, local news organizations have focused on leaders' visits, bellwether or swing ridings, seats held by incumbent ministers, and "star" candidates. Community newspapers, television and radio, third-language or ethnic media, and campus media all cover politics with scant resources and smaller audiences, but they provide some visibility for local candidates.[35] Local media might commission polls in key ridings or cover local debates, often organized by community groups.[36] In recent years, parties have been using digital media to connect directly with voters, a trend that appeared to intensify during the pandemic and in preparation for the campaign in 2021.[37] Erin O'Toole held virtual telephone town hall meetings two days a week in a studio set up in the Conservative Party's Ottawa bunker, which allowed for a more controlled environment than outdoor public events and a way to bypass the media.[38]

Electoral disinformation was mostly framed by the presence of online groups opposing vaccination and social distancing measures who organized demonstrations at Justin Trudeau's campaign stops. These groups, whose members typically hold anti-government and xenophobic views, were considered to be reproducing or adapting false narratives from the United States on COVID-19 and election fraud.[39] They were also critical of news media, especially of their coverage of the pandemic, and of government support for news organizations. Increased support for the People's Party of Canada was linked to these protests.[40]

In addition to national trends in local news coverage, the specificity of each city or region should be taken into account. The level of media diversity in a city or region accounts for considerable disparities in local coverage of candidates and issues.[41] Finally, socio-demographic characteristics[42] and local/regional political and media cultures also merit attention to offer a more granular understanding of electoral dynamics. We will examine as a case study the local news ecosystem of the Quebec City region, including Lévis and Chaudière-Appalaches south of the St. Lawrence River, which has a relatively diverse mix of TV channels, talk radio shows, and newspapers, and a large number of political pundits in traditional and digital communication spaces. Quebec City is a provincial capital that identifies as *la capitale nationale* and a mid-sized city with sprawling suburbs and rural peripheries,[43] and the local political culture – with its undertones of regional alienation, conservative views, and anti-elitism and the role of local media in forging political attitudes and behaviour – is commonly referred to as "le mystère de Québec"[44] in contrast to the rest of the province. The symbol and voice of this specific culture are found in commercial talk radio, especially Radio X (CHOI-FM), known for its right-wing libertarian politics and its irreverent, sometimes offensive tone.[45] Hosts at FM 93 and Radio X have endorsed political candidates in federal, provincial, and municipal elections, with varying levels of success. The leader of the Parti conservateur du Québec, Éric Duhaime, previously hosted talk shows at both Radio X and FM 93.

Television, newspapers, and social media are also major sources of political news in Quebec City, as in Montreal.[46] The largest media players in terms of audience are multimedia entities, which include a television network. Québecor, with its combination of TVA, LCN (all-news TV channel), tabloid newspapers *Journal de Montréal* and *Journal de Québec,* news service QMI, and digital radio QUB, dominates the overall news media market.[47] The French-language public broadcaster Radio-Canada includes RDI (all-news channel), popular morning and drive-home radio shows, as well as a local TV newscast and intensive political coverage. Both Québecor and Radio-Canada have bureaus on Parliament Hill and a stable of political analysts, with a strong focus on provincial politics.

The local daily newspaper *Le Soleil* reports intensively on local and regional aspects of the campaign. *La Presse* and *Le Devoir,* both Montreal-based dailies, also have reporters based in the provincial capital. Global, CTV, and the Montreal *Gazette* have bureaus at the National Assembly, but other English-language media, including the *Globe and Mail,* have reduced their presence in Quebec City because of budgetary constraints and possibly the reduced threat of sovereignty.[48] Finally, emerging media outlets are relatively rare in the area – hyperlocal group Monquartier.com (especially active in the young, progressive, and partially gentrified Limoilou area) and Néomédia (a rural digital news group based in Beauce, south of Quebec City) are among the most significant. Political actors outside the campaign and external events can also affect local media coverage, either intervening in or blocking out the campaign as a news story. Régis Labeaume, who served as mayor from 2007 to 2021, played an important role in giving visibility to local issues and providing candidates and parties with a "grocery list" of demands for federal investments in the region, ranging from transportation infrastructure to affordable housing to access to clean drinking water.[49]

In 2021, little attention was given to the People's Party of Canada. The party's leader, Maxime Bernier, spent little time campaigning in his own riding of Beauce, focusing his efforts on the Prairies and Southern Ontario. Several hosts at Radio X expressed libertarian views especially regarding the management of the pandemic but stopped short of endorsing the People's Party. After the election, one host took credit for the Conservative Party candidates' strong showing in the region.[50] No sizable protest was held in Quebec City or the surrounding area.

Behind the Scenes

Discussions between the author and collaborators during and after the campaign in 2021 provided insights into the production of local news from the perspective of managers in a news organization with considerable reach and impact. Indeed, despite the undeniable impact of digital technology and of social media, television remains the most popular source for election news. TVA is the most watched television network in Quebec, the flagship of a convergent media empire.[51] TVA's Quebec City studios and newsroom moved in 2016 from their previous location in Ste-Foy to a brand-new building next door to the Centre Vidéotron. The arena itself, built almost entirely with public funding at a cost of $370 million,[52] was a local issue in the election in 2011. TVA's news mandate is focused on the province of Quebec, though the channel reaches most francophone audiences throughout Canada.[53] Besides Quebec City (CFCM), TVA has four regional stations and four affiliates. News and current affairs staff at TVA and LCN totalled 781 full-time employees in 2019.[54]

From the perspective of local assignment editors, the campaign agenda is set mostly by the major parties and national media; local newsrooms play a more reactive role, covering the biggest local partisan events. In many cases, news reports focus on local issues brought up in journalists' questions to candidates rather than a candidate's or party's announcement. More generally, the campaign is framed around issues of importance to the region, such as transportation infrastructure and the maritime industry.

A regional campaign analyst has a weekly spot in the local newscast, and local candidates of the four largest parties are regularly invited as guests on the local newscast. To limit costs, TVA does not send reporters on the leaders' tours until the last week of the campaign, and it did not cover the Green Party and People's Party leaders at all in 2021; rather, it uses material from the video pool and contributes to the video pool by assigning two camera operators to the Bloc Québécois. The national desk in Montreal and the local assignment editor are in constant contact, and questions of local interest are forwarded to the correspondent to ask the leader directly. Party leaders' stops in Quebec City are covered by national correspondents, but the leader may grant an on-air interview at the local station despite a tight schedule, especially, as for Erin O'Toole, if the region – and the TVA audience – is strategically important. The Conservatives held eight of twelve seats in the region when the writ of election was issued, and the local party was considered to be particularly proactive in its media strategy during the campaign. Justin Trudeau, in contrast, had given an interview in the spring to Pierre Jobin, who left TVA Québec after twenty-eight years at the helm of the local newscast, and the Liberals preferred to focus on other local and regional media. Jagmeet Singh and Yves-François Blanchet also granted interviews to TVA Québec. The Bloc Québécois and NDP had fewer resources, with a single media officer each for the whole province. The local TVA station did not receive a single communication from the Green Party.

Events not directly related to the campaign sometimes took precedence, such as pandemic news, a six-day Amber alert, and other human interest stories that are typical fare on TVA. Aware of their responsibility for the leading news source in the region, the assignment editors made a point of maintaining the audience's interest in the election and staying in touch with an informal network of friends and family members outside the bubble, before and throughout the campaign. They favoured issues such as the federal government's contribution to a planned tunnel between Quebec City and Lévis and maintenance of the Quebec Bridge, child care, and gun control, which in their view resonated with ordinary people because they are concrete and accessible issues. During TVA's debate,[55] the moderator, veteran anchor Pierre Bruneau, asked the leaders specifically about the Quebec City–Lévis tunnel project as an example of the federal government's responsibility in transportation infrastructure.

Media competition is not a major concern. Radio-Canada's election coverage is considered to be complementary to TVA's, catering to a more urban and highly educated audience than TVA. As for talk radio, FM 93 focused on strategic analysis of campaign events, and Radio X stayed on its libertarian-pandemic message. Collaboration with *Le Journal de Québec* and *Le Journal de Montréal,* also part of the Québecor group, appears to be relatively normalized; for example, content is picked up from either newspaper without always referencing the source.

Social media are considered a useful tool for journalists to see what makes people react but not a way to find out how the campaign is playing out locally. Pressure from media managers to post news on social media had already diminished between the campaigns of 2015 and 2019, especially on Twitter, which the assignment editors perceive, in a sense, as an extension of the political-media bubble and not an ideal medium for communicating with a larger audience. TVA Québec's assignment editors did not consider either that local candidates – or even the leaders – had as strong a social media presence as in past elections. However, social messaging apps were noted as an additional point of contact with partisan sources and easier access to candidates by journalists.

For local journalists, the campaign in 2021 was their first experience in what TVA Québec's assignment editors called "hybrid election coverage," working sometimes remotely, sometimes in the newsroom or on location, though travelling to rural ridings was kept to a minimum. This made certain parts of the job easier, such as following press conferences online and securing interviews via video meeting apps, in addition to traditional reporting in the field. Because of this flexibility, the local station was able to run a daily debate with candidates from the major parties on a series of issues during the last week of the campaign, including transportation and regional mobility, labour shortage, economic recovery/development, health care, and the environment. As for many other workplaces, it is uncertain how these practices developed in the context of the pandemic will persist and develop in years to come. As for election night itself, local television news coverage of results is tightly scripted. Reporters at party assemblies are briefed in advance for their time slots, typically fifteen seconds every half hour. The segments are very short to provide for contingencies and because results come in quickly for provinces in the Eastern and Central Time Zones.

Conclusion

We have examined local media coverage of elections through a case study of Quebec City, with the collaboration of two assignment editors at a local TV station in a convergent media corporation rarely accessed by academic researchers. Despite this specific view from a predominantly francophone, relatively diverse local news ecosystem, our observations raise questions for future research on the evolving practice of political journalism in Quebec and Canada, in a variety of local contexts. For example, the assignment editors' experience suggests a certain normalization of convergence between print and TV newsrooms at Québecor and the reduced importance of social media for journalists at the local level compared with previous elections.

In 2021, the use of digital technology by local news organizations to cover the campaign – and by parties to bypass the media – followed a larger trend launched during the pandemic. Video meeting apps were an inexpensive and efficient solution to the logistical challenges of covering a relatively large geographical area comprising urban, suburban, and rural components. It is unclear to what extent these apps will be used in future campaigns and in television news in general. Also uncertain is the role of normative pressures on journalistic production, such as intermedia competition, disinformation, and social media, as well as the role of talk radio, columnists, and television pundits. It appears that outside the metropolitan media hubs and Ottawa, few cities have a local political pundit culture, especially including television.[56]

For local news organizations, the federal election sometimes comes second to other stories. By the same token, local issues occasionally rise to the national campaign level. As observed in a previous study of election coverage, television news managers tend to have a rather pragmatic perspective on their work, even in the high-stakes context of covering an election.[57] In this sense, it is not surprising that at a commercial television station the primary concern is audience interest and news stories considered to be relevant to the lives of ordinary people.

Finally, the most pressing issue for local news is its own struggle for relevance and legitimacy in the face of dwindling resources, rapidly changing technologies, and competition for attention with diverse platforms and content sources. In the digital age, local news production is no longer a profitable activity; furthermore, television and radio recently have joined print media as declining sectors of the media economy.[58] Although federal elections remain heavily driven by party leaders and national media, local news can bring substance and real-life relevance to campaigns for citizens; thus, it has an important role to play in revitalizing Canadian democratic life.

Notes

Note: Professor Brin is chairperson of Canada's Independent Advisory Board on Eligibility for Journalism Tax Measures. The Advisory Board and its work were in no way involved in this study, and the findings herein have no bearing on its assessments.

1 Taras and Waddell, "The 2011 Federal Election," 77.
2 Carty and Eagles, "Is There a Local Dimension?,"281–82.
3 Nesbitt-Larking, "The Role of the Media."
4 Carty and Eagles, "Is There a Local Dimension?"
5 Nesbitt-Larking, "The Role of the Media."
6 Stephenson et al., *Provincial Battles, National Prize?*
7 Ibid., 122.
8 Lawlor and Bastien, "La campagne vue par la presse écrite," 109; Carty and Eagles, "Is There a Local Dimension?," 285–86.
9 Brin, "La télévision publique en campagne."
10 Giasson, Le Bars, and Dubois, "Is Social Media Transforming Canadian Electioneering?"; Trottier, "Scandal Mining."
11 Dubois, *Journalisme, médias sociaux.*
12 Anderson, "News Ecosystems."
13 Hayes and Lawless, "The Decline of Local News."
14 For example, Stephenson et al., *Provincial Battles, National Prize?*
15 For example, Brunelle and Brin, *L'information locale;* Bizimana and Kane, "La presse au défi du numérique."
16 Gulyas and Baines, "Introduction," 2.
17 Unpublished data, Digital News Report Canada 2021, Centre d'études sur les médias.

18 Ibid., 83.

19 Britneff, "Parliamentary Press Gallery." Based upon the list provided on the Canadian Parliamentary Press Gallery website, there were 316 members in October 2021 compared with 320 in 2016. See https://www.press-presse.ca/en/press-gallery-members.

20 Brunelle and Brin, *L'information locale.*

21 Skogerbøa and Krumsvik, "Newspapers, Facebook and Twitter."

22 Lindgren, "What the Death of Local News Means."

23 Sampert, "Verbal Smackdown."

24 Benkler, Faris, and Roberts, *Network Propaganda,* 8–20.

25 Public Policy Forum, *Mind the Gaps;* Public Policy Forum, *The Shattered Mirror.*

26 Darr, Hitt, and Dunaway, "Newspaper Closures"; Hayes and Lawless, "The Decline of Local News."

27 Ali, *Media Localism.*

28 Napoli et al., "Local Journalism."

29 Gulyas and Baines, "Introduction"; Nielsen, *Local Journalism.*

30 Lindgren, "What the Death of Local News Means."

31 Radcliffe, "COVID-19 Has Ravaged American Newsrooms."

32 News Media Canada, "Local Journalism Initiative."

33 Income Tax Act, RSC 1985, c 1 (5th Supp), 248 (1)(a)(v).

34 Rollwagen and Shapiro, "Research from Canada Suggests."

35 Sayers, *Parties, Candidates, and Constituency Campaigns.*

36 Willing, "Ottawa Centre Debate."

37 Reynolds, "Grappling with How to Press the Virtual Flesh."

38 Le Couteur, "Analysis."

39 Cardoso, "'They Are Insurrectionists.'"

40 Karadeglija, "From COVID Conspiracies"; Pannett, "Who Is Maxime Bernier?"

41 Lindgren, Corbett, and Hodson, "Canada's Local News 'Poverty'"; Sayers, *Parties, Candidates, and Constituency Campaigns.*

42 Carty and Eagles, "Is There a Local Dimension?," 285.

43 Institut de la statistique du Québec, "Capitale-Nationale" and "Chaudière-Appalaches."

44 Thibault et al., "Is There a Distinct Quebec Media Subsystem?" and "Le 'mystère de Québec'"; Parent, *Un Québec invisible.*

45 Payette, *Les brutes et la punaise.*

46 Dubois and Gélineau, *Les motifs de la participation électorale,* 27.

47 Brin, Giroux, and Sauvageau, *Réflexions et mise en contexte.* Québecor does not subscribe to the Canadian Press/Presse canadienne wire

service, and restrictions by the Canadian Radio-Television and Telecommunications Commission do not allow the company to own a local radio station in Montreal or Quebec City.

48 Porter and Noël, "Fermeture du 'Globe and Mail' à Québec."
49 Moalla, "Élections fédérales." A list is also prepared by the mayor of Lévis, on the south shore of the St. Lawrence River.
50 Fillion, "Fillion."
51 Brin, Giroux, and Sauvageau, *Réflexions et mise en contexte.*
52 A local fundraising campaign contributed $5.4 million. Brousseau-Pouliot, "Centre Vidéotron."
53 TVA, "Profil de société."
54 Giroux, *Les médias québécois d'information*, 91. At CBC and Radio-Canada in the province of Quebec, there were 1,604 news and current affairs staff, including English and French television, radio, and digital services (94).
55 As in 2019, TVA held its own debate outside the mandate of the Leaders' Debate Commission. See DeCillia and Cormier, "Leaders' Debate Coordinators."
56 Qualitative research interviews with former journalists across Canada in 2018.
57 Brin, "La télévision publique en campagne."
58 Winseck, "Growth and Upheaval."

Bibliography

Ali, Christopher. *Media Localism: The Policies of Place.* Champaign: University of Illinois Press, 2017.

Anderson, C.W. "News Ecosystems." In *The SAGE Handbook of Digital Journalism,* edited by Tamara Witschge, C.W. Anderson, David Domingo, and Alfred Hermida, 410–23. Thousand Oaks, CA: SAGE, 2016.

Benkler, Yochai, Robert Faris, and Hal Roberts. *Network Propaganda: Manipulation, Disinformation, and Radicalization in American Politics.* New York: Oxford University Press, 2018.

Bizimana, Aimé-Jules, and Oumar Kane. "La presse au défi du numérique: Une économie politique des médias régionaux au Québec." *Les Cahiers du journalisme* 3 (2019): R141–72. https://doi.org/10.31188/CaJsm.2(3). 2019.R141.

Brin, Colette. "La télévision publique en campagne: Le plan de couverture électorale à la SRC (1997 et 1998)." PhD diss., Université Laval, 2002.

Brin, Colette, Daniel Giroux, and Florian Sauvageau. *Réflexions et mise en contexte de la situation créée par l'élection de M. Pierre Karl Péladeau.* Québec:

Centre d'études sur les médias, Université Laval, 2015. https://www.cem.
ulaval.ca/wp-content/uploads/2019/04/reflexioncontexte.pdf.

Britneff, Beatrice. "Parliamentary Press Gallery Now the Smallest It's Been
in 22 Years." iPolitics, 8 December 2016. https://ipolitics.ca/2016/12/08/
parliamentary-press-gallery-now-the-smallest-its-been-in-22-years/.

Brousseau-Pouliot, Vincent. "Centre Vidéotron: Des pertes de 5,8 millions
pour la Ville de Québec." *La Presse,* 27 July 2018. https://www.lapresse.
ca/actualites/201807/26/01-5190993-centre-videotron-des-pertes-de-58
-millions-pour-la-ville-de-quebec.php.

Brunelle, Anne-Marie, and Colette Brin. *L'information locale et régionale
au Québec: Portrait du territoire 2011–2018 et perspectives citoyennes.* Québec:
Centre d'études sur les médias, Université Laval, 2019. https://www.cem.
ulaval.ca/wp-content/uploads/2019/08/cem-infolocaleqc.pdf.

Cardoso, Tom. "'They Are Insurrectionists': Inside the Online Groups
Spreading Misinformation and Hate during the Federal Election Campaign." *Globe and Mail,* 18 September 2021. https://www.theglobeandmail.
com/politics/article-they-are-insurrectionists-inside-the-online-groups
-spreading/.

Carty, R. Kenneth, and Munroe Eagles. "Is There a Local Dimension to
Modern Election Campaigns? Party Activists' Perceptions of the Media
and Electoral Coverage of Canadian Constituency Politics." *Political Communication* 17, 3 (2000): 279–94. https://doi.org/10.1080/10584600414287.

Darr, Joshua P., Matthew P. Hitt, and Johanna L. Dunaway. "Newspaper
Closures Polarize Voting Behavior." *Journal of Communication* 68, 6 (2018):
1007–28. https://doi.org/10.1093/joc/jqy051.

DeCillia, Brooks, and Michel Cormier. "Leaders' Debate Coordinators."
In *Inside the Campaign: Managing Elections in Canada,* edited by Alex
Marland and Thierry Giasson, 71–84. Vancouver: UBC Press, 2020.

Dubois, Judith. *Journalisme, médias sociaux et intérêt public: Enquête auprès
de 393 journalistes québécois.* Québec: Presses de l'Université Laval, 2021.

Dubois, Philippe, and François Gélineau. *Les motifs de la participation électorale aux élections municipales québécoises: Le cas de 2017.* Cahier de recherche électorale et parlementaire 20. Québec: Chaire de recherche sur
la démocratie et les institutions parlementaires, Université Laval, 2021.
http://www.cms.fss.ulaval.ca/recherche/upload/chaire_democratie/
fichiers/cahier_de_recherche_chaire_democratie_no20.pdf.

Fillion, Jeff. "Fillion." Radio X, 21 September 2021. https://jefffillion.
com.

Giasson, Thierry, Gildas Le Bars, and Philippe Dubois. "Is Social Media
Transforming Canadian Electioneering? Hybridity and Online Partisan

Strategies in the 2012 Quebec Election." *Canadian Journal of Political Science* 52, 2 (2019): 323–41.

Giroux, Daniel. *Les médias québécois d'information: État des lieux en 2020.* Québec: Centre d'études sur les médias, Université Laval, 2020. https://www.cem.ulaval.ca/publications/etat-des-lieux-en-2020/.

Gulyas, Agnes, and David Baines. "Introduction: Demarcating the Field of Local Media and Journalism." In *The Routledge Companion to Local Media and Journalism,* edited by Agnes Gulyas and David Baines, 1–21. New York: Routledge, 2020.

Hayes, Danny, and Jennifer L. Lawless. "The Decline of Local News and Its Effects: New Evidence from Longitudinal Data." *Journal of Politics* 80, 1 (2018): 332–36.

Institut de la statistique du Québec. "Capitale-Nationale: Principaux indicateurs sur le Québec et ses régions." 2021. https://statistique.quebec.ca/fr/vitrine/region/03.

–. "Chaudière-Appalaches: Principaux indicateurs sur le Québec et ses régions." 2021. https://statistique.quebec.ca/fr/vitrine/region/12.

Karadeglija, Anja. "From COVID Conspiracies to Rigged Voting Machines, Misinformation Plagues Federal Election." *National Post,* 14 September 2021. https://nationalpost.com/news/politics/election-2021/from-covid-conspiracies-to-rigged-voting-machines-misinformation-plagues-the-election.

Lawlor, Andrea, and Frédérick Bastien. "La campagne vue par la presse écrite." In *Les Québécois aux urnes: Les partis, les médias et les citoyens en campagne,* edited by Frédérick Bastien, Éric Bélanger, and François Gélineau, 109–22. Montréal: Presses de l'Université de Montréal, 2013.

Le Couteur, Mike. "Analysis: O'Toole's Tele-Town Halls Seem to Be Paying Off." Global News, 5 September 2021. https://globalnews.ca/news/8168445/erin-o-toole-conservatives-analysis-tele-town-hall/.

Lindgren, April. "What the Death of Local News Means for the Federal Election." *The Walrus,* 24 April 2019. https://thewalrus.ca/what-the-death-of-local-news-means-for-the-federal-election/.

Lindgren, April, Jon Corbett, and Jaigris Hodson. "Canada's Local News 'Poverty.'" *Policy Options,* 23 January 2017. https://policyoptions.irpp.org/fr/magazines/janvier-2017/canadas-local-news-poverty/.

Moalla, Taïeb. "Élections fédérales: La protection de l'eau potable au cœur des priorités de Régis Labeaume dans sa liste d'épicerie." *Le Journal de Québec,* 31 August 2021. https://www.journaldequebec.com/2021/08/31/elections-federales-la-protection-de-leau-potable-au-cur-des-priorites-de-regis-labeaume-dans-sa-liste-depicerie.

Napoli, Philip M., Sarah Stonbely, Kathleen McCollough, and Bryce Renninger. "Local Journalism and the Information Needs of Local Communities: Towards a Scalable Assessment Approach." *Journalism Practice* 11, 4 (2017): 373–95. https://doi.org/10.1080/17512786.2016.1146625.

Nesbitt-Larking, Paul W. "The Role of the Media in Electoral Behaviour: A Canadian Perspective." *Policy and Society* 29, 1 (2010): 53–64. https://doi.org/10.1016/j.polsoc.2009.11.005.

News Media Canada. "Local Journalism Initiative: How It Works." 2020. https://nmc-mic.ca/lji/about-lji/how-it-works/.

Nielsen, Rasmus Kleis, ed. *Local Journalism: The Decline of Newspapers and the Rise of Digital Media*. New York: I.B. Tauris; Oxford: Reuters Institute for the Study of Journalism, University of Oxford, 2015.

Pannett, Rachel. "Who Is Maxime Bernier? The Far-Right Politician Compared to Trump Could Help Trudeau in Canada's Election." *Washington Post*, 13 September 2021. https://www.washingtonpost.com/world/2021/09/13/canada-election-conservative-ppc-maxime-bernier/.

Parent, Frédéric. *Un Québec invisible: Enquête ethnographique d'un village de la grande région de Québec*. Québec: Presses de l'Université Laval, 2015.

Payette, Dominique. *Les brutes et la punaise: Les radios-poubelles, la liberté d'expression et le commerce des injures*. Montréal: Lux, 2019.

Porter, Isabelle, and Dave Noël. "Fermeture du 'Globe and Mail' à Québec: Symptôme d'un désintérêt pour la politique québécoise." *Le Devoir*, 18 March 2017. https://www.ledevoir.com/politique/quebec/494280/titre-depart-du-globe-and-mail-prophete-en-son-pays.

Public Policy Forum. *Mind the Gaps: Quantifying the Decline of Local News in Canada*. Ottawa: Public Policy Forum, 2018. https://ppforum.ca/wp-content/uploads/2018/09/MindTheGaps-QuantifyingTheDeclineOfNewsCoverageInCanada-PPF-SEPT2018.pdf.

–. *The Shattered Mirror: News, Democracy and Trust in the Digital Age*. Report submitted to Industry Canada and Canadian Heritage. Ottawa: Public Policy Forum, 2017. https://shatteredmirror.ca/wp-content/uploads/theShatteredMirror.pdf.

Radcliffe, Damian. "COVID-19 Has Ravaged American Newsrooms – Here's Why that Matters." 20 July 2020. http://dx.doi.org/10.2139/ssrn.3693903.

Reynolds, Christopher. "Grappling with How to Press the Virtual Flesh, Parties Gear Up for Election Showdown." CTV News, 9 May 2021. https://www.ctvnews.ca/politics/grappling-with-how-to-press-the-virtual-flesh-parties-gear-up-for-election-showdown-1.5420259.

Rollwagen, Heather, and Ivor Shapiro. "Research from Canada Suggests Journalists' Creed Can Withstand Government Support." Nieman Lab,

21 March 2019. https://www.niemanlab.org/2019/03/research-from
-canada-suggests-journalists-creed-can-withstand-government-support/.

Sampert, Shannon. "Verbal Smackdown: Charles Adler and Canadian
Talk Radio." In *Media and Politics,* edited by David Taras and Christopher
Waddell, 295–315. How Canadians Communicate, vol. 4. Edmonton:
Athabasca University Press, 2012.

Sayers, Anthony M. *Parties, Candidates, and Constituency Campaigns in Canadian Elections.* Vancouver: UBC Press, 2011.

Skogerbøa, Eli, and Arne H. Krumsvik. "Newspapers, Facebook and Twitter:
Intermedial Agenda Setting in Local Election Campaigns." *Journalism
Practice* 9, 3 (2015): 350–66.

Stephenson, Laura B., Andrea Lawlor, William P. Cross, André Blais, and
Elisabeth Gidengil. *Provincial Battles, National Prize? Elections in a Federal
State.* Montreal and Kingston: McGill-Queen's University Press, 2019.

Taras, David, and Christopher Waddell. "The 2011 Federal Election and the
Transformation of Canadian Media and Politics." In *Media and Politics,*
edited by David Taras and Christopher Waddell, 71–107. How Canadians
Communicate, vol. 4. Edmonton: Athabasca University Press, 2012.

Thibault, Simon, Frédérick Bastien, Tania Gosselin, Colette Brin, and Colin
Scott. "Is There a Distinct Quebec Media Subsystem in Canada? Evidence
of Ideological and Political Orientations among Canadian News Media
Organizations." *Canadian Journal of Political Science* 53, 3 (2020): 638–57.
https://doi.org/10.1017/S0008423920000189.

Thibault, Simon, Colin Scott, Frédérick Bastien, and Colette Brin. "Le 'mystère de Québec' et son environnement médiatique." *Politique et société*
(forthcoming).

Trottier, Daniel. "Scandal Mining: Political Nobodies and Remediated Visibility." *Media, Culture and Society* 40, 6 (2018): 893–908.

TVA. "Profil de société." N.d. https://www.groupetva.ca/legroupe/profil
-societe.

Willing, Jon. "Ottawa Centre Debate Tests Eight Candidates on Hyper-Local Issues." *Ottawa Citizen,* 14 September 2021. https://ottawacitizen.
com/news/local-news/ottawa-centre-debate-tests-eight-candidates-on
-hyper-local-issues.

Winseck, Dwayne. "Growth and Upheaval in the Network Media Economy,
1984–2020." Digital Media and Internet Industries in Canada, Global
Media and Internet Concentration Project, Carleton University, 2021.
https://doi.org/10.22215/gmicp/2021.1.

15

Local All-Candidates' Debates
and Forums

Brooks DeCillia

Abstract · Local all-candidates' debates during federal elections get held up as an idealized expression of participatory democracy. The events are normatively imagined as means for Canadian voters to hear directly from – and question – the people vying to represent them in the House of Commons. But democratic ideals factor little in the calculations that political operatives make when deciding whether to participate in the events. Local debates, according to the people who run political campaigns, win few votes. Many political operatives, in fact, think that their candidate's finite campaign time is better spent door knocking than debating opponents. Yet all-candidates' debates remain a mainstay of local campaigns in Canadian federal elections. This chapter examines why debate organizers host the events and why political campaigns, despite their reservations, continue to participate in them. It outlines the political campaigns' vetting procedures for the debates and their political communication strategies during the debates. The chapter also discusses growing concerns about the inclusion of fringe candidates in local debates. It concludes by exploring how democratic ideals still factor into why some candidates for the House of Commons choose to participate in local debates.

Résumé · La tenue de débats locaux auxquels tous les candidats participent pendant les élections fédérales est considérée comme une expression idéalisée de la démocratie participative. Ces événements imaginés de manière normative se veulent un moyen pour les électeurs canadiens d'entendre directement les candidats qui souhaitent les représenter à la Chambre des communes, et de leur poser des questions. Or, les idéaux démocratiques ne prennent guère en compte les calculs que font les stratèges politiques lorsqu'ils décident de faire participer ou non leurs candidats aux événements. Selon ceux qui mènent les campagnes politiques, les débats locaux font gagner peu de votes. En fait, de nombreux stratèges pensent qu'il vaut mieux faire du porte-à-porte plutôt que de débattre avec les adversaires. Pourtant, ces débats demeurent un incontournable des campagnes locales pendant les élections fédérales. Ce chapitre examine pourquoi les organisateurs des débats planifient ces événements et pourquoi les candidats continuent d'y participer malgré leurs réserves. Il décrit les procédures de filtrage des campagnes politiques et leurs stratégies de communication politique pour les débats. Ce chapitre traite également des préoccupations croissantes concernant l'inclusion de candidats marginaux dans les débats locaux. Il se conclut en explorant comment les idéaux démocratiques continuent de jouer un rôle dans la décision de participer aux débats locaux de certains candidats à la Chambre des communes.

IN OUR FAST-PACED digital age, in which branded political campaigns with celebrity leaders use big data to microtarget supporters on social media, local all-candidates' debates feel quaint. The analogue events resemble the participatory democracy of an earlier time's town meetings or historical campaigns when politicians, running for a seat in the House of Commons, met citizens at train stations, village squares, and town halls to impress them with their commanding oratory.[1] An idealized democratic expression, an all-candidates' debate offers Canadian voters a chance to hear directly from – and pose questions to – the politicians who want to represent them in Ottawa. Akin to Aristotle's classic notion of rhetoric, whereby skilled debate fulfills a noble end, local all-candidates' debates or forums are normatively imagined as means of facilitating democratic communication, participation, and engagement.

At its core, politics is a contest of ideas. From Plato's ideal city-state in ancient Greece to modern-day politicians squaring off in a local all-candidates' forum, politics remains a never-ending debate. Additionally, in an increasingly polarized political environment, local debates are often held up as a much-needed public sphere for constructive and respectful political discourse. But are they? And do local federal election debates even matter? As vote getters, local debates also seem to be idiosyncratic in Canadian federal elections increasingly dominated by sophisticated, media-savvy, leader-driven national campaigns. As the introduction to this book makes plain, local candidate evaluations factor into few Canadians' vote choices. Not a lot of political science research explores the effect of or political strategy associated with a local campaign debate.[2] Most of the research focuses on national debates.[3] This chapter explores why local debates continue as a mainstay of Canadian federal election campaigns and why politicians participate in them.

A lot of the research on political debates is premised on the normative notion that debates – and the knowledge that voters glean from these exchanges of views – are healthy parts of a functioning democracy. But there is a debate about debates in political science. And, for the most part, it is about national debates, US presidential debates in particular. A meta-analysis of US presidential debates in 2003, for example, concluded that the exchanges between candidates increase voters' knowledge of issues, change their perceptions of candidates' character, and shift some of their vote intentions.[4] In contrast, a 2021 working paper analyzing dozens of television debates from 1952 to 2017 in ten countries (including Canada, the United States, the United Kingdom, and Germany) concluded that the events have no influence on vote choice.[5] Consistently, studies have found that national-level debates do not change many minds – and committed partisans, in particular, are mostly immovable.[6] Canadian political scientists have also focused on federal leaders' debates. Like in the United States, in Canada the evidence is mixed about whether the spectacle of federal leaders' debates during elections – complete with history-making gotcha moments and so-called knockout punches – really influences how Canadians eventually vote.[7] Some Canadian federal leaders, who peaked too soon, turned in glorious debate performances only to lose on election day.[8]

Much of political communication is premised on the idea that the words and actions of politicians have effects. Good or bad, what they do and what they say prompt some sort of reaction among voters. It is not that simple, though, and political scientists caution against overestimating the direct effect of debates.[9] Keep in mind that debates represent only one consideration – or one data point – in voters' deliberations. Still, longitudinal research in the United States suggests that voters think presidential debates help them to make up their minds.[10] Notably, nearly six in ten (57 percent) Canadians believed that the English-language leaders' debate during the federal election in 2019 was informative.[11] Whereas most research on political debates focuses on national-level forums, a recent field experiment in Ghana's parliamentary election suggests that policy-centred debates do have democratic benefits and help to reduce partisan polarization.[12] Theoretically, new information can change minds. A stream of competing persuasive messages, by its very nature, can prompt voters to consider new ideas, and even new candidates, leading some to new attitudes and vote intentions.[13]

Politicians running for seats in the House of Commons have complained about "trite" local debates with their packed halls filled with cheering partisans.[14] Despite these concerns, many candidates, as this chapter shows, continue to invest time and effort in the forums, likely hoping that good performances can help their campaigns. The events are not without risk, however, especially for front-runners. A poor performance can lose votes. Some candidates eschew church basement and community hall debates, once an expected ritual of local elections, believing that the events really matter only in close races. In recent federal elections, some candidates have admitted that they think their time is better spent knocking on doors and making personal connections with voters instead of performing well in front of an audience of mostly decided voters.[15] Over the past decade, some Conservative and Liberal candidates have faced criticism for skipping local debates.[16] In 2011, critics charged that the Conservative Party's national campaign instructed candidates to avoid local debates.[17] Despite these reservations, local debates were held in the federal election in 2021, even amid a surging fourth wave of the COVID-19 pandemic. The following pages examine why politicians participate in the forums, what they hope to get out of them, and why organizers continue to host the events.

Local Trends

As it did to so many aspects of our lives, the pandemic remade campaigning at the local level in the federal election of 2021, affecting everything from how politicians debate one another to how people cast their ballots. The trends detailed in this section follow from my interviews and an analysis of all the news media reports ($n = 252$) during the election pulled from the online news curation service Factiva about local debates during the election period. Local campaigns live-streamed their events and spent money on social media advertising that targeted people by postal codes. Social media, in fact, continued to play a prominent role in the promotion, delivery, and aftermath of local all-candidates' debates. Despite the public health restrictions brought on by COVID-19, all-candidates' debates and forums still took place. Some happened, as they have for generations, in town halls and school gyms, but many were virtual or a hybrid of online and in-person gatherings. Virtual debates, said some debate organizers in 2021, might not go away when the pandemic subsides. Future debates might be a blend of virtual and in-person events. Organizers welcome the potentially larger audience and the ability to control who speaks (and when) that come with online forums. Not surprisingly, COVID-19 and the federal government's response to the pandemic featured prominently in many of the local debates. Despite the relative ease for politicians of so-called Zoom debates, some candidates, as in previous federal elections, did not show up. And, as in past campaigns, the no-shows were criticized for their absences. Anti-vaccine/anti-maskers made the news in 2021 when their protests and disruptions forced some all-candidates' debates to be shut down or even cancelled in advance.

Democratic ideals continued to underpin the organization of local all-candidates' debates in the general election in 2021. There is a long history of community associations, chambers of commerce, and service and other civil society groups organizing and hosting local all-candidates' debates and forums in federal elections. These organizers believe that debates are essential to democracy – and even a pandemic was not going to stop them. Many organizers improvised during the campaign period by hosting virtual debates. In addition to an online forum, one chamber of commerce in British Columbia asked candidates for written responses to additional questions posted on the business organization's website.[18] In some ridings, the only debates that happened were hosted by news organizations or community radio and television stations. These events, such as the Lanark–Frontenac–Kingston all-candidates' debate sponsored by the Carleton Place and District Chamber of Commerce and the Lanark Federation of Agriculture, were live-streamed over the internet from YourTV studios in Smiths Falls, Ontario, and aired on a Rogers cable station. The video of the debate was also posted on various news and community websites.[19] In keeping with normative notions of informing citizens in a democracy, the chamber of commerce and agriculture group hosting the event billed it as an opportunity for voters in the riding to hear how "local candidates plan to bring forward key issues relevant to our community in the next Parliament."[20] In a similar vein, Phillip Meintzer, with the Alberta Wilderness Association, helped to organize a virtual debate as part of the "100 Debates on the Environment" project, which saw groups host environmental-themed debates across Canada during the election in 2021. Meintzer hoped that his online debate sparked a dialogue about environmental issues such as the climate crisis, calling the event a chance to hold politicians "accountable" and "incredibly important for democracy."

A crude word count of all the English news reports and commentary about all-candidates' debates and forums during the election suggests that the pandemic and related topics – such as immunization, vaccine passports, and post-pandemic economic recovery – dominated the debates. Climate change featured prominently as an issue as well. In addition to the "100 Debates on the Environment," which organizers say attracted 16,500 attendees, many of the community- and chamber of commerce–sponsored debates highlighted the climate crisis and environmental issues. For instance, climate change was a "hot topic," according to the *Campbell River Mirror,* at the all-candidates' debate hosted by the Campbell River and District Chamber of Commerce in British Columbia.[21] The economy, affordability, and the necessity of Prime Minister Justin Trudeau's election call were also conspicuous as issues in the all-candidates' debates.

Candidates who did not show up at these debates continued to garner scorn from their opponents and media attention for their absences. Taleeb Noormohamed, the Liberal candidate for Vancouver

Granville, for example, conspicuously missed some all-candidates' debates after he faced news media scrutiny for flipping housing properties, a practice that the Liberal platform promised to ban.[22] The news media connected the controversy to his absence. The Liberal "paper candidate" in the large northern BC riding (and NDP stronghold) of Skeena–Bulkley Valley, who, it turned out, lived in the province's Lower Mainland, declined an invitation to attend an all-candidates' debate when she showed up in the riding for the first time five days before the election.[23] Conservative incumbent Chris Lewis of Essex faced criticism for pulling out of the Windsor-Essex Regional Chamber of Commerce federal election debate thirty minutes before it started. A highly critical commentary in the *Windsor Star* chastised Lewis, declaring "the first rule of running for office? You show up."[24]

Security and safety concerns emerged as an issue in 2021.[25] Although debates have always been raucous events, complete with hecklers and protesters, some debates and forums were cancelled in advance because of such concerns or forced to shut down after starting because of anti-mask protesters. Campaign managers also worried about safety, wanting to limit their candidates' potential exposure to the airborne transmission of COVID-19. An all-candidates' debate in the BC riding of Chilliwack–Hope had to switch from in-person to virtual to comply with the province's vaccine requirements because the People's Party of Canada candidate was not vaccinated. In keeping with normative notions of these local debates, an editorial later called the cancellation of the in-person event "profoundly disappointing for voters in Chilliwack–Hope, and for democracy in general."[26] In Alberta, anti-mask protesters shut down a federal election forum in the Red Deer–Mountain View riding.[27] An all-candidates' debate in northeastern British Columbia was cancelled before it took place after the local chamber of commerce received a series of threats related to COVID-19 precautions. The event organizer called the decision to cancel it disappointing, noting that the chamber had hosted all-candidates' debates for more than seventy-five years.[28] Behind the scenes, local organizers, political staffers, and candidates sorted through the implications of these trends. In the next section, observations about local all-candidates' debates emerged from eleven interviews (some of them anonymous) with debate organizers, campaign workers, a pollster, and two former Liberal Members of Parliament and cabinet ministers. Some of the following conclusions represent composites of my thematic analysis of the interviews.

Behind the Scenes

By all accounts, local campaigns receive many invitations to participate in public debates and forums hosted by community groups, student organizations, and other civil society organizations during federal elections. The professional political operatives involved in multiple campaigns over many federal elections interviewed for this research believe that campaign debates are not efficient vote maximizers. For these campaign workers, door knocking or canvassing – and the potential data mining that it can bring – is far more effective at identifying voters and getting them to the polls. Veteran politicos also believe that most of the people who show up at debates are decided voters. "If it's the choice between spending three hours at a debate and an hour or two on prep, and knocking on doors in an apartment building downtown," said Alex Middleton, who has worked on NDP and Liberal campaigns, "I would go to the apartment building almost every chance I can get." Nevertheless, the debate requests trigger a process within campaigns. Campaign managers do their homework before agreeing to have their candidates take part in debates. All of the campaigns go through a similar process. They vet the debates and their organizers, asking many similar questions, including logistical questions such as where and when a debate is scheduled, who else is participating in it (including fringe candidates), what format it will take, which issues will be debated, and who is moderating the event. Campaign managers also want to know who is organizing the event and if they are partisan or have an agenda. The vetting extends to whether the organizers have produced fair debates in the past. Campaign staff are also keen to know whether the news media are expected and how many people might show up at the debate or forum.

Campaign managers use the answers to these questions to determine whether there is a strategic advantage in attending a debate. Different campaigns have disparate goals, meaning that they come to diverse conclusions. One might assume that democratic ideals about standing before voters and outlining one's vision and platform are the primary reason that candidates show up at debates. Most of the political operatives whom I interviewed said that normative notions of democracy rarely factor into their decisions about whether to advise a candidate to participate in a local debate. Middleton, for example, said that his thinking on the role of democracy in debate participation has evolved. When he began working on political campaigns, democratic ideals factored into his decision making about debate participation, but he recalled conversing with junior campaign staffers in the federal election in 2015 and telling them "it's a simple numbers game. If there's forty, fifty people at a debate, probably ten of those people are movable ... If we can go downtown and knock on fifty doors and talk to twenty people, it's a better use of our time."

Candidates do not always see it that way. Sometimes, knowing that a debate will not win them many votes, they decide to take part in the event because it is the democratic and principled thing to do. Calgary-based pollster Janet Brown, who runs Janet Brown Opinion Research, is a keen observer of politics and politicians. She suggested that ego also cannot be discounted when it comes to most politicians' belief in their skills to persuade voters. Almost all federal candidates, Brown believes, run for office convinced that their personal brands will help to win the day. Politics is a bruising contest. Politicians, said Brown, inure themselves by building up in their minds a faith in their "personal power to influence."

Incumbents (from all of the main federal parties) are a bit more cautious about participating in local debates. All of the professional political strategists interviewed stressed that the first rule of local debates is to do no harm. "You want to minimize your opportunities to do something stupid," said Neil Mackie, a veteran of many federal Liberal campaigns across the country. Debates come with risks. Local debates are often televised or live-streamed. Local news media frequently attend them, so what candidates say can be amplified outside the school gym or community hall. On top of that, smart-phones, with their high-definition cameras, are ubiquitous. Some-one in the audience can capture a gaffe or "bozo eruption" that can go viral, hurting the local candidate and forcing the national cam-paign off its message because it needs to respond to the blunder. Candidates can say things that do not align with the national party's platform or message. Also, challengers tend to pile on an incumbent, hoping to provoke an intemperate remark. Incumbents, arguably, protect themselves by not taking part in a debate. In these cases, their campaigns would rather face criticism for being "afraid to de-bate" than a potential gaffe. For these reasons, front-runners and incumbents are a bit choosier about where and when to debate. Can-didates running for re-election, however, might feel more inclined to participate in debates when riding boundaries have changed between elections. In these cases, "more serious consideration" is given to taking part in debates in the "new" parts of the riding to increase name recognition and distribute candidate material at the events, according to a Conservative Party campaign worker.

Debate organizers in Alberta, where thirty of the province's thirty-four seats went Conservative in the federal election in 2021, said that it is tough to get Conservatives, particularly in the cities, to participate in all-candidates' debates or forums. Meintzer said that the Conservative candidate whom he invited to participate in the environmental-themed debate declined the invitation. Conserv-ative campaign workers conceded that they often turn down single-issue local debates. A debate about the environment, after all, does not attract the Conservatives' "target audience," as one campaign official put it, stressing that the candidate's time is better spent door knocking.

As for general debates, the firm feeling among Conservative politicos is that most of the people who attend local debates have already made up their minds how to vote. Calgary debate organ-izer Jake Blumes recalled a Conservative campaign manager in a tight race in the federal election in 2015 telling him that he wor-ried that most of the crowd at the proposed debate would be de-cided voters. Blumes assured the campaign boss that not everyone attending the debate would be an immovable partisan, a key factor, he thought, in convincing the Conservative staffer to get his incumbent MP running for re-election in a tight race to show up at the community-sponsored debate. The story is a bit different in rural ridings. One Conservative campaign worker stressed that his incumbent MP candidate participated in just about every debate that he was invited to in his mostly rural Alberta riding in the shadow of the Rocky Mountains. Although the Conservative Party usually wins the riding with lopsided victories, the political staffer explained that part of the rationale for the candidate to attend as many debates as possible was "all about trying to be visible, taking the opportunities to be out in front of people." To that end, the campaign went out of its way to avoid an empty seat at all-candidates' debates, even driving across the large riding (almost 8,000 square kilometres) to get to two debates in a single day. The strategy in this case was about connecting with supporters, volunteers, and donors across the riding.

Underdog campaigns have a different take on local debates, leaping at any chance to be in the public or to make some news, said a Liberal campaign worker in Alberta whose candidate was running against a formidable Conservative heavyweight in one of the party's safest seats in the country. In these "no-win" situations, longshot campaigns "participate in everything," said the politico, stressing that when you are behind "you take more risks." Liberal campaign worker Mackie echoed this sentiment, stressing that underdog campaigns "leap at any debate" because the events are public, and some undecided voters might be in the crowd. More important is that debates also spark news coverage, amplifying information about the underdog candidate. Former Liberal MP and cabinet minister Kent Hehr says that he participated in an all-candidates' debate early in the election in 2015 in his first run for the House of Commons because he wanted to solidify his stature in the minds of centre-left voters in his Calgary Centre riding as the only candidate who could beat the Conservative candidate.[29]

Some campaign staff and politicians have become increasingly worried about fringe candidates participating in local debates.

Whereas debate organizers often feel compelled to invite everyone running for the House of Commons, mainstream campaigns want to avoid engaging with fringe candidates. Middleton applauds debate organizers for having the "best intentions" and wanting "to participate in a democratic process." Yet he recalled a debate in which a Christian Heritage Party candidate displayed graphic anti-abortion literature and referred to such candidates as "bad faith actors" who do not really want to participate in a democratic debate but pull stunts that spark outrage and grab attention. Middleton contended that the inclusion of fringe candidates makes participation in debates increasingly difficult and even a "waste of time" for mainstream parties if they increasingly descend into farces. For his part, Bob Nault, a former Liberal cabinet minister and MP for Kenora in Ontario, said that he even suggested to local debate organizers in his last campaign in 2019 that they not invite an independent candidate running what he called a "nasty and critical" campaign. Nault believed that the independent candidate's participation diminished the significance of the debate because it was reduced to "a mudslinging affair."

Deciding whether to attend a debate is only half the homework that campaigns complete before the event. Once a campaign accepts an invitation, its workers start prepping for the debate. Often this preparation begins with the candidate studying the party's platform. Some campaigns run mock debates and quiz their candidates on party policies. Debate preparation often depends on the candidate's experience. An incumbent Member of Parliament, whose job is essentially debating, does not usually need a lot of coaching, say the professionals who run campaigns. Local all-candidates' debates are easier, admittedly, when one has served in elected office, especially in cabinet, said Nault, because "you know the issues that you've been living with 24/7, day in and day out for years." Still, even veteran MPs running for re-election take the time to sit down and talk through their strategies for a debate, said a Conservative campaign worker in Alberta: "We would just go through the campaign book, pick a subject, and go through it." Campaigns also spend time anticipating other parties' rebuttals and formulating their candidates' rejoinders. On top of that, they try to anticipate questions in advance, believing that different organizations, depending on their location and membership, ask different questions.

For rookie politicians, it can be different. Some of them have a steep learning curve and need to spend time learning their party's platform. Sometimes the focus is on learning to speak succinctly. Yet some newly minted politicians are naturals, and their life experiences prepare them for public speaking. Many first-time candidates are not complete rookies, however, having had to win sometimes hotly contested local nomination votes to carry their party's banner in the federal election.

Rookie or veteran, candidates often receive advice about local debates from political communication experts to keep their messages simple. Middleton, who develops communication strategies for campaigns, tells his candidates to keep their answers in debates relatable. He stresses positive over negative and urges his clients to focus their responses on how their plans will make "people's lives better." Some local campaigns remain decidedly uncomplicated in their communication preparations for debates despite a national politics increasingly beholden to branding and sophisticated focus group–tested messaging.[30] Although political staffers and politicians think strategically about what they want to say during debates, they do not spend lots of time developing pithy one-liners or zingers to use during them. A long-time campaign manager working for the Conservative Party in the federal election in 2021, in fact, resists coaching her candidates to repeat so-called sound bites or talking points. "We want more sophisticated answers," she stressed; "we don't try to dumb it down at all."

Some of the coaching of candidates by political staffers focuses on staying calm and on message during debates. Debates can be heated affairs. Some candidates intentionally provoke their opponents, hoping for an ill-considered or foolish response. As noted, campaigns and candidates are desperate to avoid these gaffes or so-called bozo eruptions.

Mackie laments how too much debate prep focuses on what not to say, noting that front-runner campaigns fret about what their opponents might say during the debate to embarrass their candidates. Middleton advises candidates to stay calm and even "turn the other cheek" when the attacks come during debates, pointing out that female candidates often face unfair scrutiny of their debate performances that men do not.

Campaigns are strategic about knowing their opponents' standing in terms of public support heading into local debates. In their preparations for the events, campaigns often identify their main opposition and are guided by public and internal party polls. With this information, candidates can better contrast their responses with those of their chief rivals. Nault, for example, used polling information in debates to remind progressive voters in his northern Ontario riding that vote splitting between the New Democrats and Liberals could help the Conservatives win the riding.

Part of the strategy for debates involves preparing for the dramatic extravaganza of the events. Campaigns work hard to get their supporters to these debates. They want them to feel like a boxing match or mixed martial arts Ultimate Fighting Championship event. They want their pumped-up, t-shirt-clad supporters there to cheer on their candidates. They want "an air of spectacle" at these events, recalled one Liberal politico. Especially when the candidate is an underdog, added the former political staffer, "you want to make sure that you don't lose the theatrical element of debates."

Conclusion

Despite all of the effort – vetting the debates, prepping for them, and getting supporters to the events – "no one's mind is going to be changed by anything that's said at the debate," conceded one political campaign operative. The conventional wisdom is that the precious resource of campaign time is better spent elsewhere. Some political campaign veterans, however, insist that debates can help in tight races. Plus there is always the chance of a poignant or dramatic moment in the debate going viral and increasing a candidate's profile. But these moments are admittedly rare. So why do local all-candidates' debates persist as a mainstay of modern political campaigns?

Some candidates and their campaigns want the attention that comes with such debates. Some see a strategic advantage in participating in them, whereas others want to avoid potentially negative results of the criticism that comes from not showing up to them. Hubris and idealism about democracy cannot be discounted as well. For many politicians and political operatives, including those interviewed for this research, politics is about persuasion. People who run for a seat in the House of Commons want to talk about their plans for Canada. They want to win the argument. Former MP Hehr recalled his father taking him as a child to political debates where he heard "important ideas." For him, politics is about winning power, of course, but he also wants to influence people with the ideas that he holds dear. So, though politicians and their campaign staff know that local campaigns are not won or lost during the debates held in school auditoriums and community halls, like the people who organize the debates, they hold ideal – almost romantic – notions about democracy. Akin to Theodore Roosevelt's famous "Citizenship in a Republic" speech in 1910, local debate participants seemingly believe that "the credit belongs" to the people "actually in the arena," even if they fail while trying to win the contest.[31]

Notes

1   For a historical account of early campaigning, see Nolan, "Political Communication Methods."
2   Birdsell, "Political Campaign Debates."
3   For example, Blais and Boyer, "Assessing the Impact of Television Debates"; DeCillia and Cormier, "Leaders' Debate Coordinators."
4   Benoit, Hansen, and Verser, "A Meta-Analysis of the Effects of Viewing US Presidential Debates."
5   Le Pennec and Pons, "How Do Campaigns Shape Vote Choice?"
6   See, for example, Erickson, and Wlezien, "The Timeline of Presidential Elections."
7   Blais and Boyer, "Assessing the Impact of Televised Debates."
8   Johnston et al., *Letting the People Decide.*
9   Cho and Ha, "On the Communicative Underpinnings of Campaign Effects."
10 Heimlich, "Most Say Presidential Debates Influence Their Vote."

11 McAndrews et al., "Evaluation of the 2019 Federal Leaders' Debates."
12 Brierley, Kramon, and Ofosu, "The Moderating Effect of Debates on Political Attitudes."
13 For example, Hall Jamieson, "Creating the Hybrid Field of Political Communication"; Zaller, *The Nature and Origins of Mass Opinion.*
14 Sayers, *Parties, Candidates, and Constituency Campaigns in Canadian Elections.*
15 Labby, "'Everybody's Got a Camera Phone.'"
16 Anderson, "Liberal Candidate a No-Show"; Wilson, "Candidates Need to Resist Urge."
17 Elliott, "All-Candidate Debates."
18 Kitteringham, "Beyond the Debates."
19 Carleton Place, "Municipal Updates."
20 Carleton Place Chamber of Commerce, "Carleton Place Chamber."
21 Kitteringham, "North Island–Powell River All Candidates' Debate."
22 Kinsella, "Liberals Acted Too Slowly."
23 Paul, "Skeena–Bulkley Valley's Mysterious Liberal Candidate."
24 Jarvis, "The First Rule of Running for Office?"
25 For a summary of the increased hostility and violence during the election in 2021, see Hall, "Days of Rage."
26 Henderson, "Opinion."
27 Bachusky and Singleton, "Anti-Maskers Force Shutdown."
28 Canadian Press, "Security Concerns Shutter Candidates' Debate in Northern BC."
29 Hehr won the riding by 750 votes in 2015.
30 Marland, *Brand Command.*
31 Roosevelt, "Citizenship in a Republic."

Bibliography

Anderson, Mike. "Liberal Candidate a No-Show at York-Simcoe All-Candidates' Debate." *Georgina Post,* 14 October 2019. https://georgina post.com/2019/10/14/liberal-candidate-a-no-show-at-york-simcoe-all-candidates-debate/.

Bachusky, Dan, and Dan Singleton. "Anti-Maskers Force Shutdown of Innisfail Federal Election Forum." MountainView Today, 8 September 2021. https://www.mountainviewtoday.ca/2021-federal-election-coverage/anti-maskers-force-shutdown-of-innisfail-federal-election-forum-4315942.

Benoit, William L., Glenn J. Hansen, and Rebecca M. Verser. "A Meta-Analysis of the Effects of Viewing US Presidential Debates." *Communication Monographs* 70, 4 (2003): 335–50.

Birdsell, David S. "Political Campaign Debates." In *The Oxford Handbook of Political Communication,* edited by Kate Kenski and Kathleen H. Jamieson, 165–78. New York: Oxford University Press, 2017.

Blais, Andre, and M. Martin Boyer. "Assessing the Impact of Televised Debates: The Case of the 1988 Canadian Election." *British Journal of Political Science* 26, 2 (1996): 143–64.

Brierley, Sarah, Eric Kramon, and George Kwaku Ofosu. "The Moderating Effect of Debates on Political Attitudes." *American Journal of Political Science* 64, 1 (2020): 19–37.

Canadian Press. "Security Concerns Shutter Candidates' Debate in Northern BC." Global News, 8 September 2021. https://globalnews.ca/news/8175654/dawson-creek-debate-canceled/.

Carleton Place. "Municipal Updates." 7 September 2021. https://carleton place.ca/photos/custom/CP-Scoop-September-07-2021.pdf.

Carleton Place Chamber of Commerce. "Carleton Place Chamber along with the Lanark Federation of Agriculture Announces Local All Candidate Event for Tuesday, September 7, 2021." 27 August 2021. https://lake88.ca/wp-content/uploads/2021/08/All-Candidates-Night_Federal_PressRelease2021.pdf.

Cho, Jaeho, and Yerheen Ha. "On the Communicative Underpinnings of Campaign Effects: Presidential Debates, Citizen Communication, and Polarization in Evaluations of Candidates." *Political Communication* 29, 2 (2012): 184–204.

DeCillia, Brooks, and Michel Cormier. "Leaders' Debate Coordinators." In *Inside the Campaign: Managing Elections in Canada,* edited by Alex Marland and Thierry Giasson, 71–84. Vancouver: UBC Press, 2020.

Elliott, Louise. "All-Candidate Debates, without All the Candidates." CBC News, 19 April 2011. https://www.cbc.ca/news/politics/all-candidate -debates-without-all-the-candidates-1.98497.

Erickson, Robert S., and Christopher Wlezien. *The Timeline of Presidential Elections: How Campaigns Do (and Do Not) Matter.* Chicago: University of Chicago Press, 2012.

Hall, Chris. "Days of Rage: Angry Voters Brought New Tension to the 2021 Campaign Trail." CBC News, 2 October 2021. https://www.cbc.ca/radio/thehouse/the-house-election-anger-1.6196142.

Hall Jamieson, Kathleen. "Creating the Hybrid Field of Political Communication: A Five-Decade-Long Evolution of the Concepts of Effects." In *The Oxford Handbook of Political Communication,* edited by Kate Kenski and Kathleen Hall Jamieson, 15–45. Oxford: Oxford University Press, 2017.

Heimlich, Russell. "Most Say Presidential Debates Influence Their Vote." Pew Research Center, 11 September 2012. https://www.pewresearch.org/fact-tank/2012/09/11/most-say-presidential-debates-influence-their-vote/.

Henderson, Paul. "Opinion: Here's What Killed the Only In-Person Election Candidates Meeting in Chilliwack–Hope." *Chilliwack Progress,* 13 September 2021. https://www.theprogress.com/opinion/opinion-heres-what-killed-the-only-in-person-election-candidates-meeting-in-chilliwack-hope/.

Jarvis, Anne. "The First Rule of Running for Office? You Show Up." *Windsor Star,* 11 September 2021. https://windsorstar.com/news/local-news/jarvis-first-rule-of-running-for-office-you-show-up.

Johnston, Richard, André Blais, Henry E. Brady, and Jean Crete. *Letting the People Decide: Dynamics of a Canadian Election.* Montreal and Kingston: McGill-Queen's University Press, 1992.

Kinsella, Warren. "Liberals Acted Too Slowly on Latest Sex Scandal." *Toronto Sun,* 18 September 2021. https://torontosun.com/opinion/kinsella-liberals-acted-too-slowly-on-latest-sex-scandal.

Kitteringham, Marc. "Beyond the Debates: Candidates Submit Written Responses." *Campbell River Mirror,* 15 September 2021. https://www.campbellrivermirror.com/news/beyond-the-debate-candidates-submit-written-responses/.

–. "North Island–Powell River All Candidates' Debate: Climate." *Campbell River Mirror,* 14 September 2021. https://www.campbellrivermirror.com/news/north-island-powell-river-all-candidates-debate-climate/.

Labby, Bryan. "'Everybody's Got a Camera Phone': Navigating the Digital Minefield of Modern-Day Campaign Debates." CBC News, 3 October 2019. https://www.cbc.ca/news/canada/calgary/election-debates-social-media-missteps-1.5306956.

Le Pennec, Caroline, and Vincent Pons. "How Do Campaigns Shape Vote Choice? Multi-Country Evidence from 62 Elections and 56 TV Debates." National Bureau of Economic Research Working Paper 26572, Cambridge, MA, 2021. https://www.nber.org/papers/w26572.

Marland, Alex. *Brand Command: Canadian Politics and Democracy in the Age of Mass Control.* Vancouver: UBC Press, 2016.

McAndrews, John R., Aengus Bridgeman, Peter John Loewen, Daniel Rubenson, Laura B. Stephenson, and Allison Harell. "Evaluation of the 2019 Federal Leaders' Debates." Leaders' Debate Commission Report, 19 January 2020. https://www.debates-debats.ca/en/report/evaluation-2019-federal-leaders-debates.

Nolan, Michael. "Political Communication Methods in Canadian Federal Election Campaigns 1867–1925." *Canadian Journal of Communication* 7, 4 (1981): 28–46.

Paul, Binny. "Skeena–Bulkley Valley's Mysterious Liberal Candidate Pops Up in the Riding 5 Days before Polling." *Terrace Standard,* 14 September 2021. https://www.thestar.com/news/canada/2021/09/14/skeena-bulkley -valleys-mysterious-liberal-candidate-pops-up-in-the-riding-5-days-before -polling.html.

Roosevelt, Theodore. "Citizenship in a Republic." Speech at the Sorbonne, Paris, 23 April 1910. https://www.leadershipnow.com/leadingblog/2010/04/theodore_roosevelts_the_man_in.html.

Sayers, Anthony M. *Parties, Candidates, and Constituency Campaigns in Canadian Elections.* Vancouver: UBC Press, 1998.

Wilson, Barry. "Candidates Need to Resist Urge to Shun All-Candidates Meetings." *Western Producer,* 27 April 2011. https://www.producer.com/opinion/candidates-need-to-resist-urge-to-shun-all-candidates-meetings/.

Zaller, John. *The Nature and Origins of Mass Opinion.* New York: Cambridge University Press, 1992.

16

Campaign Signs

Gillian Maurice and Tamara A. Small

Abstract   One of the most visible manifestations that an election campaign has begun is the overnight proliferation of signs promoting local candidates. Campaign signs are a form of political advertising that expresses support for a political party, candidate, third party, or political position. Despite this common practice, neither practitioners nor researchers have produced a clear answer as to whether, let alone how, signs influence election outcomes. To what extent do campaign signs work? Or are they merely symbolic? This chapter reflects on these questions exploring the use of campaign signs in two southwestern Ontario ridings by the Green Party of Canada. It also reviews media coverage of campaign signs during the campaign in 2021 to assess broader trends. Overall, the chapter concludes that campaign signs play an important symbolic role: that is, they are critical not only in demonstrating that the candidates have active and organized campaigns but also in indicating momentum in local support.

Résumé   L'une des manifestations les plus visibles d'une campagne électorale est la prolifération, du jour au lendemain, de panneaux faisant la promotion des candidats locaux. Les affiches de campagne sont une forme de publicité politique qui exprime son appui à un parti politique, à un candidat, à un tiers, ou à une position politique. En dépit de cette pratique courante, ni les praticiens ni les chercheurs n'ont donné de réponses claires quant à savoir si les affiches influencent les résultats électoraux et encore moins la façon dont elles le feraient. Les affiches de campagne fonctionnent-elles réellement? Ou ne sont-elles que symboliques? Ce chapitre s'intéresse à ces questions en explorant l'utilisation des affiches de campagne du parti Vert dans deux circonscriptions du sud-ouest de l'Ontario. Il examine également la couverture médiatique sur les affiches de la campagne de 2021 afin d'évaluer les tendances plus générales. Dans l'ensemble, le chapitre conclut que les affiches de campagne jouent un rôle symbolique important : c'est-à-dire qu'elles sont essentielles non seulement pour démontrer que les candidats mènent des campagnes actives et organisées, mais aussi pour démontrer un élan de soutien local.

ONE OF THE MOST visible manifestations that an election campaign has begun is the overnight proliferation of signs promoting local candidates. Despite newer digital technologies, signs are a commonly used tool in Canadian campaigns. Local campaigns often have signs teams that work to place their candidate's signs around the riding. While canvassing, campaign workers ask and encourage those who indicate support to display lawn signs. Although these signs are regular features of elections in Canada and the United States, they are not used in other countries, such as Australia. Signs are such a part of campaigns in Canada that candidates even use them in winter elections, when the ground is frozen hard and snow can cause damage to the signs.[1] They are the first public revelation of what a party's communication strategy will be.

Although they are sometimes known as lawn signs, we prefer the term "campaign signs." They are a form of political advertising that expresses support for a political party, candidate, third party, or political position. In Canada, campaign signs are typically branded in party colours and feature the name of the local candidate. They can also include the candidate's image, the party represented, the leader's name and/or image, the campaign slogan, and/or a website address. As well, they might include the date of the election and the name of the riding. Campaign signs can be divided into two categories: household signs and street or road signs. The former are placed on the lawns or in the windows of householders. The latter are placed on public property, including on arterial roads or telephone poles. A typical campaign sign measures about thirty-one by forty-one centimetres and is made of coroplast, though road signs can be larger and window signs smaller. See the Appendix for examples.

Depending on where one lives in Canada, there can be minimal or extensive regulation of campaign signs during a federal election. As a form of partisan and election advertising, campaign signs are subject to the rules in the Canada Elections Act. According to Elections Canada, campaign signs must include an authorization "tagline" of the candidate's or political party's official agent, and the signs of third parties must include the third party's name, telephone number, and physical or internet address.[2] Campaign signs – like any other form of partisan advertising – are prohibited from polling places. This prohibition often includes the entire property, not just the building that contains the polling place. Property owners and condominium corporations cannot prohibit private household signs.

Despite these minimal federal rules, there can be provincial or municipal regulations for campaign signs placed on public or private property before or during an election period. Yarmouth, Nova Scotia, for instance, has banned outside campaign signs completely.[3] However, residents can display a campaign sign from a window inside their homes. Other municipalities, including Mississauga, Ontario, and Surrey, British Columbia, prohibit the placement of road signs on public property. Ottawa places time restrictions on campaign signs; household signs are restricted until sixty days before the election, and road signs on public property cannot appear until thirty days before the election.[4] Other municipalities regulate the placement of campaign signs; rules in Waterloo, Ontario, for instance, state that there needs to be at least one metre between signs in any direction.[5] This regulation limits the number of signs in a certain area, and the first local campaign to place its signs might have an advantage. All of this means that the persuasive potential of campaign signs on Canadians is affected by where they live. Some Canadians see an overwhelming number of campaign signs on public and private property, whereas others see far fewer or perhaps none at all.

Despite this common practice, neither practitioners nor researchers have produced a clear answer as to whether, let alone how, signs influence election outcomes. Indeed, the fact that we do not understand fully the persuasive potential of campaign signs might explain their continued use. As one American practitioner admitted regarding campaign signs, "you never know what will work."[6] Such signs remain understudied in Canada. However, some American studies do exist that provide justifications for why parties continue to use campaign signs, why citizens might choose to put household signs on their lawns or in their windows, and the effects of campaign signs on voters.

One reason that a local campaign would place signs on public property and encourage supporters to put them on their lawns is related to exposure and viability.[7] That is, campaign signs can increase party and candidate name recognition and signal to voters that the party or candidate is viable: that is, financially and organizationally capable. Related to this is the "bandwagon effect."[8] That is, campaign workers hope that more signs are seen as meaning more support for a local candidate, and citizens might therefore jump on the bandwagon. As mentioned earlier, campaign signs can be divided into road and household signs. The latter category is particularly interesting because supporters must choose to display the signs, thus indicating to others their political and partisan support. Although occasionally one might see signs for different parties on the same lawn, a campaign sign gives the impression of support of all members of a household whether that is true or not. Displaying household signs is considered both a form of political communication and political participation. That is, a household sign relays two messages – "a message conveyed by a displayer and received by residents of the same social space."[9]

American research suggests that education[10] and economic status[11] are positively related to displaying a household sign. As for motivation, Todd Makse and Anand Sokhey found that showing pride in one's choice also indicates that identity, whether party identification or other, is likely an important reason for supporters who display household signs. Additionally, they found that sign displayers reported a strong desire to "let neighbours know where they stand."[12] Although limited, this research can lead us to conclude that those who choose to display a household sign do so with the hope/intention of informing and influencing their neighbours.

To what extent do campaign signs work? Do they influence the electoral outcome? Or are they merely symbolic? Again, research is scant. Barbara Sommer examined ridings in a California gubernatorial election in 1978 and found that the winning candidates had higher numbers of signs, thus indicating a plausible predictive relationship.[13] Robert Huckfeldt and John Sprague determined that signs and other physical indicators of support such as bumper stickers influenced neighbours' perceptions of who would win.[14] Donald Green and colleagues conducted four experimental field studies across a series of general and primary elections from 2012 to 2015.[15] Their meta-analysis of the effects of political signs found a 1.7 percent direct effect on vote share. Overall, they found that having campaign signs in a precinct increased vote share by close to 2 percent. Not only is this American research limited, but also its applicability to Canada is questionable given differences in the electoral and political systems of the two countries. In unpublished doctoral work, Gillian Maurice took on this topic within the context of Canada's multi-party system.[16] Looking at household signs of one party within a small number of ridings in the federal election in 2019, she found them to be positively related to vote share. Not only did simply having household signs in an area show statistically significant increases in vote share, but also a predictive/correlative relationship was found in that an increasing number of household signs corresponded to proportionately increasing vote share. In addition to the limited evidence, the existing research is unclear about the extent to which campaign signs are a reflection or determinant of support for a political party.

Local Trends

Given the limited academic attention to campaign signs, we explored some of the media coverage of them in the federal election of 2021 in order to get a sense of trends across the country. We did notice two types of stories that had purchase across media outlets: sign-related criminal incidents and spoof or parody campaign signs. These types of stories are not new and have existed in Canadian campaigns for some time. Briefly discussed in *Politics on Display* is the "deluge" of news stories from the US presidential campaign in 2016 on sign-related criminal incidents, including "thefts, vandalism, and occasional escalations to assaults (or worse)," which the authors suggest is likely only a fraction of incidents that occur in the United States.[17] We find similar evidence in Canada, with news stories documenting the destruction of campaign signs and the targeting of candidates. For instance, Jenna Sudds, a candidate for Kanata–Carleton, posted photos of her damaged campaign signs on Twitter.[18] In one photo, the pole that holds up the sign was stabbed through her eye. Another candidate, Sarah Eves (Central Okanagan–Similkameen–Nicola), wrote a letter to the editor of the local newspaper describing the "unprecedented volume" of damaged and stolen signs, including some on private property. She also noted that a supporter refused to take a sign for fear of intimidation and reprisal. In the riding of Malpeque, Prince Edward Island, candidates from different parties noticed that some of their signs had been stolen once they went to collect them.[19] One candidate suspected that it was not for some nefarious political reason but for the lumber attached to the signs. The destruction of campaign signs is costly for the candidate since the damaged sign needs to be removed and, if campaign resources allow it, replaced. Indeed, in the case of sign theft in Prince Edward Island, the lumber was reported to be worth $1,000.

Although the destruction or theft of signs is a worrying aspect of the ground campaign, the number of news stories of hate-related vandalism is another troubling trend. That is, perpetrators deface campaign signs by adding slurs usually using a marker or spray paint. In the latest campaign, we found stories about transphobic slurs on signs in Manitoba,[20] anti-Muslim slurs in Montreal,[21] anti-Semitic slurs on signs in York Region,[22] and the scrawling of the swastika on the signs of racialized candidates in British Columbia.[23] In addition to the damage to property, these actions seek to intimidate candidates. The case of the transphobic slurs in Manitoba was particularly concerning on this front. The damage on the signs was a large printed sticker placed over the candidate's name, which implies a significant level of intention and organization by the perpetrators. Political scientists and commentators often lament the limited number of candidates from marginalized communities running in election campaigns in Canada, and this very public intimidation certainly does not help.

Related to these stories are those about public officials warning against this behaviour.[24] Tampering with election signs is an offence under both the Criminal Code of Canada and the Canada Elections Act. Various police services investigated many of the examples cited above. This unfortunate trend of sign-related criminal incidents might highlight the meaningfulness of campaign signs as a form of political communication: "These are instances of yard signs provoking illicit behavior. Most acts of political participation do not provoke such reactions from people who disagree with the participant's point of view."[25] Although this behaviour is not new in election campaigns, there are indications that the campaign in 2021 was more hostile than normal, with stories of local candidates facing threats, intimidation, and even violence while on the campaign trail.[26]

A much lighter trend related to campaign signs also seen in the recent election was that of spoof or parody signs. Spoof signs look very similar to regular signs in terms of materials used and design, but the "candidate" is not anyone actually running for office. For instance, a series of signs featuring different cats as candidates was placed around one Montreal community.[27] These signs drew heavily from the branding and design of signs by the major parties running in Quebec. The head of the candidate was replaced by that of a cat and included similar campaign slogans, such as "Miauler ensemble" (meow together) instead of the NDP's actual slogan, "Oser ensemble." It was reported that these signs were actually a clever piece of advertising by a local cat café in Montreal since the signs were hung conspicuously near the location. Across Ontario, there were reports of signs featuring celebrities or characters from popular culture as "candidates."[28] One example from Toronto featured the popular internet meme "Rickrolling." The sign featured a picture of 1980s pop star Rick Astley running for prime minister, promising never to "Give You Up" or "Make You Cry" (from the song "Never Gonna Give You Up"). Shrek, the Transformers, and the Canadian singer The Weeknd were also found on spoof signs across the province, often with campaign slogans related to popular culture. It is not clear who created these signs or for what purpose. Like the cat signs, many of these signs used branding and design extremely similar to the signs of the major political parties. One final example is Fernando the Cat, who unofficially ran for MP in Guelph.[29] In addition to campaign signs, Fernando had his own Instagram account.

Spoof election signs in Canada should not be surprising given that professional and amateur humour has long been a feature of campaigns. Political humour takes a number of forms, including jokes, satire, ridicule, parody, and cartoons, and it can be deployed in any number of contexts.[30] For instance, politics and elections are common topics on television shows such as *Saturday Night Live* or *This Hour Has 22 Minutes*. Newspapers regularly publish cartoons that lampoon politicians. Political humour is also a staple on the internet and is increasingly amateur.[31] There have been examples of parody or spoof websites, and political memes are often biting forms of satire against politicians.[32] Although academic research has explored the effects of political humour on citizens, less is known about why amateurs engage in it. This is partly because these online amateurs or spoof sign creators are anonymous. Why an individual would spend money to create these signs and place them around the community is a fascinating question.

Behind the Scenes

In this section, we reflect on the use of campaign signs in two southwestern Ontario ridings – Guelph and Kitchener Centre – by the Green Party of Canada. Overall, the party had a disappointing election in 2021. Despite returning two Greens to Parliament, its vote share decreased considerably to just over 2 percent nationally. In this election, the Green candidate in Guelph, Michelle Bowman, came in fourth, winning 7.5 percent of the vote, whereas in Kitchener Centre Mike Morrice was elected to the House of Commons for the first time with 34.9 percent of the vote. Both suburban ridings, Guelph has a population of 131,794 and is ninety-two square kilometres, and Kitchener Centre has a population of 105,258 and is forty-four square kilometres. These two campaigns provide an opportunity to reflect on the goals and objectives of campaign signs for candidates in smaller political parties.

What follows is based upon interviews with one member from the signs team in each campaign plus Bowman, the candidate in Guelph. It also includes insider insights from one co-author (Maurice), a long-time Green Party member who has worked on several local campaigns, including Bowman's in 2021. Overall, our conversations revealed that campaign signs played an important symbolic role: that is, they were critical in demonstrating not only that the candidates had active organized campaigns but also the momentum of support.

Practically, Green Party signs were no different from other party signs in these ridings – they included the party's branded colour(s) and prominently displayed the local candidate's name, a small version of the logo, and the necessary electoral disclaimer. The campaign workers with whom we spoke did not use photographic images, nor did they include slogans or references to the party leader on the signs. The coroplast signs typically cost just under four dollars for the smaller lawn size and about thirty dollars for the larger size. Given the Green Party's message of environmental sustainability, signs are seen as a sort of necessary evil. They are a necessary part of playing the electoral game that the dominant parties play, and the campaigns struggled with staying true to the low-carbon, low-waste practices that underlie Green values. The two campaigns attempted to address the plastic waste issue in different ways. Kitchener Centre, running the same candidate as in the previous cycle, reused about 2,000 coroplast lawn signs and bought 350–500 new large signs. Guelph, running a new candidate, ordered only 500 lawn-sized coroplast signs for streets and tested out 1,000 printed reusable canvas bags on the standard H-frame for household signs. Many of the bags were also used as giveaways at events and mainstreeting. Campaign signs accounted for about one-quarter of the budget in each campaign. The campaign workers spoke of the creative uses post-campaign for damaged or outdated coroplast signs: building chicken coops, insulating beehives, or delivery to a specialized regional recycler. Moreover, a Quebec company takes old campaign signs and turns them into plastic park benches.[33]

In terms of campaign management, each campaign had a signs team with a dedicated person in the lead role – going by the title of signs manager or signs lead – operating somewhat independently from the rest of the campaign team. The signs lead in Guelph was a part-time position, whereas in Kitchener Centre it was a full-time position. Both campaigns had from five to ten core volunteers working throughout the campaign period, but Kitchener Centre's signs team swelled to about fifty volunteers on key days of the campaign: the day the writ dropped and the day after election day because there are municipal regulations that govern sign removal. For instance, campaign signs in Toronto must be removed from both public and private property within seventy-two hours after voting on election day. Signs crew volunteers used their own vehicles, and a few walked and biked the routes.

The signs teams needed to manage both household signs and street signs in the campaigns. Both campaigns indicated that household signs are driven by direct contact with voters. Occasionally, supporters reached out to the campaigns on their own to request signs for their yards or windows. More typically, however, household signs were placed through canvassing on foot or by phone, thus bringing together different aspects of the local campaign. Once supporters were identified, and asked if they wanted signs, they were likely to say yes. The Kitchener Centre campaign signs lead went so far as to say that none of the work could happen without early foot canvassing and identification of voters. Guelph's small signs team, led by a part-time staffer, easily managed the small number of sign requests from party supporters. Morrice's campaign, conversely, had more than 700 sign requests prior to the writ dropping. The signs team sought to have all 700 delivered on the first day of the campaign and saw large spikes in sign requests after events such as the leaders' debates, culminating in over 2,000 household signs delivered during the campaign. Because of the volume, the Kitchener Centre signs team formed a customer service–style system in which each type of request had a defined response time.

For example, complaints about bylaw infractions were to be dealt with in less than three hours, and a request for a sign could take up to three days to be fulfilled. The Kitchener Centre campaign managed the signs team out of the campaign headquarters office, using a hub-and-spoke system and preplanned delivery routes across nine subdistricts in the riding. Each time a route was completed, members of the team returned to the office, entered the data, and dealt with new sign requests. The Kitchener Centre campaign reported that the original strategy was to slow down on household signs, or even stop deliveries, once get-out-the-vote efforts were needed for advance polls. However, when requests continued to come in at high rates because of continued canvassing efforts, the team decided to keep deliveries going right up to election day. It is clear from the two Green Party campaigns that campaign size in terms of volunteers is crucial. Campaigns with more volunteers can engage in increased canvassing, which identifies more potential supporters, and they can deliver more signs and deal with other sign-related issues compared with campaigns with limited human resources.

With regard to street signs, for both campaigns the goal was to maximize the number of people who saw them, but they had different ways of strategizing how to accomplish that. The team in Guelph, which received their signs later in the campaign period, mirrored another party that they believed was choosing optimal locations and made sure to have a presence at the locations where other parties placed signs. This tactic is common in municipalities where signs are not limited by local regulations. The team aimed to target the city's major intersections first and then to fill in gaps later as they were noticed. In Kitchener Centre, there were stricter municipal requirements about using and spacing signs on regional roads, meaning that prime spots for large street signs could be taken up by another party first.

To counteract the limitations on street signs, the Kitchener Centre campaign took an approach that used local traffic studies to identify high-traffic roads and then targeted private households along those roads. Those households specifically were asked if they would consider upgrading to a large sign for their lawns. This hybrid approach to household and street signs shows that even campaigners who felt that household signs were more valuable to a campaign still gave strategic consideration to sight impressions. There were some concerns that the municipal rules limiting sign placement disadvantaged smaller parties with lower levels of household support that relied on street signs for increasing name recognition. As mentioned above, there are various municipal and provincial rules regarding street signs that can constrain smaller campaigns with fewer volunteers and financial resources.

Although there were national trends of sign-related criminal incidents, both campaigns reported relatively low rates of vandalism. Signs in both ridings regularly went missing, but that was not attributed to intentional maliciousness. Campaign workers in Guelph did get a sense that signs were removed strategically given that in certain neighbourhoods sometimes only one party's signs would be left standing. The campaigners also noted some vandalism targeted at other parties, in particular the People's Party, which had many signs almost completely spray-painted black.[34]

So why even use plastic signs if they go against Green Party values? Both campaigns agreed that signs are an important part of an election campaign, though they disagreed about which type of sign – street or household – delivers the most value. The staffer in charge of the signs team in Guelph believed that street signs on major roads are more valuable in that they are seen by a greater number of people compared with maybe five to ten "pairs of eyes" for a household sign in a secluded neighbourhood. The use of street signs is about name recognition as a mechanism for building campaign momentum. In contrast, the Green Party candidate thought that household signs are more important in that they represent an endorsement or vote of confidence by the displayer. The head of the signs team in Kitchener Centre echoed the idea that a household sign is attached to a voter, making it more important, especially in the eyes of other voters.

When asked about whether campaign signs affect vote choice, workers for both campaigns were generally skeptical and thought that they would have only a small effect. Rather, campaign signs are all about demonstrating momentum. Signs were described as a visible demonstration of the momentum that a candidate was experiencing, with Bowman describing signs as a visual poll. The signs lead in Kitchener Centre echoed this thought: "Signs are important to get people to believe that you have a winning chance, but it [sic] doesn't necessarily change people's minds. If you didn't already agree ideologically with this party with a ton of signs, it doesn't make you go out and vote for them." The signs lead in Guelph believed that signs have a slight persuasive effect, especially within neighbourhoods and between neighbours. If a voter is on the edge, and sees that even one neighbour or most of the neighbours have a sign for one party, then it might give the person "permission to be another Green voter." This sentiment is supported by American research in which the clustering of signs for the same candidate is evident in certain neighbourhoods.[35]

Conclusion

It is reasonable to wonder why campaign signs, probably among the oldest forms of political communication, remain in the modern age of digital technology and social media. Indeed, the limited academic attention to campaign signs can be attributed to the notion that they are considered a marginal form of political participation.[36] Yet, in the federal election of 2021, like those before it, campaign signs proliferated along major intersections and in the yards of Canadians across the country. We have shown that campaign signs are important symbols in local election campaigns. They are less about voter effects and changing the hearts and minds of voters and more about campaign presence and momentum. Both of the campaigns that we explored highlighted that both street and household signs are important in demonstrating to local communities the viability of their candidates, the organization of their campaigns, and the momentum of those campaigns. Campaign signs were important enough to the two campaigns that a good portion of scarce financial resources was dedicated to purchasing them, and human capital in the form of volunteers and campaign staff were dedicated to making sure that the signs got to wherever they were needed. One advantage that campaign signs have compared to social media is that, unlike the latter, signs are unavoidable. That is, people can avoid political social media far more easily than they can avoid campaign signs.

We do not want to overestimate the importance of such signs. Although both campaigns saw signs as necessary and visually important, they also reported that other forms of campaign communication are more central. Social media was seen as a better mode to share information with voters, and door-to-door canvassing was seen as more important for both voter persuasion and supporter identification. At the same time, as we saw, canvassing and household signs are intimately related. Signs are more likely to be seen repeatedly by a higher number of electors in the electoral district. Moreover, we would argue that the prevalence of sign-related criminal incidents also speaks to the importance of signs in the local campaign. Some people feel the need to destroy or vandalize signs as an attempt to silence candidates or campaigns with which they disagree.

Can a local campaign do well without campaign signs? This question was certainly in the minds of workers in the two Green Party campaigns given their commitment to environmental sustainability. Indeed, a staffer in the Guelph campaign proposed an interparty agreement to do away with campaign signs in the riding. Nothing came of the proposal. Thus, the workers felt compelled to use signs because not doing so would hurt name recognition of the new Green Party candidate and favour the incumbent candidate. Despite opportunities to recycle campaign signs, workers in both local campaigns expressed hope that there might be a less wasteful way of engaging in sign publicity. Until that time, they seemed to be unwilling to give up the sense of momentum that signs can provide to the local campaign.

Notes

1 Stoodley, "The Twists of Campaigning."
2 Elections Canada, "FAQs on Elections."

3 Comeau, "Town of Yarmouth."
4 Duffy, "Should Election Signs Be Allowed?"
5 CBC News, "What You Need to Know about Election Signs."
6 Quoted in Green et al., "The Effects of Lawn Signs," 143.
7 Ibid.
8 Green et al., "The Effects of Lawn Signs," 144.
9 Makse, Minkoff, and Sokhey, *Politics on Display*, 167.
10 Makse and Sokhey, "The Displaying of Yard Signs."
11 Laband et al., "Patriotism, Pigskins, and Politics."
12 Makse and Sokhey, "The Displaying of Yard Signs," 199.
13 Sommer, "Front Yard Signs."
14 Huckfeldt and Sprague, "Political Parties and Electoral Mobilization."
15 Green et al., "The Effects of Lawn Signs."
16 Please contact the authors for further information.
17 Makse, Minkoff, and Sokhey, *Politics on Display*, 4.
18 Pringle, "'Unacceptable.'"
19 Davis, "Signs, Signs, Nowhere a Sign."
20 Bernhardt and Froese, "Hate Speech Stickers."
21 Caruso-Moro, "Montreal MP Condemns Racist Graffiti."
22 Neufeld, "Police Investigating String of Anti-Semitic Graffiti."
23 Miljure, "Hateful Graffiti."
24 Raymond, "Ottawa Police Warning Residents"; DiscoverWestman, "Elections Canada Warns against Sign Tampering."
25 Makse, Minkoff, and Sokhey, *Politics on Display*, 4.
26 Hall, "Days of Rage."
27 Belfer, "Cat Election Signs."
28 Arsenych, "These Fake Election Signs in Ontario."
29 Arsenych, "A Cat from Guelph."
30 Innocenti and Miller, "The Persuasive Force of Political Humor."
31 Baumgartner, "Humor on the Next Frontier."
32 Lalancette and Small, "'Justin Trudeau – I Don't Know Her.'"
33 Radio-Canada, "Les pancartes électorales."
34 Vivian, "Vandals Target PPC Election Signs."
35 Makse, Minkoff, and Sokhey, *Politics on Display*.
36 Ibid.

Bibliography

Arsenych, Alex. "A Cat from Guelph Is Unofficially Running in the 2021 Elections and His Campaign Is Purrfect." Narcity, 16 September 2021. https://www.narcity.com/toronto/guelph-cat-running-in-federal-elections.

—. "These Fake Election Signs in Ontario Are So Ridiculous We Kind of Wish They Were Real." Narcity, 20 September 2021. https://www.narcity. com/toronto/hilarious-fake-election-signs-in-ontario.

Baumgartner, Jody C. "Humor on the Next Frontier: Youth, Online Political Humor, and the JibJab Effect." *Social Science Computer Review* 25, 3 (2007): 319–38.

Belfer, Ilana. "Cat Election Signs Are Popping Up in Montreal and They're Pretty Purr-Suasive." MTL Blog, 4 September 2021. https://www.mtlblog. com/montreal/cat-election-signs-montreal-theyre-pretty-purrsuasive.

Bernhardt, Darren, and Ian Froese. "Hate Speech Stickers Target Election Signs of Transgender Candidate in Manitoba Riding." CBC News, 10 September 2021. https://www.cbc.ca/news/canada/manitoba/trevor -kirczenow-election-signs-hate-speech-provencher-manitoba-1.6170526.

Caruso-Moro, Luca. "Montreal MP Condemns Racist Graffiti on Campaign Sign amid 'Unprecedented' Increase in Slurs, Death Threats." CTV News Montreal, 9 September 2021. https://montreal.ctvnews.ca/montreal-mp -condemns-racist-graffiti-on-campaign-sign-amid-unprecedented-increase -in-slurs-death-threats-1.5578577.

CBC News. "What You Need to Know about Election Signs." 18 September 2019. https://www.cbc.ca/news/canada/kitchener-waterloo/federal -election-signs-need-to-know-waterloo-region-1.5288174.

Comeau, Tina. "Town of Yarmouth Approves Election Signs Ban." Salt Wire, 13 July 2020. http://www.saltwire.com/news/provincial/town-of -yarmouth-approves-election-signs-ban-472785/.

Davis, Tony. "Signs, Signs, Nowhere a Sign: Federal Election Signs Stolen from P.E.I. Ridings." CBC News, 27 September 2021. https://www.cbc. ca/news/canada/prince-edward-island/pei-signs-stolen-election-sept-2021 -1.6188989.

DiscoverWestman. "Elections Canada Warns against Sign Tampering." DiscoverWestman.com, 7 September 2021. https://chvnradio.com/ articles/elections-canada-warns-against-election-sign-tampering.

Duffy, Andrew. "Should Election Signs Be Allowed on Public Property? Take Our Poll." *Ottawa Citizen,* 14 August 2015. https://ottawacitizen. com/news/politics/should-elections-signs-be-allowed-on-public -property.

Elections Canada. "FAQs on Elections." N.d. https://www.elections.ca/ content.aspx?section=vot&dir=faq&document=faqelec&lang=e#a2.1.

Green, Donald P., Jonathan S. Krasno, Alexander Coppock, Benjamin D. Farrer, Brandon Lenoir, and Joshua N. Zingher. "The Effects of Lawn Signs on Vote Outcomes: Results from Four Randomized Field Experiments." *Electoral Studies* 41 (2016): 143–50.

Hall, Chris. "Days of Rage: Angry Voters Brought New Tensions to the 2021 Campaign Trail." CBC News, 2 October 2021. https://www.cbc.ca/radio/thehouse/the-house-election-anger-1.6196142.

Huckfeldt, Robert, and John Sprague. "Political Parties and Electoral Mobilization: Political Structure, Social Structure, and the Party Canvass." *American Political Science Review* 86, 1 (1992): 70–86.

Innocenti, Beth, and Elizabeth Miller. "The Persuasive Force of Political Humor." *Journal of Communication* 66, 3 (2016): 366–85. https://doi.org/10.1111/jcom.12231.

Laband, David N., Ram Pandit, John P. Sophocleus, and Anne M. Laband. "Patriotism, Pigskins, and Politics: An Empirical Examination of Expressive Behavior and Voting." *Public Choice* 138, 1–2 (2009): 97–108.

Lalancette, Mireille, and Tamara A. Small. "'Justin Trudeau – I Don't Know Her': An Analysis of Leadership Memes of Justin Trudeau." *Canadian Journal of Communication* 45, 2 (2020): 305–25.

Makse, Todd, Scott Minkoff, and Anand Sokhey. *Politics on Display: Yard Signs and the Politicization of Social Spaces.* Oxford: Oxford University Press, 2019.

Makse, Todd, and Anand E. Sokhey. "The Displaying of Yard Signs as a Form of Political Participation." *Political Behavior* 36, 1 (2014): 189–213.

Miljure, Ben. "Hateful Graffiti Scrawled on Surrey, B.C., Campaign Sign." CTV News British Columbia, 26 August 2021. https://bc.ctvnews.ca/hateful-graffiti-scrawled-on-surrey-b-c-campaign-sign-1.5562163.

Neufeld, Abby. "Police Investigating String of Anti-Semitic Graffiti on Election Signs in York Region." CTV News Toronto, 30 August 2021. https://toronto.ctvnews.ca/police-investigating-string-of-anti-semitic-graffiti-on-election-signs-in-york-region-1.5566717.

Pringle, Josh. "'Unacceptable': Liberal Candidate Frustrated with Vandalized Election Signs in Kanata–Carleton." CTV News Ottawa, 18 August 2021. https://ottawa.ctvnews.ca/unacceptable-liberal-candidate-frustrated-with-vandalized-election-signs-in-kanata-carleton-1.5552204.

Radio-Canada. "Les pancartes électorales, plus écologiques qu'on pourrait le penser." 14 October 2019. https://ici.radio-canada.ca/nouvelle/1345560/affiches-partis-elections-recyclage-plastique-coroplast.

Raymond, Ted. "Ottawa Police Warning Residents Not to Tamper with Election Signs." CTV News Ottawa, 30 August 2021. https://ottawa.ctvnews.ca/ottawa-police-warning-residents-not-to-tamper-with-election-signs-1.5567026.

Sommer, Barbara. "Front Yard Signs as Predictors of Election Outcome." *Political Methodology* 6, 2 (1979): 237–40.

Stoodley, Sarah. "The Twists of Campaigning in a Newfoundland and Labrador Election Hit by Pandemic Chaos." *Policy Options,* 26 May 2021. https://policyoptions.irpp.org/magazines/may-2021/the-twists-of-campaigning-in-a-newfoundland-and-labrador-election-hit-by-pandemic-chaos/.

Vivian, Richard. "Vandals Target PPC Election Signs, Spray Them with Black Paint." GuelphToday.com, 17 September 2021. https://www.guelphtoday.com/local-news/vandals-target-ppc-election-signs-spray-them-with-black-paint-4342306.

17

Local Advocacy

Thomas Collombat

A̶b̶s̶t̶r̶a̶c̶t̶   Advocacy groups' participation in electoral campaigns is framed by Elections Canada under the "third parties" regulations. Although most non-profit organizations shy away from partisan involvement, others use campaigns to raise awareness of specific issues by relying on their reputation and visibility among the public. Membership-based civil society organizations, in particular unions, focus their efforts on their members and can develop targeted local campaigns in selected ridings where they think they can make a difference. This is the case of the Public Service Alliance of Canada, the largest union representing federal public employees. Along with adopting a platform that puts forward its priorities and values, the union targets tight races in ridings where it has enough members. It deploys both digital and in-person efforts, depending on its members' will and capacity, to defeat Conservative Party candidates. Both national and regional offices are involved in this process, sometimes in different ridings. Regional offices also endorse a few individual candidates. Local campaigning remains a challenge for advocacy groups and depends on their financial capacity and the human resources that they can mobilize on the ground.

R̶é̶s̶u̶m̶é̶   La participation des groupes de défense de droits aux campagnes électorales est encadrée par les réglementations d'Élections Canada sur les « tiers partis ». Si la plupart des organismes de charité hésitent à s'impliquer de façon partisane, d'autres groupes utilisent les campagnes électorales pour mettre de l'avant des enjeux en usant de leur réputation et de leur visibilité auprès du grand public. Les organisations de la société civile disposant d'un grand nombre de membres, notamment les syndicats, concentrent leurs efforts sur leurs membres et peuvent développer des campagnes locales ciblées dans des circonscriptions où elles pensent pouvoir faire une différence. C'est le cas de l'Alliance de la fonction publique du Canada, le plus grand syndicat de la fonction publique fédérale. Outre l'adoption d'une plate-forme mettant de l'avant ses priorités et ses valeurs, le syndicat cible des circonscriptions où la course est serrée et où il dispose d'assez de membres. Il y déploie des outils virtuels et des activités en personne, suivant la volonté et la capacité de ses membres, afin de défaire les candidats du Parti conservateur. Tant le bureau national que les bureaux régionaux sont impliqués dans ce processus, parfois dans des circonscriptions différentes. Les bureaux régionaux apportent également leur appui à un nombre limité de candidatures individuelles. Conduire des campagnes locales reste un défi important pour les groupes de défense des droits et dépend de leurs capacités à la fois financières et de mobilisation sur le terrain.

EVEN IF THIRD PARTIES do not compete to get elected, they are important actors in the democratic process in Canada, including during electoral campaigns. The category of "third parties" used by Elections Canada gathers a broad range of groups and some individuals, though a significant number of them are trade unions, business associations, and professional organizations. Although Canada counts about 175,000 non-profit groups, very few of them register with Elections Canada.[1] The framing of their activities within the Elections Canada Act restricts their capacity to act during an electoral campaign. For a while, the Canada Revenue Agency's rules also largely barred organizations claiming charitable status from political activity.[2] Although this strict prohibition has been lifted, registered charities still cannot explicitly support or oppose a candidate or party. Beyond the fiscal impact, non-profits also avoid being seen as partisan in order to not jeopardize their access to government officers and resources, essential to their work, therefore creating a context termed an "advocacy chill."[3]

The imposition of spending limits on third parties is related intrinsically to the limits put on political parties themselves. Regulating their activities is supposed to avoid shortcutting the rules that candidates and their organizations have to follow by using a proxy to campaign in their names. Historically, the tendency in Canada has been to make the rules stricter by broadening the range of activities covered and lengthening the period during which regulations apply. The general election of 1988, in which civil society organizations were highly involved, in particular with issues related to free trade, represented an important moment in that process. It led to the creation of the Lortie Commission, which reasserted the need for clear and strict limits to third parties' activities during electoral campaigns.[4]

At the federal level, the period during which those activities are regulated includes not only the official electoral campaign but also a pre-election period, between 30 June of the year of a fixed-date election and the day that the election is called.[5] The activities regulated fall into three categories: "partisan advertising" (called "election advertising" during the election period), "election surveys," and "partisan activities." The last category covers a broad range of activities, including unpaid social media campaigns, canvassing, and get-out-the-vote activities. Partisan or election advertising also includes paid issue-related ads, as long as they can be clearly related to a candidate or party. Partisan activities, however, are considered as such only if they explicitly support or oppose a candidate or party, but they do include strategic voting messages and activities, since generally they are undertaken against a specific party or candidate. Membership-based organizations also have to declare as partisan those activities directed strictly to their members, as long as they explicitly support or oppose a political party or candidate.

The regulation of third parties' activities takes the form of a financial report of the regulated activities that allows for implementing spending limits. Those limits are usually higher for the pre-election period than for the election period. Ceilings are applied to the overall expense of the organization and to its spending in each riding. The limit per riding is about 1 percent of the overall limit. In all cases, these limits are much lower than those imposed on political parties and candidates.[6] For example, an individual candidate usually is allowed to spend about twenty times as much as any third party in a specific riding.

The main objective of advocacy groups during electoral campaigns is to promote the issues important for their respective mandates.[7] Most of the time, their focus is nationwide as they attempt to influence the public debate and the agenda of the campaign.

Their limited funding and the spending caps imposed by law often lead them to rely heavily on social media, though not always in a very efficient manner, for few of them are willing or able to invest enough resources in those tools.[8] Third parties' campaigns therefore rarely focus on local issues or candidates. However, considering the logic of the first-past-the-post system, "locally-targeted issue-based advertising" is sometimes seen as the most efficient option for third parties.[9] Without taking an explicit stand in favour of or against a specific candidate, a third party can target a riding where the race is expected to be close, granting more exposure to the third-party campaign and attracting the attention of the media and of political parties' national headquarters.

Registered third parties cover a broad range of issues and are spread all along the political spectrum. Many of them promote progressive policies, in particular issues related to labour, environmental protection (including climate change awareness and mitigation), social justice, and international solidarity. Other groups are associated with a more conservative vision of society, including business associations, religious groups, firearms supporters, and nationalist organizations. This diversity makes it a challenge to analyze them as a single entity. Their different sizes, resources, structures, and political orientations make them a particularly heterogeneous category. Besides, registering as a third party does not necessarily mean that an organization will indeed use its right to participate in a campaign. It is therefore appropriate to focus on one type of organization, trade unions, which consistently have represented a significant share of registered third parties while systematically becoming involved during electoral campaigns. This is not to say that unions are representative of all advocacy groups when it comes to their electoral work but that, by being particularly proactive, they offer a relevant perspective from which to approach the role of civil society organizations during campaigns.

Contrary to most non-profits, unions do not shy away from political action or even partisan involvement. In Canada, the main illustration of this dynamic is the close relationship established historically between many of them and the New Democratic Party (NDP).[10] Founded in 1961 by various groups, including a large number of unions, the NDP was long considered as the electoral arm of the labour movement and as such the main vehicle for its participation in the electoral process. The inability of the NDP to take power at the federal level, and its mixed success at the provincial level (either by not managing to form governments or by engaging in policies opposed by unions when it did), led to a loosening of that relationship.[11] However, the bond remains strong between several major Canadian unions and the party.[12]

Other unions have decided to opt for strategic voting approaches. For some of them, including many public employees' unions, this has been a long-held position. Civil servants' unions were often barred from political activism in order to maintain the neutrality of the public service, and they kept their distance from political campaigns even after the legal ban was lifted.[13] When they did get involved, often they turned to strategic voting. In the context of Canadian politics, unions that promoted strategic voting essentially campaigned against a potential Conservative Party victory by targeting a riding with a close race and putting their weight behind the candidate – whether New Democrat or Liberal – with the greatest chance of beating the Conservative candidate.[14] Beyond public employees' unions, this approach has been adopted by a rising number of labour organizations, often because they have made avoiding the election of a Conservative government their highest priority. The effectiveness of union-led strategic voting campaigns is still disputed, partly because NDP voters are less likely to be convinced to switch their votes strategically.[15] However, since this tendency is based upon voters' perceptions of the likely result of the election, it might change in time and seems to be influenced by party polarization.[16]

This diversity of strategies and tactics is reflected locally in labour councils that gather union locals active within the same region or metropolitan area. Because their affiliates' approaches can diverge, labour councils rarely become involved in federal election campaigns, but often they are active in municipal elections.[17] Several unions also prefer to focus on provincial, rather than federal, politics since about 90 percent of the workforce is under provincial jurisdiction. Unions representing federal employees or private sector workers under federal jurisdiction (e.g., interprovincial trans-portation, banking, telecommunications) are more inclined to get involved during federal election campaigns.[18]

Whether a union supports a party or adopts strategic voting tactics, some elements remain equally important when it comes to the logistics of the local campaign. As membership-based organizations, unions take into consideration local implementation when choosing ridings on which to focus. If part of their spending can be used for nationwide advertising campaigns, for instance, then their local impacts also depend heavily on the number of people whom they can mobilize. The impact of unions in a specific riding can be twofold: they can contribute to a campaign by providing human resources (e.g., for canvassing, running phone banks, distributing leaflets), and they can benefit a campaign with privileged access to their members as voters to try to influence their votes. That latter influence should not be overinflated, but it can be significant, particularly in close races. Various election studies have shown, for example, that union members are more likely than the rest of the electorate to support the NDP but that Liberals get the largest share of union members' votes when they win an election.[19]

Local Trends

The spending caps imposed on third parties as well as the limited resources that they can commit to political action often lead them to focus their efforts on the national level rather than the local level. Not having to mobilize boots on the ground in a specific riding or to elaborate a complex targeted communications strategy is the preferred option for many advocacy groups. This was even more so the case for the electoral campaign in 2021, during which the aforementioned advocacy chill was accompanied by the public health measures put in place to counter the COVID-19 pandemic.[20] A lot of the work that advocacy groups usually do at the local level, such as town hall meetings or canvassing, could not be done under those restrictions. Paradoxically, the pandemic has also put a great amount of pressure on many charities asking for support from the federal government, but they felt unheard by the parties during the campaign.[21]

The fact that this was a snap election added an extra challenge. It removed the limitations normally applied during the pre-election period for fixed-date elections, but it also took many groups by surprise, therefore preventing them from putting together elaborate campaign plans, in particular at the local level.[22] Advocacy groups that had already been turning more and more to social media to conduct their electoral work moved even further in that direction. However, sometimes they were countered by new policies adopted by those platforms to crack down on misinformation that were used to silence some groups, though they were also criticized for not being applied consistently and therefore allowing partisan advertising.[23] This extensive use of social media was particularly characteristic of groups founded to campaign against one of the political parties running.[24]

Only a handful of third-party groups registered with Elections Canada for the election in 2021 were local. Those that did identify specifically with a region usually focused their efforts on forcing the local candidates to position themselves on the issues that they promoted. Environmental issues often appear among the preoccupations of those organizations and can be of concern in the ridings in which a protected area or a site of interest is located.[25] In other cases, a local issue can span a vast area. This is the case in the Northwest Territories, represented by only one MP but where local advocacy groups have specific demands shaped by the geographic and socio-demographic realities of their vast region. Groups representing Indigenous communities, visible minorities, workers, or environmentalists all used their media access to put forward their priorities and make their voices heard by the various candidates.[26]

The restrictions put on third-party activities combined with the context of the election in 2021 meant that only the biggest players among advocacy groups were able to conduct thorough local campaigns. As was already the case in previous campaigns, unions were the most active in that category.[27] Within the labour movement, the Public Service Alliance of Canada (PSAC) is particularly concerned with federal politics. The vast majority of its 215,000 members work for the Canadian government, and as such it is the largest union representing federal public employees. It is composed of fifteen component unions, organized according to the different branches of the government, in addition to some local unions directly affiliated with the national union. Local PSAC activities are conducted mostly through the seven regional offices in British Columbia, the Prairies, Ontario, the National Capital Region, Quebec, the Atlantic, and the North. Each region is headed by a regional executive vice-president, elected from among members, who is the main representative of the union in the region. However, only the national union is registered as a third party with Elections Canada. All electoral expenses – whether made by the national union, a component union, or a regional office – have to be accounted for by the national office and have to respect the limits determined for PSAC as a single entity.

The local activities conducted by PSAC during an electoral campaign are framed by the strategies and positions adopted by the national leadership. Like several other public sector unions, PSAC is non-partisan, which means that it does not maintain a strong, formal link to the NDP, nor does it support any political party. Instead, traditionally, it has been discrete during election periods, both in order not to jeopardize its relationship with the elected government and because its members have been attached to the political neutrality of the public service. However, the years in power of the Conservative Party under the leadership of Stephen Harper led to a stronger stance of the union against the party, in particular because of the cuts made in the public sector. The general election of 2015 represented an important turning point, when the union decided to become more proactive and vocal in its opposition to the re-election of a Conservative government.

As a membership-based organization, PSAC, like most unions, focuses its efforts on convincing its members to vote in accordance with its position. This might not be the case of other civil society organizations, which – whether member based or not – might decide to rely more strongly on their public image or media presence. If unions in general, and PSAC in particular, do reach out to the broader public through their various communications, then their focus is much more on their own members to influence their decisions at the polls. To that end, the PSAC leadership adopts a national platform for each election, based upon the priorities put forward by members. The platform emphasizes the importance of public services, opposes privatization, promotes a more thorough social safety net as well as fiscal equity, pushes for measures to fight climate change, and supports stronger policies on reconciliation and discrimination.[28] Members are not only encouraged to vote for candidates committed to defending the union's platform but also explicitly discouraged to consider voting for the Conservative Party.[29] The union also insists on providing its members with information about their rights as federal public employees during an electoral campaign. This information includes the limits set in the law on what federal employees can express in public (including on social media) and that they should not fear recriminations or sanctions from their employer if they respect those limits.[30]

Despite its non-partisan stand at the national level, PSAC does allow endorsements of individual candidates by its local representatives. These endorsements have to respect criteria established at the national level, but the appraisal of each potential endorsement is left to regional offices. Formally, support for a candidate is usually made public by the regional vice-president of the union and presented as such: it is the elected official of the union who endorses the candidate, not the national union per se. Although the endorsement is of an individual and not the party for which the candidate is running, most candidates supported by a regional PSAC vice-president run for the NDP.[31] This is partly because the criteria for endorsement include prioritizing candidates active in the labour movement or those who have been involved in the community by explicitly promoting the ideas and values of the union. Local endorsements remain relatively rare. Not all regions grant them, and when they do it is rarely for more than one candidate per region. Those choices are made exclusively on the basis of the qualities of the candidate and not for strategic reasons related to the specific situation of the riding. They are made public by the union's regional office, and candidates can mention them during the campaign.

Behind the Scenes

Information presented in this section was gathered from three PSAC representatives working at the national office and in some regional offices. They are all communication staffers who were involved directly in the union's political campaigns during the general election in 2021. Data were collected through three phone interviews that I conducted.

A large part of local PSAC interventions is determined at the national level. When an election is called, a national election campaign team is formed from staffers assigned to other campaigns or files outside the electoral period. In addition to supporting the national leadership in putting together and promoting the union's platform, that team is in charge of identifying ridings where the union could have a determining impact. The work starts by comparing the membership list with voter registration lists in order to assess the number of PSAC members per riding. A threshold is established so that only ridings where the union has a significant presence (usually about 800 members) are considered. Based upon the polling done during the campaign, a list of close races in which a Conservative candidate is involved is then established. Finally, the two lists are compared to identify constituencies with both tight races and enough PSAC members so that their votes could make a difference. Those targeted ridings (usually around twenty) are where the national office will concentrate its efforts.

Considering the limited resources of the organization and the strict spending caps that it must follow, the strategic intervention happens closer to the end of the campaign period, usually the last ten days to two weeks, to make sure that the effort is still worth it: that is, if the race is still tight or if the campaign has significantly changed the odds. The tools used for this intervention are mostly digital. They include an email blast sent to all members in the riding and targeted social media ads bought to reach voters who are also PSAC members. In both cases, the union tries to customize the message as much as possible: the email is signed by the regional executive vice-president rather than by a national officer, it mentions issues particularly relevant to the region or area, and it explicitly targets the Conservative candidate in the riding, for instance by using quotations about the realities of public employees. The union can also break down its membership list by department, and therefore refine its message even more, by narrowing it down to issues that speak more precisely to members working in a specific branch of the government. The message respects the non-partisan identity of the union in that it does not tell members whom to vote for, but it does encourage them to consider not voting for Conservative Party candidates by pointing to the strong differences between the union's and that party's respective platforms.

In addition to what is done at the riding level by the national office of the union, regional offices have their own campaign plans, which usually involve more grassroots work, in direct relation to the realities of the local constituencies. For both unions and mass organizations in general that want to intervene in a federal election campaign, the focus is on members as both instruments and targets of the strategy.

At the local level, members are the ones who will be mobilized not only to do the groundwork but also to determine how the national orientations will be operationalized in their regions and ridings. Each PSAC region has established mobilization structures in order to gather members willing to contribute to the political involvement of the union. In geographically larger regions, such as British Columbia, area councils are set up in the different sectors of the province so that interested PSAC members, regardless of the component union with which they are affiliated, can get involved politically. In geographically smaller regions, such as the National Capital Region, two political action committees (one for each province composing the region) have been set up to provide spaces for activists. When an election is called, the staff and elected officials of each regional office consult these committees to determine how they would like to be involved and in which ways the national union's priorities could be operationalized in the region.

The capacity of the union to intervene locally therefore relies broadly on the will and availability of its members. The context of the campaign then becomes an important factor. If the election is called during a period when members are less available or have other priorities, such as in the summer when many members are on vacation, then they might be less willing to become involved. The challenge becomes bigger if an election is called unexpectedly, before the fixed-date election. Organizations and activists can be caught by surprise and not have the time or resources to prepare for the campaign. The duration of the campaign also matters, particularly in those cases: the shorter the campaign, the less time to plan properly the union's interventions. Contrary to political parties, civil society organizations that wish to play a role during electoral campaigns are not focused exclusively on elections and therefore are less agile to adjust to a changing political time line.

When they decide to participate actively, PSAC regional offices can organize town hall meetings during which a representative from the union will answer members' questions about the election while explaining the issues that the union has decided to put forward and inviting the audience members to keep them in mind when they go to the polls. Other activities include debates among candidates at the invitation of the union so that they can position themselves in relation to the union's platform and priorities.[32] Those debates can be targeted at one specific riding, usually chosen with logistical concerns in mind to make sure that as many members as possible can attend them, or a broader region, with the political parties then invited to delegate one of their candidates running in the area.

Where there is a high density of members in a relatively small region, such as in the National Capital Region, leafleting at the workplace can also be used. There again the idea is to reach out to as many members as possible who work in the region regardless of the specific riding in which they live – which might not be the one where they work – and to promote the positions and recommendations of the union. The fact that the vast majority of PSAC members were working from home during the election in 2021 meant that no leafleting was done this time, and the focus was on electronic communications instead.

Beyond these broader strategies, aimed at an entire region or area, regional offices can also target specific ridings. They rely on data gathered by the national office and go through a similar process of selection, but they can decide on different criteria and have different thresholds. Regions therefore usually have their own lists of targeted ridings that might or might not include some of those also targeted by the national office. They also pick constituencies where the races are close, but they might decide to apply a lower threshold of members in order to expand the potential number of races that they could try to influence. Like the national office, they rely on digital instruments such as email blasts and targeted ads on social media. But they can add phone banks and canvassing designed specifically to reach their members in the ridings and carry the messages directly to them.

The local PSAC campaign is therefore multi-layered and illustrates the diversity of approaches that can be taken by a third party to intervene in a campaign. The strategic interventions determined by the national and regional offices are also distinct from the local endorsements mentioned earlier. This can lead to a situation in which in one riding a candidate is endorsed by the regional vice-president of the union but is not among the ridings targeted by the regional office for intervention if it is not a close race involving a Conservative candidate, for example. Similarly, a riding can be selected by the regional office but not by the national one and might have no candidate endorsed by the regional vice-president. The union's intervention is therefore driven by both principles, embodied in the platform and illustrated by local endorsements, and strategic considerations based upon the numbers gathered for each constituency.

The spending caps imposed on third parties are an obstacle mostly when the union decides to become particularly active during the campaign. Having activities targeted at specific ridings means that those expenses fall under the spending limits per constituency, which are particularly low. Members who participate in the campaign work might have to take leaves of absence without pay for union business and be compensated by the union, and this compensation is considered an electoral expense. Even digital tools can get costly. Since targeted ridings are chosen because they have critical numbers of members, the costs of targeted ads can increase quickly, in particular in areas such as the National Capital Region, where a significant share of PSAC members are concentrated.

Despite the limitations of strategic voting identified in the literature, PSAC generally considers that its targeted interventions in selected ridings, whether determined at the national level or the regional level, are likely to make a difference. Without being able to reach definitive conclusions about why some of those constituencies end up electing Conservative candidates or not, the union evaluates its strategy by using internal polling and comparisons with ridings with similar socio-demographic profiles but in which it did not intervene. The general assessment is that the results on election day are usually more favourable to the objectives of the union in ridings where it campaigned, and the results are interpreted as an indication that the strategy is worth pursuing.

Spending caps also have unintended consequences for civil society organizations. Although they were designed to limit third parties' involvement in electoral campaigns, they can have broader impacts, in particular when elections do not happen as initially scheduled by the fixed-date election calendar. Some events planned by PSAC at the local level before an election is called and before anyone knows when the campaign will begin (e.g., a town hall meeting to which a local MP has been invited or a rally on a topic that could be interpreted as an electoral issue) have to be postponed so that they do not count as election-related expenses. The tightening of regulations for third parties by Elections Canada, and the inclusion of communications with members in those regulated activities, have made advocacy groups in general and unions in particular very careful about what they do and how much they spend during that period. If non-partisan actors have an influence on the campaign, the campaign also has an impact, directly or indirectly, on how these organizations work.

Conclusion

The contributions of third parties to electoral campaigns are manifold. By raising specific issues, they shed light on topics, communities, or social problems that otherwise might go undetected during the campaign, and they force political parties to position themselves on those issues. Many groups use their reputation, expertise, and media presence to carry their messages. They also rely increasingly on social media either by capitalizing on their numbers of followers or by pushing targeted ads toward the electorate. Those that are membership based, in particular unions, often focus their efforts on their own bases to make a difference on election day in specifically targeted local races.

This is when the campaign really becomes local for those organizations. Considering not only the limits imposed by law on third-party spending, but also the fact that contrary to political parties electoral politics does not represent their core activities, these groups have to gather strategic information and make choices about specifically where they want to have impacts. The means that they use depend a lot on the context of the election, the duration of the campaign, and the will and capacity of their members to get involved. If there are important issues at stake for the membership during the campaign, and if it is a tight race among parties whose platforms would have drastically different impacts on their daily lives, then chances are that members will be more inclined to become involved. Otherwise, the group's interventions will likely remain less focused and more national than local in scope.

Because they are not exclusively dedicated to electoral politics, and because their electoral activities are strictly framed by law, advocacy groups cannot participate as actively as political parties in campaigns. When they do, it is mostly at the national level, and few of them actually have the means to conduct thorough local campaigns. Those that do are usually membership based and depend heavily on their members. However, as important as electoral politics can be, campaigns are not the only moment or opportunity for civil society organizations and unions to become involved politically. Their conception of political work often goes beyond election periods and includes making representations to governments, opposing or supporting bills, joining campaigns with allied groups to promote issues in line with their values, or debating within their own governing structures about political issues that matter to their members. Electoral campaigns matter, but they comprise only one of the many sides of how advocacy groups participate in Canada's local political life.

Notes

1 Elections Canada, "Third Party Database"; Imagine Canada, "Everything You Need to Know."
2 Grosenick, "Opportunities Missed."
3 Pross, "Barriers to Third-Party Advertising."
4 Lawlor and Crandall, "Policy versus Practice."
5 Elections Canada, "New Requirements for Third Parties."
6 Lawlor and Crandall, "Policy versus Practice."
7 Laforest, "Going Digital."
8 Grosenick, "Opportunities Missed."
9 Lawlor and Crandall, "Policy versus Practice."
10 Savage, "Contemporary Party-Union Relations."
11 Walchuk, "Changing Union-Party Relations"; McGrane, *The New NDP.*
12 Jansen and Young, "Solidarity Forever?"; Pilon, Ross, and Savage, "Solidarity Revisited."
13 Savage and Smith, "Public Sector Unions."
14 Savage, "Organized Labour and the Politics of Strategic Voting"; Fowler, "Coordinated Strategic Voting."
15 Blais, "Why Is There So Little Strategic Voting?"
16 Daoust and Bol, "Polarization, Partisan Preferences and Strategic Voting."
17 Savage, "Organized Labour and the Shifting Landscape."
18 Warskett, "Federal Public Sector Unions."
19 Archer, "The Failure of the New Democratic Party"; Cross et al., *Fighting for Votes.*
20 McIntosh, "What You Need to Know"; Cameron, "Canadian Election 2021."
21 Osman, "Shore Up Charities."
22 Paas-Lang, "How Interested Outsiders Use 'Third Party' Status."
23 McIntosh, "What You Need to Know"; Al-Rawi, "Facebook's Latest Federal Election Integrity Initiative."
24 Bryden and Levitz, "New Advocacy Group Launches Pre-Election Ad Campaign."
25 Lake Winnipeg Foundation, "Canada's Election."
26 Zingel, "What Some Advocacy Groups Want."
27 Paas-Lang, "How Interested Outsiders Use 'Third Party' Status."

28 Public Service Alliance of Canada, "PSAC Members Name Their Top Election Issues."

29 Bryden, "Unions Reject O'Toole's Worker-Friendly Pitch."

30 Public Service Alliance of Canada, "Your Rights on Social Media during an Election."

31 PSAC–Atlantic, "PSAC Officially Endorses Michelle Neill"; PSAC–National Capital Region, "REVP Alex Silas Shares His Endorsement of Angella Macewen."

32 AFPC–Québec, "AFPC–Débat rencontre élections 2021."

Bibliography

AFPC–Québec. "AFPC – Débat rencontre élections 2021." Facebook, 12 September 2021. https://www.facebook.com/afpcqc/posts/1015942973 3024834.

Al-Rawi, Ahmed. "Facebook's Latest Federal Election Integrity Initiative Is Just Another Marketing Tactic." The Conversation, 29 August 2021. https://theconversation.com/facebooks-latest-federal-election-integrity-initiative-is-just-another-marketing-tactic-166849.

Archer, Keith. "The Failure of the New Democratic Party: Unions, Unionists and Politics in Canada." *Canadian Journal of Political Science* 18, 2 (1985): 353–66.

Blais, André. "Why Is There So Little Strategic Voting in Canadian Plurality Rule Elections?" *Political Studies* 50, 3 (2002): 445–54.

Bryden, Joan. "Unions Reject O'Toole's Worker-Friendly Pitch, Working to Prevent Conservative Win." *National Post,* 15 September 2021. https://nationalpost.com/news/politics/election-2021/unions-reject-otooles-worker-friendly-pitch-campaign-to-prevent-conservative-win.

Bryden, Joan, and Stephanie Levitz. "New Advocacy Group Launches Pre-Election Ad Campaign against O'Toole, Conservatives." Halifaxtoday. ca, 22 January 2021. https://halifax.citynews.ca/national-news/new-advocacy-group-launches-pre-election-ad-campaign-against-otoole-conservatives-3285019.

Cameron, John D. "Canadian Election 2021: Risk-Averse Charities, Civil Society Groups Must Show Up." The Conversation, 16 August 2021. https://theconversation.com/canadian-election-2021-risk-averse-charities-civil-society-groups-must-show-up-165424.

Cross, William, Jonathan Malloy, Tamara A. Small, and Laura B. Stephenson. *Fighting for Votes: Parties, the Media, and Voters in an Ontario Election.* Vancouver: UBC Press, 2015.

Daoust, Jean-François, and Damien Bol. "Polarization, Partisan Preferences and Strategic Voting." *Government and Opposition* 55, 4 (2020): 578–94.

Elections Canada. "New Requirements for Third Parties: Corporations, Unions, Groups and Individuals." N.d. https://www.elections.ca/content.aspx?section=pol&dir=thi&document=backgrounder&lang=e.

–. "Third Party Database." N.d. https://www.elections.ca/WPAPPS/WPR/EN/TP?referrer=PFP.

Fowler, Tim. "Coordinated Strategic Voting in the 2008 Federal Election." *American Review of Canadian Studies* 42, 1 (2012): 20–33.

Grosenick, Georgina C. "Opportunities Missed: Non-Profit Public Communication and Advocacy in Canada." In *Political Communication in Canada: Meet the Press and Tweet the Rest,* edited by Tamara A. Small, Alex Marland, and Thierry Giasson, 179–93. Vancouver: UBC Press, 2014.

Imagine Canada. "Everything You Need to Know about Canada's Charities and Nonprofits." N.d. https://www.imaginecanada.ca/en/360/sector-stats.

Jansen, Harold J., and Lisa Young. "Solidarity Forever? The NDP, Organized Labour, and the Changing Face of Party Finance in Canada." *Canadian Journal of Political Science* 42, 3 (2009): 657–78.

Laforest, Rachel. "Going Digital: Non-Profit Organizations in a Transformed Media Environment." In *Political Elites in Canada: Power and Influence in Instantaneous Times,* edited by Andrea Lawlor, Alex Marland, and Thierry Giasson, 243–60. Vancouver: UBC Press, 2018.

Lake Winnipeg Foundation. "Canada's Election: Lake Winnipeg Needs Immediate Attention." 2 September 2021. https://lakewinnipegfoundation.org/news/federalelection2021.

Lawlor, Andrea, and Erin Crandall. "Policy versus Practice: Third Party Behaviour in Canadian Elections." *Canadian Public Administration* 61, 2 (2018): 246–65.

McGrane, David. *The New NDP: Moderation, Modernization, and Political Marketing.* Vancouver: UBC Press, 2019.

McIntosh, Emma. "What You Need to Know about Third-Party Groups in the 2021 Election." *Canada's National Observer,* 26 August 2021. https://www.nationalobserver.com/2021/08/26/explainer/what-you-need-know-third-party-groups-2021-election.

Osman, Laura. "Shore Up Charities to Accomplish Platform Goals: Advocacy Group to Political Parties." CTV News, 17 September 2021. https://www.ctvnews.ca/politics/federal-election-2021/shore-up-charities-to-accomplish-platform-goals-advocacy-group-to-political-parties-1.5590041.

Paas-Lang, Christian. "How Interested Outsiders Use 'Third Party' Status to Promote Causes, Influence Election." CBC News, 30 August 2021. https://www.cbc.ca/news/politics/third-parties-election-federal-1.6137654.

Pilon, Dennis, Stephanie Ross, and Larry Savage. "Solidarity Revisited: Organized Labour and the New Democratic Party." *Canadian Political Science Review* 5, 1 (2011): 20–37.

Pross, A. Paul. "Barriers to Third-Party Advertising in Canadian Elections." *Canadian Public Administration* 56, 3 (2013): 491–505.

Public Service Alliance of Canada. "PSAC Members Name Their Top Election Issues." N.d. http://psacunion.ca/psac-members-name-their-top-election-issues.

–. "Your Rights on Social Media during an Election." N.d. http://psacunion.ca/your-rights-social-media-during-election.

Public Service Alliance of Canada–Atlantic. "PSAC Officially Endorses Michelle Neill for MP of Malpeque." News release, 2 September 2021. https://psacatlantic.ca/psac-officially-endorses-michelle-neill-for-mp-of-malpeque/.

Public Service Alliance of Canada–National Capital Region. "REVP Alex Silas Shares His Endorsement of Angella Macewen for Ottawa Centre." Facebook, 19 September 2021. https://www.facebook.com/PSACNCR/posts/4295433470505598.

Savage, Larry. "Contemporary Party-Union Relations in Canada." *Labor Studies Journal* 35, 1 (2010): 8–26.

–. "Organized Labour and the Politics of Strategic Voting." In *Rethinking the Politics of Labour in Canada,* edited by Stephanie Ross and Larry Savage, 75–87. Halifax and Winnipeg: Fernwood, 2012.

–. "Organized Labour and the Shifting Landscape of Local Politics in Ontario." *Studies in Political Economy* 93, 1 (2014): 107–26.

Savage, Larry, and Charles W. Smith. "Public Sector Unions and Electoral Politics in Canada." In *Public Sector Unions in the Age of Austerity,* edited by Stephanie Ross and Larry Savage, 46–56. Halifax and Winnipeg: Fernwood, 2013.

Walchuk, Bradley. "Changing Union-Party Relations in Canada: The Rise of the Working Families Coalition." *Labor Studies Journal* 35, 1 (2010): 27–50.

Warskett, Rosemary. "Federal Public Sector Unions in Times of Austerity." In *Public Sector Unions in the Age of Austerity,* edited by Stephanie Ross and Larry Savage, 126–38. Halifax and Winnipeg: Fernwood, 2013.

Zingel, Avery. "What Some Advocacy Groups Want from N.W.T.'s Next MP." CBC News, 17 September 2021. https://www.cbc.ca/news/canada/north/advocacy-groups-nwt-mp-1.6180234.

Conclusion

The Local Is Political ...
and (Still Mostly) Traditional

Thierry Giasson

Abstract   This conclusion reflects on how the COVID-19 pandemic affected the federal campaign in 2021 and how some of the adaptations that it imposed on local campaigns might become permanent in upcoming electoral cycles. It also highlights two common themes of local campaigning emanating from the different chapters of this book. First, it discusses how local campaigns are sometimes at odds with the national strategy and the demands that it imposes on constituency campaigning. Second, it reflects on the importance that traditional groundwork operations – such as door knocking, signage, and leafleting – still occupy in local campaigning.

Résumé   Cette conclusion revient d'abord sur les divers impacts de la pandémie de COVID-19 sur la campagne fédérale de 2021 et révèle comment certains d'entre eux pourraient s'institutionnaliser au cours des prochains cycles électoraux. Elle met également en lumière deux thèmes récurrents émanant des chapitres de l'ouvrage. Premièrement, elle montre que les actions menées au sein des campagnes dans les circonscriptions électorales entrent parfois en conflit avec la stratégie nationale des partis politiques. Enfin, elle rappelle le rôle central que revêtent encore dans les campagnes locales les opérations de terrain plus traditionnelles comme le pointage, l'affichage électoral et la distribution de matériel de campagne.

IN HIS BOOK *Winning Power,* Canadian political scientist and former Conservative strategist Tom Flanagan reminds readers that campaigns depend on specific resources in order to be successful.[1] The nature and role of these resources in winning power have evolved over time, following transformations in communication technologies and the adoption of a permanent campaigning ethos by Canadian political parties. However, the capacity of any campaign, national or local, to win a hotly contested race has always depended on a core number of electoral resources: funding, volunteers, data, and message discipline.

To win power, Canadian federal parties have to form a "minimum winning coalition" of about 40 percent of voters.[2] According to Flanagan, this coalition is achieved by allocating party resources wisely and efficiently. Efficiency is attained by adopting a triage process of electoral ridings based upon a party's probability of winning them. The lower the margin of a loss in a previous election, the higher the probability of making a gain in the riding in a forthcoming contest. Flanagan establishes a "Rule of Ten" in which parties would invest electoral resources in ridings where they had lost or won the previous elections by less than 10 percent of ballots cast. The ridings that fell within this margin would be considered battlegrounds in which to invest massively during the campaign. Money, experienced campaign managers, volunteers, canvassing data, and star candidates would be directed to these ridings to increase the probability of winning them. Less "desirable" ridings would get less attention from the national campaign because they would be considered strongholds of the party or strongholds of its opponents. The outcomes of elections in those ridings could be determined easily, so investments of costly electoral resources in them would not be efficient. Flanagan states that the guiding strategic principle in any campaign should be to concentrate resources where potential gains are the highest.[3]

This triage, or geographical targeting, of ridings establishes that constituencies are not considered equally by Canadian electoral strategists. Some are more desirable than others because they have a better chance of generating a win for a party. This rule of electability has been followed for decades by Canadian federal parties.

What Flanagan tells us, however, is that the tools and information that strategists use to establish winnable ridings have evolved considerably and made the process much more precise and therefore more efficient.

What was once done by party organizations using local folk knowledge, political intuition, or aggregated polling information is now done using granular geospatial information about voters collected during local canvassing operations that is then analyzed through algorithmic and psychometric studies. The minimum winning coalition of voters is established at the polling station level and sometimes even at the individual elector level. The more refined the data and their analysis, the more efficient a campaign can be.

As Marland presents in the introduction to this book, the quality of local campaigning, aimed at bringing voters to the polls on election day, can be the determining factor of success for a party in forming the government. The national campaign of a party leader is the driving force, the locomotive, of a party's strategy to win. It brings the party its national media exposure, and it frames its core electoral messages, promises, and policy engagements on national issues. Looking at the federal election of 2019 as a case study, our prior edited collection *Inside the Campaign: Managing Elections in Canada*[4] exposed how national campaigns are implemented by parties. It revealed a high level of centralization in decision making as the campaign runs its course. The local campaign in each riding operates as the link between the national campaign and individual electors. It is through their contact with local campaigning that electors are reminded that the election is on its way and that their votes are important. However, very little is known about how local campaigns are run, their key players, their tasks, and the processes that they follow in order to win seats for their respective parties.

Marland also reminds us in the introduction that academic knowledge of local campaigning is somewhat sparse in Canada. Most contributions on Canadian campaigning and electioneering, such as *Winning Power* or *Inside the Campaign,* focus on national electoral organization and strategy. Understanding how campaigns are run locally at the riding level is therefore less detailed in

Canadian political science. Some notable exceptions are the works of R.K. Carty, Munroe Eagles, Royce Koop, and Anthony Sayers.[5] However, it has been over a decade since the publication of the last of these volumes, and the country's political and communication environments have evolved considerably since 2011. The more recent contribution of Kaija Belfry Munroe and H.D. Munroe[6] has updated our knowledge of how local electoral district associations (EDAs) use data provided by national parties to inform their campaign operations. A significant portion of previous research on local campaigning focuses on the impacts of local candidates or incumbents on voting decisions.[7] However, scholars disagree about the extent of these impacts. In hotly contested local campaigns, in which candidates are neck and neck in support, even a limited impact can determine a win in a targeted riding.

Inside the Local Campaign aims to provide an updated look at the many trends revealed by previous works on local campaigning in Canada. It looks at how local campaigns function and at how they connect to the national campaign. Its chapters answer one simple question. How is local work carried out during a Canadian election campaign? Building upon two previous experiences of analyzing federal elections (2015 and 2019), we brought together an array of contributors to write about all aspects of constituency campaigning. Using the federal election in 2021 as their case study, the authors generated original and innovative insights into lesser-known practices such as candidate nomination, campaign management, canvassing operations, data management, signage, local debates, and candidate ambition. However, because of numerous restrictions imposed by the COVID-19 pandemic, the election of 2021 was not exactly a typical one to investigate. The pandemic brought challenges that local campaigns had to address in order to win.

Campaigning in the Time of COVID-19

Launched on 15 August 2021, the forty-fourth Canadian general election was held as the country was entering its fourth wave of COVID-19. Liberal Prime Minister Justin Trudeau justified his decision to call the election by saying that it offered Canadians an opportunity to choose which direction they wanted the country to go after the pandemic. The pandemic was therefore framed as the key theme of the election and forced all parties to engage with the issue. It also forced parties to adapt their campaign logics and practices to an uncertain, polarized, anxious, and ever-evolving social context. Some of these adaptations might remain as new campaigning staples in future election cycles.

The chapters in this collection document that the pandemic brought challenges to each aspect of the local campaign. From candidate nomination processes to canvassing operations and debate organization, every component of riding electioneering was affected, and sometimes compromised, by public health restrictions. In most provinces, public health managers established strict, and often different, guidelines for social distancing and public gatherings that the parties had to observe in each context. Therefore, the rules of engagement differed locally from one province to the next. Elections Canada also modified its practices to ensure the safety of election workers and voters. These challenges certainly complicated campaigning efforts, but as the saying goes "necessity is the mother of invention." Therefore, the pandemic context also fostered ingenuity and innovation in local campaigns.

Since the election was held in the last weeks of the summer, in mostly sunny and warm weather, partisan meetings, leaders' tour stops, and policy announcements were commonly held outside to respect safety guidelines regarding public gatherings. Outdoors, candidates and citizens could remove their masks and approach each other while respecting social distancing measures. Justin Trudeau's campaign, however, was criticized for not following social distancing when the prime minister shook hands or posed for selfies with electors during some local stops.[8] Volunteers and candidates kept canvassing in person, knocking on doors, and maintaining a distance from electors who, having suffered from limited social interactions in the past months, often happily engaged in conversations on their doorsteps. Candidates and volunteers wore buttons and pins indicating that they had been fully vaccinated in order to appease COVID-19 anxiety in electors and facilitate contact with them. Local debates were held using videoconferencing applications, which often allowed for more electors to attend the events. And some campaign events were held entirely online, such as those organized by the Conservative Party campaign in an Ottawa hotel ballroom.[9]

On the flip side, the pandemic also created complications and headaches for local campaigners. Ever since COVID-19 was declared a pandemic by the World Health Organization in March 2020, public management of the virus was criticized by vocal groups. Mandatory social distancing and face-covering guidelines as well as mass-confinement cycles were depicted by some as authoritarian manoeuvring that limited personal freedoms. The advent of vaccines and the implementation of mass-vaccination campaigns in early 2021 added new anti-vaccination critics to this group of angry Canadians. How provincial and federal governments managed the health crisis became a polarizing political issue. In his first televised debate of the campaign on the French-language network TVA, Trudeau surprised pundits by adopting a pointed position against non-vaccinated Canadians, whom he referred to as irresponsible citizens who compromised the country's recovery efforts by their refusal to get a COVID-19 vaccine. Accusations were also directed at the Conservatives, who refused to confirm whether all of their candidates were fully vaccinated.

Citizens quickly joined this polarized debate. The election campaign became a new turf on which skeptical Canadians decided to wage their ideological war against the political elite. Their anger was met with considerable popular malaise about the early snap election called by the prime minister less than two years into his mandate. This decision was criticized by opposition leaders and pundits alike as a base political way for the Liberals to gain a majority of seats in Parliament. The timing of elections has made headlines in the past, yet the Trudeau campaign proved to be incapable of shaking off the issue in 2021. The disapproval among many Canadians of the election call was sustained throughout the campaign. It was significant and dominated much of the campaign discourse and showed up in public opinion polls.[10] The prime minister's tour became a target of anti-vaccination demonstrators. Trudeau was welcomed in certain ridings by angry mobs of protesters who shouted violent slurs, waved placards, and even threw projectiles at him. Security had to be tightened for his tour events, and some campaign activities in key ridings had to be cancelled. Such public displays of anger and discontent directed at politicians had not been witnessed in recent Canadian elections. At the other end of the spectrum, Maxime Bernier, leader of the People's Party of Canada, connected with this angry electorate by presenting a populist and libertarian discourse advocating the end of lockdowns and mandatory vaccinations to large partisan crowds across Canada, often not respecting provincial COVID-19 guidelines.[11] Surprisingly, his party finished in fourth place nationally with 4.9 percent of the popular vote, an increase of 3.3 percent from the election in 2019. The party's rise in support reached nearly 8 percent of the vote in Manitoba, Alberta, and British Columbia. This represents a surge in support for the People's Party from its modest results in 2019 and indicates that a significant segment of dissatisfied voters found an outlet to express their discontent with the political system and its elite. In just two years, Bernier's populist anti-system discourse found traction within the Canadian electorate.

The pandemic also imposed logistical challenges for local organizers. As Garnett's chapter on Elections Canada attests, the organization had much difficulty securing venues for election day. Usual voting spots such as community centres or schools were not available because of the social distancing regulations. Elections Canada was also faced with a shortage of labour, with its usual number of trained employees dwindling as they became less interested in joining the workforce for the election because of anxiety about COVID-19. As a result, electors in large urban ridings in Montreal, Vancouver, and Toronto waited in long queues to vote, in some instances past the closing time of polls. The pandemic also led many Canadians to use special mail-in ballots to vote. Data from Elections Canada indicate that 1.2 million special ballot kits were sent to Canadians and that 1.078 million kits were returned,[12] out of the 16.9 million votes counted in 2021. This represents by far the largest number of special ballots used to vote in any Canadian federal election. The high number of special ballots slowed down the vote-counting process and delayed election results in some ridings.

As the country struggles with anti-vaccination movements and growing resistance to sanitary measures, Canadians might have to live with COVID-19 for many more years. The changes imposed on campaigning at all levels by the pandemic may therefore establish themselves as the new normal in campaign operations. Since the election results in 2021 brought another Liberal minority government to power, a second "pandemic election" is possible and would test the durability of the Liberal-NDP supply-and-confidence agreement struck in 2022. Masks, elbow pumps, and Plexiglas dividers – not to mention conspiracy theorists and anti-elite populists – might become the inevitable challenges with which future local campaigns will have to negotiate.

The Politics of Local Campaigning

The goal of *Inside the Local Campaign* is to reveal how Canadian federal parties implement their electoral strategies locally. With very few Canadians being members of political parties, interest in politics being rather low, and partisan flexibility characterizing a considerable portion of the electorate,[13] the local campaign becomes invested with the important task of acting as the contact point between parties and citizens. Local campaigns, candidates, and volunteers are the engines that rev up electors' attention, identify supports throughout the riding, introduce key party policy engagements, and bring citizens to polling stations. National polls indicated throughout the campaigns in 2019 and 2021 that voting intentions were extremely close between Liberals and Conservatives. In this context, every vote counted, especially in the few targeted ridings where local support seemed to be evenly split between two or three parties. The national campaign would be won in these key battleground ridings.

Flanagan and others[14] have stressed the importance of resources to generate winning campaigns. These resources are sparse and allocated to local ridings efficiently if unfairly. Candidates running in their party's strongholds and those campaigning in opponents' strongholds get limited access to resources. They campaign with less money, fewer volunteers, and fewer messaging tools. Electoral resources are sent primarily to hotly contested battlegrounds where campaign efforts on the ground make a difference. These strategic political decisions can affect the relationship between national and local campaigns. This concentration of resources in targeted winnable constituencies can cause tensions.

R.K. Carty's research presents party organization and campaigning in Canada as a franchise model in which the national party acts as the central decision-making headquarters and EDAs are tasked with implementing in each riding the strategic master plan designed for them by central command. Adding some local flavour and colour is allowed, but communication and messaging in a constituency usually follow strict guidelines imposed by the national campaign. However, as some chapters of this book indicate, this distribution of responsibilities also creates tension points between local campaigns and the national party war room. The account is one of antagonism between local organizations and federal parties' command centres. Hence, the local campaign is intrinsically political and implies constant negotiation.

Three key areas seem to cause the most political tension in local campaigns. The first is the candidate nomination process. Chapters by Wagner, Esselment and Bondy, de Clercy, and Lewis attest that the most contentious political aspect of the local campaign is determining who will stand for the party. As Esselment and Bondy indicate, most federal parties delegate the nomination process to an EDA's members. However, prior to having the right to run for a party nomination, all potential candidates must be vetted by the party, not the EDA. This vetting process represents an opportunity for central command to put aside suspicious, difficult, or potentially harmful candidates. The timing of a snap election call also provides central party authority with the opportunity to bypass the nomination process altogether and impose candidates on EDAs. In some instances, parties also impose star candidates on EDAs or protect incumbents from a contested nomination process by rejecting applications from opposing candidates.

But this is not always the case. As de Clercy depicts in her chapter, some star candidates, such as Arielle Kayabaga in the riding of London West, have to withstand a contested nomination process to be selected as the party's candidate. Through invasive vetting protocols, parties scrutinize potential candidates' past social media posts, professional backgrounds, criminal records, and personal relations to ensure that a selected candidate will positively represent the party brand and not harm the national campaign. Candidates are the local spokespersons for a party, and their selection is therefore a crucial political decision. The capacity of central command to bypass EDAs' decision making in the nomination process can therefore create a climate of suspicion or resentment among local organizers, candidates, and volunteers.

The second area of political tension relates to message discipline. If local candidates are the official spokespersons for a party brand in the ridings, then they are expected to relay and amplify the party's message in its purest form to electors. Message discipline is a key principle in campaigning, both nationally and locally. Party engagements and policy platforms are developed based upon extensive research and intelligence prior to the election. They are crafted and selected to stimulate specific reactions in targeted segments of the electorate that the party knows it needs to mobilize to win the election. Therefore, as elements of the chapters written by Yates, Lalancette and Raynauld, and Crandall and Blois demonstrate, the national party position on an issue might be at odds with that of the local campaign. In looking at the campaign of the sole NDP MP in Quebec, incumbent Alexandre Boulerice, Yates states that an original campaign slogan and signs were developed for Quebec and that the Boulerice campaign in the Montreal riding of Rosemont was given significant leeway for communication on social media. Talking points from central command were often put aside in favour of a more negative style of campaigning that Boulerice preferred to use in his local communications. The NDP allowed him to steer away from the national script because he was a star candidate and a close adviser of party leader Jagmeet Singh. In the chapter that he wrote with Crandall, Blois, the incumbent Liberal MP for the Nova Scotia riding of Kings–Hants, also recounts an instance when his personal position regarding the local issue of the Windsor Causeway put him at odds with his party's official stance. Blois stood his ground and expressed his concern about the issue – a concern shared by many of his constituents. Both Blois and Boulerice were incumbents who won re-election, but their respective campaigns indicate how tensions in messaging or in defending a party position or brand can cause conflict between national and local organizations. Their relative defiance of central command campaign directives would probably be unlikely from a rookie candidate or non-incumbent.

Finally, a third and more novel area of political dissent between national and local campaigns is depicted in Belfry Munroe and Munroe's chapter on data collection and use in the riding of Charlottetown. Studies of recent electoral cycles in Canada have indicated that federal parties collected and analyzed large data sets of personal voter information to allocate resources better and to target messages efficiently to specific groups of electors during campaigns.[15] Parties are said to manage large databases to help inform their electoral decision making. In their previous analysis of local data campaigning in a BC riding, Belfry Munroe and Munroe found that data collection and analysis were conducted with varying degrees of professionalism among Canadian parties, which led them to question the real ability of these parties to undertake effective data-driven campaigning.[16] In their analysis of data use in three campaigns in Charlottetown in 2021, they provide new insights that further question the assertion that Canadian electioneering is largely data driven.

Their account indicates, rather, that some local organizers flatly refuse to collect personal data when canvassing, that others do not use data analysis provided to them by central command to inform their canvassing operations, and that some parties – the NDP in particular – impose access fees on local campaigns interested in using their central databases to better their operations. Data-driven campaigning has been presented in recent Canadian research as the new normal,[17] with every party and its local candidates and volunteers canvassing their ridings to identify support and prepare get-out-the-vote operations on election day. Prior research did not identify such apparent political conflict between local campaigns and central command on this issue. This chapter presents insights into how data-driven campaigning might be evolving in Canada, at least in smaller places where candidates and canvassers already know a lot about local electors.

Hence, telling the story of local campaigning in Canadian federal elections is telling the story of political conflict and its negotiation. Pressure points arise between the party's national command centre, which expects its political marketing goals to be achieved and the party's electoral communication and messaging amplified in every riding, and local organizations that might be faced with regional specificities putting them at odds with the national strategy or some partisan policy positions. In each instance, the conflict must be resolved quickly so as not to harm the leader's tour. National campaigns are heavily scripted, fine-tuned, and fast-paced exercises. Each stop of the leader's tour in a local riding is predetermined and expected to generate electoral gains there. Pressure points and political conflicts must therefore be ironed-out to allow the desired campaign to be implemented.

The Traditions of Local Campaigning

Despite an extensive body of research[18] stating that political organization and campaigning are hybrid endeavours carried out both online and offline, many chapters in this book make the case for the importance of traditional in-person groundwork in local campaigning in Canada. From placing electoral signs to door knocking and phone calling to reach voters and to taking part in local candidates' debates, traditional forms of campaigning are still key at the riding level.

In their chapter on campaign signs, Maurice and Small reveal that campaigns and their staff are annoyed at having to carry out this tradition of posting electoral placards and signs throughout the riding. Yet, even though the effectiveness of signs in generating voter support is disputed, campaigns keep posting them in public spaces to remind voters that the election is under way. The authors also highlight the useful content on the signs, such as riding and candidate names as well as the party slogan, usually the first revelation of the organization's communication strategy. Citizens' interest in politics is average in Canada,[19] and many of them need the visual reminders that campaign signs bring to their environments that an election is under way.

Canvassing, the ultimate traditional form of campaigning, is also a key feature of local contests. Robbins-Kanter's chapter on this central operation indicates that most of a local campaign's resources are dedicated to reaching out to voters. Canvassing, achieved through door-to-door knocking or phone calling, helps to monitor the level of support for a party and its candidate during the campaign. These operations, developed using precise data (including phone numbers and civic addresses of voters) and carried out by volunteers, are aimed at determining whether voters located in specific areas of the riding, where the race might be close, support the party's candidate or not. Looking at a variety of urban and rural ridings (including in Toronto, Montreal, Ottawa, and Labrador), Robbins-Kanter reveals that different canvassing approaches are used, often guided by the geography of the riding. Urban ridings with high population densities are not canvassed in the same way as rural ridings, where voters can be separated by hundreds of kilometres. Undecided electors will be followed more closely and be contacted numerous times during the campaign. Robbins-Kanter's interviews indicate that many local campaign managers primarily follow canvassing instructions provided by the national campaign, in which voter data analysis and geographical targeting are implemented. Finally, the interviews confirm previous research[20] indicating that volunteers collect voter information during canvassing that is fed directly into the party's databases to be used later to refine get-out-the-vote operations.

However, as mentioned, Belfry Munroe and Munroe's chapter tells a different story of local candidates and campaign managers in Charlottetown who resisted using data to coordinate their canvassing. Stating that they preferred to let the terrain guide them, they chose to knock on as many doors as possible in the riding to meet as many electors as they could. Canvassing is the purest form of personal political communication. It allows for real interaction between a campaign (through a volunteer or the candidate) and an elector. It is in this social encounter that persuasion can most actively manifest itself.

This potential for persuasion in direct, in-person campaigning explains why candidates still take part in local debates, why they join their teams of volunteers on street corners to wave to electors bright and early in the morning, why they hand out partisan leaflets at subway stations or grocery stores, and why, before COVID-19, they used to shake hands with citizens and held babies in their laps. Local campaigning is grounded in tradition and folk knowledge. Online technologies and social media strategies, such as the personalization tactics that Lalancette and Raynauld describe in their chapter, are also present in constituency campaigning. However, digital tools are used mostly to inform field operations, especially to get electors out to vote on election day. And sometimes there is strong resistance to digital and data-driven campaigning in certain local organizations.

Writing about the Local Campaign

Inside the Local Campaign offers novel and up-to-date reflections on how campaigns are run in Canadian federal ridings. Several chapters are collaborations between an academic and a practitioner. In our previous project, this unusual writing partnership caused friction in some cases. This time we let our academic contributors decide whether to team up with practitioners. These collaborative contributions are based upon direct accounts provided by the professional collaborators in interviews during and after the campaign in 2021. Some professionals are credited as co-authors, whereas others provided valuable insights on the condition of anonymity. In both cases, though, the collaborations provide analytical depth and local colour.

Other academics decided to go it alone, basing their research on original empirical data analyses. These chapters help us to understand better how different socio-economic and contextual factors condition candidacy ambition, how campaign staff are recruited and assigned to different tasks, which different canvassing strategies are adopted by parties to identify their supporters in the ridings, and how campaign managers implement national strategies locally.

This volume covers all aspects of local campaigning and provides direct insights from the five federal parties represented in the House of Commons.

As with *Inside the Campaign*, we wanted this new book to reach audiences quickly. An expedited process imposed two challenges. First, our contributors had to commit to turning in first drafts of their chapters two weeks after the election. This meant that those working with practitioners – including incumbent MPs, campaign directors, regional managers, candidates, or political reporters – had to secure final post-electoral interviews in the days following the vote. Despite having just finished a gruelling electoral sprint over thirty-nine days, the professional collaborators proved to be accessible. All contributors were therefore able to file their chapters in a timely manner. The two co-editors then reviewed each contribution and provided the authors with requests for editing. The revised drafts were submitted a few days later and assembled into a cohesive manuscript, including both an introduction and a conclusion.

Second, we had to ensure a quick external review. Based upon our prior project, UBC Press quickly secured three anonymous external evaluators tasked with swiftly reviewing the first complete draft of the book. They were in turn very responsive. The final manuscript was sent into production just a few months following the vote.

Bringing such an ambitious project to fruition is a collaborative effort. It reflects the cohesiveness and cooperative spirit of a vibrant community of Canadian politics and political communication scholars. It also highlights the understanding shared by members of this community that local campaigning is an understudied and poorly understood component of politics in our country. Some important work had been produced in past decades about constituency campaigning, but it was clear to all contributors – academics and political practitioners alike – that an update was long overdue. In the past decade, technological tools, communication strategies, and campaign practices evolved. New political issues – such as the climate change crisis, identity politics, and anti-elite sentiment –

have become prevalent in Canadian politics. And since 2020 the COVID-19 pandemic has forced innovations in political campaigning, both locally and nationally.

Inside the Local Campaign helps make sense of these recent transformations and trends in federal politics. Building upon the work of Carty, Koop, Sayers, and a few others, it reveals the ongoing political tensions and pressure points that exist between the centralizing force of national campaigning and the idiosyncratic nature of local campaigning in federal ridings. This paradoxical push-and-pull nature defines what it means to campaign locally in Canada.

Notes

1   Flanagan, *Winning Power.*
2   Ibid., 71.
3   Ibid., 73.
4   Marland and Giasson, *Inside the Campaign.*
5   Carty, *Canadian Political Parties in the Constituencies;* Carty and Eagles, *Politics Is Local;* Koop, *Grassroots Liberals;* Sayers, *Parties, Candidates, and Constituency Campaigns.*
6   Belfry Munroe and Munroe, "Constituency Campaigning in the Age of Data."
7   See, for instance, Blais et al., "Does the Local Candidate Matter?"; Roy and Alcantara, "The Candidate Effect"; and Stevens et al., "Local Candidate Effects in Canadian Elections."
8   Tasker, "O'Toole Attacks Trudeau."
9   Thibedeau, "Conservatives Say 'Virtual' Campaign Is Paying Off."
10 Schere and Ljunggren, "Canada's Trudeau Sought an Election"; Austin, "Trudeau Seeks a Fresh Start."
11 Pauls and Liewicki, "People's Party Leader Maxime Bernier."
12 Elections Canada, "Data on Special Voting Kits."
13 Gidengil, "The Diversity of the Canadian Political Marketplace."
14 Flanagan, *Winning Power;* Cross, "The Importance of Local Party Activity"; Bernier, *Gérer la victoire.*
15 See, for instance, Giasson, Le Bars, and Dubois, "Is Social Media Transforming Canadian Electioneering?"; Giasson and Small, "Online All the Time"; Patten, "Databases, Microtargeting, and the Permanent Campaign"; and Delacourt, *Shopping for Votes.*

16 Belfry Munroe and Munroe, "Constituency Campaigning in the Age of Data."

17 See, for instance, Flanagan, *Winning Power;* Giasson and Small, "Online All the Time"; Patten, "Databases, Microtargeting, and the Permanent Campaign"; and Delacourt, *Shopping for Votes.*

18 See, for instance, Giasson, Le Bars, and Dubois, "Is Social Media Transforming Canadian Electioneering?"; Marland and Mathews, "'Friend, Can You Chip in $3?'"; Kreiss, *Prototype Politics;* Flanagan, *Winning Power;* Chadwick, *The Hybrid Media System;* Gibson, "Party Change, Social Media"; and Vaccari, "Technology Is a Commodity."

19 Gidengil, "The Diversity of the Canadian Political Marketplace," 41–42.

20 See, for instance, Belfry Munroe and Munroe, "Constituency Campaigning in the Age of Data"; Patten, "Databases, Microtargeting, and the Permanent Campaign"; and Delacourt, *Shopping for Votes.*

Bibliography

Austin, Ian. "Trudeau Seeks a Fresh Start but Many Voters See a Power Grab." *New York Times,* 18 September 2021. https://www.nytimes.com/2021/09/18/world/canada/justin-trudeau-snap-election.html.

Belfry Munroe, Kaija, and H.D. Munroe. "Constituency Campaigning in the Age of Data." *Canadian Journal of Political Science* 51, 1 (2018): 135–54.

Bernier, Robert. *Gérer la victoire: Organisation, communication, stratégie.* Montréal: Gaëtan Morin, 1991.

Blais, André, Elisabeth Gidengil, Agnieszka Dobrzynska, Neil Nevitte, and Richard Nadeau. "Does the Local Candidate Matter? Candidate Effects in the Canadian Election of 2000." *Canadian Journal of Political Science* 36, 3 (2003): 657–64.

Carty, R.K. *Canadian Political Parties in the Constituencies.* Toronto: Dundurn Press, 1991.

Carty, R.K., and Munroe Eagles. *Politics Is Local: National Politics at the Grassroots.* Oxford: Oxford University Press, 2005.

Chadwick, Andrew. *The Hybrid Media System: Politics and Power.* Oxford: Oxford University Press, 2013.

Cross, William. "The Importance of Local Party Activity in Understanding Canadian Politics: Winning from the Ground Up in the 2015 Federal Election: Presidential Address to the Canadian Political Science Association Calgary, 31 May 2016." *Canadian Journal of Political Science* 49, 4 (2016): 601–20.

Delacourt, Susan. *Shopping for Votes: How Politicians Choose Us and We Choose Them.* Toronto: Douglas and McIntyre, 2016.

Elections Canada. "Data on Special Ballot Voting Kits: 44th General Election – September 20, 2021." https://www.elections.ca/content.aspx? section=ele&dir=pas/44ge/vbm&document=index&lang=e.

Flanagan, Tom. *Winning Power: Canadian Campaigning in the Twenty-First Century.* Montreal and Kingston: McGill-Queen's University Press, 2014.

Giasson, Thierry, Gildas Le Bars, and Philippe Dubois. "Is Social Media Transforming Canadian Electioneering? Hybridity and Online Partisan Strategies in the 2012 Quebec Election." *Canadian Journal of Political Science* 52, 2 (2019): 323–41.

Giasson, Thierry, and Tamara A. Small. "Online All the Time: The Strategic Objectives of Canadian Opposition Parties." In *Permanent Campaigning in Canada,* edited by Alex Marland, Thierry Giasson, and Anna Lennox Esselment, 109–26. Vancouver: UBC Press, 2017.

Gibson, Rachel K. "Party Change, Social Media and the Rise of 'Citizen-Initiated' Campaigning." *Party Politics* 30 (2013): 1–15.

Gidengil, Elisabeth. "The Diversity of the Canadian Political Marketplace." In *Political Marketing in Canada,* edited by Alex Marland, Thierry Giasson, and Jennifer Lees-Marshment, 39–56. Vancouver: UBC Press, 2012.

Koop, Royce. *Grassroots Liberals: Organizing for Local and National Politics.* Vancouver: UBC Press, 2011.

Kreiss, Daniel. *Prototype Politics: Technology-Intensive Campaigning and the Data of Democracy.* Oxford: Oxford University Press, 2016.

Marland, Alex, and Thierry Giasson, eds. *Inside the Campaign: Managing Elections in Canada.* Vancouver: UBC Press, 2020.

Marland, Alex, and Maria Mathews. "'Friend, Can You Chip in $3?': Canadian Political Parties Email Communication and Fundraising." In *Permanent Campaigning in Canada,* edited by Alex Marland, Thierry Giasson, and Anna Lennox Esselment, 87–108. Vancouver: UBC Press, 2017.

Patten, Steven. "Databases, Microtargeting, and the Permanent Campaign: A Threat to Democracy?" In *Permanent Campaigning in Canada,* edited by Alex Marland, Thierry Giasson, and Anna Lennox Esselment, 47–64. Vancouver: UBC Press, 2017.

Pauls, Karen, and Nathan Liewicki. "People's Party Leader Maxime Bernier Attends 3 Manitoba Rallies, Doesn't Quarantine upon Entering Province." CBC News, 6 September 2021. https://www.cbc.ca/news/canada/manitoba/maxime-bernier-rally-1.6166298.

Roy, Jason, and Christopher Alcantara. "The Candidate Effect: Does the Local Candidate Matter?" *Journal of Elections, Public Opinion and Parties* 25, 2 (2014): 195–214.

Sayers, Anthony. *Parties, Candidates, and Constituency Campaigns in Canadian Elections*. Vancouver: UBC Press, 1999.

Schere, Steve, and David Ljunggren. "Canada's Trudeau Sought an Election He Risks Losing with Only a Week to Go." Reuters, 14 September 2021. https://www.reuters.com/world/americas/canadas-trudeau-sought-an -election-he-risks-losing-with-only-week-go-2021-09-13/.

Stevens, Benjamin Allen, Md Mujahedul Islam, Roosmarijn de Geus, Jonah Goldberg, John R. McAndrews, Alex Mierke-Zatwarnicki, Peter John Loewen, and Daniel Rubenson. "Local Candidate Effects in Canadian Elections." *Canadian Journal of Political Science* 52 (2019): 83–96.

Tasker, John Paul. "O'Toole Attacks Trudeau for Holding a Large Campaign Event Indoors." CBC News, 15 September 2021. https://www.cbc.ca/news/politics/otoole-rips-trudeau-campaign-event-1.6176747.

Thibedeau, Hannah. "Conservatives Say Their 'Virtual' Campaign Strategy Is Paying Off Already." CBC News, 27 August 2021. https://www.cbc.ca/news/politics/otoole-conservative-election-virtual-campaign-town-hall -pandemic-1.6154822.

Vaccari, Cristian. "Technology Is a Commodity: The Internet in the 2008 United States Presidential Election." *Journal of Information Technology and Politics* 7, 4 (2010): 318–39.

Appendix
Constituency Campaign Photographs

Candidate Campaign Headquarters

Aside from being the nucleus for supporters and volunteers, a candidate's campaign headquarters acts as a publicity tool and is used to generate excitement about an election.

Liberal MP Kody Blois's campaign headquarters. Wolfville, Nova Scotia. | *Kristina Shannon*

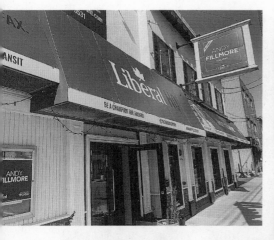

Liberal MP Andy Fillmore's campaign headquarters. Halifax, Nova Scotia. | *Alex Marland*

Liberal MP Anthony Rota's campaign headquarters. North Bay, Ontario. | *Dinty Garnett*

Candidate Websites

Each party's website features candidate biographies and may link to candidate websites, some of which use party-supplied templates.

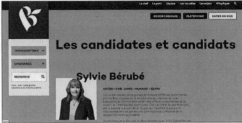

Campaign Signs

Campaign signs are the most visible indication that an election is under way. The use of party templates is common, but there are variances across Canada in how signs are displayed.

During concurrent elections for different levels of government, competition increases for sign real estate. St. John's, Newfoundland and Labrador. | *Alex Marland*

In some urban centres, campaign signs feature unofficial languages. Vancouver, British Columbia. | *Michael Marland*

In Quebec, campaign signs are routinely affixed to utility poles. Montreal, Quebec. | *Sean Grogan*

Sherbrooke, Quebec. | *Jacob Robbins-Kanter*

Signs become anchors for photos, as shown in these images from Liberal MP Kody Blois's re-election campaign. Clarksville and Elmsdale, Nova Scotia. | *Kristina Shannon*

Social Media

Candidates' use of social media includes posting photos showing participation in all-candidates' debates, reminding constituents to vote, and sharing photos of mingling in the community.

Liberal minister Mélanie Joly mingling with constituents. Montreal, Quebec. | *Mélanie Joly, via Twitter*

Conservative candidate Kailin Che posted photos of herself canvassing with supporters. Vancouver, British Columbia. | *Kailin Che, via Twitter*

Ministers' Tours

High-profile candidates whose re-election is reasonably assured often visit other electoral districts to give a boost to party candidates. The local candidates rally supporters and promote the visit on social media.

Toronto MP and Deputy Prime Minister Chrystia Freeland in Alberta with Liberal candidate Tanya Holm. Fort Saskatchewan, Alberta. | *Chrystia Freeland, via Instagram*

Minister Freeland in Newfoundland with Minister Seamus O'Regan and Liberal MP Churence Rogers. Clarenville, Newfoundland and Labrador. | *Seamus O'Regan, via Twitter*

Campaign Ephemera

Across the country, constituency campaign workers distribute pamphlets, postcards, and voting reminder cards.

People's Party, Bloc Québécois, and NDP pamphlets. Sherbrooke, Quebec. | *Jacob Robbins-Kanter*

Postcard distributed by the re-election campaign of Liberal MP Kody Blois. Kings–Hants, Nova Scotia. | *Office of MP Kody Blois*

"This is unacceptable."

–Kody Blois, M.P. for Kings–Hants

"I will fight for all stakeholders on this issue. Businesses like Ski Martock are threatened and local residents have been impacted and have suffered. As Member of Parliament I have stood up for our communities, and I will continue to make their voices heard while also supporting improved fish passage."

Kody Blois

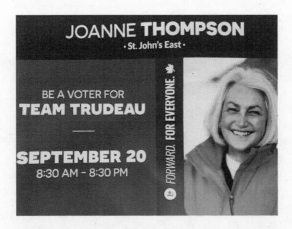

Liberal candidate Joanne Thompson's voting reminder card. St. John's, Newfoundland and Labrador. | *Alex Marland*

Pamphlets from the campaigns of Bloc Québécois candidate Nathalie Bresse and Conservative candidate Andrea Winters. Sherbrooke, Quebec. | *Jacob Robbins-Kanter*

The Pandemic Election

Some aspects of the 2021 federal election were unique to constituency campaigning in a pandemic.

Physical distancing was observed when NDP MP Alexandre Boulerice addressed crowds of supporters and held news conferences. Montreal, Quebec. | *Jean-Philippe Sansfaçon*

Conservative Party badge. | *Anonymous staffer*

In some areas of Canada, physical distancing requirements resulted in outdoor lineups to vote. Kingston, Ontario. | *Madison MacGregor*

NDP MP Alexandre Boulerice, wearing a facemask, takes part in the Marche de la Fierté. Montreal, Quebec. | *Jean-Philippe Sansfaçon*

Contributors

KAIJA BELFRY MUNROE is a principal and co-founder of Politikos Research, a social science research and analysis firm. Her academic expertise is in Canadian politics and public policy.

KODY BLOIS is a Canadian Member of Parliament who represents the riding of Kings–Hants. He was elected in the federal elections of 2019 and 2021 as a member of the Liberal Party. He has an educational background in commerce, law, and public administration.

MATTHEW BONDY is an executive leader in Canada's tech sector. He is a frequent commentator on public policy and national security and has vied for the federal nomination in the riding of Kitchener–Conestoga.

COLETTE BRIN is a professor of journalism at Université Laval, the director of Centre d'études sur les médias, and the chairperson of Canada's Independent Advisory Board on Eligibility for Journalism Tax Measures. She coordinates the Canadian edition of the *Digital News Report* and co-edited *Journalism in Crisis* (University of Toronto Press, 2016).

THOMAS COLLOMBAT is an associate professor of political science and the chair of the Department of Social Sciences at Université du Québec en Outaouais. His research focuses on the socio-political role of the labour movement, both in Canada and in Latin America.

FRANÇOIS CORMIER is the news director at FM93 radio in Quebec City, formerly the assignment editor with TVA Nouvelles Québec.

ERIN CRANDALL is an associate professor in the Department of Politics at Acadia University. Her research focuses on Canadian politics, law, and election policy. She has published articles in the *Canadian Journal of Political Science, Canadian Public Administration,* and *Canadian Journal of Law and Society,* among others.

CRISTINE DE CLERCY is an associate professor of political science at Western University. She studies political leadership, Canadian politics, and comparative politics. She is a regular media commentator on issues in Canadian and Ontario politics.

BROOKS DECILLIA reported and produced news at CBC for two decades. These days, he's an assistant professor at Mount Royal University's School of Communication Studies.

MYRIAM DESCARREAUX is an assistant assignment editor with TVA Nouvelles Québec.

ANNA LENNOX ESSELMENT is an associate professor in the Department of Political Science at the University of Waterloo. Her research interests include elections and campaigns, political parties, and political marketing.

HOLLY ANN GARNETT is an associate professor of political science at the Royal Military College of Canada in Kingston. She is cross-appointed faculty at Queen's University (Canada) and an honorary research fellow at the University of East Anglia (United Kingdom). She is co-director of the Electoral Integrity Project.

THIERRY GIASSON is a professor in and the chair of the Department of Political Science at Université Laval. He is the director of the Groupe de recherche en communication politique. His research focuses on political journalism, online technologies, and political marketing. He is the co-editor, with Alex Marland, of the series Communication, Strategy, and Politics from UBC Press.

ROYCE KOOP is a professor of political studies at the University of Manitoba. He researches representation and political parties in Canada and other developed democracies.

MIREILLE LALANCETTE is a professor of political communication at Université du Québec à Trois-Rivières. She has published research on the mediatized images of politicians and the uses of social media by citizens, grassroots organizations, and political actors.

J.P. LEWIS is an associate professor in the Department of History and Politics at the University of New Brunswick (Saint John). His work on cabinet government has appeared in *Governance, Canadian Journal of Political Science,* and *Canadian Public Administration.*

RICHARD MAKSYMETZ is the principal of ALAR Strategy and a veteran political adviser. He has worked in almost all federal ridings in western and northern Canada, and was a national field director for the Liberal Party of Canada in 2015.

ALEX MARLAND is a professor in and the head of the Department of Political Science at Memorial University. He is the author of *Brand Command: Canadian Politics and Democracy in the Age of Message Control* (UBC Press, 2016) and *Whipped: Party Discipline in Canada* (UBC Press, 2020).

GILLIAN MAURICE is a PhD candidate in the Department of Psychology, University of Guelph. She undertakes research in applied social psychology, with a focus on group influence on environmentally responsible behaviour. She is a long-time volunteer political campaigner, with primarily local campaign experience.

H.D. MUNROE is a principal and co-founder of Politikos Research, a social science research and analysis firm. His academic expertise is in international politics and strategic studies.

ANTHONY OZORAI was the social media and publicity campaign manager for Martin Francoeur, the Liberal Party candidate in 2021 in Trois-Rivières.

VINCENT RAYNAULD is an associate professor in the Department of Communication Studies at Emerson College and an affiliated professor in the Département de lettres et communication sociale at Université du Québec à Trois-Rivières.

JACOB ROBBINS-KANTER is an assistant professor in the Department of Politics and International Studies at Bishop's University. His research examines Canadian party politics, political communication, and representation.

ANTHONY M. SAYERS teaches in the Department of Political Science at the University of Calgary and has published widely on political representation and federalism.

TAMARA A. SMALL is a professor in the Department of Political Science at the University of Guelph. In addition to conducting research on digital campaigning in the past seven Canadian federal elections, she has published work on political memes and on the regulatory framework for digital technologies in elections in Canada. She is the co-editor of *Digital Politics in Canada: Promises and Realities* (University of Toronto Press, 2020).

ANGELIA WAGNER is an instructor at the University of Alberta. Her research areas are Canadian politics, gender and politics, political communication, and political representation. Wagner is a former journalist, having worked for newspapers in Alberta and Saskatchewan.

JARED WESLEY is a professor of political science at the University of Alberta. He researches the links between elections and community values. He is the author of *Code Politics: Campaigns and Cultures on the Canadian Prairies* (UBC Press, 2011).

PAUL WILSON is an associate professor in the Clayton H. Riddell Graduate Program in Political Management at Carleton University. Formerly the director of policy in the Prime Minister's Office under Prime Minister Stephen Harper, he focuses his research on ministerial and parliamentary political staffers.

STÉPHANIE YATES is a professor of communication at Université du Québec à Montréal. She works on lobbying, public participation, and social acceptability and is the editor of *Introduction aux relations publiques: Fondements, enjeux et pratiques* (Presses de l'Université du Québec, 2018).

Index

Note: (f) after a page number indicates a figure.

74; as brand ambassadors, 9; and campaign managers, 192–93, 200–2; campaign teams as concentric circles surrounding, 192; candidate-only campaign, 254; canvassing, 200, 201–2, 240, 256–57; data collection by, 257; dissent from party issues, 296; diversity of, 21, 80; door-to-door canvassing, 215, 258–59; "ethos," 150; factors mattering most, 7; focus on, vs. data-driven campaigning, 256–57; as franchisees, 25; full slate, 176; interaction with voters, 201; and knowledge of voters' preferences, 257; and local vs. national issues, 292, 300; media appearances, 240; mistakes, 176, 201; and national vs. local issues, 291; outstanding, 15; party loyalty, 292; and polls/news stories, 200–1; PSAC endorsements, 373–74; quality, and image of party, 176; socializing by, 200; strengths vs. struggles, 201–2; third parties and, 363, 364, 365; time off, 202; turnover, 130, 131; and voter identification, 257. *See also* incumbent candidates; star candidates

canvassing, 227, 241, 393; app-based, 236–37, 241; cabinet ministers and, 121; campaign leaflets in, 227; campaign managers and, 215; candidates and, 200, 201–2, 230, 240, 256–57, 258–59; central/federal parties and, 229, 230–31, 232–34; and close races, 228; COVID-19 and, 18–19, 196, 212, 233, 255, 385; and data collection, 11–12, 219, 228, 255, 332, 391; digital technologies and, 195–96; between election periods, 237; and electoral success, 228; geography and, 231–33, 238, 240; goals, 231; GOTV, 219, 220–22; Green Party and, 258; importance of, 227–28, 240; independent service providers and, 195; and in-person campaigning, 393; "leapfrogging," 219; local knowledge vs. data-driven, 258–59; local party support, 229–30; local support of municipal figures for, 121; marginal seat targeting, 233–34; ministerial incumbents and, 138; party leaders and, 121; permanent campaigning and, 237; polling firms and, 195; PSAC and, 374; in public places, 232; reduction in relevance, 4; resources for, 227, 230, 237–39, 240–41; in rural ridings, 232, 241, 393; shorter campaign periods and, 238–39; and signs, 353, 354, 357; social media in, 236, 241; in stronghold vs. uncompetitive ridings, 229–30; targets, 203; in urban ridings, 232, 393; voter data errors and, 237; and voter engagement/mobilization, 228; and voter identification, 219–20, 332; and voter information collection, 228, 393. *See also* door-to-door canvassing; telephone canvassing

Cavallaro, Frank, 114
celebrity politicians, 110, 112
Cerasuolo, Lisa, 293
Chagger, Bardish, 132

Chahal, George, 184–85, 233

Champagne, François-Philippe, 155, 159

Chang, Michael, 78

Che, Kailin, 406(f)

chief electoral officer (CEO), 46, 47, 56

Chrétien, Jean, 268

Christian Heritage Party, 336

close races: canvassing and, 228; debates and, 334–35; limited impacts and, 384; local campaigning and, 7, 185–86, 286; local candidates and, 131; local debates and, 328, 338; and minority vs. majority government, 8; PSAC and, 371, 374; regional campaign directors in, 175, 182–83, 185–86; resources and, 183; third parties and, 365, 376; unions and, 367

Coenraad, Melissa, 235, 236, 240

Coletto, David, 12

communications: cabinet ministers and, 131–33; campaign managers and, 215–16; centralization of, 130, 131, 135; directors, 215–16; local campaign teams and, 287; micro-targeting of, 248; ministerial incumbents and, 138; prime minister and, 131. *See also* messages/messaging

concentration of power: in party leaders, 174, 175; prime minister and, 130; Prime Minister's Office (PMO) and, 130, 135

Conservative Party: average donations to, 273; campaign managers, 192; campaign spending, 194; in Charlottetown, 253, 258–59; and COVID-19, 386; digital campaign-ing, 11; and "electoral urgency" candidate appointments, 91; funding transfers to local ridings, 269; fundraising, 271; local campaign volunteers, 214; and local debates, 334–35; marginal seat targeting, 234; and media, 315; national campaign office, 202; and national vs. Quebec platform, 290; nominations process, 90; PSAC and, 369, 370, 371, 372, 374; and Quebec partnership federalism, 290; riding vacancies, 92; star candidates in, 113, 114, 115, 122; unions and, 366; vetting process in, 94–97

constituencies. *See* ridings

contractors/specialists, 195, 196, 197–99

COVID-19: campaign managers and, 196; and canvassing, 18–19, 196, 219, 233, 255, 258, 385; and data use, 258; and debates, 328–29, 331, 385–86; disinformation regarding, 312; and electoral administration, 52; and federal election of 2021, 16–20, 44, 51–54, 56, 196; and fundraising, 271, 275–76; and GOTV, 19; and leaders' tours, 184–85; and local campaigns, 16–20, 211–12, 384–88; media and, 311, 313, 316; and online campaign activities, 17; polarization of public opinion regarding, 386–87; political parties and, 212, 385; and polling stations, 52–53, 56; protests against, 17–18, 311–12, 386–87; and recruitment of poll workers, 52; safety protocols/guidelines,

51–52; social media and, 19, 196, 235, 329–30; and timing of election, 120, 384–85, 386–87; unions and, 367–68

Cummings, James, 183

in participation, 328, 333–34; rookie politicians in, 337; in rural ridings, 335; security/safety concerns, 331; strategic advantages, 333; underdog candidates in, 335; US presidential, 327–28; video conferencing technology, 17; and vote choices, 326–27, 334–35, 338, 339

Deltorto-Russell, Bianca, 75–76

democracy: candidate diversity and, 67; citizen choice of representative and, 86; debates and, 26, 326, 327, 328, 329–30, 333, 339; local campaigns and, 9–10; local issues and, 286; local news media and, 309, 318; party unity and, 13; third parties and, 363

Le Devoir, 313

digital campaigning. *See* data-driven campaigning

digital media: in canvassing, 236–37, 241; legacy news organizations vs., 309; and local news production, 318; political parties and, 311; size of audience, 309; video, 74, 76, 77, 152, 317

digital technologies: campaign managers and, 191, 194–95, 204; and canvassing, 195–96; and centralization, 4; effect on local campaigns, 4–5; and quantitative research, 5; signs vs., 356

diversity: among candidates, 21, 80; and democracy, 67; in social characteristics, 66–67

door-to-door canvassing, 138, 214, 229; aides and, 215; campaign leaflets in, 233; candidates and, 215, 256–57, 258–59; COVID-19

and, 219, 255, 258; efficiency in, 217–18; on election day (e-day), 221; local debates vs., 328, 332, 333, 334; local knowledge vs. data in, 255; messages for distribution, 216; microtargeting vs., 258; ministerial incumbents and, 138; policy and, 217–18; telephone canvassing vs., 219–20, 229

Duhaime, Éric, 312

Easter, Wayne, 13

E-Canvasser, 250

election day (e-day): benefits for campaign workers on, 200; "bingo sheets," 221; campaign managers on, 200; campaign workers on, 220, 221–22; door knocking on, 221; GOTV and, 220, 221–22, 239; ministerial incumbents and, 140

election outcomes: canvassing and, 228; fundraising and, 270; nationwide campaigns and, 185; political marketing and, 185; signs and, 346–47; voter identification database management and, 185

elections, 6; administration, 44, 52; frequency, 213, 271, 276; management, 44–46; officials, 47. *See also* ballots; close races; federal elections; provincial/territorial elections; snap elections; voters/voting

Elections Canada: and "bingo sheets," 221; "Campaign Guidance for Canvassing during COVID-19," 211–12; COVID-19 and, 385; election management,

45; low profile, 46; PSAC registration with, 369; role/responsibilities, 22, 44; on signs, 346; and third parties, 363, 375

electoral district associations (EDAs), 13–14, 178–79; candidate nominations committees (CNCs), 96–97; candidate recruitment by, 96; and candidate selection, 23, 100, 153; and fundraising, 270; in local nomination contests, 100; and national party data, 384; and nomination process, 389–90; nomination vetting, 95–97; regional campaign directors and, 177; responsibilities, 6

electoral districts. *See* ridings

Ellis, Neil, 182–83

email, 236, 371–72

environmental issues, 293–94, 298, 330

Erskine-Smith, Nathaniel, 237

Eves, Sarah, 349

Eylofson, Doug, 183

Fair Elections Act (2014), 46

federal election (1988), 363–64

federal election (2015): data-driven campaigning in, 247, 249; length of campaign, 202; media coverage, 308; microtargeting in, 252; PSAC and Conservative Party in, 369; social media and, 316

federal election (2019): COVID-19 and, 233; leaders' debates, 328; social media and, 316; vote gap between first- and second-place candidates, 209

federal election (2021): advocacy groups, 367–68; ballot errors, 55–56; canvassing during shorter campaign period, 238–39; COVID-19 and, 16–20, 44, 51–54, 56, 196; fundraising in, 271–72; as leader-centred campaign, 135; local news media coverage, 314–17; media coverage, 52; poorly performing national campaigns in, 203; racism and, 119–20; regional campaign directors in, 182–85, 186; social media coverage, 316; star candidates in, 113, 115–16; television coverage, 314–16; timing, 120, 384–85, 386–87; vote gap between first- and second-place candidates, 209

federal elections: central management of, 56; hybrid media coverage, 316; local issues in, 286; local news media and, 317, 318; localized elections within, 172, 286; media coverage in Quebec, vs. provincial elections, 308; national media setting campaign agenda, 314; overlapping provincial/territorial elections, 213; political parties setting campaign agenda, 314; post-Confederation, 172–73; provincial overlapping with, 272; turnover rate in, 131; unions and, 366–67

federal government/politics: candidate motivations for entering, 70, 71–72, 73; issues, 80; policy, 71–72

field liaison officers (FLOs), 49–50

Fillmore, Andy, 401(f)

Fonda, Jane, 15

Francoeur, Martin, 154–61, 156(f), 159(f), 160(f), 162–63

21, 191–92, 383–84; challenges, 197; changing attitudes toward, 4–5; COVID-19 and, 16–20, 384–88; and democracy, 9–10; in digital environment, 21; goals of, 194–95; in-person, 393–94; as link between national campaigns and electors, 383; as link between parties and people, 388; politics of, 388–92; resurgence, 6–12; traditions of, 392–94; trends, 12–16
local news media. *See under* media
local parties: candidate selection, 86–87; and canvassing, 229–30; fundraising and, 269; presidents, 14; responsibilities of, 86
Lortie Commission, 364

Mackie, Neil, 333, 335, 337–38
"mainstreeting," 218–19
marginal seats, 8, 178, 186, 233–34
Martin, Paul, Jr., 129–30
Mathyssen, Lindsey, 17
McCrimmon, Karen, 183
McKenna, Catherine, 121, 132
media, 26; candidate appearances in, 240; and celebrity politicians, 110; competition, 315–16; and debates, 333–34; election coverage, 52; evolution of, 308; and fate of ministerial incumbents on election night, 140; government funding, 311; and high- vs. low-profile candidates, 111; hybrid coverage of elections, 316; importance of traditional, 161; legacy organizations, 309–10; local news, 311–18; local vs. national, 15; meaning of "local," 309; meaning of "regional," 309;

and ministerial incumbents, 135; multimedia, 312–13; national, and local/regional issues, 310; national, setting federal election campaign agenda, 314; newspapers in Quebec City, 313; and party leaders, 6, 150; and personalization, 147, 148; political parties and, 315; on signs, 348–51; star candidates and, 110, 120–21; talk radio, 310, 312, 315. *See also* digital media
Meintzer, Phillip, 330, 334
Members of Parliament (MPs): candidate appointments and, 91; and data collection, 261; diminishing influence of, 4; and local debates, 336; ongoing constituent contacts, 261; personal constituency contacts/services, 253; political staff, 210; social standing, 70; turnover, 200. *See also* cabinet ministers; incumbent candidates
Mendicino, Marco, 134
messages/messaging, 25–26; branding and, 390; centralized decision making/control over, 287–88; development of local, 289; deviation from national, 288; digital vs. printed, 216; local, and national campaigns, 289; mass texting, 235–36, 241; matching to voter preferences, 11; microtargeting and, 251–52; national-local tensions in, 390–91; political parties and, 216; PSAC and, 371–72; regional, 289; social media and local, 287. *See also* communications

microtargeting: candidate knowledge of local culture vs., 259; of communications, 248; conflation of possible vs. actual in, 252; and data uses, 251; defined, 246, 251, 252; door canvassing vs., 258; and GOTV, 259–60; Green Party and, 258; identification of individuals, 251; as limiting vs. expanding voter contacts, 261–62; and messaging, 251–52; and voter identification, 259

Middleton, Alex, 332, 333, 336, 337, 338

Miller, Marc, 132

ministerial incumbents, 23; about, 129; advantages/disadvantages, 130, 135, 140–41; as attack dogs, 133; and branding, 141; campaign managers and, 135–36, 137, 141; campaign staff, 138; caretaker convention and, 134; centralization of power and, 135; and communications, 138; and constituencies, 133–34, 138–39; double duty, 132, 133, 135; on election night, 140; government popularity and, 135; information access, 136–37; interest groups and, 136; and leader's campaign, 139; and local campaigns, 137, 138–39; media and, 135; and ministerial work, 137, 140–41; and national campaign, 134–35, 136, 139, 141; opposition and, 133, 136; party headquarters and, 138; policy announcements, 139; political staff and, 134, 136; schedules, 138; seat loss, 136; snap elections and, 137; as star candidates, 130; tours, 133, 138; un-

expected political developments and, 134. *See also* cabinet ministers

minority governments: and candidate appointment, 91, 100; and election management, 45

Montreal *Gazette,* 313

Morrice, Mike, 351, 353

motivation(s): altruistic, 67; communal goals, 68, 80; dissatisfaction with incumbents, 81; extrinsic, 67; gender and, 22, 71–73, 80; giving back to community, 75, 77; having impact, 72, 73; intrinsic, 67; issues, 75, 77; making a difference, 71, 80; in nomination contests, 99; policy/policy making, 22, 71, 75, 77, 80; political/personal values, 75–76, 77–78; power goals, 68; public service, 75, 77; quality of representation, 76, 78–79, 81; race and, 22, 80; research on, 67; social characteristics and, 76–77; values promotion, 80–81; variety, 79; voter choice, 78. *See also* ambition

Mulroney, Brian, 108

municipal government/politics: candidate motivations for entering, 69, 70, 71, 72, 73; nonpartisan nature, 71

Munro, Devin, 121, 384

Mustapha, Jennifer, 120

national campaigns: benefits for local campaigns, 202; campaign managers and, 191, 202–3; and campaign professionals, 202; centralization of, 174; contact information, 202; and election outcomes, 185; emergence of, vs.

and, 80; white heterosexual men and, 67; women and, 71

political parties: and branding, 9, 112–13, 286; cabinet ministers and, 129; and campaign managers, 192–93, 231; and campaign workers, 230–31; and candidate nomination/selection, 23, 86, 94–97, 100, 389; and canvassing, 229; caucus and, 87, 174; centralization of, 185; COVID-19 and, 212, 385; data collection/management, 11, 228, 241, 249, 250, 255, 391; and digital technology/media, 5, 175, 310, 311; and election campaign agenda, 314; flexible allegiance to, 259; franchise model, 9, 86, 174–75, 191, 271, 286, 389; funding transfers from, 269; image, 176–77; incumbent candidates as standard bearers for, 129; independent candidates vs. belonging to, 298, 301; individualization vs. discipline, 150–51; insiders as archetype, 21; internal polling, 175; and local campaigning, 5; local candidate dependence on, 131; and local canvassing, 230–31, 232–34; and local issues, 286; and local-level campaigning, 4; marginal seat targeting, 233–34; and messaging, 216, 287–88; and national campaigns, 383; national conventions, 88; national organization development, 87–89, 174; national party campaigns, and fundraising, 272; and national vs. local issues, 300; and patronage, 87; and personalization, 148; and poll workers, 50; professionaliza-

tion of, 185; public funding, 267, 268–69; regional campaign directors and, 174, 176–77; and regionalization, 172–74; responsibilities of, 86; smaller, 230; and star/front-runner candidates, 97–98, 109, 110–11, 112–13, 115–16, 123; stratarchical model, 86, 89; third parties and, 363, 364, 376; unity, and democracy, 13. *See also* party leaders

political staff, 24–25, 136, 210, 337

politicians, image in US vs. Canada, 109–10

polling, 175, 195

polling stations: campaign workers at, 221–22; COVID-19 and, 52–53, 56; lineups at, 53–54, 387; locations, 19, 54, 387; numbers, 53; poll workers, 45, 47, 50–51, 387; robocall incidents, 46; scrutineering at, 212, 221–22, 239; signs and, 346

PolyRemembers, 291

Postmedia, 310

La Presse, 313

prime ministers: and communications, 131, 135; concentration of power, 130, 135

Progressive Conservative Party, as regional brokerage party, 173–74

provincial government/politics: candidate motivations for entering, 70, 71, 72, 73; policy, 71–72

provincial/territorial elections: federal elections overlapping, 213, 272; poll worker shortages, 52

public service: neutrality, 366, 369; unions, 366

Public Service Alliance of Canada (PSAC), 26–27, 369–75

Qualtrough, Carla, 132
Québecor, 312–13, 316, 317

racialized people: and activist nominees, 99; barriers to political involvement, 67; candidate motivations, 22, 73, 75, 77–79, 80–81; and communal goals, 68; in federal election (2021), 119–20; and federal government/politics, 73; and levels of government, 69; as nominees/candidates, 92; and policy, 73, 77
Radio X, 312, 313, 315
Radio-Canada, 308, 313, 315
RDI, 313
recruitment: for data skills, 250; Green Party and, 78; leader's office and, 177; local party presidents and, 14; of poll workers, 52; post-Confederation, 172–73; pre-writ seat triage and, 177; regional campaign directors and, 172, 177–78; and size/diversity of set of candidates, 92–93; of specialists, 198; of star candidates, 177; of women as nominees/candidates, 80, 93. *See also* appointment(s); candidate selection; nomination contests
regional campaign directors, 13, 24; and campaign managers, 177, 182; candidate identification and handling, 176; in close elections, 175; and electoral district associations, 177, 178–79; in federal election of 2021, 182–85, 186; and

GOTV, 175; history of, 172–75; as intermediaries between local and national campaigns, 178–81, 184–86; and leaders' tours, 174, 180–81; and local campaign workers, 182, 183–84; and national campaigns/teams, 172, 174–75, 184–85; and national strategy, 175, 179, 186; and nominations, 177; and party image, 176–77; and political parties, 174; premiers as, 173; provincial lieutenants and, 173; and recruitment, 177–78; resource distribution among local campaigns, 182–85; role, 172–75, 186; titles, 172; triaging riding competitiveness, 182
remote ridings, 193, 241, 288
Rempel Garner, Michelle, 18
returning officers (ROs), 45, 46–47, 48–49, 50, 52
ridings: boundary changes, 334; candidate's rootedness in, 152–53; canvassing in stronghold vs. uncompetitive, 229–30; Charlottetown as, 253–62; electability, 177, 178, 203, 229–30, 382–83; geographical targeting of, 382–83; ministerial incumbents and, 137, 138–39; PSAC and, 371, 373–75; scale, and data-driven campaigning, 247; three tiers of, 177–78; triaging competitiveness of, 182. *See also* remote ridings; rural ridings; urban ridings
Robarts, John, 173
Robinson, Shirley, 114
Rodriguez, Pablo, 155, 290
Rogers, Churence, 407(f)
Roosevelt, Theodore, 339

Rota, Anthony, 401(f)
Royal Commission on Electoral Reform and Party Financing, 20, 209–10
rural ridings: campaign managers in, 193, 198; candidate-driven fundraising in, 272; canvassing in, 232, 241, 393; data-driven campaigning in, 262; fundraising in, 267; local debates in, 335; local issues in, 277; specialists in, 198; star candidates in, 115, 122, 123; wedge issues with urban areas, 291

Sahota, Jag, 184
Sajjan, Harjit, 121, 134, 135
Salih, Mohammed, 120
Samara Centre for Democracy, 13, 23, 89, 90–93
scrutineering, 212, 221–22, 239
Sherbrooke Declaration, 294–95
Sidhu, Maninder, 232
signs, 26, 216–17, 345, 392–93, 403–5(f); and advertising, 345; "bandwagon effect," 347; canvassing and, 353, 354, 357; as demonstrating momentum, 355–56, 357; digital technology vs., 356; effectiveness, 348; and election outcomes, 346–47; environmental sustainability and, 357; GOTV and, 354; household, 345, 347, 353, 354–55, 357; independent service providers and, 195; media coverage of, 348–51; and party/candidate visibility, 347, 356; and party's communication strategy, 345; phone canvassing and, 255; plastic, 352–53, 355; and polling

stations, 346; recycling, 352–53, 357; removal, 353; rules/regulations, 346, 355; social media vs., 356, 357; spoof/parody, 350–51; star candidates and, 120; street/road, 345, 347, 354–55; symbolic value, 26, 352, 356; tampering with, 17–18, 19, 349–50, 355, 357; teams, 353–54; as visual polls, 356; and vote choice, 355–56; and vote share, 348
Simidzija, Adis, 155
Sinclair Desgagné, Nathalie, 91
Singh, Jagmeet, 15, 121, 294–95, 296, 315, 390
smaller ridings, 247–48, 253, 262
Smallwood, Joey, 173
snap elections, 14, 91, 137, 176, 212, 368, 389
social media, 406(f), 407(f); advocacy groups/third parties and, 368, 376; and branding, 120; candidates' aides and, 215; in canvassing, 236, 241; COVID-19 and, 19, 196, 235, 329–30; as data source, 250; and disinformation, 309, 311–12; election campaign coverage, 316, 317; Green Party and, 254; information sharing, 357; and local issues, 293; and local messages, 287; messaging apps, 316; and national vs. local issues, 297; and personalization, 150, 151, 153–54, 156–60, 162–63; political parties and, 310; PSAC and, 371; in Quebec, 308–9; reduced importance of, 316, 317; role, 308–9; and scandals, 308; scrubbing accounts, 178; signs vs., 356, 357; star candidates and, 120–21, 161,

162; Trudeau and, 24, 153–54, 156–57, 158, 159, 161; and voter data, 216, 234–35

Sohi, Amarjeet, 134

Le Soleil, 313

spending, campaign, 194, 267, 268, 269

star candidates, 23, 108, 111; appointment, 110, 389; Boulerice as, 294; and branding, 112–13, 116–17, 120; in British Columbia, 114, 115, 122; campaign managers and, 194; campaign teams, 120–21; and causes, 122; crossing floor, 109; in federal election (2021), 113, 115–16; Francoeur as, 154; independence of, 288, 294, 296; Liberal Party and, 111; local news media and, 311; local support for, 123; and media, 110, 120–21; ministerial incumbents as, 23, 130; national campaign and, 121, 123; as national leaders, 108; numbers winning, 107; as political outsiders, 122; political parties and, 109, 110–11, 112–13, 115–16, 123; provincial representation, 114–15, 122; recruitment, 108–9, 110, 112, 177; in rural ridings, 115; and social media, 120–21, 161, 162; stars to make stars, 122; studies regarding, 110–13; success rates, 123; in urban/suburban ridings, 112, 115, 122, 194

stopgap candidates, 21, 288

Stronach, Belinda, 109

suburban ridings, 115, 193. *See also* urban ridings

Sudds, Jenna, 183, 349

Suzuki, David, 15

telephone canvassing, 12, 219–20, 229, 235–36, 241, 255, 257

television: and federal election of 2021, 314–16; and local issues, 317; print convergence with, 317; in Quebec City region, 312–13

Thatcher, Ross, 173

third parties: activities regulation, 364; and advertising, 364, 365; and candidates, 363, 364, 365; choices regarding impacts, 376; and close races, 376; conception of political work, 376–77; contributions to electoral campaigns, 375–76; and democracy, 363; diversity among, 365; Elections Canada and, 363, 375; issues raising, 364–65, 375–76; and local campaigns, 376–77; and ministerial incumbents, 136; national vs. local interventions, 376; and national vs. local level political activity, 367; and political parties, 363, 364, 376; and social media, 376; spending limits, 363, 364, 365, 367, 374–75, 376. *See also* advocacy/advocacy groups

Thompson, Allan, 211

Thompson, Joanne, 409(f)

Tk'emlúps te Sacwépeme First Nation, 119

Tollar, Maryem, 114

Toth, Susan, 120

tours: cabinet ministers on, 131–32; ministerial incumbents and, 133, 138; shadow leader's, 133. *See also* leaders' tours

trade unions. *See* unions

Trans Mountain Pipeline, 292, 298

majority, 67; and municipal government/politics, 73

Wickr Pro, 16

Wilkinson, Jonathan, 132

Windsor-Essex Regional Chamber of Commerce debate, 331

Winters, Andrea, 235, 237, 238, 240, 409(f)

women: barriers to political involvement, 67; candidate motivations, 69, 71, 78–79, 81; and gender stereotypes, 68; in local debates, 338; and local issues, 69; as nominees/candidates, 92, 93; online harassment/trolling, 93, 101; recruitment of, 80

Young, Kate, 118, 121

Yousef, Ahmed, 78

Zann, Lenore, 15

Printed and bound in Canada by Friesens

Set in Bodoni, Baskerville, and Myriad
by Artegraphica Design Co. Ltd.

Copy editor: Dallas Harrison

Proofreader: Judith Earnshaw

Indexer: Noeline Bridge

Cover designer: Kimberley Devlin